Contributions to Economics

The series *Contributions to Economics* provides an outlet for innovative research in all areas of economics. Books published in the series are primarily monographs and multiple author works that present new research results on a clearly defined topic, but contributed volumes and conference proceedings are also considered. All books are published in print and ebook and disseminated and promoted globally. The series and the volumes published in it are indexed by Scopus and ISI (selected volumes).

Ilona Bartuseviciene · Buracas Antanas ·
Anastasios Karasavvoglou ·
Persefoni Polychronidou
Editors

Building Economic Resilience

Strategies for Sustainable Growth and Competitiveness

Springer

Editors
Ilona Bartuseviciene
Mykolas Romeris University
Vilnius, Lithuania

Buracas Antanas
Mykolas Romeris University
Vilnius, Lithuania

Anastasios Karasavvoglou
Democritus University of Thrace
Kavala, Greece

Persefoni Polychronidou
Economic Sciences Department
International Hellenic University
Serres, Greece

ISSN 1431-1933 ISSN 2197-7178 (electronic)
Contributions to Economics
ISBN 978-3-031-96427-5 ISBN 978-3-031-96428-2 (eBook)
https://doi.org/10.1007/978-3-031-96428-2

This Springer imprint is published by the registered company Springer Nature Switzerland AG
The registered company address is: Gewerbestrasse 11, 6330 Cham, Switzerland

Preface

By embracing continuous learning, fostering innovation, and prioritizing sustainability, Europe can navigate the turbulence of the twenty-first century and achieve long-term prosperity. Hence, this volume presents the works of researchers who share their advances in a nuanced understanding of economic resilience and sustainable development beyond conventional recovery models. The scientific findings prompt critical arguments about the dynamic approaches emphasizing transformative capabilities, adaptive restructuring, competency development among economic agents, and the ability to leverage disruptive experiences as competitive advantages. The studies critically examine the intersection of economic growth and environmental sustainability. Key observations include challenges aligning consumer sustainability preferences with actual behaviors, the European Union's Green Deal as a strategic framework for climate neutrality, and complex decision-making processes surrounding sustainable choices. Emerging research highlights the pivotal role of digital technologies in economic resilience: Artificial intelligence as a strategic management tool, Machine learning for organizational performance evaluation, and Smart grid technologies as innovative investment strategies.

The volume includes 11 articles presented at the 16th International Conference "Economies of the Balkan and Eastern European Countries (EBEEC)," held in Vilnius, Lithuania, in 2024. The book consists of three parts: Part I focuses on economic and Regional Resilience, Part II is dedicated to Organizational and Industrial Resilience, and Part III is related to Sustainability and Environmental Governance.

Part I—Economic and Regional Resilience

Part I converges on critical themes of economic resilience, regional stability, sustainability, and social progress in the context of recent global disruptions, including the COVID-19 pandemic and the war in Ukraine. Researchers from various Eastern

European and Balkan countries explore interconnected challenges of economic adaptation, policy responses, and the potential for financial resilience during crises, and regional competitiveness using advanced analytical methods, technological innovation, and sustainable development. Key focal points include:

1. Economic resilience: studies examine how regions and organizations can transform and adapt to unexpected shocks, emphasizing the need to develop dynamic capabilities beyond traditional recovery strategies.
2. Sustainable development: researchers investigate sustainable competitiveness, exploring how countries can balance economic growth with environmental protection and social equity.
3. Technological transformation: papers highlight the role of digital technologies, artificial intelligence, and smart grid innovations in driving sustainable economic development.
4. Governance and policy: multiple studies underscore the critical role of institutional frameworks, EU policies, and strategic interventions in facilitating economic resilience and sustainable transitions.

This research collection demonstrates remarkable methodological sophistication, employing advanced analytical techniques across different domains of quantitative network analysis to understand regional economic interdependencies. **Vesna Lukovic's** (*independent researcher from Poland*) research explores the impact of geopolitical shifts, particularly the war in Ukraine, on EU cohesion policy. The study demonstrates a sophisticated understanding of the multilayered challenges inherent in cohesion policy implementation. It highlights the need for a balanced approach to enlargement and the importance of strengthening economic resilience in the EU's eastern regions. The study's emphasis on economic resilience, especially in border regions, represents a forward-looking approach to understanding territorial development within the EU framework.

Gökhan Berk Özbek's (*Harmancık Vocational School, Bursa Uludağ University, Turkey*) study examines the financial resilience of sectoral indices in the Borsa Istanbul Exchange (BIST) during financial crises. BIST 100 serves as a benchmark for a financial resistance index, and measures the sensitivity of sectoral indices to financial crises from 2000–2001 to 2018. The structural reform decisions for the banking sector implemented relatively rapidly after crises and the rapid enactment of legal regulations, particularly those aimed at boosting exports, have proved crucial. Indeed, according to the recovery index, these sectors have demonstrated the most significant success in mitigating the effects of crises. Wholesale withdrawal from capital markets will, over time, indirectly compromise the entire country's economic stability. The research identifies the sectors that have shown resilience and those that have been more vulnerable to economic shocks.

Pagona Filenta, Dimitrios Kydros, Persefoni Polychronidou, and George Magoulios (*School of Economics and Management, International Hellenic University, Greece*) utilize social network analysis to study the interconnectedness of EU regions based on macroeconomic indicators. The analysis aims to identify regional disparities and potential areas for targeted policy interventions to improve cohesion. By mapping correlations between NUTS2 regions using the Python programming language, the researchers introduce an innovative method to visualize complex economic relationships, identify potential policy interventions to reduce regional imbalances, and propose strategic connections to enhance EU cohesion. The study's originality lies in its computational approach to regional economic integration, moving beyond traditional economic analysis by treating regions as interconnected network nodes.

Aleksandra Fedajev's (*University of Belgrade, Serbia*) publication on Balkan countries introduces a comprehensive evaluation framework using the Global Sustainable Competitiveness Index. The methodology's distinctiveness emerges from multi-criteria decision-making techniques, an entropy-based PROMETHEE method, and a dynamic assessment of countries' sustainable development across multiple dimensions. By assigning variable weights to different criteria, the research provides a nuanced understanding of sustainable competitiveness that goes beyond simplistic economic metrics.

Part II—Organizational and Industrial Resilience

The research findings in this part of the collection converge on the critical themes of organizational resilience, strategic adaptability, and digital innovation in the face of contemporary challenges, including economic volatility and evolving market conditions. Researchers emphasize the interplay between robust quality management, leadership dynamics, and the transformative power of emerging technologies to bolster competitiveness and long-term sustainability. Key focal points include:

1. The refinement of quality management frameworks: these studies highlight the need for more nuanced, category-based analysis of nonconformities, recognizing that organizations must move beyond traditional defect tracking to uncover more profound operational vulnerabilities.
2. The potential of the assessment of organizational resilience: the scholars explore how organizations can proactively evolve structures and processes, showing that alignment between leadership, culture, and continuous learning is essential for sustained resilience and responsiveness to external shocks.
3. Digital transformation and AI-driven decision-making: the researchers reveal how digital technologies can foster resilience and adaptability while navigating uncertain times. By applying artificial neural networks, they reveal that leadership development, employee engagement, and digital transformation better prepare organizations to reorient themselves in turbulent environments, offering new pathways for organizations to remain agile and competitive.

By employing advanced methodological approaches and focusing on adaptive leadership, proactive governance, and data-driven insights, these studies provide valuable guidance for policymakers, managers, and stakeholders to strengthen resilience in an increasingly volatile global environment.

Olga Snarskė and **Birute Mockeviciene** (*Mykolas Romeris University, Lithuania*) emphasize the importance of quality management frameworks and adaptive operational strategies in ensuring organizational resilience. Their research demonstrates that organizations must prioritize the establishment of comprehensive quality management frameworks and the development of an adaptive operational strategy. These approaches are critical for maintaining sustained competitiveness and ensuring effective responses to environmental changes. While companies traditionally assess quality by tracking overall defect rates, a more nuanced examination of nonconformities can provide deeper insights into specific areas requiring management intervention. This study explores and evaluates potential nonconformity categories within a logistics service provider, aiming to help organizations proactively identify, rectify, and prevent operational issues. Organizations can proactively mitigate risks by identifying and addressing nonconformities and enhancing their ability to respond to changes.

Ilona Bartuseviciene's (*Mykolas Romeris University, Lithuania*) organizational resilience modeling study employs structural equation modeling to explore organizational resilience. It reveals complex interactions between leadership, culture, and adaptive capabilities. Key insights include positive correlations between leadership dimensions and employee awareness, quantifiable impacts of organizational change, and the identification of critical factors in maintaining organizational dynamism.

The correlation analysis highlights the positive impact of these factors on employee engagement, decision-making, and overall organizational performance. A one-standard-deviation increase in leadership and culture can significantly enhance employee situational awareness and leadership, with a moderate impact on management situational awareness and employee decision-making. Similarly, such an increase in network dimensions can significantly improve unity of purpose in both groups and foster a proactive posture among managers. A one-standard-deviation increase in change readiness and learning can have a moderate impact on all indicators, including staff engagement, breaking down silos, and leveraging knowledge in both groups. However, it is demonstrated that the network dimension does not directly influence change readiness and learning among managers. Enhancing dimensions of organizational resilience can substantially impact employee situational awareness, leadership, unity of purpose, and decision-making, with a less pronounced effect on other indicators.

Several papers highlight the transformative potential of technological innovations and sustainability. **Lidija Kraujaliene** and **Alytis Gruodis** (*Mykolas Romeris University, Lithuania*) focus on the role of digital technologies, using artificial neural networks as a cutting-edge approach to organizational development. They identify key organizational performance indicators by developing a set of digital indicators and utilizing artificial neural networks and sophisticated digital evaluation models. Their study demonstrates the potential of machine learning in strategic management, enabling organizations to evaluate their performance and effectively target areas for improvement.

These research findings provide valuable insights for organizations seeking to foster resilience and adaptability while navigating uncertain times. Strong leadership and a positive organizational culture are crucial. By focusing on quality management, leadership development, employee engagement, and digital transformation, organizations can position themselves for long-term success. Empowering employees and investing in their development can enhance organizational resilience. Leveraging digital technologies can help organizations identify, analyze, and address challenges more effectively. By fostering leadership development, employee engagement, and digital transformation, organizations can position themselves for long-term success.

Part III—Sustainability and Environmental Governance

The papers in Part III of this collection respond to the challenges associated with sustainable and environmental governance by focusing on the intersection of these two phenomena. This includes key areas such as energy transitions, climate change mitigation, and sustainable investment strategies. The collected studies suggest several promising research trajectories and potential future directions:

1. Advancing renewable energy integration: expanding renewable energy in Central and Eastern Europe is vital for reducing carbon emissions and fostering green development. Overcoming barriers requires targeted policies, fiscal incentives, and modernized energy systems.
2. Strengthening governance for climate mitigation: effective governance and institutional reforms are crucial in order to maintain sustainability and reduce CO_2 emissions. Strong policy frameworks and improved governance can drive sustainable development across regions.
3. Innovating regarding smart grid technologies: smart grids are key to integrating renewable energy and improving power system efficiency. Exploring their scalability, digital advancements, and investment potential can accelerate sustainable energy transitions.

These research directions highlight the importance of promoting sustainability through innovative energy solutions, strong governance, and advanced technologies, ensuring balanced growth, environmental preservation, and resilience.
Petar Mitic and **Aleksandar Zdravković** (*Institute of Economic Sciences, Belgrade, Serbia*) emphasize that strong reliance on energy-intensive industrial processes and cost-effective energy supply characterizes Central and Eastern European (CEE) countries. Their research highlights the positive impact of increasing renewable electricity generation on green development in CEE countries, which is critical for reducing carbon emissions in the region. Despite the significant potential for renewable energy expansion in CEE economies, these countries encounter substantial technical, economic, and social barriers to generating electricity from renewable sources. Consequently, public policies must create robust incentives for investment in renewable energy projects. The successful implementation of targeted policy measures

and comprehensive institutional frameworks—including public-private partnerships and fiscal incentives—is essential to promote greater renewable energy use and production, thereby driving the modernization of the power sector.

Eirini Triarchi (*University of Ioannina, Greece*), **Dimitrios Kolias** (*Hellenic Open University, Greece*), and **Efstratios Kypriotelis** (*University of Ioannina, Greece*) demonstrate how EU membership positively influences environmental policies, showing that institutional governance significantly impacts strategies for CO_2 emission reduction. Empirical evidence supports the proposition that EU membership plays a crucial role in enhancing climate mitigation efforts through comprehensive policy frameworks and improvements in governance quality. The research highlights how EU integration encourages more stringent environmental regulations in the Balkan states, and calls for further detailed investigations into the influence of policy interventions and institutional backgrounds on climate resilience.

Ewelina Idziak (*Kazimierz Wielki University, Poland; Azerbaijan State University of Economics,* and *Vilniaus kolegija, Lithuania*) examines sustainable practices in the packaging industry and assesses their economic impact based on real business case studies. From a practical perspective, this is important due to the growing emphasis on measuring the effects of sustainability activities and their economic outcomes.

Cristiana Tudor and **Robert Sova** (*Bucharest University of Economic Studies, Romania*) reveal that smart grid technology plays a pivotal role in advancing sustainability and achieving the goals of the 2030 Agenda for Sustainable Development. By integrating advanced digital technologies, smart grids improve the efficiency and reliability of electricity transmission while supporting large-scale renewable energy integration. This paper analyzes the financial landscape of smart grid technologies through a comprehensive examination of Exchange-Traded Funds (ETFs) that invest in this sector. Using portfolio optimization techniques, including Monte Carlo simulation and efficient frontier analysis, the study evaluates the risk-return profiles and diversification benefits of smart grid ETFs compared to traditional diversified portfolios. The results show that smart grid ETFs like GRID exhibit annualized returns of approximately 20% with a volatility of around 25%, significantly higher than the returns of traditional energy sector ETFs like XLE, which show a return of 8% but with a higher volatility of around 35%. This study provides valuable insights for investors and policymakers by demonstrating that smart grid ETFs offer a strategic opportunity to enhance portfolio performance while aligning with sustainable investment objectives.

Vilnius, Lithuania	Ilona Bartuseviciene
Vilnius, Lithuania	Buracas Antanas
Kavala, Greece	Anastasios Karasavvoglou
Serres, Greece	Persefoni Polychronidou

Introduction: Navigating Disruption for a Resilient and Sustainable Future

It is turning into a norm that never-ending turmoils, constant uncertainty, and unexpected shocks increasingly determine the contemporary economic landscape. The COVID-19 pandemic compelled our economies to undergo profound transformations, acquire new skills, and adapt to a drastically altered environment. It is unfortunate, but distressing events, such as the war in Ukraine, became one of the most significant events that substantially reconfigured economic trajectories, leading to disruptions in energy supply chains and complex realignment towards new markets. Inevitably, such disruptions have highlighted the vulnerabilities of European economies and exposed disparities in recovery patterns across different regions.

On the positive side, these occurrences also resulted in us working harder towards a resilient and sustainable European economy capable of resisting these turmoils.

The Industry 5.0 principles emphasize that resilience and sustainability are cornerstones of societal and economic development until at least 2050. Hence, it provides a vision of the future of European industry to achieve societal goals beyond jobs and growth. The core message of this initiative is oriented to the industry, which, by becoming a resilient provider of prosperity, would be better equipped with the capacity to make production more sustainable and place the worker's well-being at the center of the production process. However, this approach calls for new ways of thinking, which shift from simply safeguarding economies from disruptions to developing strategies that enable them to thrive in volatile environments. Researchers advocating for economic resilience call for an emphasis on transformation and restructuring, allowing economies to adapt and emerge stronger from crises.

The ambitious nature of these objectives necessitates immediate action towards developing strategies specifically designed to address VUCA (Volatility, Uncertainty, Complexity, and Ambiguity) scenarios. Researchers delving into economic resilience emphasize the need for economies to progress in their ability to transform in the face of disruptions. They argue that the capacity to transform goes beyond projected resistance, recovery, and adaptation, focusing instead on reconfiguration and restructuring in new settings (Martin et al., 2016). Furthermore, researchers contend that it is essential to redirect attention away from merely safeguarding economies from challenging situations. Instead, it is crucial to learn how to cope with adversity by cultivating the competencies of economic agents, thus empowering them to adapt to changed environments, aftershocks, or threats, return to normal activities, and use the acquired experience as a driving force that will provide a unique competitive advantage.

Sustainable development is critical for addressing long-term challenges like climate change and resource scarcity. The European Union's Green Deal, with its goal of achieving climate neutrality by 2050, underscores the importance of transitioning from a growth-at-all-costs approach to one that prioritizes environmental protection. Consumer choices regarding sustainability are complex and multifaceted, as the desire for sustainable products does not always align with their stated preferences (Elmor et al., 2024). An experiment by Vringer et al. (2017) revealed that individuals prefer others to bear the cost of sustainability despite recognizing its collective benefits. These findings raise important questions about the global pursuit of sustainability: Why do priorities differ across regions, and how do cultural and economic factors shape these approaches?

Fostering knowledge transfer through education and policy strengthens the social market economy. Empowering employees within organizations by promoting flatter structures can further unlock valuable ideas and drive innovation. The Strategic Agenda 2024–2029 shows that the European Union is reshaping its growth strategy based on sustainability as a driver of change through ecological and digital transitions (Council of the European Union, 2023). It strongly focuses on education for personal fulfillment, employability, and active and responsible citizenship. Education and scientific inquiry are fundamental to the European paradigm of existence. They are pivotal in bolstering the social market economy and democratic governance through the principles of liberty, plurality, human rights, and social equity (European Commission, 2024).

As a result, building a resilient and sustainable European economy requires a multifaceted approach. By embracing continuous learning, fostering innovation, and prioritizing sustainability, Europe can navigate the turbulence of the twenty-first century and achieve long-term prosperity. Hence, this volume presents the work of researchers who share their advances in creating a nuanced understanding of economic resilience that goes beyond conventional recovery models. These scientific findings prompt critical arguments surrounding dynamic approaches that emphasize transformative capabilities, adaptive restructuring, competency development among economic agents, and the ability to leverage disruptive experiences to turn them into competitive advantages. These studies also critically examine the intersection of economic growth and environmental sustainability. Key observations include challenges aligning consumer sustainability preferences with actual behaviors, the European Union's Green Deal as a strategic framework for climate neutrality, and complex decision-making processes surrounding sustainable choices. Emerging research highlights the pivotal role of digital technologies in economic resilience: artificial intelligence as a strategic management tool, machine learning for organizational performance evaluation, and smart grid technologies as innovative investment strategies.

This volume includes 11 selected manuscripts presented at the 16th "Economies of the Balkan and Eastern European Countries (EBEEC)" International Conference held in Vilnius, Lithuania, in September 2024. The book consists of three parts: Part I focuses on Economic and Regional Resilience, Part II is dedicated to Organizational and Industrial Resilience, and Part III is entitled Sustainability and Environmental Governance.

Part I—Economic and Regional Resilience

Research on economic and regional resilience plays a key role in social sciences, as it is linked to the ability of economies to cope with unexpected shocks, such as recessions, natural disasters, technological disruptions, or market shifts while maintaining or even improving their long-term development trajectories (Hundt & Grün, 2022).

In the spring of 2020, the global community faced the COVID-19 pandemic—an extraordinary event that particularly impacted the health sector while simultaneously paralyzing economies worldwide. In light of subsequent economic deceleration, nations endure substantial financial losses and strive to restore conditions like those preceding the pandemic. In February 2021, the European Council enacted a regulation establishing the Recovery and Resilience Facility, a foundational element of the European Union's recovery strategy. This initiative allocated €672.5 billion[1] in grants and loans to facilitate public investment and reforms across the Member States, thereby assisting them in addressing the ramifications of the COVID-19 pandemic through six distinct components: the green transition, digital transformation, intelligent, sustainable, and inclusive economic growth and employment creation, social and territorial cohesion, health and resilience, and policies directed towards children and youth, including education and skills development (CITATA). Nevertheless, as articulated by Dr. Juergen Voegele, Vice President for Sustainable Development at the World Bank, a return of four dollars can be anticipated for every dollar allocated towards resilient development. Thus, rather than adhering to conventional financial planning, investment strategies should prioritize the enhancement of resilience across all tiers, given that the promotion of resilience transcends mere investment in infrastructural projects such as roads, bridges, and factories, instead constituting a systemic phenomenon that encompasses the entire ecosystem, including organizations, societies, and people.

These initiatives align with the findings of Kapitsinis et al. (2022), who noted that while crises and shocks can have a negative impact on regional economies, they should primarily be perceived as opportunities while anticipating future growth prospects. However, the situation here is more complex than it may initially appear:

[1] https://www.europarl.europa.eu/news/en/press-room/20210204IPR97105/parliament-gives-go-ahead-to-EU672-5-billion-recovery-and-resilience-facility

different regions are treated homogeneously regardless of their size, economic performance, or industrial structure, thus failing to address the region's resources, capabilities, and limitations (Sutton et al., 2023). As a result, it is often assumed that the factors contributing to resilience operate uniformly across all types of regions, neglecting the possibility that some aspects may be more relevant or practical in certain regional contexts than others (Hundt & Grün, 2022). Another complex notion worth addressing is that most empirical investigations are treated as closed systems and explored using aspatial models, which limits our knowledge of the factors that exert a spatial and hierarchical influence on regions' resilience. Moreover, the nature of these influences is little explored in the existing literature (Sutton et al., 2023).

As illustrated in the seminal study by Martin et al. (2016), economies must address both their short- and long-term potential to rebound after facing disruption. The prevailing consensus in the scientific community reveals that short-term recovery deals with resistance and recoverability and concerns the regional ability to withstand disruptions with as minor damage as possible. Resistance, also recognized as engineering resilience (Caro & Fratesi, 2023), combines robust physical designs characterized by specific limits beyond which the system becomes unsustainable. Hence, to rapidly rebound from adversity, it is vital to ensure the adaptability competence of the economic system, i.e., to empower ecological resilience. The latter equips the economic system with the capacity to absorb shocks and maintain its current equilibrium by undergoing minimal structural and/or functional change after reaching the limits of its possibilities. Although this concept of evolutionary resilience is limited, ensuring economic regional resilience in the short term remains vital (Boschma, 2015).

However, when delving into the potential of the economic resilience of regions in the long term, assessing their ability to resist or recover as quickly as possible is insufficient. Therefore, Balland et al. (2019) suggest analyzing the economic resilience of regions in the form of evolutionary or transformative resilience. Reinforcing the perspective of Sutton et al. (2023) that crises and shocks should primarily be viewed as opportunities to predict future growth prospects, the phenomenon of evolutionary resilience becomes vital as it reveals the ability of regions to develop foresight and adapt to new circumstances in the event of a crisis, move to a new normal, and continue to develop with a newly established economic performance rhythm, also referred as a new normal (Bristow & Healy, 2018; Webber et al., 2017). Undoubtedly, the development of regional economic resilience in terms of transformative resilience also brings to bear essential arguments about the benefits of resilience, as it emphasizes the ability of regions to reconfigure the structure of their economies in the face of uncertainty in order to respond to the most favorable economic growth prospects (Capello & Dellisanti, 2023). A seminal study by Martin (2012) revealed that regional economies demonstrate a twofold approach in terms of long-term recovery. First, they acknowledge the response to the shock by renewing themselves—the degree to which regions reestablish their old growth path or move to a new one. Second, they consider the reorientation capacity, which departs from the growth path perspective towards a structural approach. The aforementioned study also demonstrates the capacity to examine how regions modify their economic structures in response to shocks.

Hundt and Grün (2022) argue that the four approaches introduced as cornerstones of Martin's (2012) study—resistance, recovery, renewal, and reorientation—are not equally specific. Although resistance and recovery constitute the fundamental essence of the concept, renewal, and reorientation, pertain more closely to broader considerations of growth and development. Furthermore, the indicators that investigate the potential of evaluating a region's capacity for renewal and reorientation are frequently utilized to elucidate economic growth in general. These indicators include social capital, cultural capital, education, innovation, sectoral diversification, industrial diversity, and institutional support.

However, as Hundt and Grün (2022) indicate, regional specialization is one of the most relevant areas for assessing regional economic resilience and growth. The reasoning here is straightforward: the goal of smart specialization is not to make regions' economic structures more specialized (i.e., less diversified) but rather to capitalize on existing competencies, identify hidden opportunities, and generate novel platforms upon which regions can build competitive advantage in high-value-added activities (Balland et al., 2019).

In conclusion, economic and regional resilience is a multifaceted construct that cannot be straightforwardly exploited. The existing literature indicates that although the different types of regional economic resilience are not equal, each is instrumental in shaping an economy's response to shocks. Without the ability of regions to resist and recover, distinct economies cannot evolve and transform. Consequently, while the latter have an advantage in terms of their potential to secure economic resilience in the long term, the ability of regions to cope with and absorb shocks cannot be undervalued.

Part II—Organizational and Industrial Resilience

As many of the world's economies have grappled with challenges stemming from the COVID-19 pandemic, energy crises, global security concerns, and military tensions in recent years, there has been a growing focus on resilience research, which is based on the fundamental notion that crises, shocks, and unexpected turbulence are an inevitable part of evolution. Hence, rather than trying to avoid challenging circumstances entirely, developing the capacity of countries, organizations, societies, and systems to adapt to altered conditions and leverage the insights gained as catalysts for innovation and sustained competitive advantage is crucial.

Nevertheless, many scholars question the relevance of existing strategies for rationalizing and predicting complex environments, particularly in a tightly intertwined world. Thus, the scholarly discourse stresses the necessity of fundamentally different management, behavior, and decision-making models.

Retrospectively, it is apparent that the COVID-19 pandemic exposed a critical shortfall in the capacity to function effectively under shock conditions. Most organizations were unprepared to function appropriately in conditions of high turbulence. They experienced a lack of the skills that would have enabled them to transform their routines during this crisis. While most public services became inaccessible or were disrupted, the OECD (2021) reported that organizations with a higher level of resilience, i.e., the ability to respond quickly to a crisis environment, managed the COVID-19 pandemic more effectively. The OECD also noted that more resilient organizations have effectively employed digital technologies, enabling public service continuity, control, and accountability.

As the concept of resilience continues to gain prominence in research—facilitating insights into how individuals, organizations, and other ecosystem actors adapt to an ever-changing environment—Holling's (1973) seminal work, which first introduced resilience within an ecological framework, remains indispensable. One of Holling's pivotal insights, which laid the groundwork for further development, is that resilience reflects an ecosystem's capacity to absorb disturbances while preserving the core relationships among its constituent elements. Although the concept of resilience became a research object among social science researchers a few decades later, its popularity only garnered heightened focus in 2020, when researchers and practitioners sought strategies to sustain effective, stable, and proactive operations in contexts marked by instability and complexity.

In a broad sense, organizational resilience equips organizations with the capacity to function in environments of uncertainty and adapt to constantly changing conditions. This perspective is rooted in the fundamental premise that uncertainty, crises, and shocks of various natures are integral aspects of evolutionary development. Consequently, the focus shifts from shielding against every possible disruption to developing the capacity to manage and learn from them. Strengthening such capacities helps entities and societies reestablish new normal conditions after crises and leverage new experiences to secure a competitive edge (Bartuseviciene & Butkus, 2024).

We find that different theoretical perspectives shed light on the various perceptions of resilience development levels. For instance, Duit et al. (2010) reveal that an organization's resilience level determines its ability to tackle unforeseen challenges and return to a pre-crisis state as quickly as possible. Achieving this state is not effortless, as it requires proactive preparation from all levels and planning for "unknown unknowns" (Näswall et al., 2019), also referred to as black swan events (Adobor et al., 2021). By enhancing their capacity to operate in uncertainty, organizations gain the advantage of foresight, perceiving potential threats, and adapting management strategies. Thus, rather than concentrating solely on crisis prevention, it is more prudent to strengthen the ability to function under high uncertainty and complexity conditions.

Many researchers concur that resilient organizations can respond more swiftly and recover from crises, returning to or surpassing their pre-crisis state faster and more efficiently (Franken et al., 2020; Elston & Bel, 2022; Fischer et al., 2022). This capacity is often attributed to their ability to reallocate resources promptly and focus on managing critical resources (Lund & Andersen, 2022; Mazzucato & Kattel, 2020). Notably, resource optimization in this context does not equate to budget cuts; instead, it involves identifying alternative solutions (Plimmer et al., 2023) that enable organizations to act not merely "better" than before but in fundamentally different ways (Rajala & Jalonen, 2022). Crucially, the capacity to act differently emerges more readily in organizations, encouraging employees to step outside their comfort zones, improvise, and propose new performance-enhancing ideas (Termeer & van den Brink, 2013). By incorporating the insights and experiences gained during a crisis into post-crisis operations, organizations gain a unique advantage: transforming their former equilibrium into a new stable state that serves as the foundation for ongoing activities informed by updated knowledge and competencies (Duit et al., 2010).

Reichenbach et al. (2021) propose a framework of adaptive action that evaluates an organization's capacity to adapt at three key levels: (a) What happened? *(b)* How will recent events influence the organization's future activities? and *(c)* Whose experiences are most significant and valuable for integration into the organization's future operations? Building on this, Rajala and Jalonen (2022) posit that an organization's resilience hinges primarily on leadership and the willingness to act in fundamentally new ways rather than merely reverting to pre-crisis norms. They underscore the critical role of integrating lessons learned from disruptive events.

However, good intentions are not always sufficient to assess the benefits of resilience, and the lack of unified methodologies for evaluating this phenomenon is widely regarded as a barrier to building resilience (Phillips et al., 2021). Existing methods for evaluating organizational resilience typically involve a three-stage approach:

1. preparation for change (e.g., crisis readiness);
2. response and adaptation (e.g., rapid reorientation of operational practices, adoption of novel processes);
3. Transformative adaptation entails leveraging insights from the crisis to bolster future resilience (e.g., incorporating newly gained knowledge into daily activities, thereby creating equilibriums in the new normal).

Preparedness, response, and adaptation focus on measuring resilience both before and immediately following a crisis, striving to optimize readiness for unforeseen disruptions (Mazzucato & Kattel, 2020; Termeer & van den Brink, 2013) and to restore organizational operations at minimal cost (Leite & Hodgkinson, 2021; Ticlau et al., 2020; Fehrer & Bove, 2022). Transformative adaptation, meanwhile, highlights the importance of an organization's ability to learn from crisis episodes as a vehicle for improvement (Williams et al., 2020; Kramer et al., 2018). This process involves integrating crisis-derived knowledge into routine operations—an essential factor in facilitating positive adaptation (Brykman & King, 2021). This leads to a distinct organizational transformation (Hoegl & Hartmann, 2021), also called antifragility. To be antifragile means to succeed in the face of randomness, uncertainty, and disorder, benefiting from various shocks, especially black swan events (Bartuseviciene & Butkus, 2024). Antifragile capability equips organizations with the capacity to maintain dynamic stability during crises and exploit these events as opportunities for breakthroughs (Bajaba et al., 2024). However, although antifragility is acknowledged as a driver for innovation management, its empirical connections have yet to be fully explored. Future research could delve into the potential of antifragility as a catalyst for innovation management, further expanding our understanding of how organizations can leverage antifragility to enhance their capacity for innovation in disruptive environments.

To sum up, organizational resilience is evolving from a discretionary asset to an essential attribute, driven by rapidly intensifying geopolitical tensions and threats. Although these threats are increasingly difficult to anticipate, their consequences can significantly disrupt organizational activities. Thus, the ability to address these challenges effectively and to derive strategic benefits from them has become a critical source of competitive advantage.

Part III—Sustainability and Environmental Governance

The field of sustainable management and decision-making responds to the needs of today's society and can produce a transformative impact. Expanding and justifying this paradigm of thinking, it should be noted that reconciling economic, ecological, and social goals is crucial to achieving a responsible and sustainable modus operandi (construction of the whole). The paradigm of sustainable management requires that decision-making is directed towards the field of sustainability, creating a legitimate environment for decision-making. However, sustainable solutions will be legitimized when decision-makers have clear policies, governance structures, and methodologies to address trade-offs and potential value conflicts.

One of the key frameworks guiding sustainable development efforts is the European Green Deal, which is inextricably linked to the United Nations Sustainable Development Goals. It outlines ambitious goals in clean energy, sustainable agriculture, biodiversity protection, and the circular economy to foster economic growth while reducing environmental impact. By encouraging green innovation, regulatory changes, and socially just policies, the European Green Deal seeks to ensure that both people and the planet benefit from the transition to a more sustainable future.

However, despite the integrity of the link between its strategic orientations, implementing the Green Deal will be a challenge—both for the scientific community and in a political and practical sense—due to regional and cultural differences that influence how these strategies are perceived and implemented (Kruhlov et al., 2024). Nevertheless, enhancing sustainable practices will be impossible without robust governance mechanisms, as they provide knowledge and equip countries with tools to redirect traditional activities towards sustainability.

Promoting sustainable development and environmental protection through governance mechanisms involves a multifaceted approach integrating economic, social, and environmental strategies. Effective governance mechanisms are crucial in balancing present needs with future resource conservation, ensuring sustainable development through practical and inclusive strategies.

Lisenko (2024) indicates that sustainable growth can coexist with environmental preservation by implementing green investments, supportive policies, and inclusive development strategies. Moreover, a comparative analysis of governance models from the Nordic countries, Germany, France, and the Netherlands, revealed that these inclusive development strategies can successfully balance economic growth with environmental preservation. These results suggest that economic development does not have to come at the expense of environmental health and vice versa. This aligns with the findings of Kruhlov et al. (2024), who observed a moderate positive correlation between the environmental indicators of European countries and the quality of governance, suggesting that capable state institutions can contribute to achieving sustainable development goals. These results sound promising; however, challenges related to the implementation and compliance of global governance mechanisms should receive careful attention.

Adanma (2024) concluded that adaptive governance structures that are responsive to evolving environmental issues and stakeholders are encountering challenges. The involvement of civil society and non-governmental organizations is crucial for the success of governance frameworks but often remains inadequate. Thus, Yang et al. (2024) suggested the promotion of sustainable development through governance mechanisms by (1) enlarging board size, providing managerial incentives, establishing sustainability committees, and enhancing corporate transparency; (2) promoting board diversity alongside similar mechanisms; (3) reducing ownership concentration while maintaining managerial incentives and sustainability committees; and (4) encouraging individual investment with the exact supportive mechanisms. This proposed strategy would involve interested parties in managing organizations and ensure that sustainable practices become organizational routines, not declarative strategies.

Wei and Wang (2024) also offered insights to overcome the challenges faced by stakeholder inclusion by introducing the green+ strategy, which integrates ecological civilization into all aspects of economic, political, cultural, and social construction. It advocates for the "four comprehensive" strategic layout and the "five in one" overall layout to address challenges in sustainable development. By fully incorporating the green+ strategy into national economic and social development processes, effective governance mechanisms can promote sustainable development and environmental protection, reflecting our deepened understanding of economic and social development laws.

According to existing knowledge, achieving sustainable development requires us to integrate robust governance mechanisms with inclusive and adaptive strategies to balance economic growth, environmental preservation, and social equity. The European Green Deal, supported by research insights, exemplifies a transformative framework that aligns global goals with local needs. Although challenges are inevitable in implementing and harmonizing these strategies across diverse cultural and regional contexts, practical achievements for a sustainable future are impossible without robust governance mechanisms. By embedding sustainability into decision-making processes, societies can move from declarative strategies to actionable practices, fostering a resilient and sustainable future for all.

In summary, the introduction to this collected book emphasizes that the selected papers highlight the value of holistic and interdisciplinary approaches for understanding and tackling modern economic challenges, showcasing the potential of strategic interventions. The studies offer a comprehensive roadmap for navigating increasingly complex global economic landscapes by emphasizing interdisciplinary approaches and strategic interventions. The fundamental message offers a transformative vision: Economic resilience is not merely about withstanding shocks but concerns cultivating adaptive capabilities that convert challenges into sustainable growth and opportunities for societal well-being.

Ilona Bartuseviciene
Buracas Antanas
Anastasios Karasavvoglou
Persefoni Polychronidou

References

Adobor, H., Darbi, W. P. K., & Damoah, O. B. O. (2021). Strategy in the era of "swans": The role of strategic leadership under uncertainty and unpredictability. *Journal of Strategy and Management*, ahead-of-print(ahead-of-print). https://doi.org/10.1108/JSMA-09-2020-0242

Bajaba, A., Bajaba, S., & Simmering, M. J. (2024). When resilience is not enough: Theoretical development and validation of the antifragility at work scale. *Personality and Individual Differences, 231*, 112818. https://doi.org/10.1016/j.paid.2024.112818

Balland, P.-A., Boschma, R., Crespo, J., & Rigby, D. L. (2019). Smart specialization policy in the European Union: Relatedness, knowledge complexity and regional diversification. *Regional Studies, 53*(9), 1252–1268. https://doi.org/10.1080/00343404.2018.1437900

Bartuseviciene, I., & Butkus, M. (2024). The effect of digital governance to stimulate the antifragile capabilities of public sector organizations. *Economics & Sociology, 17*(3), 41–61. https://doi.org/10.14254/2071-789X.2024/17-3/3

Boschma, R. (2015). Towards an evolutionary perspective on regional resilience. *Regional Studies, 49*(5), 733–751. https://doi.org/10.1080/00343404.2014.959481

Bristow, G., & Healy, A. (2018). Innovation and regional economic resilience: An exploratory analysis. *The Annals of Regional Science, 60*(2), 265–284. https://doi.org/10.1007/s00168-017-0841-6

Brykman, K. M., & King, D. D. (2021). A resource model of team resilience capacity and learning. *Group & Organization Management, 46*(4), 737–772. https://doi.org/10.1177/10596011211018008

Capello, R., & Dellisanti, R. (2023). Chapter 2: Creativity in cultural and creative industries as a source of regional adaptive resilience. Retrieved from https://www.elgaronline.com

Caro, P. D., & Fratesi, U. (2023). The role of cohesion policy for sustaining the resilience of European regional labour markets during different crises. *Regional Studies, 57*(12), 2426–2442. https://doi.org/10.1080/00343404.2022.2118252

Council of the European Union. (n.d.). Strategic Agenda 2024–2029. Retrieved from https://www.consilium.europa.eu/media/yxrc05pz/sn02167en24_web.pdf

Duit, A., Galaz, V., Katarina, E., & Ebbesson, J. (2010). Governance, complexity, and resilience. *Global Environmental Change*. https://doi.org/10.1016/j.gloenvcha.2010.04.006

Elmor, L., Ramos, G. A., Vieites, Y., Andretti, B., & Andrade, E. B. (2024). Environmental sustainability considerations (or lack thereof) in consumer decision making. *International Journal of Research in Marketing*. https://doi.org/10.1016/j.ijresmar.2024.08.003

Elston, T., & Bel, G. (2022). Does inter-municipal collaboration improve public service resilience? Evidence from local authorities in England. *Public Management Review*. https://doi.org/10.1080/14719037.2021.2012377

European Commission. (2023). The European Pillar of Social Rights in 20 principles. Retrieved from https://ec.europa.eu/social/main.jsp?catId=1226

Fehrer, J. A., & Bove, L. L. (2022). Viewpoint: Shaping resilient service ecosystems in times of crises—A trans-Tasman perspective. *Journal of Services Marketing, 36*(4), 489–498. https://doi.org/10.1108/JSM-06-2021-0216

Fischer, C., Siegel, J., Proeller, I., & Drathschmidt, N. (2022). Resilience through digitalisation: How individual and organisational resources affect public employees working from home during the COVID-19 pandemic. *Public Management Review*. https://doi.org/10.1080/14719037.2022.2037014

Franken, E., Plimmer, G., & Malinen, S. (2020). Paradoxical leadership in public sector organisations: Its role in fostering employee resilience. *Australian Journal of Public Administration, 79*(1), 93–110. https://doi.org/10.1111/1467-8500.12396

Hoegl, M., & Hartmann, S. (2021). Bouncing back, if not beyond: Challenges for research on resilience. *Asian Business & Management, 20*(4), 456–464. https://doi.org/10.1057/s41291-020-00133-z

Holling, C. S. (1973). Resilience and stability of ecological systems. *Annual Review of Ecology and Systematics, 4*, 1–23.

Hundt, C., & Grün, L. (2022). Resilience and specialization—How German regions weathered the Great Recession. *ZFW – Advances in Economic Geography, 66*(2), 96–110. https://doi.org/10.1515/zfw-2021-0014

Kapitsinis, N., Poulimas, M., Emmanouil, E., & Gialis, S. (2022). Spatialities of being a young NEET in an era of turbulence: A critical account of regional resilience across the Mediterranean EU South. *Journal of Youth Studies, 27*, 1–22. https://doi.org/10.1080/13676261.2022.2101355

Kramer, D., Thierry, J., & van Hooren, F. (2018). Responding to free movement: Quarantining mobile union citizens in European welfare states. *Journal of European Public Policy, 25*(10), 1501–1521. https://doi.org/10.1080/13501763.2018.1488882

Leite, H., & Hodgkinson, I. (n.d.). Examining resilience across a service ecosystem under crisis. *Public Management Review*. https://doi.org/10.1080/14719037.2021.2012375

Lund, C. S., & Andersen, L. B. (2022). Professional development leadership in turbulent times. *Public Administration*. https://doi.org/10.1111/padm.12854

Martin, R., Sunley, P., Gardiner, B., & Tyler, P. (2016). How regions react to recessions: Resilience and the role of economic structure. *Regional Studies, 50*(4), 561–585. https://doi.org/10.1080/00343404.2015.1136410

Martin, R. (2012). Regional economic resilience, hysteresis and recessionary shocks. Journal of Economic Geography, 12(1), 1–32. https://doi.org/10.1093/jeg/lbr019

Mazzucato, M., & Kattel, R. (2020). COVID-19 and public-sector capacity. *Oxford Review of Economic Policy, 36*, S256–S269. https://doi.org/10.1093/oxrep/graa031

Näswall, K., Malinen, S., Kuntz, J., & Hodliffe, M. (2019). Employee resilience: Development and validation of a measure. *Journal of Managerial Psychology, 34*(5), 353–367. https://doi.org/10.1108/JMP-02-2018-0102

Phillips, W., Roehrich, J., & Kapletia, D. (n.d.). Responding to information asymmetry in crisis situations: Innovation in the time of the COVID-19 pandemic. *Public Management Review*. https://doi.org/10.1080/14719037.2021.1960737

Plimmer, G., Kuntz, J., Berman, E., Malinen, S., Näswall, K., & Franken, E. (2023). The negative relationships between employee resilience and ambiguity, complexity, and inter-agency collaboration. *Australian Journal of Public Administration, 82*(2), 248–270. https://doi.org/10.1111/1467-8500.12587

Rajala, T., & Jalonen, H. (2022). Stress tests for public service resilience: Introducing the possible-worlds thinking. *Public Management Review*. https://doi.org/10.1080/14719037.2022.2048686

Reichenbach, R., Lynn, J., & Heeg, J. (2021). Learning amid disruption: Bouncing forward into a changed world. *The Foundation Review, 13*(3). https://doi.org/10.9707/1944-5660.1577

Sutton, J., Arcidiacono, A., Torrisi, G., & Arku, R. N. (2023). Regional economic resilience: A scoping review. *Progress in Human Geography, 47*(4), 500–532. https://doi.org/10.1177/03091325231174183

Termeer, C. J. A. M., & van den Brink, M. A. (2013). Organizational conditions for dealing with the unknown unknown. *Public Management Review, 15*(1), 43–62. https://doi.org/10.1080/14719037.2012.664014

Ticlau, T., Hintea, C., & Andrianu, B. (2020). Adaptive and turbulent governance: Ways of governing that foster resilience – The case of the COVID-19 pandemic. *Transylvanian Review of Administrative Sciences*, 167–182. https://doi.org/10.24193/tras.SI2020.10

Vringer, K., van der Heijden, E., van Soest, D., Vollebergh, H., & Dietz, F. (2017). Sustainable consumption dilemmas. *Sustainability, 9*(6), Article 6. https://doi.org/10.3390/su9060942

Webber, D., Gissing, A., Dufty, N., & Bird, D. (2017). Community participation in emergency planning: NSW State Emergency Service case study. *Australian Journal of Emergency Management, 32*(2), 28–34.

Williams, D., Rosendo, S., Sadasing, O., & Celliers, L. (2020). Identifying local governance capacity needs for implementing climate change adaptation in Mauritius. *Climate Policy, 20*(5), 548–562. https://doi.org/10.1080/14693062.2020.1745743

Contents

Sustainability and Environmental Governance

Economic and Regional Resilience

Cohesion Policy for Economic Resilience in Eastern Members of the European Union in the Context of Geopolitics

Vesna Lukovic

Abstract The European Union (EU) has been hit with unexpected challenges since February 2022. The war in Ukraine and its territorial impact on certain EU countries have led to many questions, including with regard to the implications for the EU budget and the "flexibility" of cohesion policy. The EU candidate status awarded to Ukraine, one of the world's largest agricultural producers, has generated new calls for changes in EU governance. This paper has a policy-oriented approach. It explores cohesion policy in the context of current geopolitics and EU enlargement. The analysis looks at cohesion policy with a view to resilience and economic security in the eastern regions of the EU. The research methodology is qualitative and includes the case study of Poland. The research finds that there are many intertwined and complex issues. From the perspective of economic policymaking some solutions may require changes of the EU Treaties, if new candidate countries become full members of the EU. Certain options may not be appealing to EU candidate countries, while there isn't a lot of enthusiasm for those solutions that would require amendments of the EU Treaties.

Keywords Resilience · Cohesion policy · EU budget · Integration · Candidate countries

JEL classification H72 · O23 · R58

1 Introduction

The process of enlargement of the European Union (hereinafter: EU) is typically a complex technical and political process that takes years (Ludlow, 2013). In the case of the last EU entrant Croatia, that became a member in 2013, it took 10 years of negotiations and preparations (Mrak & Zuber, 2022; Wankiewicz, 2023).

V. Lukovic (✉)
Thessaloniki, Greece
e-mail: lukove@yahoo.com

I. Bartuseviciene et al. (eds.), *Building Economic Resilience*, Contributions to Economics, https://doi.org/10.1007/978-3-031-96428-2_1

A decision to open negotiations with a candidate country on the recommendation of the European Commission must be approved with unanimity of all EU member states. The application of Ukraine that opened EU negotiations in December 2023 has been fundamentally different from any other application in the whole history of the EU. Despite the expectation of unanimity when it comes to granting a candidacy status to a country (European Commission, 2023c) one EU member state was clearly voicing its objections to Ukraine becoming an EU candidate (RFE/RL, 2023). As a result, the decision to open the negotiations with Ukraine on 14 December 2023 (European Council, 2023) was taken without all representatives of EU member states being present at the time of that decision-making. Hungarian President, Viktor Orban abstained from the vote on accession of Ukraine (O'Carroll, 2023) and later described the decision to grant the candidate status to Ukraine as very bad (Sanchez Nicolas & Soler, 2023). This has never happened before in previous enlargement rounds. Moreover, the EU accession negotiations with Ukraine start at the time when the candidate country is at war. This is a large deviation from usual EU's policy towards enlargement (Klimkin & Miklos, 2023). Typically, the EU has insisted on resolving bilateral border and other issues before joining the EU (e.g. Slovenia-Croatia border dispute). It is obvious that the candidate status of Ukraine reflects geopolitical concerns and interests. It is difficult to imagine any other reason why a country at war that had been denied the EU candidate status for years (Parandii, 2023; Walldén, 2017) suddenly becomes a suitable candidate overnight.

The focus of this research is on the economic and social security in regions of the EU that border on Ukraine. The case study of Poland is presented in this respect. The paper examines certain questions of economic resilience in the context of current developments by looking at the EU's cohesion policy for the period 2021–2027, it's "flexibility" for the period 2014–2020 and the distribution of cohesion funds to member states. These questions build on the possibility of future leaning of the weight of cohesion funds towards Ukraine and other new candidates that may lead to certain imbalances vis-à-vis current net recipients of the EU budget. Possible solutions and relevant legal and enlargement implications are explored in this respect. The paper does not venture into the latest discussions on new avenues of budgetary powers and the financial constitution of European integration (Weber, 2023) considering that the fiscal legal framework that has been traditionally considered a technical field, now appears to have become more "politicised" (Mongouachon, 2023).

The paper is structured as follows. Section 2 presents research methodology and data sources, while Sect. 3 introduces the background of cohesion policy. Section 4 elaborates on the flexibility of the current cohesion policy, and Sect. 5 presents the distribution of cohesion funds in selected member states in the current EU budget cycle. Section 6 presents the case study of Poland. Section 7 discusses various policy implications while the final section draws on some conclusions.

2 Methodology and Data Sources

This research draws on theories on geopolitics and theories on EU enlargement. The methodology is qualitative and exploratory. The main method is textual analysis of legal acts such as the Treaty on the European Union (hereinafter: TEU), Treaty on the functioning of the European Union (hereinafter: TFEU) and other documents and processes related to the accession to the EU, the EU governance and EU budget. The analytical approach looks at the context and constraints of the new EU enlargement round if the risks of various negative consequences are minimised. The research also examines various country reports, recommendations and other documents by the European Commission, European Parliament, Court of Auditors, other EU institutions and authorities, press releases, news and similar.

In line with the established methods of qualitative research in political science (Blatter et al., 2016), the research approach evolves around the political phenomena of granting a candidate status to the country that is at war. The research is focused on certain complexities that cannot be captured with the use of quantitative methods (Brinkmann et al., 2014). In addition to textual and interpretative analysis of various legal texts and reports, the research also includes a case study. It presents the case of people's resilience and economic security in regions in Poland that border on Ukraine. The case study looks at their needs for cohesion funds and the impact on local population due to measures introduced by the European Commission in 2022 and 2023 in response to the war in Ukraine. Case studies may be quite efficient at presenting causal linkages (George & Bennett, 2005). This case study looks at policy formulation with regard to certain unintended consequences.

Although the methodology highlights the importance of context that is not numerical or statistical in nature, statistical data about the distribution of cohesion funds are also examined. This is particularly relevant in those EU member states that have been affected by economic and social consequences of the war in Ukraine. By looking into various parameters (e.g. GDP per capita), this part of analysis aims to highlight financial challenges for the current EU member states and possible future issues with regard to maintaining their status of net recipients of EU cohesion funds. That touches upon the question about the need to change EU governance and the change of EU Treaties if Ukraine, Moldova, and Western Balkans are to become full members of the EU in the near future.

3 Background

The Treaty of Rome that established the European Economic Community (hereinafter: EEC) in 1957 did not specifically mention cohesion policy, but it did establish the task of promoting solidarity among the member states by referring to the economic and social cohesion (EUR-Lex, 1957). The Treaty established the European Social Fund (ESF) with the objective to improve employment opportunities for workers in the internal market and contribute to raising the standard of living (EUR-Lex ESF, 2023). The Treaty of Rome also established the European Investment Bank (EIB) whose primary task was to improve economic and social cohesion. The EIB provides loans to the member states to support development (EUR-Lex EIB, 2023).

Since economic disparities among the six founding member states were small, cohesion policy did not have an important political priority within the first decade of the EEC (Court of Auditors, 2022). That changed when UK, Denmark and Ireland joined in 1973. As a result, in 1975 the European Regional Development Fund (ERDF) was established with the goal to reduce regional imbalances by creating jobs and investing in infrastructure, education and health. In 1981 Greece became a member and in 1985 Portugal and Spain joined which led to new regional disparities. More financing of less developed members was needed to reduce the development gap vis-à-vis the average of the EEC. The Single European Act enforced in 1985, established cohesion policy as a full-fledged policy that led to reform of structural funds in 1988. The idea was to complete the internal market so as to aid it by a geographically redistributive social policy.

From 1988 to 1992, the cohesion policy evolved from a simple project-by-project financial support to a policy instrument based on principles such as multi-annual programming (Court of Auditors, 2022). In 1992, the Cohesion Fund (CF) was set up to finance projects to improve the environment and transport infrastructure in member states whose gross national product (GNP) per capita was below 90% of the EU average (Mrak & Zuber, 2022). The establishment of this fund completed the institutional architecture of cohesion policy until 2021 when the Just Transition Fund (JTF) was added.

With the aim of achieving the objective of EU climate neutrality and as part of the European Green Deal, the European Commission in 2020 proposed the creation of a Just Transition Fund that "should focus on the regions and sectors that are most affected by the transition due to their dependence on fossil fuels, including coal, peat and oil shale, and on greenhouse-gas-intensive industrial processes" (European Parliament, 2021). This is the fourth fund intended for the implementation of the EU cohesion policy objectives.

In summary, key legal documents of the EU established cohesion policy as an important principle in the EU. In the Treaty on European Union (TEU), the importance of cohesion is depicted in Article 3 which states that the "Union shall promote economic, social and territorial cohesion and solidarity among Member States" (TEU, 2012). More details on social, economic and territorial cohesion are set in TFEU, known as the Lisbon Treaty that articulates the following:

> In order to promote its overall harmonious development, the Union shall develop and pursue its actions leading to the strengthening of its economic, social and territorial cohesion.
>
> In particular, the Union shall aim at reducing disparities between the levels of development of the various regions and the backwardness of the least favoured regions (TFEU 2012, Article 174, para. 1 and 2).

4 "Flexibility" of Cohesion Policy to Assist Ukraine

EU budget is not only a question of complex financial rules; it is a field of EU law with the principles of constitutional value that is the key in shaping the paths for integration (Gregorio Merino, 2023). Cohesion policy and its programmes have certain rules such as eligibility and allocation criteria that must be applied.

The flexibility of cohesion funds in this paper is viewed through the lens of measures proposed by the European Commission in response to the war in Ukraine. After the start of the war in Ukraine, the EU budget was mobilised to provide emergency assistance and humanitarian support to Ukraine (European Commission, 2022c). Hence, in addition to hundreds of millions of EUR in humanitarian and early recovery assistance to Ukraine since 2014 (European Commission, 2022a), on 8 March 2022 the European Commission proposed the Cohesion's Action for Refugees in Europe (hereinafter: CARE) (European Commission, 2022b). The aim of CARE was to use cohesion policy funds to ease the burden on national and regional budgets with regard to the influx of refugees from Ukraine, especially in the EU's eastern regions. CARE provided "exceptional changes" to the overall 2014–2020 Multiannual Financial Framework (European Commission, 2023c). It introduced extra flexibility in re-allocation of cohesion funds by enabling member states to speed up the deployment of all un-programmed funding under the 2014–2020 Multiannual Financial Framework and introduced new flexibility to cohesion policy rules:

i) the possibility of 100% EU co-financing for 2014–2020 cohesion policy funding. That framework was extended for the accounting year 2021–2022;
ii) the possibility to use resources from either the regional fund ERDF or social fund ESF for any type of measures to support refugees from Ukraine. Therefore, either fund would also be able to support projects that would normally be funded by the other one;
iii) the possibility to spend on all actions for refugees from Ukraine retroactively as of the start date of the Russian invasion (24 February 2022); and
iv) the reporting and the programme modifications were simplified (European Commission, 2022a).

The "flexibility" of cohesion policy was also established when the European Commission announced on 8 March 2022 another possibility to assist Ukraine via cohesion funds. This possibility was the Recovery Assistance for Cohesion and the Territories of Europe (hereinafter: REACT-EU). These funds which originally aimed to provide assistance to crisis repair in the context of the COVID-19 pandemic and its social consequences and for preparing a green, digital and resilient recovery of the economy, were allowed to be used to address the new Ukraine-related demands (European Commission, 2022a). A large part of 10 billion EUR from the 2022 REACT-EU has been made available to member states to support projects to assist refugees from Ukraine without the need for legislative changes. The REACT-EU resources have been provided with a number of implementation flexibilities.

Moreover, on 29 June 2022 the European Commission adopted the Flexible Assistance to Territories Package (FAST–CARE), a new set of legislative and non-legislative proposals to make cohesion policy funds more accessible and flexible (European Commission, 2022b). FAST-CARE provides maximum flexibility with regard to the implementation of EU-funded projects. About 30% of the funding support was supposed to go to local authorities and civil society organisations. Further, additional 3.5 billion euros were made available in advance payments to alleviate the burden on public finances of the EU member states (European Commission, 2022c). The proposed changes included a co-financing rate of up to 100% for activities promoting the socio-economic integration of third-country nationals (European Commission, 2022c). This was possible under the Multiannual Financial Framework (hereinafter:MFF) for 2014–2020 and 2021–2027 programming periods, at least until the next review of the provision in 2024. EU member states were also allowed to benefit from extra flexibility to interchangeably use the unspent resources from the 2014–2020 Cohesion Fund (in addition to ERDF and ESF + already allowed under CARE) to finance projects regardless of their traditional eligibility scope. Other changes included the increase of the unit cost for temporary protection beneficiaries -a simplified way to calculate project costs-, from 40 to 100 euros per week for 26 weeks (European Commission, 2022c).

In summary, cohesion policy instruments that typically aim to achieve economic convergence of less developed EU member states, were in 2022 and 2023 provided with particular flexibility to be used so to assist EU member states to cope with humanitarian crisis following the influx of refugees from Ukraine.

5 Distribution of Cohesion Funds in Eastern EU Close to Ukraine

The enlargement of the EU with Ukraine, Moldova and Western Balkan countries mean large adjustments to the EU budget. On the expenditure side, the enlargement will require a large re-allocation of EU funds, in particular for cohesion policy and the common agriculture policy. Cohesion policy accounts for about a third of the EU budget for the period 2021–2027. Since the aim of cohesion policy is to enhance socio-economic convergence, and candidate countries from east Europe have a considerably lower GDP per capita compared to the current EU member states, a large part of cohesion funds would have to be re-allocated to new EU members. That means that current net beneficiaries would be affected unless the overall budget increases. If not, every country gets a smaller amount of the cohesion funds.

It must be noted that the EU budget has gradually evolved over the years, together with adding new member states and the integration process in the EU. The MFF for 2021–2027 is the largest ever in the history of EU. The EU's 2021–2027 long-term budget (i.e. MFF) and the NextGenerationEU (NGEU) recovery instrument together amount to €2.018 trillion in current prices. About 30.4% of MFF is allocated to

"Economic, Social and Territorial Cohesion" (European Commission, 2023a). The total budget for 2021–2027 for cohesion policy stood at 392 billion EUR as of end of December 2023 (European Commission Cohesion data, 2023). The allocations under the goals and headings were 361,056.8 million euros for *IJG: Investment for jobs and growth goal* (the European Regional Development Fund (ERDF), the European Social Fund + (ESF +), the Cohesion Fund (CF)), and 19,236.9 million euros for the *Just Transition Fund (JTF).* The allocation of cohesion funds in the period 2021–2017 for selected central and eastern European countries is presented in Table 1.

There are growing concerns about politicisation of the EU budget as fiscal rules are becoming more and more politicised despite the fact that they have been traditionally considered a technical field (Mongouachon, 2023).This questions the democratic decision-making in a multi-level EU system that is transforming the financial constitution of European integration significantly (Weber, 2023). With regard to Ukraine the European Commission in June 2023 proposed to reinforce the EU's 2021–2027 EU's long-term budget with:

i. setting up of an Ukraine facility, of €50 billion for 2024–2027 to cater for Ukraine's immediate needs, recovery and modernisation on its path towards the EU and
ii. €15 billion to help the EU address internal and external dimensions of migration, needs arising from the global consequences of Russia's war of aggression in Ukraine, and stronger partnerships with key third countries (European Commission, 2023a).

The European Commission explains that "it has also been instrumental to provide support to Ukraine and to EU countries welcoming refugees" (European Commission, 2023a).

There are legitimate questions about the impact of possible Ukraine's full EU membership on the rest of the EU. Ukraine has a lower GDP per capita than the average of the EU based on purchasing power parity in 2017 international dollar, as calculated by the International Monetary Fund (Fig. 1). The GDP per capita of Ukraine is even worse in comparison to the least developed EU member states

Table 1 Cohesion funds by selected countries in planned budget for 2021–2027 in EUR, as of 20 March 2025

	Poland	Romania	Czechia	Slovakia	Hungary
Total	**92,024,356,677**	**44,430,371,289**	**26,710,816,749**	**16,147,152,251**	**26,135,680,439**
ERDF	58,368,790,950	25,461,381,862	13,815,703,704	9,734,340,776	16,445,998,251
ESF +	15,603,800,951	9,153,933,668	3,157,597,866	2,835,251,420	6,321,197,906
CF	13,274,282,520	7,284,317,701	7,806,348,106	2,923,567,267	3,061,362,686
JTF	4,777,482,256	2,530,738,058	1,931,167,073	653,992,788	307,121,596

Source European Commission, Cohesion policy overview, 2024

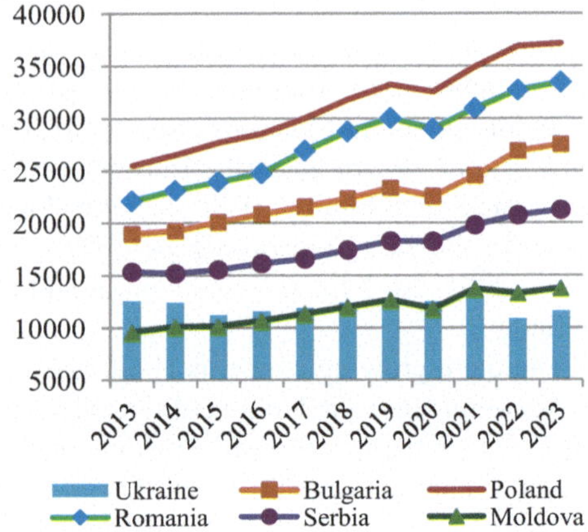

Fig. 1 GDP per capita, constant prices in Ukraine compared to some EU members and candidate countries (*Source* Author's compilation of data from IMF databases, September 2024)

(European Commission Ukraine Report, 2023) and even worse than some other EU candidates (Fig. 1).

A comparison of Ukraine's GDP per capita with some of the most advanced EU member states paints a very gloomy picture (Fig. 2). Taking that into account, it will be painful to allocate funds in the long-term EU budget with regard to future distribution of EU funds between the "old" and "new" EU member states. The gap is larger compared to the previous rounds of enlargement in 2004, 2007 and 2013. Many, if not all, current EU countries that are net recipients from the EU budget may become net contributors to the EU budget because contributions to the budget depend on GDP and new EU members have low GDP. Without a significant change of the EU governance with regard to the EU long-term budget, cohesion funds could be absorbed by Ukraine alone, if it joins as a full EU member state. That may be a particular issue as conflicts between current EU members about the future distribution of EU's structural and cohesion funds have already started (Jones et al., 2023).

6 Helping Ukraine but Still Respecting EU Treaties and the Case of Poland

The MFF is a conventional budgetary basis, based on "programme" spending. However, as some authors have already argued, budgetary spending of the EU evolved in recent years from programme spending to emergency spending and strategic spending, reflecting a shift from "rules-politics" to "events-politics" (Middelaar, 2023). In case of events-politics, the idea is to respond to unanticipated and unforeseen situations. Legal and other researchers have already raised questions on the EU's innovative law making that appears to be on the edge of legalitity (Leino-Sandberg, 2023; Wutscher, 2023). The danger is that "executive decision-making, paired with opportunistic exercise guided by institutional ambition" leads to derogating from

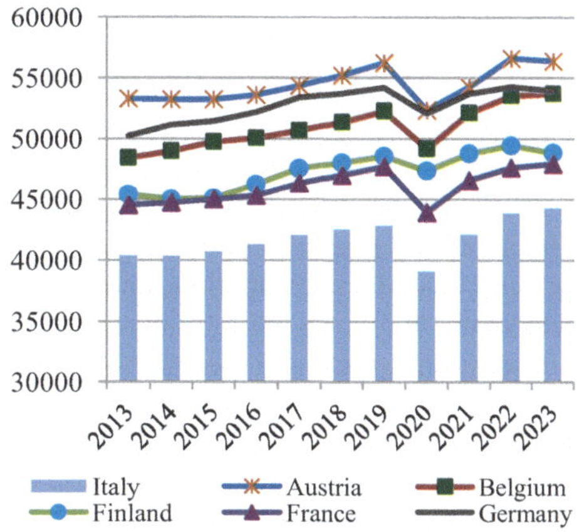

Fig. 2 GDP per capita, constant prices in some advanced EU members (*Source* Author's compilation of data from IMF databases, September 2024)

the EU Treaties and thus expanding EU competence replacing budgetary democracy by technocratic executive action (Leino-Sandberg, 2023). There have been questions of democratic legitimacy, including with regard to creating new EU's "crisis" instruments that allowed the decisions to be taken with qualified majority instead of unanimity. It is no wonder then that concerns about the lack of transparency at the European Commission and the European Council have grown, including with regard to the lack of clear political responsibility for the implementation of the new instruments (Ondarza, 2023).

6.1 Case Study: Poland (and Some Other Countries Next to Ukraine)

Questions about cohesion and economic resilience with regard to the war in Ukraine surfaced particularly in Poland, but not only there; in other eastern EU members there has been a growing discontent as well. It started with certain measures proposed by the European Commission. For example, on 30 May 2022 the EU introduced the Regulation (EU) 2022/870 enforcing trade liberalisation measures applicable to Ukrainian products. Article 1 of this Regulation provisioned the full removal of preferential customs duties on importation into the EU on certain industrial products originating in Ukraine and the suspension of the application of the entry price system to products as specified in Annex I-A to the Association Agreement. Therefore, no customs duties were to be applied to imports of those products and there was the suspension of tariff-rate quotas in addition to the full removal of import duties on products covered by those quotas. Moreover, Article 1 of this Regulation (Regulation, 2022/870, 2022) established that anti-dumping duties on imports originating in Ukraine should not be collected at any point in time, including after the expiry of this Regulation and that there was temporary suspension of the application of Regulation (EU) 2015/478 of the European Parliament and of the Council which enforces rules with regard to surveillance or safeguard measures.

All this aimed to help products from Ukraine reach certain destinations considering that usual traveling routes, particularly via Black Sea, were not available any more. In practice, these measures meant that products from Ukraine were imported into the EU under very favourable conditions. They flooded not only the bordering regions, but the markets in the whole EU. As they were cheaper, EU's producers' products became less competitive and as they increased supply they drove down local prices in the bordering regions, as reported in the news.

In addition to the mentioned measures, in 2022 the European Commission waived the transport permits system and set up special corridors in order to facilitate the transportation of goods between EU member states and Ukraine. The main idea was to facilitate humanitarian and military aid into Ukraine, and also to get Ukrainian grain out. The European Commission introduced "Solidarity Lanes" for extending transport infrastructure network asking EU member states to prioritise Ukrainian agricultural exports along busy freight corridors and to increase inspection capacity at border posts to deal with arrivals 24/7 (European Commission Speech, 2022). In addition, restrictions on Ukrainian drivers were eased and Ukrainian certificates for professional drivers and driving licences have been recognised across the EU.

All this became a problem for the neighbouring EU member states. Due to complaints from Poland, Hungary, Slovakia and Romania, the European Commission adopted exceptional and temporary preventive measures on imports of wheat, maize, rapeseed and sunflower seed originating and imported from Ukraine (European Commission, 2023b). The measures entered into force on 2 May 2023 and were supposed to last until 5 June 2023. During this period those products could be released for free circulation in the whole of EU except in Bulgaria, Poland, Hungary, Slovakia and Romania.

However, on 15 September 2023 the European Commission decided not to extend a ban on Ukrainian grain imports to EU that applied to Poland, Hungary, Slovakia, Romania and Bulgaria (European Commission, 2023b). Since the problem was large for the mentioned countries, on September 16, 2023 Poland, Hungary and Slovakia said they would impose their own bans on Ukrainian grain. Poland introduced national measures because it did not agree with the decision of the European Commission not to extend a ban on certain Ukrainian products. Slovakia banned the import of wheat, corn, rapeseed and sunflower seeds citing excessive pressure on the Slovak farmers (Gijs, 2023). Hungary also imposed an import ban on Ukrainian grains, rapeseed and sunflower seeds, certain meat products, honey and eggs while Poland excluded Ukrainian agricultural wheat, corn and rapeseed. Romania also decided to ban the import of Ukrainian grain and other food products. Poland, Hungary and Slovakia stated that bans were necessary in order to protect their farmers from the extra-large supply from Ukraine that drove down local prices and hurt the wellbeing of local people (Gijs, 2023).

Ukraine complained at the World Trade Organization against Hungary, Poland and Slovakia after they unilateraly imposed bans on imports from Ukraine in September 2023 (World Trade Organization, 2023). The request by Ukraine over the continued imposition of import bans by Hungary, Poland and Slovakia was circulated to World Trade Organization members on 21 September 2023 (World Trade Organization, 2023).

6.2 *Case Study: Poland's Regions Lubelskie and Podkarpackie*

The situation obviously threatened the wellbeing of people in regions bordering Ukraine. It was not just about large quantities of cheap agricultural products being imported, it was also about the transportation problem. In November and December 2023 Polish truckers blocked the largest freight border crossings with Ukraine. They protested against what they saw as their government inaction over a loss of business to Ukrainian competitors. People from the region formed a Committee to Protect Transporters and Transport Employers in the logistics sector. They demanded the reintroduction of entry permits for Ukrainian drivers (Sieradzka, 2023). There have been reports of issues such as that some customs agencies specialised in registering vehicles carrying commercial goods as part of humanitarian or military aid convoys that were free to pass without any restriction (Sieradzka, 2023). Other reports were about the "expansion" of Ukrainian transport companies in the EU market. In Polish border regions of Lubelskie and Podkarpackie, protesters complained because Ukrainians didn't have to meet any European standards, and they were allowed to carry any load in Europe for less, while Polish transport companies had to meet all EU standards. As a result, Ukrainian companies squeezed Polish companies out of the market, which before had accounted for 38% of cross-border transportation but now account only 8% (Euronews, 2023). The main demand by Polish truckers was to stop truckers from Ukraine having permit-free access to the EU. Major cargo border crossings (e.g. Dorohusk-Jagodin, Korczowa-Krakovetz, Medyka-Shehyni and Hrebenne-Rava) are located in the south east of Poland, in the regions Lubelskie and Podkarpackie.

These two regions are among the poorest regions in Poland (OECD, 2018; PBU, 2020). Since they are less developed regions, they have been recipients of cohesion funds, particularly with regard to infrastructure and education. Data from the 2014–2020 MFF show those for Lubelskie region (Table 2) before the war in Ukraine.

Cohesion policy is the EU's main long-term investment framework aimed to promote social, economic and territorial development in the EU (European Court of Auditors, 2023). The eligibility and funding for cohesion funds are granted in line with geographical criteria. The outcomes are assessed in terms of the performance in administrative regions. Within the MFF, which is a planning framework for periods of 7 years, annual ceilings for expenditure are set in each broad heading of the budget (European Court of Auditors, 2022). Funds are pre-allocated to individual EU member states as a result of the various formulae to determine where spending is allocated (European Parliament Budget, 2023).

Table 2 Lubelskie, programming period 2014–2020

Date	Project	Total investment in EUR	EU funding in EUR
28 June 2016	Construction of S19 express road Lublin —Rzeszow, section Lublin Sławinek—Lublin Węglin	149 648 817	CF: 66 149 817
28 July 2017	Works on the railway line No. 7 Warszawa Wschodnia Osobowa—Dorohusk, section: Warszawa—Otwock—Dęblin—Lublin, Phase I	1 085 922 875	CF: 750 434 507
05 October 2017	Construction of S3 express road: Gorzów Wielkopolski—Nowa Sól (section Sulechów Kruszyna—Nowa Sól)	324 967 126	CF:180 615 171
09 May 2018	Construction of the S17 express road, section Garwolin—Kurów	529 721 579	CF: 273 510 962
22 November 2018	Improving the labour market relevance of upper secondary education through the construction of a new building for practical vocational training in the existing upper secondary school complex in Radzyń Podlaski—stage I and the purchase of equipment for vocational training workshops and classrooms	1 540 276	ERDF: 700 055
14 October 2020	Remote School—support of the National Education Network in the remote education system	82 110 951	ERDF: 82 110 951
14 October 2021	Improved Rail Connections and Smart Mobility In Central Europe	2 602 924	ERDF: 2 142 529

Source European Commission, project database, 2024

According to the government of Poland, the value of GDP per capita in eastern Poland ranges from 67 to 84% of the national average (Ministry of Development Funds & Regional Policy, 2021). These figures indicate why both regions, Lubelskie and Podkarpackie, were allocated significant amount of cohesion funds. Funding from the European Regional and Development Fund (ERDF) and the Cohesion Fund (CF) were provided or have been committed to for the period 2014–2020 for Lubelskie (Table 2) and Podkarpackie (Table 4). Funding provided for both regions is in line with the Treaty on the functioning of the EU (TFEU) which states that:

> Among the regions concerned, particular attention shall be paid to rural areas, areas affected by industrial transition, and regions which suffer from severe and permanent natural or demographic handicaps such as the northernmost regions with very low population density and island, cross-border and mountain regions. (TFEU, Article 174, para. 3)

Lubelskie and Podkarpackie are two regions in Poland that border on Ukraine and have a high percentage of population at risk of poverty (Table 3).

Table 3 Percentage of population at risk of poverty (2020–2023) by regions as of 20 March 2025

	2020	2021	2022	2023
Poland	17.0	16.8	15.9	16.3
Makroregion południowy	13.0	15.1	12.5	12.5
Małopolskie	15.1	16.0	15.0	14.8
Śląskie	11.4	14.5	10.5	10.7
Makroregion północno-zachodni	16.7	16.9	16.5	16.4
Wielkopolskie	18.1	17.8	16.4	16.4
Zachodniopomorskie	15.0	14.6	16.5	16.8
Lubuskie	14.2	17.3	16.7	16.0
Makroregion południowo-zachodni	13.6	12.0	12.5	13.8
Dolnośląskie	12.7	12.1	12.1	14.4
Opolskie	16.3	11.4	13.8	11.9
Makroregion północny	17.9	19.9	19.3	21.3
Kujawsko-pomorskie	19.7	23.3	19.9	24.1
Warmińsko-mazurskie	24.2	22.5	23.8	24.7
Pomorskie	12.4	15.3	16.2	16.9
Makroregion centralny	16.7	15.4	17.1	18.0
Łódzkie	16.4	157	17.4	16.1
Świętokrzyskie	17.2	14.7	16.6	22.0
Makroregion wschodni	24.0	21.6	22.9	21.3
Lubelskie	26.0	24.4	25.3	22.1
Podkarpackie	22.0	19.2	19.0	17.2
Podlaskie	24.2	21.0	25.6	27.0
Makroregion województwo mazowieckie	17.9	15.5	11.9	12.6
Warszawski stołeczny	12.8	10.7	7.7	8.9
Mazowiecki regionalny	24.0	22.0	18.0	18.0

Source Eurostat, 2025

Cohesion policy has clearly helped convergence between the average of the EU and other regions, including Poland, but the war in Ukraine has obviously tested the coherence, economic resilience and economic security in certain regions.

According to the government of Poland, in the MFF for 2021–2027 it was earmarked that Lubelskie would receive 1.768 billion euros and Podkarpackie 1.661 billion euros (Ministry of Development Funds & Regional Policy, 2021). However, that was envisaged in 2021, before the start of the war in Ukraine, which changed the situation in these two regions.

Data in Table 4 shows that projects in labour market and investment in infrastructure in Podkarpackie in 2014–2020 MFF period (before the war in Ukraine) were large, exceeding one billion euros.

Table 4 Podkarpackie, programming period 2014–2020

Date	Project	Total investment in EUR	EU funding in EUR
29 November 2016	Modernizacja linii kolejowej E30/C-E30, odcinek Kraków-Rzeszów, etap III—Faza II	196 133 650	CF: 109 727 850
29 November 2017	Construction of S8 express road Wyszków-Białystok, section Wyszków—Mazowieckie/ Podlaskie border	317 523 087	CF: 154 182 783
21 February 2019	Modernization of the railway line E30/C-E 30, Kraków-Rzeszów section, stage III	959 015 230	ERDF: 571 374 843
01 March 2019	Implementation of product innovation in the form of high definition texture-based spatial 2.5D and 3D printing of medals on the European market, based on R&D	1 560 000	ERDF: 820 000
10 May 2019	Implementation of an integrated low-carbon emission transportation system: Sanok-Lesko	6 958 176	ERDF: 4 954 830
14 August 2019	Development of low-carbon transport in the Municipal Functional Area Krosno	9 023 345	ERDF: 6 412 715
05 November 2019	Purchase of platform wagons for intermodal transport by PKP CARGO S.A	106 362 534	CF: 43 209 359
11 May 2020	PIONIER-LAB—National Platform for Integration of Research Infrastructures for Innovation Ecosystem	122 127 142	ERDF: 71 074 361
31 May 2022	Employment in ZAZ (Vocational Rehabilitation Unit) is my chance	533 821	ERDF: 453 748
20 April 2022	Installation of renewable energy systems in the area belonging to the Association of Municipalities of the Wisłoka River Basin	3 515 594	ERDF: 2 246 214
27 August 2020	Modernisation of the Terrain Centre for Ecological Education of Bieszczady National Park in Suche Rzeki	444 882	CF: 307 450
27 September 2019	Innovative platform for recruiting IT specialists—Challengerocket.com	243 521	ERDF: 187 404

Source European Commission, project database, August 2024

However, certain regional statistics by NUTS2 classification[1] that are relevant to look for an impact of the conflict in Ukraine on both regions, are not available at the Eurostat database. For example, as of March 2025 data for economic accounts for agriculture for Lubelskie and Podkarpackie end with the year 2019 (Eurostat

[1] NUTS abbreviation stands for the nomenclature of territorial units for statistics. The EU developed this system for statistical and policy purposes. NUTS nomenclature divides each country intro three levels. NUTS2 mentioned here relates to basic regions (for regional policies) as regions eligible for support from cohesion policy have been defined at NUTS2 level.

database, 2025b). There are some auxiliary data for 2023. For example, according to the database on domestic product indicators, the data on average annual population to calculate regional GDP data shows the decline of population in both regions since 2014 and that that trend has not reversed in 2022 and 2023 (Eurostat database, 2025a). Still, due to short time frame and non-availability of certain data, no firm conclusions can be made for Lubelskie and Podkarpackie regions in relation to the impact of the war in Ukraine.

However, some indications about the people's perception of economic resilience and economic security in those two regions are provided by the EU survey from the beginning of 2024. According to the Flash Eurobarometer survey carried out between 11 January and 15 February 2024 in EU regions, people in Lubelskie and Podkarpackie provided answers that show that their concerns about economic situation and unemployment were larger compared to the average of the EU27 (Table 5).

According to the same survey, only 8% of people in Lubelskie and 9% of people in Podkarpackie were very optimistic about the future of their region compared to the average of the EU27 where that figure was higher, standing at 13% (European Commission Eurobarometer, 2024).

It appears that today, even if people are still generally pro-European, they are increasingly more concerned with their standard of living. For example, six months before the 2024 European Elections, the European Parliament's Autumn 2023 Eurobarometer survey revealed that Europeans continued to value EU membership but wanted the European Parliament to prioritise the fight against poverty and social exclusion (36%) and public health (34%) as the main topics, followed by action against climate change and support to the economy and creation of new jobs (both 29%). 73% of respondents thought that their standard of living would decrease in the next year (European Parliament Eurobarometer, 2023). Over a third of Europeans (37%) experience difficulties paying bills either sometimes or most of the time Their disaffection was expressed in the European elections in June of 2024, as parties that are EU-sceptic made huge gains in many countries.

Table 5 What do you think are the most important issues facing your region at the moment?

	EU27	Lubelskie	Podkarpackie
Immigration	13%	20%	20%
Economic situation and unemployment	26%	38%	31%
People and/or business going away from the region	8%	13%	16%
Cost of living	31%	37%	31%

Source European Commission, flash eurobarometer FL539, 2024

7 Looking Ahead

The EU launched its European Neighbourhood Policy in early 2000s to deal with the EU's neighbours with tools other than promises of accession (Brunet, 2013). This policy was "not designed as a clear alternative to membership, but as an indefinite, composite and multidirectional policy that remained ambivalent about its ultimate purpose" (Cadier, 2013, p.57). That approach obviously changed after February 2022.

Despite the fact that the EU has emphasised, particularly since 2013 onward, that accession to the EU depends on fulfilling the accession criteria and is therefore a merit-based process, the EU has made it clear that Ukraine's membership is a geopolitical decision. Such an approach may exacerbate tensions between the widening and deepening of the EU because of an "illusion that EU membership creates more homogeneity amongst its members" (Verheugen, 2013, p.8). New member states, if they become full members of the EU, are likely to increase tensions in economic and social cohesion and threaten economic resilience not only because of their lower level of GDP per capita, but also because they have large financing needs, particularly Ukraine. The EU budgetary exposure to Ukraine more than doubled in 2022 compared to 2021 (from €7 billion to €16 billion) and exposure for future budgets will significantly increase (European Court of Auditors, 2022).

Over the last few years, the introduction of certain instruments in the EU in response to various crises, shocks and/or perceived new needs has significantly increased the overall size and complexity of the EU's public finances. Budgetary operations outside the EU's budget provide more flexibility because they can be created (or activated) relatively quickly by using Article 122 of TFEU (European Parliament Budget, 2023). However, there is a question of transparency and efficiency because for many of the newly introduced instruments, the European Parliament has almost no or a very limited role in decision-making and oversight (European Parliament Budget, 2023). As some authors noted the "emergency Article 122" of TFEU which was rarely used before recent crises "largely excludes the involvement of the European Parliament" (Ondarza, 2023, p.1).

As stated by the European Court of Auditors in its reports, the MFF budget allocations for cohesion are intended for the EU member states (ECA, 2022). Although some may argue that it is necessary to modify cohesion policy in the context of the current challenges, the EU Treaties are clear about the aim and purpose of cohesion policy instruments. Cohesion funds are envisaged as funds that support regions in the EU member states.

It may be a difficult methodological question to assess the precise socio-economic impact of cohesion policy. However, from the policy viewpoint, it is clear that the new round of EU enlargement should be supported by adequate EU policies, notably in the area of cohesion, particularly in certain regions and sectors of the current EU member states. Applying "flexibility of cohesion policy" and its occasional, incremental instruments similar to those introduced by the European Commission in 2021, 2022 and 2023 may not be adequate. The performance and eligibility criteria of cohesion policy should focus on regional development priorities from the perspective of economic security and resilience of people, particularly in regions bordering on Ukraine. Further, the emergence of anti-EU and EU-sceptical parties in EU member states must be considered seriously. The obvious policy implication of accession of new member states is that the EU governance must change, particularly with regard to majority voting. That implies the changes of EU Treaties.

Moreover, some "old" EU member states might not be supportive of the new enlargement due to the democratic backsliding, government instability and corruption in some of the newer member states, such as Bulgaria, Croatia, Hungary, Poland, and Romania (Bernhard, 2021; Cianetti et al., 2019; Stanley, 2019). Developments in these countries raised questions about how to keep them committed to the EU fundamental values once there was no conditionality of the pre-accession period.

After it lost the UK that was one of the largest net contributor to the EU budget, accepting new members that are far below the EU average in terms of GDP per capita will be clearly a challenge for the EU. It is no wonder then that it has been argued that the solution to a "shock" of the new members is to undertake a major reform of the EU policies, processes and institutions (Bossong et al., 2022).

The EU's capacity to absorb additional member states is one of key factors in the accession process. Previous rounds of EU enlargements were not easy, but the addition of up to ten more members with many open questions means even more challenges for the EU which is currently already burdened with a number of economic and other problems.

The impact of enlargement on the EU's effectiveness in decision-making will be even more problematic in view of unanimity voting requirement in certain areas. With more EU members, there is a higher probability of vetoes being exercised to block decisions. It might be then more efficient to take decisions in an enlarged EU by qualified majority. Today, many decisions require a qualified majority that is at least 55% of EU member states, representing at least 65% of the EU population. However, decisions about EU budget and enlargement still require unanimity. The unanimity principle in the EU enlargement process can be exploited, for instance with a veto power in enlargement negotiations.

A set of constitutional changes, including the change of EU Treaties with regard to unanimity and majority voting rights, were proposed by the Conference on the Future of the European Union (European Parliament, 2023). Some EU governments are likely to block this path. Poland, Czechia and Hungary have already clearly indicated their opposition to EU Treaty changes (Krzysztoszek, 2023). Smaller central and eastern EU members are worried that they may lose influence over EU decision-making if unanimity principle changes into the qualified majority voting principle. That means that a wider application of qualified majority (for example in decision-making on EU budget) erodes the voice of the smaller EU countries. Therefore, EU member states that are against amending the EU Treaties but are in favour of Ukraine's accession to the EU may find themselves in a position that they will have to agree with the adjustment of EU's decision-making procedures.

There are various ideas in regard to future EU enlargement. One of them, called "staged accession" has been suggested by Pierre Mirel. It is about "progressing towards accession in stages according to reforms achieved, with each stage giving access to increased funds; establishing a consolidation phase at the end of the negotiations before full membership" (Mirel, 2022, p.1). The first stage would be the implementation of the association agreements and some symbolic reforms. The candidate country would then receive a fraction of the structural funds. The second step would be the integration of the country into the EU internal market. This, combined with the parallel completion of the regional common market, should accelerate investment. Reforms in the various sectors/chapters would lead to the next steps and progress on fundamental elements of the rule of law should be made throughout the process, for example in the fight against corruption in relation to the EU internal market (public procurement and conflicts of interest in particular) (Mirel, 2022).

This "differentiated integration" may not be appealing to some candidate countries that want nothing else but full EU membership, and possibly immediately. If the EU is going to insist on full compliance with regard to the accession criteria, as it has insisted with the Western Balkans so far, time and circumstances may play an important role. Can the accession with Ukraine last for years or decades, as has been with the Western Balkans? On the other hand, if the EU ignores serious issues and deficiencies in the progress of Ukraine, it risks being burdened with unresolved problems that have no solutions. Ignoring the merit-based criteria for enlargement may deal a serious blow to the functioning and survival of the EU as a bloc.

The EU cannot do much to help eliminate certain structural issues in EU member states. For instance, corruption. Some authors have found that the EU is not only incapable to eliminate structural reasons for corruption in any member state, it may even add to the problem through its transfers to member states (Mungiu-Pippidi, 2013).

Finally, how to strengthen economic resilience in border regions in the current EU member states? An example of Poland is illustrative enough. Changes introduced by European Commission's "Solidarity Lanes" in 2022 have considerably reduced the competitiveness of Polish truckers. Although their protests were not supported by the government of Poland, the European Commission threatened the government of Poland to resolve this issue soon (Liboreiro, 2023). But it was people who protested, not the government. Unfortunately, some politicians in the EU do not seem to be listening to people. The mood of people is changeable and it is not guaranteed that the solidarity with Ukraine shown after February 2022 translates into strong support for EU enlargement in the future.

8 Conclusion

This paper looks at the cohesion policy of the EU through the lens of EU enlargement. From this perspective policy implications are many and they are complex. The EU must respect the EU law and therefore cannot deviate too much in its creativity about the EU budget in order to accommodate Ukraine. On the other hand, eastern EU member states bordering on Ukraine are facing special circumstances that have threatened their economic security and resilience. Finally, if the EU is serious to enlarge the EU with Ukraine, Moldova and the Western Balkans, it will have to change its governance. That implies amending the EU Treaties. However, there is not a lot of enthusiasm about that option in certain EU member states.

The key objective of cohesion policy is to enhance economic convergence and support long-term sustainable development in all EU regions, including the most deprived regions. Looking at the current enlargement round, particularly with regard to Ukraine, the EU cannot ignore "narrow" questions connected with the EU budget. In order to act in line with the main principles of cohesion policy and instruments set by the EU Treaties, economic security and resilience of the local population in bordering regions must be taken into account seriously and properly.

Enlargement should not exacerbate existing inequalities in the EU, particularly in the border regions vis-à-vis the rest of the EU. That would create unpleasant picture of winners and losers. In either case, relevant cohesion and other policies aiming to strengthen economic security and resilience in the EU, particularly in bordering regions, will be crucial in years to come.

Future research would benefit from relevant data for Lubelskie and Podkarpackie in order to assess the impact of war in Ukraine in order to adjust relevant policies at the EU and national level.

References

Bernhard, M. (2021). Democratic backsliding in Poland and Hungary. *Slavic Review, 80*(3), 585–607. https://doi.org/10.1017/slr.2021.145

Blatter K. J., Haverland, M., & Hulst, V. M. (2016). *Qualitative research in political science.* SAGE Publications.

Bossong, R., Geden, O., Härtel, A., Kempin, R. et al. (2022). Ukraine's possible EU accession and its consequences. *Stiftung Wissenschaft un Politik.* German Institute for International and Security Affairs. https://www.swp-berlin.org/en/publication/ukraines-possible-eu-accession-and-its-consequences

Brinkmann, S., Jacobsen, M. H., & Kristiansen, S. (2014). Historical overview of qualitative research in the social sciencies. In P. Leavy (Ed.), *The Oxford Handbook of Qualiative Research* (pp. 17–42). Oxford University Press.

Brunet, L. A. (2013, November). Executive summary. *LSE Ideas, Special Report, SR018.* https://www.lse.ac.uk/ideas/Assets/Documents/reports/LSE-IDEAS-Crisis-of-EU-Enlargement.pdf

Cadier, D. (2013). Is the European neighbourhood policy a substitute for enlargement? *LSE Ideas, Special Report,* 52–58. https://www.lse.ac.uk/ideas/Assets/Documents/reports/LSE-IDEAS-Crisis-of-EU-Enlargement.pdf

Cianetti, L., Dawson, J., & Hanley, S. L. (2019). *Rethinking 'democratic backsliding' in Central and Eastern Europe—Looking beyond Hungary and Poland*. Routledge.

Court of Auditors. (2022). *Cohesion policy—Where has it come from? Where is it going?* https://euauditors.medium.com/cohesion-policy-where-has-it-come-from-where-is-it-going-79aa681dd583

ECA. (2022). *2022. EU audit in brief*. https://www.eca.europa.eu/ECAPublications/AIB-2022/AIB-2022_EN.pdf

EUR-Lex. (1957). *Treaty establishing the European Economic Community*. https://eur-lex.europa.eu/eli/treaty/teec/sign

EUR-Lex EIB. (2023). *European Investment Bank (EIB).* https://eur-lex.europa.eu/EN/legal-content/glossary/european-investment-bank-eib.html#:~:text=Established%20in%201958%20under%20the,projects%20which%20further%20EU%20objectives.
EUR-LexESF. (2023). *European Social Fund (ESF).* https://eur-lex.europa.eu/EN/legal-content/glossary/european-social-fund-esf.html
Euronews. (2023). Explanied: Why truckers are blockading the EU's eastern border with Ukraine. 4/12/2023. https://www.euronews.com/my-europe/2023/12/04/explained-why-truckers-are-blockading-the-eus-eastern-borderwith-ukraine
European Commission. (2022a). *Ukraine: EU coordinating emergency assistance and steps up humaritarian aid.* https://ec.europa.eu/commission/presscorner/detail/es/ip_22_1462
European Commission. (2022b). *Ukraine: Cohesion funding to support people fleeing Russia's invasion of Ukraine.* https://ec.europa.eu/commission/presscorner/detail/en/ip_22_1607
European Commission. (2022c). *EU assistance to Ukraine.* https://eu-solidarity-ukraine.ec.europa.eu/eu-assistance-ukraine_en
European Commission. (2023a). *EU budget today. Midterm review of the MFF 2021–2027.* https://www.commission.europa.eu/strategy-and-policy/eu-budget/motion/today_en
European Commission. (2023b). *Following the expiry of the restrictive measures on Ukrainian exports of grain and other foodstuff to the EU, Ukraine agrees to introduce measures to avoid a renewed surge in EU imports.* https://ec.europa.eu/commission/presscorner/detail/en/IP_23_4497
European Commission. (2023c). *European leaders decide to open accession negotiations with Ukraine and Moldova in a historic summit.* https://ec.europa.eu/commission/presscorner/detail/en/ac_23_6711
European Council. (2023). *European council conclusions on Ukraine, enlargement and reforms.* https://www.consilium.europa.eu/en/press/press-releases/2023/12/14/european-council-conclusions-on-ukraine-enlargement-and-reforms/
European Commission Cohesion Data. (2023). *2021–2027 Cohesion policy overview.* https://cohesiondata.ec.europa.eu/cohesion_overview/21–27
European Commission Eurobarometer. (2024). *Flash eurobarometer FL539: Public opinion in the EU regions.* https://www.data.europa.eu/data/datasets/s3218_fl539_eng?locale=en
European Commission Speech. (2022). *Speaking points press conference EU- Ukraine.* Solidarity Lanes. https://ec.europa.eu/commission/presscorner/detail/en/SPEECH_22_3036
European Commission Ukraine Report. (2023). *Commission staff working document. Brussels, 8.11.2023. SWD (2023).699 final.* https://neighbourhood-enlargement.ec.europa.eu/system/files/2023-11/SWD_2023_699%20Ukraine%20report.pdf
European Court of Auditors. (2022). Cohesion policy reflects what the EU is all about—and will remain for the ECA one of the most important areas to audit. *Interview with Martin Weber, ECA Director.* https://euauditors.medium.com/cohesion-policy-reflects-what-the-eu-is-all-about-and-will-remain-for-the-eca-one-of-the-most-c5242da816c9
European Court of Auditors. (2023). *Financing through cohesion policy and the recovery and resilience facility: A comparative analysis.* https://www.eca.europa.eu/en/publications?ref=RW23_01
European Parliament. (2021). *Just transition fund.* https://www.europarl.europa.eu/factsheets/en/sheet/214/just-transition-fund#:~:text=The%20final%20text%20of%20the,Journal%20on%2030%20June%202021
European Parliament. (2023). *Proposals of the European Parliament for the amendment of the treaties.* https://www.europarl.europa.eu/doceo/document/TA-9-2023-0427_EN.html
European Parliament Budget. (2023). Options for a stronger and more agile EU budget. https://www.europarl.europa.eu/RegData/etudes/STUD/2023/755099/IPOL_STU(2023)755099_EN.pdf
European Parliament Eurobarometer. (2023). EP Autumn 2023 Survey: Six months before the 2024 European Elections. https://europa.eu/eurobarometer/surveys/detail/3152

Eurostat Database. (2025a). *Average annual population to calculate regional GDP data (thousand persons) by NUTS3 region*. https://ec.europa.eu/eurostat/databrowser/view/nama_10r_3popgdp/default/table?lang=en&category=reg.reg_eco10.reg_eco10gdp

Eurostat Database. (2025b). *Economic accounts for agriculture by NUTS2 region*. https://ec.europa.eu/eurostat/databrowser/view/agr_r_accts/default/table?lang=en&category=reg.reg_agr.reg_agr_

George, L. A., & Bennet, A. (2005). *Case studies and theory development in the social sciences*. MIT Press.

Gijs, C. (2023, September 16). Poland, Hungary, Slovakia impose own Ukraine grain bans as EU measure expires. *Politico*. https://www.politico.eu/article/poland-hungary-slovakia-extend-grain-bans-despite-blocs-lift/

Gregori Merino, A. (2023). Follow the money, follow the values. In R. Weber (Ed.), *The Financial Constitution of European Integration* (pp. 113–130). Hart Publishing.

Jones, M. G., Tidey, A., & Liborerio, J. (2023, December 15). Hungary's Orbán blocks €50bn EU long-term financial support to Ukraine. *Euronews*. https://www.euronews.com/my-europe/2023/12/15/hungarys-orban-blocks-eus-50bn-long-term-financial-support-to-ukraine

Klimkin, P., & Miklos, I. (2023). Why Ukraine delayed integration and reforms. And why it's high time to get serious. *VoxEU CEPR*. https://cepr.org/voxeu/columns/why-ukraine-delayed-integration-and-reforms-and-why-its-high-time-get-serious

Krzysztoszek, A. (2023, November 22). Poland's Tusk opposes treaty changes. *Euroactiv*. https://www.euractiv.com/section/politics/news/polands-tusk-opposes-eu-treaty-changes/

Leino-Sandberg, P. (2023). Constitutional imaginaries of solidarity: Framing fiscal integration post-NGEU. In R. Weber (Ed.), *The Financial Constitution of European Integration* (pp. 161–188). Hart Publishing.

Liboreiro, J. (2023, November 29). Brussels threatens Poland with legal action over 'unacceptable' truckers blockade at Ukraine border. *Euronews*. https://www.euronews.com/my-europe/2023/11/29/brussels-threatens-poland-with-legal-action-over-unacceptable-truckers-blockade-at-ukraine

Ludlow, N. P. (2013). Hard-won but Vital: EU enlargement in historical perspective. *LSE Ideas. Special Report, SR018:12–18*. https://www.lse.ac.uk/ideas/Assets/Documents/reports/LSE-IDEAS-Crisis-of-EU-Enlargement.pdf

Middelaar, V. L. (2023). Investment Politics: A new capacity to project union action into the future? In R. Weber (Ed.) *The Financial Constitution of European Integration* (pp. 237–258). Hart Publishing

Ministry of Development Funds and Regional Policy. (2021). *European funds for Eastern Poland—What will they look like in 2021–2027?* https://www.gov.pl/web/funds-regional-policy/european-funds-for-eastern-poland---what-will-they-look-like-in-2021-2027

Mirel, P. (2022). In support of a new approach with the Western Balkans: Staged accession with a consolidation phase. *Foundation Robert Schuman. European issues, no.633*. https://old.robert-schuman.eu//en/doc/questions-d-europe/qe-633-en.pdf

Mongouachon, C. (2023). The debate on the revision of the European fiscal rules: Towards more political governance of the EMU? In R. Weber (Ed.), *The Financial Constitution of European Integration* (pp. 69–92). Hart Publishing.

Mrak, M., & Zuber, P. (2022). Ukraine's EU accession process in the field of regional and local development. *ULEAD with Europe*. https://u-lead.org.ua/en/news/234

Mungiu-Pippidi, A. (2013, April 9). The good, the bad and the ugly: Controlling corruption in the European Union. *Advanced Policy Paper for Discussion in the European Parliament*. https://www.againstcorruption.eu/wp-content/uploads/2013/03/ANTICORRP-Policy-Paper-on-Lessons-Learnt-final.pdf

O'Carroll, L. (2023, December 15). Hungary blocks €50bn in EU aid for Ukraine hours after membership talks approved. *The Guardian*. https://www.theguardian.com/world/2023/dec/15/hungary-blocks-50bn-in-eu-aid-for-ukraine-hours-after-membership-talks-were-approved

OECD. (2018). *Regions and cities at a Glance 2018—Poland*. https://www.oecd-ilibrary.org/governance/oecd-regions-and-cities-at-a-glance-2018_reg_cit_glance-2018-en

Ondarza, V. N. (2023). The crisis governance of the European Union. *SWP Research Paper 2023/RP 10*. https://doi.org/10.18449/2023RP10

Parandii, K. (2023). Eastern Europe joins the Western Balkans. *GMF Report*. https://www.gmfus.org/sites/default/files/2023-06/Parandii%20-%20EU%20Enlargement%20-%20Report.pdf

PBU. (2020). *Socio-economic analysis for the programme area PL-BY-UA*. https://www.pbu2020.eu/files/uploads/pages_en/pbu2021-2027/documents/PBU%202021-2027%20Socio–economic%20analysis%20of%20the%20Programme%20area.pdf

Regulation 2022/870. (2022). Regulation (EU) 2022/870 on temporary trade-liberalisation measures supplementing trade concessions applicable to Ukranian products under the association agreement between the European Union and the EAEC and their member states, of the one part, and Ukraine, of the other part. *Official Journal of the EU L 152*, 3.6.2022

RFE/RL. (2023, December 1). Orban says Ukraine's EU accession not currently in Hungary's interest. *RadioFreeEurope/RL* https://www.rferl.org/a/orban-ukraine-eu-membership-hungary-interest-partnership/32710057.html

Sanchez Nicolas, E., & Soler, P. (2023, December 14). EU agrees Ukraine accession talks as Orbán leaves room. *Euobserver*. https://euobserver.com/eu-political/157830

Sieradzka, M. (2023, November 29). Deadlock: Polish truckers' border protest enters third week. *DW*. https://www.dw.com/en/polish-truckers-protest-unfair-competition-by-blocking-ukraine-border-crossings/a-67580337

Stanley, B. (2019). Backsliding away? The quality of democracy in Central and Eastern Europe backsliding away? The quality of democracy in Central and Eastern Europe. *Journal of Contemporay European Research, 15*(4), 1–11.

TEU. (2012). Consolidated version of the treaty on European Union. *Official Journal of the European Union C* 326/13, 26.10.2012.

TFEU. (2012). Consolidated version of the treaty on the functioning of the European Union. *Official Journal of the European Union C 326/47*, 26.10.2012

Verheugen, G. (2013). Enlargement since 2000: Too much too soon? *LSE Ideas. Special report, 8–12. SR018*. https://www.lse.ac.uk/ideas/Assets/Documents/reports/LSE-IDEAS-Crisis-of-EU-Enlargement.pdf

Walldén, A. S. (2017). The demise of EU enlargement policy. https://www.eliamep.gr/wp-content/uploads/2017/03/Enlargement-policy-1701-fin.pdf

Wankiewicz, P. (2023). The fading star pupil: Ten years of Croatia's membership in the European Union. *Centre for Eastern Studies, OSW Commentary 2023–08–18*. https://www.osw.waw.pl/en/publikacje/osw-commentary/2023-08-18/fading-star-pupil-ten-years-croatias-membership-european-union

Weber, R. (2023). Follow the money! In R. Weber (Ed.), *The Financial Constitution of European Integration* (pp. 1–16). Hart Publishing.

World Trade Organization. (2023). *Ukraine initiates WTO dispute complaints against Hungary, Poland and Slovak Republic*. https://www.wto.org/english/news_e/news23_e/ds619_620_621rfc_21sep23_e.htm

Wutscher, C. (2023). When size matters: On the legality of the recovery instrument "next generation EU' in light of its unprecedented volume. In R. Weber (Ed.), *The Financial Constitution of European Integration* (pp. 131–144). Hart Publishing.

Measuring the Financial Resilience of Sectoral Indices: An Analysis of Financial Crises in Turkey

Gökhan Berk Özbek

Abstract In the last quarter-century, Turkey has faced three significant financial crises, one of which originated entirely from its own reasons. The first one occurred during 2000–2001, resulting from its internal dynamics. The second was the 2008–2009 Crisis, a global crisis with effects felt worldwide. The last one, again specifically due to its internal dynamics, started in 2018 and was further compounded by the negative impacts of the pandemic. The effects of this crisis still persist in Turkey today. This study comparatively examines the financial resilience of sectoral indices in BIST (Borsa Istanbul—formerly known as Istanbul Stock Exchange) against the mentioned financial crises. Financial resistance and financial recovery are considered as indicators of financial resilience. For the measurement of financial resistance, the performances of sectoral indices have been examined during the pre-crisis and post-crisis periods. In this context, the BIST 100 has been used as a benchmark for a financial resistance index. Through this resistance index, the sensitivity of sectoral indices to financial crises compared to the BIST 100 has been measured. Additionally, a financial recovery index is employed, using the performance of sectoral indices within the 3 years following each crisis. This allows for a comparative analysis in terms of financial recovery. In the study, the 2000–2001 Crisis and the 2008–2009 Crisis were empirically examined, while the 2018 Crisis was theoretically examined due to its ongoing impact on Turkey. For the 2000–2001 Crisis, the start date of the post-crisis period is chosen as 27.11.2000 (the date when some bank owners were featured in the news with their hands handcuffed due to bank embezzlement charges) and for the 2008–2009 Crisis, it is selected as 15.09.2008 (the date of Lehman Brothers' collapse). According to the research results, the sectors most affected by the 2000–2001 Crisis were, in order, the service sector, technology sector, real estate investment trusts sector, and wholesale & retail trade sector. Banking sector and industrial sector, on the other hand, demonstrated a higher level of resistance compared to the benchmark index. The underlying reason for this is believed to be the structural reform decisions taken for the banking sector in a relatively short period following the crisis and the swift implementation of legal regulations, especially

G. B. Özbek (✉)
Lecturer of Accounting and Finance, Department of Accounting and Taxation, Harmancık Vocational School, Bursa Uludağ University, Bursa, Turkey
e-mail: gbozbek@uludag.edu.tr

I. Bartuseviciene et al. (eds.), *Building Economic Resilience*, Contributions to Economics, https://doi.org/10.1007/978-3-031-96428-2_2

aimed at enhancing exports. Indeed, these two sectors have been the most successful in overcoming the effects of the crisis according to the recovery index. In the 2008–2009 Crisis, the two sectors that were unsuccessful according to the resistance index were the real estate investment trusts sector and the industrial sector. The limited impact of the crisis on developing economies was also applicable to Turkey. In this regard, despite many sectors overcoming this crisis with minimal difficulty, adverse events in international markets, especially negatively affecting exports, have harmed the industrial sector. Additionally, it is believed that the crisis, originating from mortgage-related issues, has negatively impacted the real estate sector as well.

Keywords Financial crisis · Financial resilience · Sectoral indices

Jel Classification Codes · G01 · G15 · O17

1 Introduction

Since the early years of the Republic, ensuring stability in the Turkish economy has been one of the primary goals of all governments that have come to power. Because given the great sacrifices made by the population during the war years and the subsequent period of building a new country, the longing of the people for economic prosperity has increased significantly. Nevertheless, achieving this has never been easy. The Turkish economy has faced numerous financial crises throughout its historical past. In addition to global crises, it has also experienced many crises originating from its internal dynamics. Among these internal dynamics, long-standing issues such as exchange rate problems, high inflation, and flawed interest rate policies have been at the forefront for many years (Cömert & Yeldan, 2018; Temiz & Gökmen, 2009; Yurdakul, 2014). Especially in the years before the 2000s, political instability that prevailed in the country's agenda has brought about financial instability as well. Short-term populist economic decisions have led to the inability to implement long-term economic development.

The impact of financial crises on capital markets, with relatively limited depth and breadth, is quite significant. During financial crisis periods, the increase in volatility and downside risk in the stock market (Gazioğlu, 2008; Sekmen, 2015) leads savers to turn to alternative investment instruments perceived as safe havens. Consequently, this makes the transfer of capital to the real sector more challenging. Additionally, expectations of a rise in exchange rates and high inflationary processes create an increasing effect on dollarization in national economies (Havrylyshyn & Beddies, 2003; Korhonen, 1996). The Turkish economy, in particular, has frequently been drawn into the spiral of dollarization during financial crisis periods (Barbuta-Misu et al., 2020; Metin-Özcan & Us, 2007). One of the fundamental reasons for this situation is the loss of investors' confidence in the country's healthy macroeconomic balances and financial stability. Therefore, maintaining a confident atmosphere in the market as much as possible during financial crisis periods will ensure that both the real sector and the financial sector emerge from this process with minimal damage. To achieve this, it is necessary to clearly and transparently demonstrate the effects of financial crisis periods on capital markets to savers. Because the human mind generally has a stronger tendency to recall positive things than the negative impacts of adverse processes (Baumeister et al., 2001). This situation can strengthen the panic atmosphere in the market and lead investors to make decisions with the Bandwagon Effect.

In this regard, the fundamental motivation behind the execution of the study is to shed light on an element that creates uncertainty for investors by examining stock market movements during financial crisis periods. In this context, sector indices have been scrutinized in the study, aiming to determine which sectors exhibit higher financial resilience during financial crisis periods. Thus, the study seeks to present a guiding work for savers to make rational financial decisions during economic depressions. Additionally, the consideration of different financial crisis periods based on various causes provides an insight into what might occur in the future due to similar macroeconomic developments. The inadequacy in the national literature on the subject constitutes another source of motivation for the study.

Despite the 2000–2001 Crisis being originated from the financial sector, it had serious adverse effects on the real sector as well. A significant contraction in consumer demand, especially, adversely affected the trade and service sectors (Erdönmez, 2003; Yıldırım, 2019). Additionally, while the effects of the 1999 Istanbul Earthquake persisted, the subsequent financial crisis caused significant damage to the tourism sector (Göçen et al., 2011). As the crisis was already originated from the financial sector, its most significant impacts were evident on the banking sector. The sector's loss, which was $560 million in 1999, reached $4 billion at the end of 2000 and $3.5 billion at the end of 2001. Additionally, the number of banks operating in the sector decreased from 81 in 1999 to 61 in 2001 as a result of liquidations (Coşkun & Eken, 2015). Following the 2000–2001 crisis, the banking sector underwent restructuring through legal regulations and structural reforms (Yiğitoğlu, 2005). As a result, the banking sector demonstrated a much more robust stance against the 2008–2009 crisis. There were no deteriorations in the asset structures of banks, and the continuity of sector profitability was ensured. This enabled the global crisis to be weathered by the banking sector with minimal damage (Aras, 2010; Bostan & Bölükbaş, 2011; Kale & Eken, 2017; Selçuk, 2010). However, the situation has not been the same for the real sector. The contraction in global trade volume has adversely affected all production enterprises, especially those engaged in export-oriented activities. With the global crisis dragging the Eurozone into a recession, there has been a significant decline in exports, reaching rates as high as 25%. Capacity utilization and employment rates in production facilities have decreased significantly. Additionally, the weakening of international capital's risk appetite has led to a substantial outflow of foreign capital and restricted investments for growth. Problems in the international financial sector have led to the contraction of external financing channels and increased access to financing sources for companies at higher costs (Çabuk & Özkan, 2010; Hepaktan & Çınar, 2011; Öztürk & Gövdere, 2010). The construction sector has been significantly adversely affected by the crisis as well. Due to the contracting demand and cost increases, housing stocks have increased, housing prices have retreated, and companies in the sector have faced significant losses (Kılıç et al., 2013). The tourism sector has managed to offset profit losses due to demand elasticity by attracting relatively cheaper holiday destinations like Turkey, especially as higher-income tourists chose it during the crisis period (Yıldız & Durgun, 2010).

An examination of national literature reveals that studies addressing the effects of crisis periods on sectors in a general and comparative manner are quite limited. Additionally, it has been found that these studies do not focus on the recovery performance of sectors in the subsequent periods. Thanks to the study, advisory results have been presented regarding how savers can manage their investments more rationally during financial crisis periods. Additionally, the study contributes to the potential actions that can be taken to maintain more robust capital markets during crisis processes. Since the foundation of financial stability relies on establishing an economic confidence atmosphere, and the major factor destroying the confidence environment is the uncertainties in that regard.

2 The Recent History of the Turkish Economy and Financial Crises

1970s, the inadequacy of Keynesian Theories in providing solutions to stagflationary processes led to their declining relevance. Consequently, with the global emergence of financial liberalization trends during this period, a new era began for the global economy. The evolution of financial deregulation trends in the 1980s towards financial liberalization led to the dismantling of limitations in the financial context of national economies, resulting in the internationalization of finance. This situation not only brought advantages to national economies but also made developing economies, in particular, more sensitive to the external market. This system, which opened the way for international capital movements, also contributed to the rapid globalization of adverse events in financial markets. The volatile nature of international capital flows has made it challenging to maintain macroeconomic balances in developing economies. This situation has significantly increased the frequency of financial crises. Turkey is one of the countries with a developing economy and is highly sensitive to international capital movements. Indeed, the Turkish economy has a rich structure in terms of financial crises.

The 1980s is also a significant period in Turkey's economic history. The year 1980 can be considered the starting point for a profound change in both the pursued economic philosophies and implemented monetary policies. The lack of action in implementing correct structural reforms after the 1973 Oil Crisis increased the impact of the second Oil Crisis on the Turkish economy. Attempting to overcome the adverse effects of the Oil Crisis on the current account deficit through external borrowing increased the burden of short-term external debt. The decrease in domestic savings and the industrialization based on imports led to a decline in real investments. Shortages in production due to the inadequacy of oil and energy resources resulted in material scarcities. This situation gradually dragged the national economy into high inflation. Additionally, the fixed exchange rate regime resulted in the national currency being more valuable than necessary, acting as a complete deterrent to exports. As a result of the mentioned economic conjuncture, in 1980, a set of radical structural reforms known as the January 24 decisions were implemented and entered into the economic literature. This decision aimed to increase domestic savings and implement interest rate policies to control inflation. Legal regulations were made to boost exports. Additionally, a high-rate devaluation was implemented, and a transition to a flexible exchange rate regime was attempted to reduce the current account deficit. Incentives for the entry of foreign capital were applied, and a shift was made towards a system where market conditions prevailed instead of public interventions (Parasız & Eroğlu, 2017: 226,250). With this period, the foundations of financial liberalization were laid for Turkey. The 1990s were a period in which both goods and capital movements were completely liberalized for Turkey. However, events such as the Gulf War and the dissolution of the USSR negatively affected the Turkish economy (Telli, 2015: 35). The country's economy entered a foreign exchange bottleneck due to significantly narrowing external markets. Additionally, early elections during this period and the resulting political instability limited the entry of foreign capital into the economy. Increases in public debt stock due to high-interest rates led to liquidity problems for the government. High budget deficits, external debts, insufficient central bank reserves, and a high inflationary environment laid the groundwork for a financial crisis. Indeed, the inevitable occurred with the 1994 Crisis. Following the crisis, economic stability measures known as the April 5 decisions were implemented on April 5, 1994, to prevent the transformation of high inflation into hyperinflation. However, the positive effects of these stability measures on economic growth were short-lived; both the real and financial sectors were adversely affected by the Southeast Asian Crisis.

By the 2000s, the country's economy began to experience serious liquidity problems. The rapid increase in interest rates led banks to transfer a significant portion of their resources to government bonds, resulting in a weak liquidity structure. As a result, the first shock of the 2000–2001 Crisis occurred in November 2000. Despite attempts to overcome the shock with a $10.4 billion credit from the International Monetary Fund (IMF), the financial crisis deepened with the added impact of political tensions in February 2001.

Although the impact of the Southeast Asian Crisis on the Turkish economy was initially limited, it began to be felt indirectly over time. Initially perceived as a regional crisis, it eventually took on a nature perceived for all emerging markets. Indeed, this perception led to international investors withdrawing their funds from Turkey. This situation made access to foreign capital more challenging, consequently leading to problems in the balance of payments. The situation of the Turkish economy before the crisis was quite bleak. The ratio of public debt stock to gross domestic product had reached high levels, foreign exchange reserves were inadequate, dollarization prevailed in the market, economic contraction had occurred, the current account deficit had reached alarming levels, inflation rates had reached around 70%, and the threshold of hyperinflation was approached. In the summer of the year 2000, a new economic program was implemented with the goal of reducing inflation and achieving sustainable economic growth. A stand-by agreement was also reached with the IMF. The stand-by agreement primarily foresaw structural reforms in six areas: social security, agriculture, tax policy and administration, capital markets, transparency in financial management, and the banking sector. However, especially in the last two areas, serious difficulties were encountered. The regulations regarding the banking sector gained momentum after this stage, leading banks to make much sharper moves to close their open positions. In this context, banks increased their liquidity demands to acquire foreign currency, leading to a rapid upward spike in money market interest rates. Many banks with a high percentage of government domestic debt securities in their assets were forced to fund their treasury securities after the liquidity crisis, resulting in significant losses. With the increasing risk, demand for treasury securities substantially contracted in the secondary market. At the same time, foreign investors also noticed that something was going wrong with the country's economy, and a trend of withdrawal from international investments in Turkey began. During the same period, financial investigations into the transparency of bank structures and rumors of the liquidation of some banks created a serious crisis of confidence in the market. This situation brought the interbank credit flow to a halt and deepened the crisis in banks facing liquidity problems. Each stage of the process led to further increases in interest rates. While such a liquidity crisis was happening in the market, the Central Bank of the Republic of Turkey (CBRT) was slow to take action because one of the performance criteria of the stand-by agreement was based on the CBRT releasing Turkish Lira only in exchange for foreign currency inflows. This situation led the CBRT to refrain from intervening in banks facing liquidity problems for a considerable period. Eventually, with a new loan opened by the IMF, the foreign exchange reserves of CBRT increased from $18 billion to $28 billion, providing a temporary relief for the markets. However, the significant rise in interest rates due to loss of confidence continued. While the process maintained its pessimism, the political tension between the president and the prime minister during the National Security Council meeting on February 19, 2001, made it extremely difficult to overcome the crisis. On February 21, 2001, the interbank overnight interest rate reached a record-breaking 6200%. The financial crisis rapidly manifested its impact on the real sector. The unstoppable rise in interest rates significantly contracted demand in the real sector, leading the economy into a recession (Eğilmez, 2020: 217, 221; Özatay, 2020: 96, 112).

Although the 2000–2001 crisis is fundamentally based on internal factors, certain international factors have also been triggering elements of the crisis (Alper, 2001: 73). The 100 basis point increase in the federal funds rate in the United States in the year 2000 (from 5.5 to 6.5 percent) significantly impacted developing economies and increased the risk of a crisis. Additionally, the gradual doubling of oil prices in the year 2000 increased production costs, negatively impacting the real sector and contributing to the widening current account deficit. Another factor contributing to the increase in the current account deficit was the weakening of the Euro/Dollar exchange rate. This is because Turkey's import dependence is dollar-denominated, while a significant portion of its exports is to the Eurozone (especially to Germany).

Starting from 2002, Turkey implemented an economic development program named the "Strong Economy Transition Program" with the support of the IMF. The program aimed to achieve sustainable growth and macroeconomic stability, with a primary focus on ensuring fiscal discipline. In the elections held at the end of 2002, a political party came to power alone, preventing political instabilities and contributing to an increase in economic confidence. Structural reforms in the banking sector significantly strengthened the capital structures of banks. Measures supporting the real sector increased the private sector's share in the economy. Fiscal discipline was implemented, reducing budget deficits, and inflation dropped to single digits for the first time in 2004. Uninterrupted economic growth was achieved over a four-year period starting from 2002. Reforms in the social security system contributed significantly to budget balance. Additionally, during this period, a transition to a floating exchange rate regime was made. Exchange rates remained stable for an extended period due to stringent monetary and fiscal policies.

The fight against inflation constituted a major element of the economic program implemented during this period. Steps were taken to make the CBRT independent from political authority, and effective monetary policies were pursued. The tight monetary policies implemented during this period and the decrease in the cost of imported inputs contributed to a rapid reduction in inflation. The current account deficit, resulting from the overvaluation of the Turkish Lira, was financed through inflows of hot money, including privatization revenues. Another significant development during this period was Turkey starting negotiations for full membership with the European Union. With the impact of this development, access to international capital was greatly facilitated, and international direct investments reached record levels.

From the second half of 2007, problems that started in the U.S. mortgage markets quickly turned into a liquidity crisis affecting the entire world. With a volume of $10 trillion, the mortgage market became the world's largest market at that time. However, the indiscriminate issuance of subprime mortgage loans eventually created a bubble effect in housing prices, significantly increasing the market's risk. Households demanding subprime mortgage loans opted for variable-rate borrowing with the expectation that interest rates in the United States would generally remain low. However, the Federal Reserve System (FED) raising interest rates after a while led to difficulties, especially for individuals in the low-income groups, in repaying their loans. As individuals facing problems in repaying their loans increased, a trend towards selling their homes as collateral emerged. However, this situation initially caused housing prices to plummet due to an increase in supply, leading to a problem where the sale proceeds of the homes used as collateral were insufficient to cover the loans. The main factor deepening the financial crisis, however, was the derivative instruments used as collateral for these mortgage loans. These derivative financial instruments caused a serious impact on the entire financial sector during the financial crisis.

The global crisis period was relatively weathered with less damage by Turkey compared to the 2000–2001 Crisis. Structural reforms implemented, especially in the banking sector, ensured that the banking sector acquired a very robust structure. Indeed, while banks in developed economies struggled with serious problems during the crisis period, Turkish banks went through this period with high profitability rates. Additionally, the absence of derivative instruments based on mortgage loans in the assets of Turkish banks contributed to navigating the crisis with minimal damage. However, the situation has not developed as smoothly for the real sector as it has for the banking sector. The contraction of export markets and financing problems resulting from global financial issues primarily reduced the economic growth rate to 0.8% in 2008. The main effects of the crisis on Turkey were felt in 2009, leading to a negative economic growth of minus 4.7%.

Following the 2008–2009 crisis, Turkey experienced a rapid economic recovery thanks to the ample liquidity provided to the global markets after the crisis. However, especially after 2013, the country lost its momentum in economic growth. Simultaneously, there was an upward trend in the inflation rate during this period. The contradictory nature of the monetary policies and fiscal policies implemented during this period is seen as the main reason for the emerging negative macroeconomic indicators (Eğilmez, 2020: 235,237). The tight monetary policies continued alongside inflation targeting, and at the same time, loose fiscal policies supported by tax cuts, public incentives, and increased public spending created a contradiction in the economic policies.

During the same period, i.e., in the post-global crisis era, both the United States and Europe kept interest rates low and expanded the money supply, leading to credit expansion in developing economies. A similar credit expansion occurred in Turkey, with significant increases in foreign currency borrowing, especially in the private sector. This situation contributed to the rising financial fragility in Turkey as we entered the year 2018 (Özatay, 2020: 259,266). Subsequently, the tension between the United States and Turkey, triggered by the case of Pastor Andrew Brunson and the economic sanctions declared by the United States against Turkey, led to a rapid increase in the exchange rate. As a result, companies with significantly more foreign currency liabilities than assets experienced significant damage to their balance sheets due to the exchange rate spike. The negative developments in the real sector quickly affected the financial sector due to their adverse impact on companies' credit repayments. While the Turkish economy was in the process of overcoming this problem, the first Covid-19 case in Turkey was announced on March 10, 2020. Subsequently, as in almost all economies globally, problems such as economic contraction, a significant decrease in employment, the halt of foreign trade and tourism revenues, and losses in industrial production emerged. Turkey, unlike other countries, had limited maneuverability against these issues, primarily due to the existing economic difficulties. In the subsequent periods, Turkey attempted to overcome the effects of the pandemic through a highly debated economic orientation. In this context, the CBRT implemented expansionary monetary policies for a specific period to achieve economic growth and reduce the current account deficit. However, due to the unbearable inflationary environment, in June 2023, the CBRT, after approximately a two-year period, raised interest rates and transitioned to a tight monetary policy to bring inflation under control.

3 Measurement of Financial Resistance and Financial Recovery

In his study, Martin (2012) examines regional economic resilience against recessionary shocks. In this context, he examines economic resilience in four dimensions: resistance, recovery, renewal, and re-orientation. For the measurement of economic resistance in the study, he proposed the following formulation;

$$\Delta E_r/E_r = \beta_r(\Delta E_n/E_n) \tag{1}$$

In Eq. 1, β_r is defined as an indicator of the sensitivity index. Thus, it calculates the employment decline of the respective region in the face of recession shocks by comparing it to the overall employment decline in the country. ΔE/E represents the percentage change in employment. If the β_r of the region is greater than the β_r of unity, it indicates higher sensitivity (lower resistance) to shocks. If the β_r of the region is smaller than the β_r of unity, it indicates lower sensitivity (higher resistance) to shocks.

Lagravinese (2015) also worked on regional resilience and proposed the following equations for the measurement of resistance and recovery;

$$\beta_{res} = [(\Delta E_r/\ E_r) - (\Delta E_n/E_n)]/|\Delta E_r/E_r| \tag{2}$$

$$\beta_{rec} = \ (\Delta E_r/E_r)\ /\ (\Delta E_n/E_n) \tag{3}$$

In Eq. 2, (ΔEr/Er) represents the percentage change in the employment level in the region, and (ΔEn/En) represents the percentage change in the employment level in the country. A positive β_{res} value indicates a better resistance level against shocks, while a negative β_{res} value indicates a worse resistance level against shocks. In Eq. 3, a β_{rec} value greater than 1 indicates a better recovery performance in the post-shock period.

Oliva and Lazzeretti (2018) measured the economic resistance and recovery performances of regions in response to shocks caused by earthquakes in Japan. In this context, they utilized employment levels in regions and adapted the resistance and recovery indices used in the study by Faggian et al. (2018) to their own research;

$$\beta_{res} = \left(E_{p,t}/E_{p,t-1}\right)/(E_{w,t}/E_{w,t-1}) \tag{4}$$

$$\beta_{rec} = \left(\Delta E_p/E_{p,t}\right) \tag{5}$$

Equation 4 defines $\left(E_{p,t}/E_{p,t-1}\right)$ as the ratio of the employment level in the relevant prefecture during the shock period to the pre-shock period. $(E_{w,t}/E_{w,t-1})$ represents the same ratio covering all prefectures. If β_{res} obtains a value greater than 1, it indicates that the region exhibits high resistance to the shock, while if β_{res} obtains a value less than 1, it indicates that the region shows low resistance to the shock. Equation 5 measures the recovery performance by comparing the change in the employment level in the region during the post-shock period to the period during the shock.

4 Literature

Yiğitoğlu (2005), which evaluates the economic effects of the 2000–2001 Crisis, it was found that the banking sector experienced a significant recovery after the crisis and an increase in the profitability of banks.

Tanrıöven and Aksoy (2009), a sectoral analysis of the effects of crises in Turkey was conducted, and it was found that the most significant impacts were on the technology, communication, food, and textile sectors.

Aras (2010), which addressed the impact of the 2008–2009 Crisis on the banking sector, it was found that the Turkish banking sector was less affected by the crisis compared to the banking sectors of other developed and developing countries.

Bostan and Bölükbaş (2011), which examined the profitability of the banking sector after the 2008–2009 crisis, it was found that the banking sector was relatively minimally affected by the crisis and experienced a rapid recovery afterward.

İskenderoğlu and Karakozak (2013), which addressed the manufacturing sector in Turkey after the 2008–2009 Crisis, it was found that there was a significant increase in the bankruptcy risk of companies operating in the manufacturing sector following the crisis.

Gümüş and Aydemir (2014), which examined the sectoral impacts of the 2008–2009 Crisis, it was found that the textile and food sectors were particularly among the most affected by the crisis.

Kesebir (2018), which addresses the state of the banking sector after the 2000–2001 Crisis, it was concluded that the financial performance of the banking sector improved as a result of the economic reforms implemented.

Çakmak and Öztürk (2023), which examined the effects of the 2008–2009 Crisis on sector profitability, it was found that the profitability of the manufacturing, construction, and transportation sectors was most significantly affected by the crisis.

Pilatin and Karamustafa (2023), which examined the equity profitability of sectors after the 2008–2009 crisis, it was concluded that all sectors except the trade sector were affected by the crisis in terms of equity profitability.

Table 1 Informations of indices

Index name	Index code	Base value of index
BIST 100	XU100	01.01.1986 = 0,01
BIST INDUSTRIALS	XUSIN	28.12.1990 = 0,33
BIST SERVICES	XUHIZ	27.12.1996 = 10,46
BIST REAL EST. INV. TRUSTS	XGMYO	28.12.1999 = 211,81
BIST TECHNOLOGY	XUTEK	30.06.2000 = 144,66
BIST W. AND RETAIL TRADE	XTCRT	27.12.1996 = 10,46
BIST BANKS	XBANK	27.12.1996 = 9,14

Source Author's construction based on the Borsa Istanbul index data

5 Data and Methodology

5.1 Data

The study used the main sectoral indices calculated on the Borsa Istanbul Stock Market; BIST Industrials, BIST Services, BIST Real Estate Investment Trusts, BIST Technology, BIST Wholesale and Retail Trade, BIST Banks. The BIST 100 has been used as the benchmark index. The names, codes, and base values of the indices are summarized in Table 1.

In the subsequent sections of the study, indices will be expressed through index codes. Daily closing data of indices have been used as the index values, and arithmetic averages have been utilized for the period values (the starting date of the XUTEK is considered as the start date of the index calculation). The data is sourced from Refinitiv Eikon.

For the 2000–2001 Crisis, the pre-crisis period covers the date range from 04.01.2000 to 24.11.2000, and the post-crisis period covers the date range from 27.11.2000 to 28.12.2001. The period used for the recovery index is the year 2004. For the 2008–2009 Crisis, the pre-crisis period covers the date range from 02.01.2008 to 12.09.2008, and the post-crisis period covers the date range from 15.09.2008 to 31.12.2009. The period used for the recovery index is the year 2012. The starting date for the 2000–2001 Crisis was selected as the date when some bank owners were featured in the news with their hands handcuffed due to bank embezzlement charges. The starting date for the 2008–2009 crisis was selected as the date of Lehman Brothers' collapse.

5.2 Methodology

In this study, the resistance and recovery dynamics of sector indices in Turkey during financial crisis periods were measured using the resistance index and recovery index borrowed from the study of Olivia and Lazzeretti (2018). This version of the indices overcomes possible issues related to the concordance or discordance of signs, as suggested by the authors.

In this context, Formula 6 was used to measure the financial resistance of sector indices compared to the benchmark index during financial crisis periods.

$$\beta_{res} = (V_{i,t}/V_{i,t-1})/(V_{w,t}/V_{w,t-1}) \quad (6)$$

In formula;
β_{res} as the score of the financial resistance,
t as the year of the financial crisis,
t_{-1} as the year before financial crisis,
i as single sectoral index,
w as benchmark index.

When β_{res} takes a value greater than 1, it indicates that the sector index exhibits higher resistance compared to the benchmark index during the crisis period, while a value less than 1 indicates lower resistance.

For the measurement of financial recovery, Formula 7 has been used.

$$\beta_{rec} = (\Delta V_i / V_{i,t}) \quad (7)$$

ΔV_i represents the change in the value of the sector index over a 3-year period.

The desired condition for financial recovery performance is to have the β_{rec} score as high as possible. A high β_{rec} score indicates that the sector index experienced a successful recovery process compared to its situation during the crisis in the following 3-year period.

6 Results

The financial resistance and financial recovery performances of six sectoral indices compared to the benchmark during the 2000–2001 and 2008–2009 crises were examined using resistance and recovery indices. The results are summarized in Table 2.

When Fig. 1 is examined, it is observed that two indices, XUSIN and XBANK, outperformed the benchmark during the 2000–2001 Crisis. The other indices show a less successful resistance performance compared to the benchmark. The index with the worst score is XUHIZ. In the 2000–2001 Crisis, the benchmark index has a financial recovery score of 0.9757. Only XUSIN has exceeded this score. XUSIN achieved higher growth than its average during the crisis in the three-year period following the crisis. Although XBANK lagged behind the benchmark performance, it became the second-best index in terms of recovery performance. XUTEK, on the other hand, obtained a negative recovery score and experienced a decline compared to its average during the crisis period.

Table 2 Resistance and recovery scores of indices

Index	Resistance	Recovery
2000–2001 Crisis		
XUSIN	1,1037	1,1726
XUHIZ	0,7268	0,7259
XGMYO	0,8659	0,4708
XUTEK	0,8620	-0,0723
XTCRT	0,9188	0,4361
XBANK	1,0909	0,9279
XU100		0,9757
2008–2009 Crisis		
XUSIN	0,8942	1,0988
XUHIZ	1,0832	0,5692
XGMYO	0,8891	0,8776
XUTEK	1,0676	2,6312
XTCRT	1,2041	1,6336
XBANK	1,0996	0,6657
XU100		0,7976

Source Author's construction

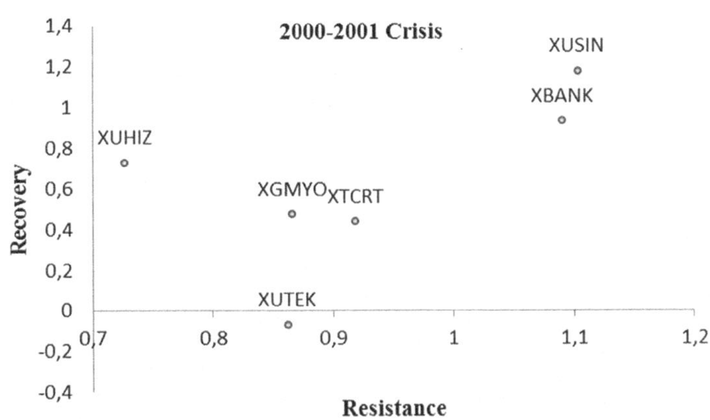

Fig. 1 The scatter of 2000–2001 crisis (*Source* Author's construction)

When Fig. 2 is examined, it is observed that, except for XUSIN and XGMYO, other sectoral indices showed better resistance performance compared to the benchmark index during the 2008–2009 Crisis. The best performance is seen in XTCRT. The worst performance is shown by XGMYO. In the three-year period following the crisis, although no index has a negative recovery score, the recovery performance of XUTEK stands out with a score of 2.6312. In terms of recovery performance, all

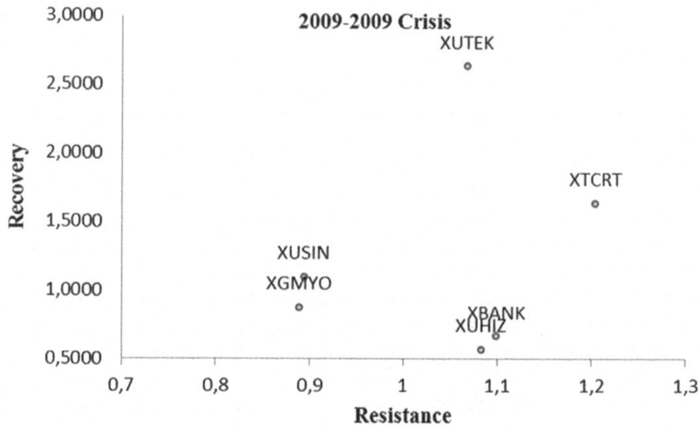

Fig. 2 The scatter of 2008–2009 crisis (*Source* Author's construction)

indices except XUHIZ and XBANK surpass the recovery score of the benchmark index (0.7976).

XGMYO exhibited lower resistance performance compared to the benchmark index in both crisis periods and is the only index showing this characteristic during the research period. On the other hand, the XBANK index demonstrated better resistance performance than the benchmark in both crisis periods, and its resistance scores during both crisis periods are quite close to each other. In this regard, for the research period, it can be interpreted that XGMYO has the lowest resistance against crises, while XBANK has the highest resistance among the indices.

7 Conclusion

The chronic problems of the Turkish economy include high inflation, volatility in exchange rates, high unemployment rates, and a dependency on external financing. High inflation has been a prominent and unresolved economic issue for Turkey for many years, with an average inflation rate of 38.29% between 1985 and 2022, approximately 4 times the world average and 17 times the average of developed economies (the data in this section, unless otherwise specified, has been accessed from the IMF-World Economic Outlook Databases). Although inflation showed a declining trend after 2002 and reached single digits for most of the period between 2004 and 2016, it started to rise again after 2016. These recurring periods of high inflation have led to high-interest rates and, consequently, the accumulation of high public debt. Unexpected devaluations in periods of fixed exchange rate regimes have exposed the real sector to financial crises unprepared. In floating exchange rate periods, the high volatility of exchange rates has negatively affected the risk appetite for investment in the real sector. Another chronic issue for Turkey over the years has been high unemployment, peaking during the 2000–2001 Crisis. The average unemployment rate in Turkey between 1985 and 2022 is 9.1%, which is about 1.5 times the average of developed economies. Another chronic issue that the Turkish economy has been grappling with for many years is the current account deficit. In Turkey, domestic savings are insufficient to finance investments, leading to a continuous reliance on savings imports. The predominant structure of this savings import consists of portfolio investments and borrowing rather than direct investments. This situation significantly increases the sensitivity and vulnerability of the Turkish economy to external factors. The current account deficit forces both the public sector and the private sector into a high level of external borrowing. This situation particularly significantly increases the risk for the private sector due to exchange rate volatility. Indeed, during the 2018 Crisis, unlike the global crisis, there was a substantial outflow of foreign capital from Turkey despite no decrease in the international investor's risk appetite (according to VIX index). Similarly, during the 2018 crisis period, Turkey's CDS (Credit Default Swap) premiums rapidly increased. There are two ways to reduce dependency on external financing and the current account deficit. The first is to cut investments. However, for Turkey, economic growth has always been a priority. Achieving economic growth to catch up with developed economies and providing employment for the young population should indeed be the primary goals for Turkey. In this context, there is only one way left: to increase domestic savings. The first step that needs to be taken in this direction for Turkey is to ensure the inclusion of idle funds in the financial system. Because these funds do not gain the qualification of savings unless they are included in the financial system. To achieve this, it is necessary to implement encouraging methods for households and provide the trust in the financial system. The study is particularly crucial in this regard. Indeed, even in normal times, Turkey's idle capital capacity is quite high, but panic movements during crisis periods lead to an even further shrinkage of capital markets. At this point, actions need to be taken to address the uncertainties in the minds of savers. Because the foundation of the risk element is uncertainties. Each enlightening piece of information aimed at dispelling uncertainties will help maintain confidence in the markets.

In times of crisis, the first macroeconomic reactions typically involve upward spikes in interest rates and a rapid depletion of central banks' foreign exchange reserves. This is because foreign investors tend to sell their portfolios to exit the market quickly during such periods. Simultaneously, domestic investors, anticipating a sharp decline in the value of their savings in foreign currency, sell their financial assets denominated in Turkish lira and turn to buying foreign currency. Both of these trends increase the demand for foreign exchange. The central bank intervenes in the foreign exchange market by increasing interest rates and selling foreign exchange to try to maintain the exchange rate at a certain level. However, the sustainability of this situation is limited, and significant increases in the exchange rate occur after a certain point. In a way, there is a "self-fulfilling expectations" dynamic in the market. The negative impacts observed in the capital markets spread rapidly to the real sector in a domino effect.

However, during the pandemic period, while many sectors were adversely affected, the trade sector achieved high profitability rates. The wholesale & retail trade index provided positive returns to investors. According to the study results, during the 2000–2001 Crisis period, the service sector, technology sector, real estate investment trusts sector, and wholesale & retail trade sector exhibited financial resistance below the benchmark index. The recession in the economy has led to a significant decrease in domestic market demand, negatively affecting almost the entire real sector. The industrial sector, particularly supported by export-generated revenues, has been able to exhibit a more robust stance against the crisis. Similarly, with the elimination of weaknesses within the banking sector and the establishment of confidence-inspiring reforms, a rapid recovery process has taken place. Indeed, according to the study results, both the banking sector and the industrial sector demonstrated financial resistance above the benchmark index. Similarly, the industrial sector and banking sector have been the two indices showing the best performance according to the financial recovery index during the 2000–2001 Crisis. During the 2008–2009 Crisis, especially the contraction of export markets and problems in accessing international finance caused the industrial sector to exhibit a worse financial resistance than the benchmark index. The crisis, with its real estate-related nature, also negatively affected the real estate investment trusts sector, and it demonstrated a worse financial resistance than the benchmark index. Other indices, however, felt the effects of the global crisis much less and showed a financial resistance higher than the benchmark index. After the crisis, especially the technology sector showed a highly successful financial recovery index performance. The acceleration of technological developments during the relevant period had a significant impact on this situation. The wholesale & retail trade sector and the industrial sector were other indices that showed successful financial recovery after the 2008–2009 Crisis.

It is believed that the determination of investment policies by savers in Turkey based on sectoral considerations during financial crisis periods would be beneficial. In this context, although individual pragmatic solutions are sought by investors in the initial stages of crisis periods, it should not be forgotten that a wholesale escape from capital markets, over time, will indirectly adversely affect the entire country's economy. Studies on macroeconomic and financial movements during crisis periods are thought to provide investors with predictions, eliminating uncertainties and helping them remain more composed.

Acknowledgements This study was supported by the Scientific and Technological Research Council of Turkey (TUBITAK) [Grant Number 1919B022400529].

References

Alper, C. E. (2001). The Turkish liquidity crisis of 2000: What went wrong. *Russian & East European Finance and Trade, 37*(6), 58–80.

Aras, O. N. (2010). Effects of the global economic crisis on Turkish banking sector. *International Journal of Economics and Finance Studies, 2*(1), 113–120.
Baumeister, R. F., Bratslavsky, E., Finkenauer, C., & Vohs, K. D. (2001). Bad is stronger than good. *Review of General Psychology, No., 5*, 323–370.
Barbuta-Misu, N., Guleç, T. C., Duramaz, S., & Virlanuta, F. O. (2020). Determinants of dollarization of savings in the Turkish economy. *Sustainability, 12*(15), 6141.
Bostan, A., & Bölükbaş, M. (2011). Küresel Finansal Kriz ve Bankacılık Sektörüne Etkileri; Türkiye Örneği. *Finans Politik Ve Ekonomik Yorumlar Dergisi, 48*(562), 1–16.
Çabuk, A., & Özkan, G. (2010). Küresel Finansal Krizin Türk Reel Sektörüne Etkileri: Bursa Örneği. *Uluslararası Yönetim İktisat Ve İşletme Dergisi, 6*(12), 1–23.
Çakmak, İ., & Öztürk, S. (2023). 2008 Küresel Ekonomik Krizi ve Türkiye'de Sektör Karlılığı. *Fiscaoeconomia, 7*(2), 1700–1720.
Cömert, H., & Yeldan, E. (2018). *A tale of three crises in Turkey: 1994, 2001 and 2008–09* (ERC Working Papers 1809). ERC-Economic Research Center, Middle East Technical University.
Coşkun, Ö. A., & Eken, M. H. (2015). 2001 ve 2008 Krizlerinin Türk Bankacılık Sektörüne Etkilerinin Karşılaştırılması. *Maliye Ve Finans Yazıları, 1*(104), 105–130.
Eğilmez, M. (2020). *Türkiye Ekonomisi.* Remzi Kitabevi, Istanbul. Turkey.
Erdönmez, P. A. (2003). Türkiye'de 2001 Yılındaki Mali Kriz Sonrasında Kurumsal Sektörde Yeniden Yapılandırma. *Bankacılar Dergisi, No., 47*, 38–55.
Faggian, A., Gemmiti, R., Jaquet, T., & Santini, I. (2018). Regional economic resilience: The experience of the Italian local labor Systems. *The Annals of Regional Science, No., 60*, 393–410.
Gazioğlu, S. (2008). Stock market returns in an emerging financial market: Turkish case study. *Applied Economics, 40*(11), 1363–1372.
Göçen, Ö. G. S., et al. (2011). Türkiye'de Krizler ve Krizlerin Turizm Sektörüne Etkileri. *Süleyman Demirel Üniversitesi İktisadi Ve İdari Bilimler Fakültesi Dergisi, 16*(2), 493–509.
Gümüş, F., & Aydemir, L. (2014). 2008 Küresel Finans Krizinin Sektörel Bazda Şirket Bilançolarına Etkilerinin Analizi. *İşletme Bilimi Dergisi, 2*(45), 37–64.
Havrylyshyn, O., & Beddies, C. H. (2003). Dollarisation in the former soviet union: From Hysteria to Hysteresis. *Comparative Economic Studies, No., 45*, 329–357.
Hepaktan, C. E., & Çınar, S. (2011). Mali Krizler ve Son Mali Krizin (2008) Reel Sektöre Etkileri. *Dumlupınar Üniversitesi Sosyal Bilimler Dergisi, No., 30*, 155–168.
İskenderoğlu, Ö., & Karakozak, Ö. (2013). 2008 Küresel Finansal Krizinin Finansal Oranlar Üzerine Etkisi: BIST'de İşlem Gören İmalat Sanayi İşletmeleri Üzerine Bir Uygulama. *Dokuz Eylül Üniversitesi İktisadi İdari Bilimler Fakültesi Dergisi, 28*(2), 98–129.
Kale, S., & Eken, M. H. (2017). Türk Bankacılığında Krizler ve Çıkarılan Dersler (Turkish Banking Crisis and Inferences). *Kırklareli Üniversitesi, İktisadi Ve İdari Bilimler Fakültesi Dergisi, 6*(5), 11–23.
Kesebir, M. (2018). Türkiye'de 2001 Krizi Sonrası Bankacılık Sektörünün Durumu, Yapısal Reformlar ile Son Yıllardaki Gelişmeler. *Akademik İzdüşüm Dergisi, 3*(2), 1–19.
Kılıç, C., et al. (2013). Küresel Finansal Krizin Türkiye'nin İnşaat Sektörü Üzerindeki Etkileri. *Uluslararası Alanya İşletme Fakültesi Dergisi, 5*(3), 95–104.
Korhonen, I. (1996). Dollarization in Lithuania. *Review of Economies in Transition, 5*(96), 53–59.
Lagravinese, R. (2015). Economic crisis and rising gaps north–south: Evidence from the Italian regions. *Cambridge Journal of Regions, Economy and Society, 8*(2), 331–342.
Martin, R. (2012). Regional economic resilience, Hysteresis and recessionary shocks. *Journal of Economic Geography, 12*(1), 1–32.
Metin-Özcan, K., & Us, V. (2007). Dedollarization in Turkey after decades of dollarization: A myth or reality? *Physica a: Statistical Mechanics and Its Applications, 385*(1), 292–306.
Oliva, S., & Lazzeretti, L. (2018). Measuring the economic resilience of natural disasters: An analysis of major earthquakes in Japan. *City, Culture and Society, No., 15*, 53–59.
Ozatay, F. (2020). *Finansal Krizler ve Türkiye (6. Baskı).* Doğan Kitap, Istanbul. Turkey.
Öztürk, S., & Gövdere, B. (2010). Küresel Finansal Kriz ve Türkiye Ekonomisine Etkileri. *Süleyman Demirel Üniversitesi İktisadi Ve İdari Bilimler Fakültesi Dergisi, 15*(1), 377–397.

Parasız, I., & Eroğlu, I. (2017). *Tarihsel Süreçte Türkiye Ekonomisi.* Ekin Yayınevi, Bursa. Turkey.

Pilatin, A., & Karamustafa, O. (2023). 2008 Küresel Finans Krizinin Borsa İstanbul'da İşlem Gören Şirket Kârlılıklarına Etkisi. *Journal of Economics, Finance and Sustainability, 1*(1), 32–62.

Sekmen, T. (2015). Effect of the subprime crisis on return and volatility of the Turkish stock market. *Journal of Economics and Behavioral Studies, 7*(3), 23–29.

Selçuk, B. (2010). Küresel Krizin Türk Finans Sektörü Üzerindeki Etkileri. *Ekonomi Bilimleri Dergisi, 2*(2), 21–27.

Tanrıöven, C., & Aksoy, E. E. (2009). Krizlerin Reel Sektör İşletmeleri Üzerine Etkileri: İMKB'de Sektörel Bazda İnceleme. *Gazi Üniversitesi İktisadi Ve İdari Bilimler Fakültesi Dergisi, 11*(2), 79–114.

Telli, R. (2015). *Türkiye Ekonomisi ve Avrupa Birliği.* Ekin Yayınevi, Bursa. Turkey.

Temiz, D., & Gökmen, A. (2009). The 2000–2001 financial crisis in Turkey and the global economic crisis of 2008–2009: Reasons and comparisons. *International Journal of Social Sciences and Humanity Studies, 1*(1), 1–16.

Yıldırım, C. (2019). The development of service sector in Turkey after 2001 crisis. *Bolu Abant İzzet Baysal Üniversitesi Sosyal Bilimler Enstitüsü Dergisi, 19*(2), 347–387.

Yıldız, Z., & Durgun, A. (2010). 2008 Küresel Ekonomik Krizi ve Turizm Sektörü Üzerine Etkileri. *Süleyman Demirel Üniversitesi Vizyoner Dergisi, 2*(1), 1–15.

Yiğitoğlu, A. İ. (2005). 2001 Krizi Sonrası Dönemde Türkiye Ekonomisinin ve Bankacılık Sektörünün Değerlendirilmesi. *Sosyoekonomi, 1*(1), 115–125.

Yurdakul, F. (2014). Factors that trigger financial crises: The case of Turkey. *Procedia-Social and Behavioral Sciences, No., 109*, 896–901.

A Social Network Analysis of Certain Macroeconomic Indicators of European Union NUTS 2 Regions

Pagona Filenta, Dimitrios Kydros, Persefoni Polychronidou, and George Magoulios

Abstract Social Network Analysis investigates the relationships formed between different nodes, i.e. between units that can be individuals, groups, or organizations. The nodes and links between them that form a network, are taken as interdependent units. In this paper, the nodes are the NUTS2 regions of the EU, and we seek to study the degree of correlation between them in terms of certain macroeconomic indicators. In addition, we present the visualization of networks based on the degree of correlation of the indicators and calculate metrics and measures of centrality, as well as the resulting groupings (communities) of regions. Could the existence of more communities of regions be translated as a lack of cohesion between regions? The results show that the Analysis of Social Networks could help to identify specific regions, where the implementation of targeted policies could lead to a reduction in regional imbalances and thus improve cohesion in the EU.

Keywords Social Network Analysis (SNA) · Economic and regional development · European regions NUTS2 · Macroeconomic indicators

JEL Codes C82 · R11 · E60

1 Introduction

The regional problem is a complex phenomenon with political, social, and cultural dimensions, determining the level of regional disparities, as it expresses the lack of balanced development between regions or countries, which results in regional economic and social asymmetry of a geographical area. In a competitive environment, human and capital mobility, as trade between regions, will reinforce the negative relationship between growth and regional imbalances (Petrakos et al., 2005). Numerous studies use a variety of quantitative and statistical analysis techniques

---

P. Filenta (✉) · D. Kydros · P. Polychronidou · G. Magoulios
School of Economics and Management, Department of Economic Sciences, International Hellenic University, Serres, Greece
e-mail: pagofile2@ihu.gr

I. Bartuseviciene et al. (eds.), *Building Economic Resilience*, Contributions to Economics, https://doi.org/10.1007/978-3-031-96428-2_3

to concentrate on the structural and spatial variations between regions. The study of economic and regional development examines the intricate dynamics of regions rather than focusing on a static image (Nijkamp & Abreu, 2009).

According to Wasserman and Faust (1994), Social Network Analysis (SNA), also known as network science, is a theory that facilitates the comprehension and investigation of units that have formed a relationship or connection with one another. Since its inception by sociologists over a century ago, the theory has developed into a significant area of sociological research (Jackson, 2005). Nevertheless, the theory has proven to be effective not only in the scientific discipline of sociology but also in computer networks, biology, economic science, and political science. Moreover, researchers have applied social media theory analysis techniques to literary and cultural works in recent years (Kydros et al., 2014). SNA has its roots in graph theory, and a basic form of it is the visualization of a network.

The main objective of this study is to integrate SNA with regional and economic analysis. For this purpose, we collected raw data from GDP per capita and total unemployment rate of EU NUTS2 regions from 2010 to 2021, to generate networks (graphs) using the visualization software package NodeXL Pro combined with SNA methodologies (Smith et al., 2010). Using appropriate metrics and centrality measures, we will be able to examine the NUTS2 regions of the EU.

In particular, we try to draw conclusions about specific macroeconomic indicators: can regions be grouped based on the correlation of GDP per capita and unemployment rate? Which areas are included in each group, and how are they grouped? Can the clustering of regions be compared with the existence or lack of cohesion between regions?

2 Regional Development Through SNA

In the next section, we will present Regional Analysis in the EU, as well as SNA.

2.1 Regional Development in the EU

Regional Development states the achievement of changes in the economic and social activity of the citizens of a region to eliminate any disparities with other regions due to historical, social, or economic reasons. The term reflects a general attempt to improve prosperity and living standards in every type of region, from rural areas to cities, and to increase their impact on national performance and more general and resilient societies. In a competitive environment, the mobility of human resources and capital, as well as trade between regions, will reinforce the negative relationship between growth and regional imbalances (Petrakos et al., 2005).

The EU is not a homogeneous economic area, as the regions that make it up have different levels of development and development potential (Monford et al., 2013).

The disparities observed are significant and demonstrate the different levels at which the economies are, which is an obstacle to the integration being attempted (Polyzos, 2019). In their research, Spulbar et al. (2020) concluded that the lack of integration in the EU is explained by various factors. They emphasized, among other aspects, the great degree of variability in macroeconomic and financial stability, which is reflected in various country risks. Examples of this diversity include variations in sovereign risk, public and private debt, etc. (Matuzeviciute et al., 2023). According to research by Psycharis et al. (2020) Central and Eastern EU countries followed a largely uniform development path after joining the EU. Growing inequalities hurt the economic development of the EU and threaten social peace and political stability (Widuto Agnieszda, 2019). These inequalities are observed both at the national and regional levels. The majority of studies related to spatial disparities in the EU emphasize disparities between the regions of different Member States and are less concerned with the corresponding disparities within countries. However, according to Ezcurra (2019) the existence of inequalities within a country is a key factor in the existence of inequalities between regions in the EU.

The Cohesion Policy pursued by the EU aims to eliminate inequalities and economic convergence of regions. This means in practice that the per capita income of the poorer regions will tend to grow faster than the richer regions in order to close the gap and achieve an increase in the living standards of citizens. Although income is considered an important indicator to compare the well-being of citizens, it is considered that there are other data that should be taken into account when assessing well-being, such as nutrition, health, housing, education, etc. (Das, 2016). The EU's Cohesion Policy is about strategic investment in all regions and cities to stimulate and develop economies and improve the living standards of citizens, boost the competitiveness of businesses and create jobs. Cohesion Policy, which aims to support European solidarity, is implemented through the European Structural and Investment Funds (ESIF), which are essentially the funds of the Union's Cohesion Policy European Regional Development Fund (ERDF), Cohesion Fund (CF), European Social Fund Plus (ESF +), Just Transition Fund (JTF). The economic, social, and geographical cohesion of the EU is strengthened under the EU's Cohesion Policy, as it aims to address the disparities that exist between nations and geographical areas. At the same time, it attempts to fulfill the Union's policy objectives, with a particular emphasis on the digital and green transition. (European Commission, 2022).

2.2 Social Network Analysis

SNA studies the connections between individuals or groups within a social network using graph theory. Networks require several nodes or vertices interacting with each other, which are denoted by edges or links (O'Malley & Marsden, 2008) and are often depicted through sociograms to reflect characteristics of interest (Wasserman & Faust, 1994).

A social network G = (N, A) consists of units, the "nodes", i.e. the set of vertices N = {n1, n2, n3,…,nN}, that interact with each other through social relations, and the "links", the corresponding set of edges A = {l1, l2, l3,…, lL}. A network G can be represented by an adjacency matrix, of dimensions nxn, with values of 1 or 0. A value of 1 is given when there is a connection between nodes and a value of 0 in case there is no connection. (Jackson, 2005).

In graph theory, some descriptive indicators and centrality metrics that allow us to draw useful conclusions about the role and position of nodes can be calculated. Specifically, network density equals to the fraction of the number of edges to the total number of edges that could exist in a network. The closer the density is to 1, the denser the network we are studying. The degree centrality denotes the number of immediate neighbors of a node. In case a node has no neighbors, it is called an isolated node. Betweenness centrality is a measure of the influence of nodes in network. Specifically, it identifies the nodes that are most frequently located between other nodes and act as bridges from one part of a graph to another, i.e. are present on most paths and are defined as the number of shortest paths between pairs of other nodes that pass through it. The greater the betweenness centrality of a node, the greater its importance for the overall graph as it controls the interactions between other nodes (Girvan & Newman, 2002; Rusinowska et al., 2011).

One of the important characteristics of networks is node clustering, which refers to the process of segmenting a graph to identify high density of links between nodes within a group, i.e. nodes that are locally densely connected and have low edge density between nodes in different groups. Such highly interconnected groups are commonly denoted as communities, and the process of identifying them is known as community detection (McNulty, 2022). Detecting communities has become highly important problem in network science with multiple applications, as it allows for revealing the structure of a network and then further inferring specific relationships between nodes that may not be easily accessible (Yang et al., 2019).

In addition, structural hole theory refers to the groupings of nodes, noting that communities of nodes between which there are no links form holes in the structure of a network, i.e. they do not interact with each other. Despite the existence of these holes, there are some nodes that occupy bridge positions between different communities and are called brokers and have advantages as they control the main information diffusion paths. In other words, nodes that act as bridges fill the structural holes, resulting in the benefits of accessing different kinds of views and ideas, diffusing information between different communities, synthesizing more potentially feasible methods and more effectively coordinating multiple tasks of different communities (Burt, 2015; Lin et al., 2021). Several indicators are proposed that measure whether a node is considered a bridge in a network, as the constraint index, the size of which is influenced by the size and density of the network. A node has a low constraint index when there is an alternative path along which information can be carried, i.e. there are alternative neighboring nodes that are connected to other nodes. On the contrary, a node's high constraint means that this node has no other possibility to channel information in the network than a neighboring node. Therefore, the higher the constraint index of a node, the more restricted a node's opportunities to communicate with neighboring nodes are (Buskens & van de Rijt, 2008; Burt, 2004).

3 Methodology

This paper studies certain macroeconomic variables for the NUTS2 regions for the period 2010–2021. In particular, it studies the indicators of GDP per capita, and the total unemployment rate for citizens aged from 15 to 64 years. These indicators were chosen as they are two of the most frequently studied indicators in Regional Development. Clearly, there is a strong correlation between poverty, long-term unemployment, employability, and education. Many long-term unemployed people face multi-faceted problems, many of which include low levels of motivation and educational skills (Bejakovic & Mrnjavac, 2018).

We collected data from the Eurostat database (https://ec.europa.eu/eurostat/data/database). However, there were some missing values in the time series due to the modification of the NUTS classification. More specifically, there were gaps in the total unemployment rate in certain regions, which have been edited to complete as follows: the average of the Irish regions of Border, Midland and Western and Southern and Eastern (NUTS, 2013) was used to fill in the gaps in the Northern and Western, Southern and Eastern, and Midland (NUTS, 2016). A similar methodology was applied in Sostines regionas (LT) and Vidurio ir vakaru Lietuvos regionas (LT) (NUTS, 2016), which according to the NUTS 2013 classification were included in Lietuva (LT), for the period 2010–2012. Lietuva data for the years 2010 to 2012 was therefore used to fill in the gaps of the two regions. The Lietuva region ceased to exist with the 2016 classification. Budapest (HU) and Pest (HU) (NUTS, 2016) were included in the Közép-Magyarország (HU) region, which ceased to exist with the 2016 classification. We used data for Közép-Dunántúl (HU) for the years 2010 to 2012 to fill in the gaps of the two regions. Kontinentalna Hrvatska (HR) (NUTS, 2021) was abolished and replaced by three new regions: Panonska Hrvatska, Grad Zagreb, and Sjeverna Hrvatska. However, in the Eurostat database there is no data for the new regions for the years 2010 to 2020, but only for 2021. Therefore, we used data from the Kontinentalna Hrvatska region, resulting in two regions for Croatia: Kontinentalna Hrvatska and Jadranska Hrvatska for the whole period.

There were also other missing values, which we filled in with linear regression. As regards the total unemployment rate, this was the case in the following regions: Trier (DE) for 2020–2021, Mazowiecki regionalny and Warszawski stoleczny (PL) for 2010–2012, Mayotte (FR) for 2010–2012 and Lubuskie for 2020–2021.

Finally, missing values were identified in the total unemployment rate data in some regions for the year 2020. To fill them in, we calculated the average of the previous and next year's data for the German regions Niederbayern, Oberpfalz, Oberfranken, Unterfranken, Bremen, Kassel, Koblenz, Saarland, Chemnitz and the French one of Corse. In addition, the French overseas department of Mayotte was completely missing from the database of the total unemployment rate.

After this process, the final samples of the work resulted in, which consists of 239 NUTS2 regions for the total unemployment rate, whereas the final sample of the GPD consists of 242 NUTS2 regions.

Next, we converted the data to construct correlation tables, i.e. tables showing the correlation coefficient of the regions, which was calculated from the following function:

$\rho_{ij} = cov_{ij}/\sigma_i\sigma_j$, where

cov_{ij} = the covariance of regions i and j, where $cov_{ij} = [P_i - E(P_i)][P_j - E(P_j)]/n - 1$

E(P) = the average of each region, n = the count of the regions,

σ_i = the standard deviation of region i and σ_j = the standard deviation of region j

The coefficient can take values from −1 to + 1, which indicates the degree of correlation between the data: when the correlation coefficient tends to −1, the two regions move inversely, i.e. when the size of one region increases, the corresponding size of the second region tends to decrease and vice versa. When the correlation coefficient tends to 1, the two regions move in the same direction, and when the coefficient is zero, which means that the two regions are changing randomly.

As a result, we obtained a symmetric correlation matrix of dimensions 242×242. In the next step, we processed the table by setting a threshold θ with the possibility to take values between −1 and 1. In particular, for each correlation coefficient greater than the threshold θ, the value 1 appears in the table, while when the value is less than the threshold θ, the value 0 appears. In practice, this means that when the degree of correlation between the data of the regions is greater than the threshold θ, a link (edge) between the regions is created.

Finally, we ended up with an adjacency table, which allows us to create a network with the contribution of the NodeXL Pro software package (Smith et al., 2010), with a key feature of visualizing the nodes and the edges.

We applied the same procedure for GDP per capita, and the total unemployment rate for NUTS2 regions for 2010–2021.

A main purpose of this paper is to identify a way to reduce the number of communities of regions in their networks. Such a reduction would practically mean greater homogeneity between regions, i.e. a small number of communities in a network implies the elimination of regional disparities and cohesion between regions, the purpose of EU Cohesion Policy. For this reason, a process was applied to identify which links could connect specific pairs of nodes for more homogeneous networks, i.e. networks consisting of a smaller number of communities. The homogeneity of networks could be compared to economic and social cohesion between regions, i.e. the elimination of regional disparities. According to the constraint index, we implemented an algorithm using the Python programming language to add links between nodes with a high constraint index of different communities (**Appendix**). Consequently, new edges were created between pairs of regions to bridge the communities and reduce their number. The process is repeated until the number of communities reaches the desired number, resulting in a more homogeneous network with greater cohesion.

4 Network Analysis, Results, and Discussion

In this section, we will attempt to study the networks constructed for certain values of θ (threshold). The procedure was applied for the indices of GDP per capita and the total unemployment rate for NUTS2 regions of EU for the period of 2010–2021. In addition, we calculated degree centrality and betweenness centrality for every created network and their correspondent density. The size of the nodes was based on betweenness centrality, i.e. the higher the centrality, the larger the size of nodes (Brandes, 2001).

4.1 GDP Per Capita

When studying GDP per capita, we choose a high correlation coefficient of 0.94, as for lower correlation coefficients the networks created are too dense, which does not allow us to draw conclusions. In this network (Fig. 1), the number of communities of regions created is six, two of which include the majority of regions, while the remaining communities consist of far fewer regions, belonging exclusively to Greece and Spain. There are 13 isolated nodes in this network, and there are 11.944 links between the regions. The most important nodes in terms of betweenness centrality are Jadranska Hrvatska (HR) and Aragón (ES), while in terms of degree centrality are Noord-Holland (NL) and Alsace (FR). Finally, the density of the network equals 0,409.

This paper aims to find a way to reduce the number of communities of regions in the networks, which means more homogeneity between regions. Again, a small number of communities in a network implies the elimination of regional disparities and cohesion between regions, which is what the EU is working on through its regional policy. For this reason, we used Python (programming language) to reduce the number of communities. Specifically, in the network where the correlation coefficient $\theta = 0.94$, the number of communities is 6, the Python code (annex) is applied based on the constraint index to reduce the number of communities to 2. In this case, the number of edges required is only 12, i.e. an increase from 11.944 to 11.956. It should be noted that proportionally only a small number of edges is required, i.e. only 0.1% of the existing edges, to create a more homogeneous network, which

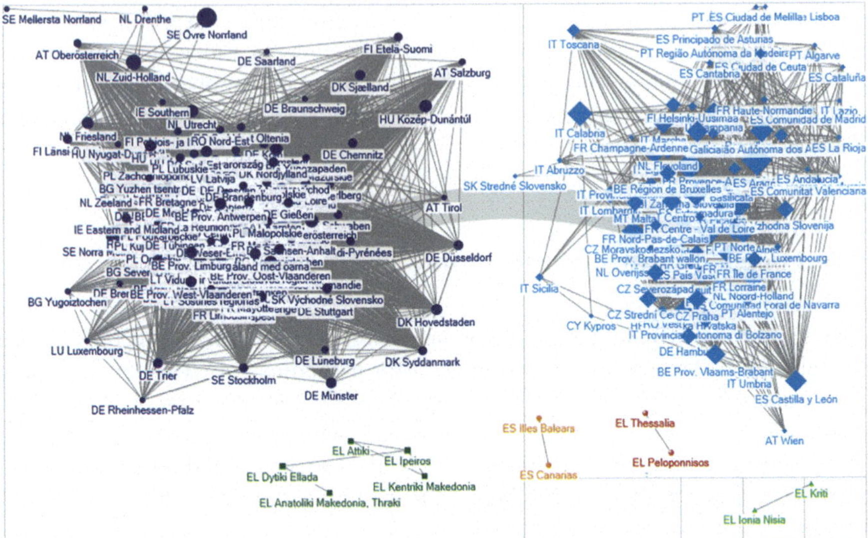

Fig. 1 Network of GDP per capita, correlation coefficient $\theta = 0.94$

reflects greater cohesion between regions. The EU could apply targeted policies and strategies through the European Structural and Investment Funds (ESIF) to specific regions, to reduce the regional disparities. In the following (Table 1) is a list of the specific edges:

The question that arises is how do we interfere in the regions to achieve greater cohesion between the regions? The fact that the model we use is based on creating edges between pairs of regions means that intervention will be done on a pair-by-pair basis. In other words, it is proposed to reinforce programs in one of the regions

Table 1 New links added in the network of GDP, correlation coefficient $\theta = 0.94$

EL Attiki	EL Kriti
EL Anatoliki Makedonia	EL Thessalia
EL Ionia Nisia	ES Illes Balears
EL Peloponnisos	SE Mellersta Norrland
ES Canarias	IT Lazio
EL Kentriki Makedonia	CY Kypros
EL Attiki	EL Anatoliki Makedonia
EL Kriti	EL Thessalia
EL Ionia Nisia	EL Peloponnisos
EL Dytiki Ellada	ES Illes Balears
ES Canarias	CY Kypros
SE Mellersta Norrland	NL Drenthe

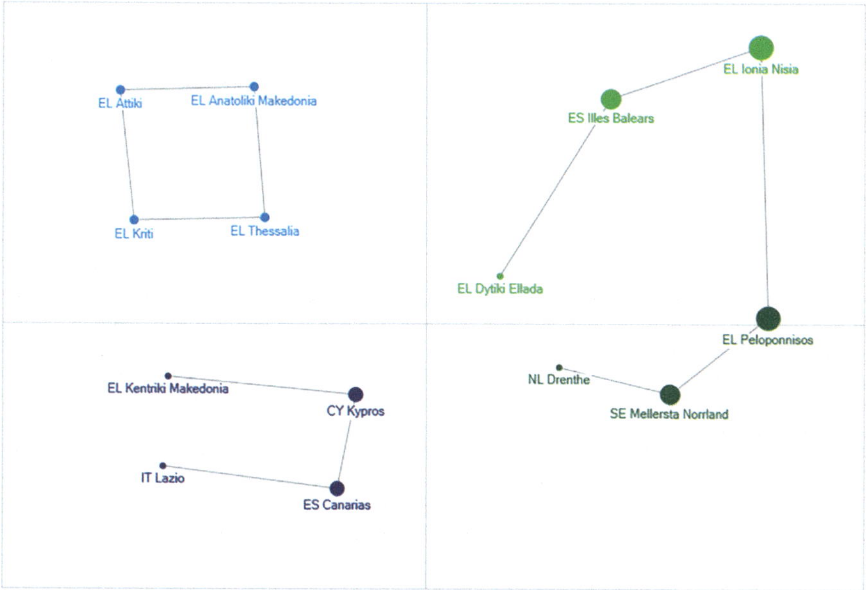

Fig. 2 Network of the new links (GDP per capita)

in each pair to achieve greater correlation between them, i.e. to create a new edge. Therefore, we decided to visualize the resulting edges again using the NodeXL software package in a network, for a better understanding of the interaction of the regions through visualization (Fig. 2).

It is important to stress that through the EU policies and strategies in these regions, higher cohesion is aimed at the territory and not only between specific regions. For greater cohesion, intervening in pairs means increasing (decreasing) Cohesion Policy in specific regions. Consequently, the neighboring regions of a given region will suffer a decrease (increase), the next regions of neighboring regions will receive an increase (decrease) in the Cohesion Policy exercise, and so on. In other words, the change (increase or decrease) in the Cohesion Policy exercise must be applied alternately to the regions according to the following graph. In this way, an efficient use of important resources could be achieved, as it would avoid their massive application to all the regions of the Union.

Starting from the network's most central node (region), we increase the Cohesion Policy implementation in the region of Ionia Nisia (EL), as it has the highest betweenness centrality (=4). Consequently, its neighboring regions will suffer a decrease; the next neighboring regions will receive an increase in the Cohesion Policy exercise, and so on. In other words, the change (increase or decrease) in the Cohesion Policy exercise should be applied alternately to the regions based on the graph below, which shows the modification, which will lead to a more coherent network of GDP per

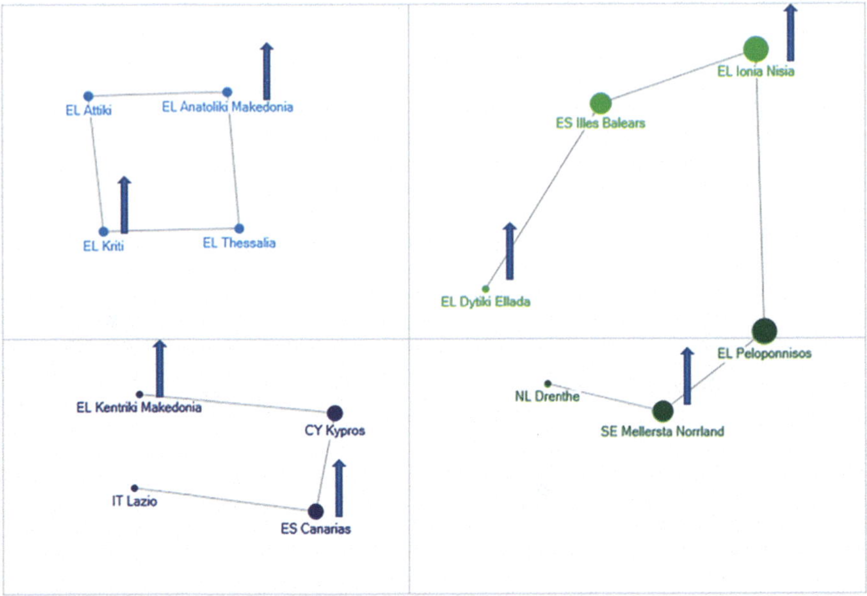

Fig. 3 Network of the new links (GDP per capita) with the modification in the implementation of Cohesion policy

capita. After this procedure, we can see in Fig. 3 the changes in the Cohesion Policy exercise for each of the proposed regions.

As far as the EU is concerned, this fact means that specific and targeted strategies and policies for improving and increasing GDP per capita could be implemented, with the ultimate aim of reducing regional disparities throughout the Union. In this way, the efficient use of important resources could be achieved, as it would avoid their massive application to all the regions of the territory.

The Time Factor in the Implementation of Policies in the GDP Per Capita Indicator

The question then arises as to how the above policies could be implemented in time in the specific regions. Time is an important factor in the implementation of cohesion policy, as the effectiveness of the measures depends on it. At this point, we decided to pursue alternative approaches to the implementation of measures in terms of timing.

First, there is the possibility of implementing policies that will simultaneously increase overall cohesion. In other words, we propose that the increase should go hand in hand with a corresponding reduction in measures when implementing Cohesion Policy and in all the regions for which the new extremes are proposed. In other words, from the ERDF, CF, ESF + , and JTF programs of Cohesion Policy to improve regional disparities, it is proposed to increase them in the following regions: Ionia

Nisia (EL), Mellersta Norrland (SE), Dytiki Ellada (EL), Anataloki Makedonia (EL), Kriti (EL), Kentriki Makedonia (EL), and Canarias (ES). At the same time, it is proposed to weaken the Cohesion Policy exercise for the other regions, i.e. Attiki (EL), Thessalia (EL), Lazio (IT), Kypros (CY), Illes Balears (ES), Drehnte (NL) and Peloponnisos (EL).

According to another approach, Cohesion Policy support could be applied only in the regions where a positive change is proposed, without reducing the corresponding policies in neighboring regions. More specifically, about the GDP per capita measure, there could be a reinforcement of measures and policies in the regions: Ionia Nisia (EL), Mellersta Norrland (SE), Dytiki Ellada (EL), Anataloki Makedonia (EL), Kriti (EL), Kentriki Makedonia (EL), and Canarias (ES).

That is, by implementing reinforcing policies in some regions and bypassing their neighboring regions, after a certain period the evolution of the GDP per capita could be observed. Since after the intervention, the index between these regions and their neighbors may move more in parallel, as a higher correlation between them is expected to follow, it could be captured by an edge between regions in the network. In other words, increasing policies in specific regions and avoiding any change in the Cohesion Policy of their neighboring regions causes a parallel movement in the GDP per capita index, essentially depicted by an edge between regions. The expected effects of this intervention will start to appear in a reasonable period.

Finally, another suggestion is that the policies should be implemented gradually rather than simultaneously, following the order in which the edges were derived using the Python programming language (Table 2). In detail, starting from the first edge, i.e. for the pair Attiki (EL) and Kriti (EL), we propose to increase the measures to Kriti (EL) with a corresponding decrease in Attiki (EL). In the next step, the edge between the regions Anatoliki Makedonia (EL) and Thessalia (EL) follows. In this edge, we propose to increase the measures in the region Anatoliki Makedonia (EL) and to decrease them in the region Thessalia (EL). The process continues by increasing and decreasing the measures in the regions, in line with the change proposed in the previous model. The table below shows the edges in order, as obtained by applying a methodology using the Python programming language.

In Table 2, there are regions that repeat in more edges, i.e. there are edges that join regions that have already been intervened in a previous step. In this case, there is no need to increase the measures in these regions again, but only to reduce the neighboring ones. For example, the region of Kriti (EL) exists at the first and eighth edges. Since the region has suffered an increase in measures in the first vertex, it would be unnecessary to reapply reinforcing measures in the eighth vertex, with the result that only the cuts in the neighboring regions of Attiki (EL) and Thessalia (EL) would be applied. The same is to happen with the regions in the subsequent vertices. That is, the increase of measures in the region of Ionia Nisia (EL) will take place in the third vertex with a simultaneous reduction in the region of Illes Balears (ES), while in the ninth vertex only the reduction in the region of Peloponnisos (EL)

Table 2 Reinforcing-reducing regional policies (GDP per capita)

	Regions for which supportive policies are proposed	Regions for which reducing policies are proposed
1	EL Kriti	EL Attiki
2	EL Anatoliki Makedonia	EL Thessalia
3	EL Ionia Nisia	ES Illes Balears
4	SE Mellersta Norrland	EL Peloponnisos
5	ES Canarias	IT Lazio
6	EL Kentriki Makedonia	CY Kypros
7	EL Anatoliki Makedonia	EL Attiki
8	EL Kriti	EL Thessalia
9	EL Ionia Nisia	EL Peloponnisos
10	EL Dytiki Ellada	ES Illes Balears
11	ES Canarias	CY Kypros
12	SE Mellersta Norrland	NL Drenthe

will take place. In terms of timing, for this approach, we foresee that it requires a certain period between the implementation of the measures in each pair of vertices. It becomes noticeable that to complete all edges, the time interval required is long. Of course, in this way, the expected results could be gradually evaluated until all possible edges leading to homogeneity of the GDP per capita network are exhausted.

Regardless of the approach finally applied, the GDP per capita network will end up consisting of two communities of regions, and i.e. it will be a more coherent network than the original one.

4.2 *Total Unemployment Rate*

In the network of the total unemployment rate (Fig. 4) with a correlation coefficient $\theta = 0.80$ the network density equals 0,175. The communes of the regions are six, and the isolated nodes, i.e. nodes that have no edge with other nodes in the network, are also six: the French regions Limousin and Mayotte, two Romanian regions, Nord-Est and Sud-Vest Oltenia and Burgenland (AT) and Luxembourg (LU). The most important regions in terms of centrality measures appear to be Norte (PT), with a high betweenness centrality and degree centrality, Région de Bruxelles (BE), with a high betweenness centrality and Podkarpackie (PL) with a high degree centrality. Finally, a characteristic feature of this network is that six of the eight Swedish regions form a community, to which no other European region belongs. These are the regions

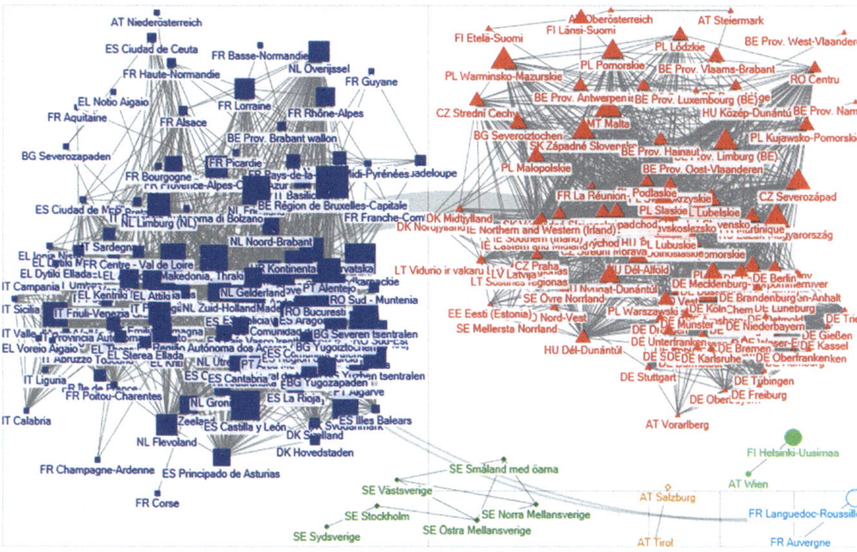

Fig. 4 Network of total unemployment rate, correlation coefficient $\theta = 0.8$

of Stockholm, Sydsverige, Östra Mellansverige, Småland med öarna, Västsverige, and Norra Mellansverige.

In this network (Fig. 4) there are two large communities of regions and four smaller ones, and this work aims to reduce the number of communities from six to two. In this case, the edges required are 29, i.e. they increase from 4.983 to 5.012. That is, using the code (**A**ppendix) in the programming language of Python, the following edges of regions are created (Table 3), so that the network has a higher cohesion.

The visualization of the above links (Table 3) follows in Fig. 5.

Our approach for this indicator is the same as that of the GDP network, i.e. to achieve future cohesion in the network of the total unemployment rate pairwise intervention means increasing and decreasing Cohesion Policy in specific regions. We increase the Cohesion Policy exercise in the regions of Notio Aigaio (EL), Stockholm (SE), and Niederösterreich (AT) starting with the most central nodes (regions) of the network, as they score the highest centrality metrics (degree centrality and betweenness centrality). As a result, the adjacent regions will experience a decline; the next regions that follow will see an increase in the Cohesion Policy exercise, and so on. In other words, the change (increase or decrease) in the Cohesion Policy exercise should be applied alternately to the regions based on the graph below, which illustrates the change, creating a more coherent network of the total unemployment rate (Fig. 6).

Table 3 New links added in the network of total unemployment rate, correlation coefficient θ = 0.80

BE Prov. Namur	FR Auvergne
FR Corse	AT Wien
AT Niederösterreich	AT Salzburg
AT Tirol	SE Sydsverige
SE Småland med öarna	EL Notio Aigaio
SE Västsverige	FR Basse-Normandie
SE Norra Mellansverige	BE Prov. West-Vlaanderen
BE Prov. Namur	FR Aquitaine
FR Languedoc-Roussillon	FR Corse
FR Auvergne	AT Niederösterreich
AT Wien	AT Steiermark
AT Oberösterreich	FR Guyane
AT Salzburg	EL Notio Aigaio
AT Tirol	FR Champagne-Ardenne
FI Helsinki-Uusimaa	BG Severozapaden
SE Stockholm	FI Länsi-Suomi
SE Sydsverige	AT Steiermark
SE Östra Mellansverige	FI Etelä-Suomi
SE Småland med öarna	SE Stockholm
SE Västsverige	BE Prov. Namur
SE Norra Mellansverige	EL Notio Aigaio
SE Småland med öarna	BE Prov. Vlaams-Brabant
FR Basse-Normandie	FI Länsi-Suomi
SE Östra Mellansverige	FR Aquitaine
SE Norra Mellansverige	FR Languedoc-Roussillon
BE Prov. West-Vlaanderen	AT Vorarlberg
FR Auvergne	EE Eesti
FR Corse	SE Stockholm
AT Niederösterreich	BG Severozapaden

The Time Factor in the Implementation of Policies in the Indicator of the Total Unemployment Rate

The following are the alternative approaches to the implementation of time-based measures. First, there is the possibility of implementing simultaneously the policies that will increase overall cohesion. In other words, it is proposed that the increase should be made in parallel with a corresponding reduction of measures in the implementation of the Cohesion Policy in all 29 regions. In other words, from the Cohesion Fund, which is implemented through specific Funds (ERDF, CF, ESF + , JTF), it is

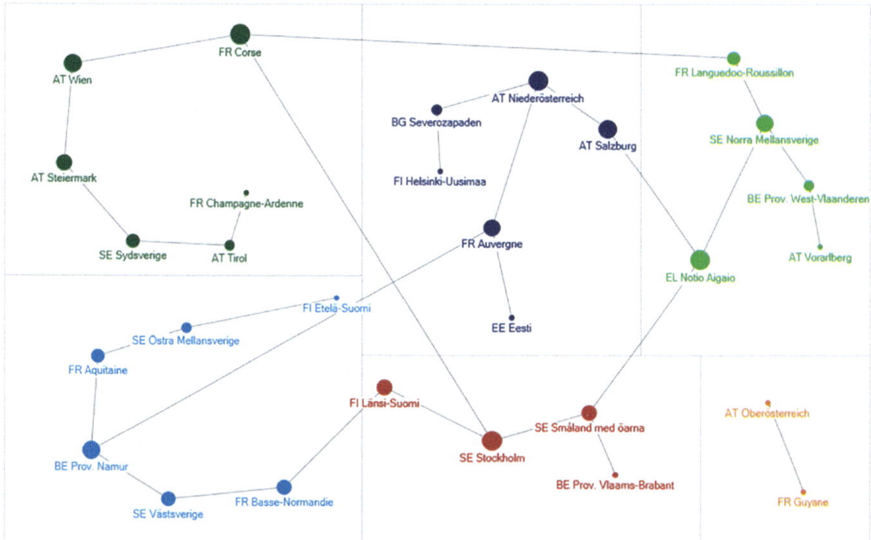

Fig. 5 Network of the new links (total unemployment rate)

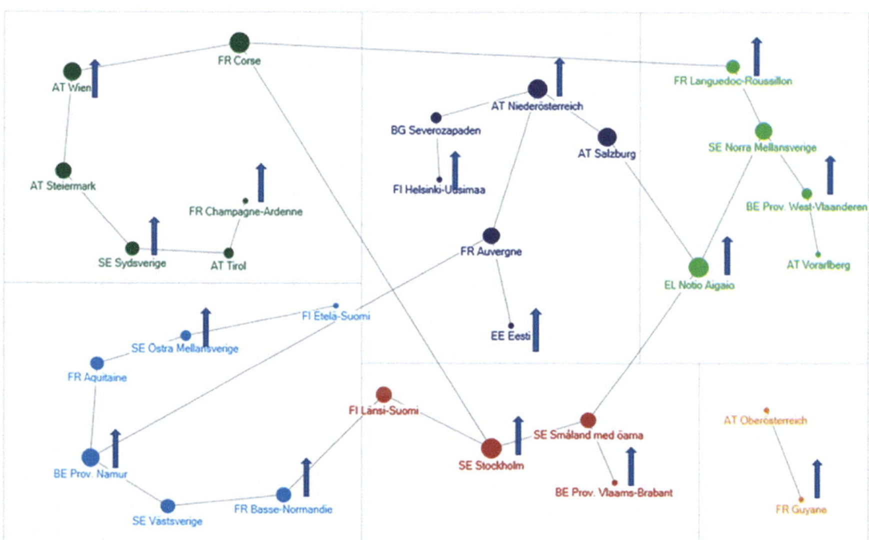

Fig. 6 Network of the new links (unemployment rate) with the modification in the implementation of Cohesion Policy

proposed to strengthen the regions: Notio Aigaio (EL), Stockholm (SE), Niederösterreich (AT), Languedoc-Roussillon (FR), Prov. West-Vlaanderen (BE), Wien (AT), Sydsverige (SE), Champagne-Ardenne (FR), Prov. Vlaams-Brabant (BE), Basse-Normandie (FR), Prov. Namur (BE), Esti (EE), Helsinki (FI), and Guyane (FR). At the same time, a reduction is proposed in the regions of: Corse (FR), Steiermark (AT), Tirol (AT), Östra Mellansverige (SE), Salzburg (AT), Auvergne (FR), Aquitaine (FR), Etelä-Suomi (FI), Västsverige (SE), Länsi-Suomi (FI), Småland med öarna (SE), Norra Mellansverige (SE), Severozapaden (BG), Oberösterreich (AT), and Vorarlberg (AT). In this case, if the measures are applied in parallel, the results are expected.

Another method would be to reduce the equivalent measures in neighboring regions and limit the support for the Cohesion Policy to the regions where positive changes are planned. More precisely, policies and initiatives in the areas may be strengthened to lower the total unemployment rate: Notio Aigaio (EL), Stockholm (SE), Niederösterreich (AT), Languedoc-Roussillon (FR), Prov. West-Vlaanderen (BE), Wien (AT), Sydsverige (SE), Champagne-Ardenne (FR), Prov. Vlaams-Brabant (BE), Basse-Normandie (FR), Prov. Namur (BE), Esti (EE), Helsinki (FI), Östra Mellansverige (SE), and Guyane (FR). On the other hand, the regions in which there will be no corresponding reduction: Auvergne (FR), Corse (FR), Salzburg (AT), Tirol (AT), Småland med öarna (SE), Västsverige (SE), Norra Mellansverige (SE), Aquitaine (FR), Steiermark (AT), Oberösterreich (AT), Severozapaden (BG), Länsi-Suomi (FI), Etelä-Suomi (FI), Vorarlberg (AT). That is, after a specific period, the trend of the region's overall unemployment index could be influenced by enacting supporting policies in some regions and avoiding their neighboring regions. Since a larger correlation between the given regions and their closest neighbors is predicted to follow the intervention, the unemployment rate between those regions and their neighboring regions may move more in parallel, which might be recorded by a link between the regions in the network. To put it another way, tightening policies in one location while resisting changes to the cohesiveness policies of nearby regions results in a parallel trend in the unemployment rate index, which is effectively a link between regions. Within an appropriate period, the anticipated outcomes of this intervention will start to show.

Lastly, an alternative suggestion is to apply the policies separately instead of all at once, in the same sequence that the edges were determined using the Python programming language (Table 4). To be more specific, it is suggested to raise the measures in Namur (BE) and decrease them in Auvergne (FR) for the pair Namur (BE) and Auvergne (FR). The border between the Wien (AT) and Corse (FR) areas is the next stage. It is suggested to enhance the measures at this edge in the Corse (FR) region and decrease them in the Wien (AT) region. According to the variation suggested in the previous model, the process proceeds by raising and lowering the measurements in the respective regions. The edges are arranged in the table below according to a methodology that was implemented with the Python computer language.

Table 4 Reinforcing-reducing regional policies (total unemployment rate)

	Regions for which supportive policies are proposed	Regions for which reducing policies are proposed
1	Namur (BE)	Auvergne (FR)
2	Wien (AT)	Corse (FR)
3	Niederösterreich (AT)	Salzburg (AT)
4	Sydsverige (SE)	Tirol (AT)
5	Notio Aigaio (EL)	Småland med öarna (SE)
6	Basse-Normandie (FR)	Västsverige (SE)
7	Prov. West-Vlaanderen (BE)	Norra Mellansverige (SE)
8	Prov. Namur (BE)	Aquitaine (FR)
9	Languedoc-Roussillon (FR)	Corse (FR)
10	Niederösterreich (AT)	Auvergne (FR)
11	Wien (AT)	Steiermark (AT)
12	Guyane (FR)	Oberösterreich (AT)
13	Notio Aigaio (EL)	Salzburg (AT)
14	Champagne-Ardenne (FR)	Tirol (AT)
15	Helsinki-Uusimaa (FI)	Severozapaden (BG)
16	Stockholm (SE)	Länsi-Suomi (FI)
17	Sydsverige (SE)	Steiermark (AT)
18	Östra Mellansverige (SE)	Etelä-Suomi (FI)
19	Stockholm (SE)	Småland med öarna (SE)
20	Prov. Namur (BE)	Västsverige (SE)
21	Notio Aigaio (EL)	Norra Mellansverige (SE)
22	Prov. Vlaams-Brabant (BE)	Småland med öarna (SE)
23	Basse-Normandie (FR)	Länsi-Suomi (FR)
24	Östra Mellansverige (SE)	Aquitaine (FR)
25	Languedoc-Roussillon (FR)	Norra Mellansverige (SE)
26	Prov. West-Vlaanderen (BE)	Vorarlberg (AT)
27	Eesti (EE)	Auvergne (FR)
28	Stockholm (SE)	Corse (FR)
29	Niederösterreich (AT)	Severozapaden (BG)

There are regions in the above table that are repeated on many edges, which means that some edges connect regions that have already been interfered with in a previous step. In this case, there is no need to increase the measures in these regions again, only to reduce the adjacent ones. For example, the first, eighth, and twentieth edges connect certain regions to Namur (BE). Only reductions will be applied to the neighboring regions of Aquitaine (FR) and Västsverige (SE) since the region has already experienced an increase in measures at the first edge. This would reduce the need to reapply reinforcing measures to face unemployment in links number 8 and 20. The regions of the coming edges will experience the same situation. In other words, the second link will see an increase in measures in Wien (AT) and a concurrent decrease in Corse (FR), whereas the eleventh peak will only see a decrease in Steiermark (AT). Considering timing, we estimate that this method will need a specific amount of time between applying the measures to each edge pair. Completing every edge takes a significant period. Naturally, in this case, the anticipated outcomes might be progressively assessed until all potential edges that could lead to the homogeneity of the total unemployment network are exhausted.

The overall unemployment rate network will ultimately comprise of two communities of areas, meaning that it will be a more cohesive network than the first one, regardless of the methodology ultimately used.

5 Conclusions

In this paper, we have attempted to study the economic and regional development of the EU with the contribution of SNA. In particular, we studied two macroeconomic indicators, GDP per capita and the total unemployment rate in the NUTS2 regions for the period 2010–2021.

We first tried to draw some conclusions about the degree of correlation of the indicators between regions. Through the NodeXL software package, we achieved the visualization of our data, i.e. the groupings (communities) created based on the degree of correlation that we defined (threshold θ). For both indicators, the number of communities was such that it leads us to the conclusion of the lack of regional cohesion. In other words, when more communities of regions exist in a network, we cannot talk about homogeneity between our data. Given that the Cohesion Policy pursued by the EU aims at homogeneity and parallel development of regions and not only of Member States, it is reasonable to compare the homogeneity of the networks we have constructed with the homogeneity of macroeconomic indicators i.e. with the cohesion in the EU.

In the next step, the question arose whether we could again use SNA to implement a Cohesion Policy more concentrated in specific regions, to achieve homogeneity across the territory of the Union. Using the Python programming language, we propose to create new edges between specific regions to reduce the number of communities in the regions, thus increasing cohesion. It is important to stress that the pursuit of policies in specific regions improves cohesion across the territory, resulting in valuable savings from the European Structural and Investment Funds (ESIF).

This study has been presented at the 16th International Conference "Economies of the Balkan and Eastern European Countries", EBEEC 2024, Vilnius, Lithuania (http://ebeec.ihu.gr/).

Appendix

To add links between nodes with a high constraint index of different communities, we used Python (a programming language), by introducing the following code:

```
#I add links with the highest betweenness or the highest constraints from different

communities.

#I stop as soon as I have only 2 communities



#the networkx operates in 3.2.1



#option to remove isolates. What will these become? Why are there?
```

```
import time
import openpyxl
import pandas as pd
import networkx as nx
import matplotlib.pyplot as plt
from networkx.algorithms import community
import numpy as np
from scipy import sparse
from pyvis.network import Network

#the following to read real data
def readGraph():
    from tkinter.filedialog import askopenfilename
    filename = askopenfilename()
    mydata = pd.read_excel(filename)
    labels = mydata['Unnamed: 0']
    mydata = mydata.drop('Unnamed: 0', axis = 1)
    A = np.array(mydata)
    G = nx.from_numpy_array(A)
    d = {}
    for node in G.nodes:
        d[node]=labels[node]
    G = nx.relabel_nodes(G, d)
    sel = input('remove isolates?(y/n)')
```

```
    if sel in 'yY':
        G.remove_nodes_from(list(nx.isolates(G)))

    return G



#the following to draw graph
def drawGraph(graph, between, communities):
    #general position pos for reproduction
    pos = nx.spring_layout(graph)
    #some colors for communities
    col=['r', 'g', 'b','c', 'm', 'silver','salmon', 'bisque', 'khaki',
         'olive', 'lime', 'azure', 'violet']
    #print(constraints)

    #print(communities)
    #draw basic graph
    nx.draw_networkx(graph, pos, verticalalignment = 'bottom', with_labels = True)
    #now draw betweeenness above each edge
    nx.set_node_attributes(graph, between, 'labs')
    labels = nx.get_node_attributes(graph, 'labs')
    nx.draw_networkx(graph, pos, verticalalignment = 'top', labels = labels)

    #now color communities
    i=0
```

```
    for com in communities:
        colo = col[i]
        nl = []
        for n in com:
            nl.append(n)
        nx.draw_networkx_nodes(graph, pos, nodelist=nl, node_color=colo)
        i=i+1
        if i == len(col)-1:i = 0

    plt.show()



#the following to fastly compute constraints
def local_constraint(g):
    A = nx.to_scipy_sparse_array(g)
    n = nx.number_of_nodes(g)
    A = A - sparse.dia_array((A.diagonal(), [0]), shape = (n,n))

    ones = np.ones(n)

    x = (A+A.T)@ones
    y = ones / x

    diag_y = sparse.dia_array((y, [0]), shape = (n, n))
```

```
    P = diag_y @ (A + A.T)
    L_temp = P + P@P.multiply(A)

    return L_temp.multiply(L_temp)

def constraint(g):
    A = nx.to_scipy_sparse_array(g)
    n = nx.number_of_nodes(g)
    A = A - sparse.dia_matrix((A.diagonal(), [0]), shape = (n, n))

    L = local_constraint(g)

    C = (L.multiply(A)).sum(axis = 1)
    C = np.squeeze(np.asarray(C))

    return dict(zip([name for name in g.nodes], C))



###main###
g = readGraph()
print(g)
e1 = len(g.edges()) #num of edges at the beginning

#first pass
```

```
selector = input('Betweenness (b) - OK or Constraint (c)')
if selector in 'bBcC':
    if selector in 'bB':
        c = nx.betweenness_centrality(g)
    elif selector in 'cC':
        c = constraint(g)

minComs = int(input('Ελάχιστο πλήθος τελικών Communities?'))



coms = community.greedy_modularity_communities(g)
sel = input('Do you want to draw? (y/n)')
if sel in 'yY':
    #draw_pyvis(g, coms)
    drawGraph(g, c, coms)
print('Starting number of communities:', len(coms))

#c is dictionary of betweenness or constraints
#coms is dictionary of communities

added_links = []
####here the new graph
g1 = nx.Graph()
####
```

```
start_time = time.time()
#now repetitively add links between nodes with highest betweenness from different
communities
while True:
    added = False
    x = sorted(c.items(), key=lambda x:x[1], reverse=True) #sort descending
    l1=[]
    for i,j in x:
        l1.append(i)

    for u in l1:
        for v in l1:
            if v!=u:
                if (u, v) not in g.edges():
                    for com in coms:
                        if v in com:
                            c1 = com
                    for com in coms:
                        if u in com:
                            c2 = com
                    if c1 != c2: #must be in different community
                        g1.add_edge(u, v)
                        odd_cycles = False
                        cycles = sorted(nx.simple_cycles(g1))
                        for c in cycles:
```

```
                #print(c)
                    if len(c)%2==1:
                        odd_cycles = True
                        break
                if odd_cycles == True:
                    g1.remove_edge(u, v)
                    continue

                g.add_edge(u, v)
                ####
                #print(u, v)
                added = True
                added_links.append([u, v])
                break
        if added:break

    if len(coms)==minComs:break  # here is the number of final communities I want.

    if selector in 'bB':
        c = nx.betweenness_centrality(g)
    else:
        c = constraint(g)

    coms = community.greedy_modularity_communities(g)
```

```
end_time = time.time()
print('total time = ', end_time-start_time)
e2 = len(g.edges()) #num of edges at the end
print('from:', e1, '->', e2, 'edges. Difference is:', e2-e1)
print('Final number of communities:', len(coms))


sel = input('Do you want to draw? (y/n)')
if sel in 'yY':
    drawGraph(g, c, coms)
    #draw_pyvis(g, coms)
sel = input('Do you want to see the list of added edges? (y/n)')
if sel in 'yY':
    print(added_links)


# From now on test, new network only with added links
#g1 = nx.from_edgelist(added_links)
cycles = sorted(nx.simple_cycles(g1))
for c in cycles:
    #print(c)
    if len(c)%2==1:
        print(c, ' odd')
nt = Network('1000px', '1000px')
# populates the nodes and edges data structures
nt.from_nx(g1)
nt.show('nx.html', notebook=False)
```

While running the Module, we have to response to the next questions:

```
remove isolates?(y/n)

Graph with X nodes and Y edges

Betweenness (b) - OK or Constraint (c)

Minimum number of final Communities?

Do you want to draw? (y/n)

Starting number of communities: A

total time =  1.5318477153778076

from: 5013 -> 5021 edges. Difference is: 8

Final number of communities: 2

Do you want to draw? (y/n)

Do you want to see the list of added edges? (y/n)
```

References

Agnieszda, W. (2019). *European Parliament Research Service, ERPS*. (E. Parliament, Editor) Retrieved 02 13, 2020, from https://www.europarl.europa.eu/RegData/etudes/BRIE/2019/637951/EPRS_BRI(2019)637951_EN.pdf

Bejakovic, P., & Mrnjavac, Z. (2018). The danger of long-term unemployment and measuresfor its reduction: The case of Croatia. *Economic Research-Ekonomska Istraživanja, 31*(1), 1837–1850. https://doi.org/10.1080/1331677X.2018.152129

Burt, R. (2004). Structural holes and good ideas. *American Journal of Sociology, 2*, 349–399. https://doi.org/10.1086/421787

Burt, R. (2015). Reinforced structural holes. *Social Networks, 43*, 149–161.

Buskens, V., & van de Rijt, A. (2008). Dynamics of networks if everyone strives for structural holes. *American Journal of Sociology, 114*(2), 371–407. https://doi.org/10.1086/590674

Das, R. C. (2016). *Handbook of research on global indicators of economic and political convergence*. IGI Global.

European Commission. (2022). *Shaping Europe's digital future*. Retrieved 01 22, 2024, from https://digital-strategy.ec.europa.eu/el/activities/funding-digital

Ezcurra, R. (2019). Regional disparities and within-country inequality in the European Union. *Revista De Econimia Mundial, 51*, 139–162. https://doi.org/10.33776/rem.v0i51.3907

Girvan, M., & Newman, M. (2002). Community structure in social and biological networks. *Proceedings of the National Academy of Sciences, 99*(12), 7821–7826. https://doi.org/10.1073/pnas.122653799

Jackson, M. (2005). The economics of social networks. *Advances in Economics and Econometrics*, (pp. 1–56). https://doi.org/10.1017/CBO9781139052269.003

Kydros, D., Athianos, S., & Dimadis, D. (2014). Corporate governance analysis and social networks: A case study in Greek firms. *MIBES Transactions, 8*, 84–99.

Lin, Z., Zhang, Y., Gong, Q., Chen, Y., Oksanen, A., & Ding, A. (2021). Structural hole theory in social network analysis: A review. *IEEE Transactions on Computational Social Systems*.

Matuzeviciute, K., Mironikovaitė, I., Garšvienė, L., & Ruplienė, D. (2023). Threshold effects of public debt on the tax burden: Evidence from EU member states. *Intellectual Economics, 17*(2), Article 2. https://doi.org/10.13165/IE-23-17-2-03

McNulty, K. (2022). *Handbook of graphs and networks in people analytics: With examples in R and Python*. Taylor & Francis Ltd.

Monford, M., Cuestas, J., & Ordonez, J. (2013). Real convergence in Europe: A cluster analysis. *Economic Modelling, 33*, 689–694. https://doi.org/10.1016/j.econmod.2013.05.015

Nijkamp, P., & Abreu, M. (2009). Regional development theory. *International Encyclopedia of Human Geography*, (pp. 202–207).

O'Malley, J., & Marsden, P. (2008). The analysis of social networks. *Health Serv Outcomes Res Methodol, 8*(4). https://doi.org/10.1007/s10742-008-0041-z

Petrakos, G., Rodriguez-Pose, A., & Rovolis, A. (2005). Growth, inmtegration, and regional disparities in the European Union. *Environment and Planning A*, 1837–1855. https://doi.org/10.1068/a37348

Polyzos, S. (2019). *Regional development* (2nd ed.). Kritiki Publications.

Psycharis, Y., Kallioras, D., & Pantazis, P. (2020). Regional inequalities in Central and Eastern European countries: The role of Capital regions and Metropolitan Areas. In Contributions to Economics. In A. Śliwiński, P. Polychronidou, & A. Karasavvoglou (Eds.), *Economic development and financial markets*. Springer. https://doi.org/10.1007/978-3-030-32426-1

Rusinowska, A., Berghammer, R., de Swart, H., & Grabish, M. (2011). Social networks: Prestige, centrality, and influence. In *Conference: Proceedings of the 12th International Conference on Relational and Algebraic Methods in Computer Science*. https://doi.org/10.1007/978-3-642-21070-9_2

Smith, M., Ceni, A., Milic-Frayling, N., ShneidermaN, B., Mendes Rodrigues, E., Leskovec, J., & Dunne, C. (2010). *NodeXL: A free and open network overview, discovery and exploration add-in for Excel 2007/2010/2013/2016 from the Social Media Research Foundation*. https://www.smrfoundation.org

Spulbar, C., Tenea, A.-C., Stanciu, C., & Birau, R. (2020, Mar 02). Is there a common path for the integration of EuropeanUnion banking systems? *Economic Research-Ekonomska Istraživanja, 33*(1), 399–419. https://doi.org/10.1080/1331677X.2019.1700386

Wasserman, S., & Faust, K. (1994). *Social network Analysis: methods and applications*. Cambridge University Press. https://doi.org/10.1017/CBO9780511815478

Yang, Z., Algesheimer, R., & Tessone, C. (2019). A comparative analysis of community detection algorithms on artificial networks. *Scientific Reports, 6*. https://doi.org/10.1038/srep30750

Assessing Sustainable Competitiveness of Balkan Economies Using the Entropy-Based PROMETHEE Method

Aleksandra Fedajev

Abstract Over the last two decades, Balkan countries have faced a multitude of challenges, encompassing economic recovery, structural weaknesses, socio-economic disparities, and environmental sustainability. Intense global competitive pressures compel these economies to strive for a stronger competitive position, a struggle exacerbated after the pandemic crisis, which significantly weakened their development capabilities and resulted in social and environmental problems due to an exclusive focus on economic performance. While this strategy may yield short-term effects, it ultimately undermines long-term competitiveness by neglecting environmental and social dimensions of development. Consequently, the concept of sustainable competitiveness has gained prominence, necessitating a comprehensive understanding of a country's strengths and weaknesses across various dimensions beyond traditional economic indicators. Recognizing the importance of measuring sustainable competitiveness for policymakers globally, the Global Sustainable Competitiveness Index (GSCI) has been developed. The index evaluates the performance, trends, and growth prospects of countries by analyzing a variety of quantitative indicators categorized into five pillars of national development, including natural capital, resource efficiency, social capital, intellectual and innovation capital, and governance performance. However, considering variations in number of indicators, pillars (in 2022, new pillar is introduced), and analyzed countries over time, along with some methodological constraints mentioned in the current literature, such as uniform weights for all pillars and aggregation procedures, a comparative analysis of Balkan countries' sustainable competitiveness is conducted using the Entropy-based PROMETHEE method. The Entropy approach, an objective weighting is employed to calculate the relative importance of each pillar, assigning higher weights to criteria with greater differences across countries and lower weights to those with similar states among countries. PROMETHEE method, as one of the most commonly used Multi-Criteria Decision Making (MCDM) methods, is used for ranking countries, enabling a comparative analysis of observed countries (Albania, Bosnia and Herzegovina, Bulgaria, Croatia, Greece, Montenegro, North Macedonia, Romania, and

---

A. Fedajev (✉)
Technical Faculty in Bor, University of Belgrade, Bor, Serbia
e-mail: afedajev@tfbor.bg.ac.rs

I. Bartuseviciene et al. (eds.), *Building Economic Resilience*, Contributions to Economics, https://doi.org/10.1007/978-3-031-96428-2_4

Serbia). Given the paramount importance of ensuring sustainable competitiveness, particularly in the aftermath of the COVID-19 pandemic, the aim of this paper is to conduct a comparative analysis of Balkan economies in 2020 and 2023. The objective is to derive appropriate policy implications based on changes in rankings and graphical representations of the advantages and disadvantages of each country derived by the applied methodology. The results reveal significant shifts in rankings between 2020 and 2023, indicating that economic measures implemented for recovery from the pandemic crisis have significantly impacted sustainable competitiveness in these countries. While Croatia retained its first position in 2023 as it did in 2020, other countries experienced substantial changes in their positions, accompanied by alterations in their advantages and disadvantages compared to 2020. Analyzing these differences provides a deep and comprehensive insight into the sustainable competitiveness of these economies, forming the basis for developing policy implications.

Keywords Sustainable competitiveness · Balkan countries · Pandemic crisis · GSCI · Entropy method · PROMETEE method

Jel Classification Codes Q56

1 Introduction

The dynamic development of the global economy, and of the human civilization itself, accompanied by many challenges, including growing income inequalities, increasing disparities in productivity resulting from unequal access to education, health care, and innovation, increasing social exclusion, or even climate change and its negative consequences, have all contributed to the introduction of the concept of "sustainable competitiveness" into economic discourse (Falkowski, 2023). In the wake of the COVID-19 pandemic, the resilience and adaptability of economies worldwide have come under intense scrutiny (Karpook et al., 2020). Nowhere is this more evident than in the Balkan region (Mitreva & Koleva, 2021), where countries have grappled with a myriad of challenges, ranging from economic recovery to environmental sustainability. The pandemic crisis exacerbated pre-existing structural weaknesses and socio-economic disparities, prompting a reevaluation of traditional approaches to development. Therefore, it is imperative for these countries to prioritize the nurturing of factors conducive to economic growth. These factors encompass: robust institutions (such as secure property rights, a reliable legal system, transparent governance, a competitive market, and political stability), the establishment of new incentives for growth (improved business environments, enhanced investment in research and development—R&D), and the optimization of production factors, including human and physical capital, organizational efficiency, and technological advancement (Cowen & Tabarrok, 2021).

In this context, the concept of sustainable competitiveness has emerged as a critical framework for assessing a country's ability to thrive in an increasingly interconnected and resource-constrained world (Adamowicz, 2022). It doesn't entirely neglect the traditional viewpoint that equates competitiveness with a country's economic development level and its capacity to enhance living standards more rapidly than other countries through favorable changes in productivity (Porter, 1990), the sustainable competitiveness goes beyond narrow measures of economic performance to encompass a holistic understanding of a country's strengths and weaknesses across multiple dimensions (Balkytė & Tvaronavičienė, 2010; Cheba et al., 2020; Mamipour et al., 2019; Petkovski et al., 2022).

An essential concern regarding sustainable competitiveness revolves around its measurement. Much like competitiveness itself, there is no singular, universally accepted method for quantifying it (Bilbao-Terol et al., 2017; Doyle & Perez-Alaniz, 2017; Popescu et al., 2017). The Swiss-Korean think-tank SolAbility, renowned for its publication of the Global Sustainable Competitiveness Index (GSCI) since 2012, has proposed its own methodology for this purpose. GSCI has been developed as a tool for policymakers and analysts to assess countries' performance and prospects. SolAbility defines sustainable competitiveness as the capacity to generate and maintain inclusive wealth without depleting future prospects for sustaining or increasing current levels of wealth, within an environment of ever-increasing competition among countries (SolAbility, 2017).

SolAbility's approach to measuring sustainable competitiveness is rooted in the three-dimensional model of sustainability, where three primary dimensions—economic, social, and environmental—coexist and interact (SolAbility, 2017). Consequently, the level of sustainable competitiveness is gauged through five key groups of factors, or pillars: natural capital (comprising natural resources, their accessibility, and depletion levels), social capital (encompassing health, security, freedom and equality levels, and life satisfaction), resource efficiency (pertaining to the utilization of available resources), intellectual capital (reflecting the capacity to generate wealth and employment via innovation and value-added sectors in global markets), and governance performance (focused on establishing a framework for sustainable and equitable wealth distribution). Indicators within each category receive weighting and are combined to generate a composite score for each country, subsequently utilized to rank countries based on their sustainable competitiveness (Januškaitė & Užienė, 2018).

However, while the GSCI provides valuable insights, it is not without its limitations, including methodological constraints and variations in the number of indicators and pillars over time. A commonly cited issue is that the GSCI is composed of scores for five sub-indexes, corresponding to the five groups of factors (pillars) mentioned above, all of which are given the same weighting (Falkowski, 2023). This equal weighting might oversimplify the complex interactions between different pillars, potentially obscuring nuanced differences in a country's sustainable competitiveness. The changing number of pillars is another significant limitation, as it complicates comparative analysis over time. Specifically, in 2022, a new pillar related to economic sustainability was introduced. While this pillar is crucial as it reflects a country's ability to generate wealth through sustainable economic development, its inclusion disrupted the continuity of the GSCI results, making it difficult to compare with previous years' scores, which were calculated without this pillar. Moreover, the GSCI's reliance on available data can also be a limitation, as not all countries have the same level of data transparency or quality. This discrepancy can lead to biased results, particularly for countries with less robust data collection practices. Additionally, the GSCI might not fully capture the unique socio-economic contexts of different regions, leading to an oversimplified view of sustainable competitiveness that may not be entirely applicable to all countries. Another limitation lies in the GSCI's static nature, as it often fails to account for dynamic changes in a country's socio-economic environment, such as sudden political shifts or environmental crises, which can drastically alter a nation's competitiveness. The index's methodological rigidity can also be a limitation, as it may not adapt well to evolving concepts of sustainability, which are increasingly emphasizing aspects like technological innovation and social equity (Škuflić et al., 2024).

In light of these limitations, this paper aims to undertake a comparative analysis of the sustainable competitiveness of Balkan economies in 2020 and 2023, utilizing the Entropy-based PROMETHEE method to rank countries according to the pillars of the Global Sustainable Competitiveness Index. By employing this methodology, the study aims to offer methodological framework to take insight into the relative performance of Balkan countries, and identify areas requiring enhancement for providing tailored recommendations to policymakers and stakeholders for fostering economic growth, social cohesion, and environmental sustainability. It's crucial to determine relative position of each country compared to its neighbors, emphasizing strengths and areas requiring enhancement. With this knowledge, targeted initiatives can be implemented to improve favorable conditions and promote growth and development within these nations.

The structure of the paper is organized as follows. After the introduction in Sect. 1, the literature review is presented in Sect. 2. Section 3 is dedicated to elaboration of applied data and methodology. Section 4 presents the obtained results and provides appropriate discussion, while Sect. 5 concludes the paper.

2 Literature Review

The evolution of sustainable competitiveness discourse reflects a reevaluation of traditional economic metrics, with scholars emphasizing the integration of environmental and social dimensions into competitiveness studies. Porter and Linde (1995) initiated this shift, advocating for the inclusion of environmental considerations in competitive strategies, while Thore and Tarverdyan (2016) and Doyle and Perez-Alaniz (2017) underscored the importance of social aspects in competitiveness assessments.

Conventional economic indicators offer valuable insights but often overlook critical factors like environmental sustainability and social equity (Kolluru & Suresh, 2020; Melnyk et al., 2020). Sustainable competitiveness emerged as a strategic paradigm, emphasizing the harmonization of economic growth with environmental and social considerations (Vasiljević et al., 2018). The GSCI serves as a comprehensive tool for evaluating nations' environmental, social, and governance (ESG) performance (Ng et al., 2023). It assesses factors such as economic sustainability, environmental stewardship, social capital, and governance effectiveness (Kostakis et al., 2023; Mishchuk et al., 2022). The GSCI's utility in shaping policy decisions and fostering sustainable development has been recognized by researchers and policymakers (Aiginger & Vogel, 2015; Çifçi & Sönmez, 2023). By providing a nuanced understanding of national competitiveness beyond GDP, the GSCI enables informed decision-making and facilitates dialogue on sustainability issues.

Researchers have focused on examining the impact of individual pillars of sustainable competitiveness on economic performance (Qazi & Al-Mhdawi, 2024). Factors like intellectual capital, governance quality, and social cohesion are highlighted for their role in driving national growth and sustainability (Alvino et al., 2021; Omri & Mabrouk, 2020). Moreover, scholars have explored the nexus between global competitiveness pillars and sustainable development goals, identifying critical factors such as innovation capability and labor market dynamics (Qazi, 2024). Governance practices play a pivotal role in shaping the environment for sustainable competitiveness, with transparent, accountable, and law-abiding governance fostering stability and investment attractiveness (Omri & Mabrouk, 2020). Conversely, corruption and inefficiency can impede sustainable development efforts, eroding trust and diverting resources from critical initiatives (Biggs et al., 2013; Owusu et al., 2020). Scholars have extensively explored the impact of effective institutions and political stability on competitiveness, emphasizing the importance of good governance in nurturing a conducive business environment (Groşanu et al., 2015).

Social capital, encompassing trust, cooperation, and social cohesion, is another key determinant of sustainable competitiveness, facilitating collaboration on environmental and social welfare initiatives (Turok & Bailey, 2004). Conversely, low social capital characterized by social fragmentation and distrust can hinder collective action for sustainability (Ballet et al., 2020; Del-Aguila-Arcentales et al., 2022). Intellectual capital, comprising education and innovation, is crucial for driving sustainable growth through technology advancements and knowledge-based industries (Bąk et al., 2022; Yusliza et al., 2020). Insufficient investment in education and innovation may leave countries ill-prepared to address environmental and societal challenges, limiting their sustainable competitiveness (Ávila et al., 2017). Studies underscore the significance of fostering innovation and knowledge-based economies for long-term competitiveness (Alvino et al., 2021; Bąk et al., 2022).

Within the GSCI framework, natural capital and resource efficiency are central to sustainable development discussions, with effective resource management contributing to greater competitiveness (Song et al., 2019; Sun et al., 2023). Improvements in resource efficiency have been shown to positively impact economic performance, underlining the importance of sustainable resource management (Liu et al., 2018; Yang & Zhang, 2018). Similarly, research on social capital within the GSCI context highlights the correlation between social well-being, education, healthcare, and overall competitiveness (Despotovic et al., 2019). These findings emphasize the multidimensional nature of sustainable competitiveness, underscoring the interplay between governance, social cohesion, intellectual capital, and natural resource management in shaping a country's competitive position.

The literature demonstrates the expanding discourse on sustainable competitiveness and the evolving application of MCDM methods in this context (Gautam et al., 2020; Lahane & Kant, 2022; Tian et al., 2023; Verma et al., 2022), offering structured approaches for analyzing multifaceted problems involving diverse criteria and stakeholders. These methods enable researchers to objectively evaluate countries' performances, identify improvement areas, and formulate targeted policies for sustainable development (Lahane & Kant, 2022). Such frameworks facilitate decision-making by systematically comparing and prioritizing alternatives across various criteria. Authors used various subjective and objective methods for definition of criteria's weights. For instance, employing the PF-AHP and PF-CODAS methods, Tian et al. (2023) subjectively determined criteria weights and ranked countries based on sustainability competitiveness. On the other hand, Escandon-Barbosa et al. (2019) objective weight determination and ranking are achieved through methods like CRITIC and CTOPSIS, aiding in the identification of countries' strengths and weaknesses in economic sustainability, environmental preservation, social capital, and governance effectiveness. By quantifying and comparing these dimensions, researchers can discern countries excelling in specific areas and those necessitating enhancement.

Studies delve into the intricate relationship between sustainable development, competitiveness, and the integration of environmental and social considerations into decision-making frameworks (Gautam et al., 2020). Noteworthy examples include Širá et al.'s (2020) investigation into competitiveness, knowledge economy, and sustainability in European Union countries using the TOPSIS method. Similarly, Hu et al. (2018) developed the Air Cargo Terminal Quality System to enhance Taiwan's global competitiveness, employing the ANP and DEMATEL methods. Deng (2023) utilized CRITIC and TODIM methods, integrating fuzzy number intuitionistic fuzzy sets, to rank financial centers across countries. The study of Mate et al. (2022) aimed to investigate the interconnectedness between economic competitiveness and sustainability by integrating indicators from the Global Competitiveness Index (GCI) and the GSCI to refine country rankings across both dimensions. Through the application of Deep Ranking Analysis by Power Eigenvectors (DRAPE) with Variable Clustering (VARCLUS), it was found that economic competitiveness, particularly institutional environment and innovation capabilities, tend to align with a greater degree of sustainability. These studies underscore the significance of embracing multidimensional assessments and holistic approaches to foster sustainable development and competitiveness.

The Balkan region has witnessed significant changes since the political and economic transitions of the 1990s. While progress has been made in various areas, the challenge of achieving sustainable development remains paramount (Jakovljevic et al., 2021). Economic studies focusing on the Balkans have shed light on critical issues such as demography, brain drain, underemployment, and regional peripheralization (King & Oruc, 2018; Malaj & de Rubertis, 2017; Petreski et al., 2017). The phenomenon of brain drain, where skilled individuals emigrate in search of better economic prospects, has significantly impacted Balkan countries. The migrations not only leads to a loss of human capital but also exacerbates issues of underemployment and brain waste, where individuals are compelled to work in sectors that do not utilize their full skill set.

Addressing economic security is very important for Balkan economies, particularly those in the Western Balkans, to advance and compete more effectively (Zeneli, 2014). Challenges such as poverty, unemployment, and inequalities need to be effectively addressed through accelerated socio-economic reforms, modernization efforts, and institutional transformations. Additionally, deeper regional cooperation and integration with the EU market are essential to enable these economies to catch up with technological advancements and adopt market-oriented institutions that foster growth and development. Efforts to enhance sustainable competitiveness in the Balkans also require a focus on redirecting remittances towards investment rather than personal consumption, creating more business-friendly environments, combating corruption, and improving government effectiveness, particularly in upholding the rule of law (Jushi et al., 2021; Nedić et al., 2020; Ziberi & Alili, 2021). Furthermore, fostering the process of automation and digitalization is essential, as domestic enterprises often lag behind foreign firms in terms of competitiveness. The impact of EU membership on economic development in the Balkans was interesting research topic in previous literature, with studies suggesting that EU membership correlates with lower income inequality (Velkovska et al., 2021).

The most similar paper to this research is study of Štilić et al. (2023) where an assessment of sustainable competitiveness in Balkan countries using the GSCI and Entropy-based MARCOS method was conducted, highlighting the significance of criteria such as Natural Capital and Resource Efficiency & Intensity. However, despite the expanding literature on sustainable competitiveness, there remains a notable dearth of studies dedicated to the Balkan countries. This paper aims to fill this research gap by providing a comprehensive analysis of sustainable competitiveness in the Balkans.

3 Data and Methodology

The research is grounded in the ranking of Balkan countries based on sustainable competitiveness in both 2020 and 2023, aiming to compare the results and identify differences. The rankings are determined through the application of the Entropy-based PROMETHEE II method, using Visual PROMETHEE software (academic edition). This software offers valuable graphical representations, allowing for the identification of each country's strengths and weaknesses. The application of the PROMETHEE method is the most appropriate methodology for this research because it offers a balanced approach to evaluating multiple, often conflicting criteria, which is essential in assessing sustainable competitiveness across diverse countries. PROMETHEE allows for a detailed comparison of alternatives without the need for complex mathematical transformations, preserving the integrity of original data (Oubahman & Duleba, 2021). Additionally, PROMETHEE provides clear, understandable rankings and visualizations, enabling policymakers to easily identify strengths, weaknesses, and areas for improvement in different countries. Its robustness in handling sensitivity analysis further ensures that the results are reliable and can be confidently used to inform policy decisions.

3.1 Data

A data used in this research are from The Global Sustainable Competitiveness Index reports from 2020 and 2023 on basic pillars of sustainable competitiveness that are used for index calculation in both years: Natural Capital (NC), Resource Intensity (RI), Intellectual Capital (IC), Social Capital (SC) and Governance Performance (GP).

3.2 Methodology

Given that there are five criteria to consider for the comparative analysis of nine countries, it's evident that this study falls within the domain of multi-criteria analysis. In this regard, the PROMETHEE II method, recognized as one of the most commonly employed multi-criteria decision-making (MCDM) methods.

(Bari & Karande, 2021; El-Araby et al., 2022; Jati & Dominic, 2017; Niu et al., 2024), is utilized to rank the countries. This method is coupled with the Entropy method, which is employed to objectively define weights.

PROMETHEE II, proposed by Brans, is a Multi-Criteria Decision Making (MCDM) method based on outranking relations, utilized for ranking a finite set of alternatives (Barns et al., 1986). One of PROMETHEE's strengths lies in its ability to rank and select among conflicting criteria (Behzadian et al., 2010). Alidrisi (2021) introduced four variations of PROMETHEE: I, II, III, and IV. Given the problem's nature, PROMETHEE II emerges as the most suitable and applicable method in this scenario.

The foundation of PROMETHEE II lies in pairwise comparisons between each pair of criteria. This method considers differences in evaluations of each pair of alternatives on a specified criterion. When differences are substantial, decision-makers may assign greater preference to the superior alternative. The degree of preference correlates with the magnitude of deviation, calculated using a preference function (Kabir et al., 2013). PROMETHEE II offers flexibility in selecting the preference function, with six recommended types (Özkaya, 2022; Song & Peng, 2019).

Furthermore, the calculation of preference levels incorporates the use of indifference and preference thresholds (Nikouei et al., 2017; Ostovare & Shahraki, 2019). The indifference threshold denotes the maximum difference deemed insignificant, while the preference threshold indicates the minimal difference considered as preference. Additionally, the evaluation procedure involves weighting criteria to signify their importance.

To complete the method, the calculation of positive and negative preference flows is conducted. These flows are then used to derive the net preference flow, representing the overall preference of one alternative over another across all criteria. A higher net flow signifies a superior alternative.

In the PROMETHEE method, it's essential to have a method for evaluating the weights of the criteria. This study utilizes the Shannon Entropy method (Hsu, 2013), which is widely recognized as one of the most common objective-weighting methods, extensively employed by decision-makers to determine criteria weights. The concept of Entropy, originally introduced by Shannon (1948) in communication theory to handle uncertain information and missing data, found additional applications in describing irreversible motion in thermodynamics. Subsequently, it proved effective in addressing decision-making problems (Azadfallah, 2020).

The method relies on numerical data provided by decision-makers to assess the relative importance of each criterion (El-Araby et al., 2022). Essentially, Shannon's Entropy was adapted into the Entropy weight method, assigning higher weights to criteria with significant differences among alternatives, while criteria where the situation among alternatives is similar receive lower weights. The criterion assigned the highest weight carries greater importance compared to others (Xu et al., 2018).

3.3 Evaluation Matrix Definition

The first step in the analysis is definition of evaluation matrix for 2020 and 2023, where parameters of MCDM problem and input data are inserted. The evaluation matrix for 2020 is presented in Table 1.

The data from Table 1 indicate that all criteria should be maximized, and V-shape preference function with absolute preference thresholds set at standard deviation level. Weights calculated by Entropy method indicate the highest differences among analyzed countries are recorded in the level of IC, while the lowest differences are recorded for NC. The significant differences in IC among Balkan countries in 2020 can be attributed to varying levels of investment in R&D, disparities in development of education and skills, and differences in support for entrepreneurship. The relatively low differences among Balkan countries in 2020 concerning natural capital, which encompasses a country's given natural environment and resource availability, including depletion levels, are partly influenced by the overarching impact of the COVID-19 pandemic. The pandemic likely led to a slowdown in economic activities across the region, resulting in reduced exploitation of natural resources and environmental pressures. Additionally, shared environmental challenges arising from the pandemic, such as shifts in consumer behavior towards sustainability and heightened awareness of the importance of preserving natural ecosystems, have prompted

Table 1 Evaluation matrix for 2020 data

Parameters and alternatives	NC	RI	SC	IC	GP
Direction of preference	max	max	max	max	max
Weight	0.1522	0.2433	0.1559	0.2822	0.1664
Preference function	V-shape	V-shape	V-shape	V-shape	V-shape
Thresholds measure	absolute	absolute	absolute	absolute	absolute
Preference threshold	4.98	5.39	2.73	3.61	4.67
Croatia	61.09	57.70	52.28	50.91	63.92
Romania	56.90	57.48	53.72	42.69	61.69
Bulgaria	56.08	43.23	47.18	49.43	61.93
Serbia	52.46	44.43	53.46	48.03	55.25
Bosnia and Herzegovina	60.11	42.60	52.47	43.11	54.05
North Macedonia	51.55	49.29	51.95	43.05	56.24
Greece	44.74	46.03	50.01	49.88	59.15
Montenegro	49.18	45.46	51.56	41.98	52.15
Albania	51.43	49.72	45.25	41.66	49.14

in some extent coordinated efforts among Balkan countries to mitigate environmental degradation and conserve natural resources uniformly.

In the same way, the evaluation matrix for 2023 is defined and it is presented in Table 2.

Table 2 Evaluation matrix for 2023 data

Parameters and alternatives	NC	RI	SC	IC	GP
Direction of preference	max	max	max	max	max
Weight	0.1929	0.1876	0.1749	0.2504	0.1942
Preference function	V-shape	V-shape	V-shape	V-shape	V-shape
Thresholds	absolute	absolute	absolute	absolute	absolute
p	4.98	5.39	2.73	3.61	4.67
Croatia	55.59	44.24	55.81	46.37	64.69
Romania	53.62	45.17	51.86	35.02	61.42
Bulgaria	50.14	35.64	48.97	38.77	66.23
Serbia	54.62	25.49	52.65	41.01	57.88
Bosnia and Herzegovina	54.30	34.53	51.89	34.01	55.47
North Macedonia	41.72	30.82	60.81	33.50	59.04
Greece	38.84	43.93	51.08	45.47	62.74
Montenegro	46.10	44.24	53.02	36.08	58.02
Albania	57.59	40.02	57.31	39.56	53.92

To obtain comparability of the results between two observed years, the same preference function with preference thresholds amounting as much as standard deviation is used (Table 2). Weights of criteria indicate that differences in IC are again the highest, indicating that Balkan countries still didn't manage to reduce gap in this area. The uneven distribution of recovery efforts and resources among Balkan countries have resulted in disparities in investment in R&D and support for innovation ecosystems. Additionally, structural challenges within certain countries, such as inadequate education and skills development or limited access to funding for innovative projects, have hindered their ability to enhance IC effectively. Moreover, the lingering economic uncertainties and disruptions caused by the pandemic have exacerbated existing disparities in innovation capabilities among Balkan countries.

On the other hand, the deviations are lowest in terms of SC. The decrease in differences in SC among Balkan countries in 2023 can be attributed to various factors influenced by the diverse recovery measures enacted in response to the pandemic crisis. Firstly, the heightened awareness of the importance of social cohesion and well-being during the crisis have led to concerted efforts by governments and communities to address disparities in healthcare access, security provisions, and overall societal satisfaction across the region. Secondly, the implementation of targeted policies aimed at mitigating socio-economic inequalities exacerbated by the pandemic have contributed to a narrowing of disparities in health outcomes, freedom, and equality among Balkan countries in 2023. Additionally, the collaborative nature of regional and international initiatives focused on rebuilding social infrastructure and fostering resilience in the aftermath of the crisis may have facilitated greater convergence in SC indicators among Balkan countries by 2023.

The definition of these evaluation matrixes enabled ranking of alternatives for both considered years.

4 Results and Discussion

The ranking of countries for 2020 enables a comparative analysis of the sustainable competitiveness of Balkan countries during the pandemic crisis, while the ranking in 2023 provides insight into the most accurate state of sustainable competitiveness in these countries. By comparing the ranking results, it can be identified which countries were most resilient to the pandemic crisis, which managed to recover swiftly from it, and which suffered the most afterward. The ranking results for both years (with net preference flow is presented in Table 3).

The first insight in Table 3 shows that only Croatia retained its position from 2020. The countries that worsened their position are Romania, Bulgaria, Serbia, North Macedonia, and Bosnia and Herzegovina. On the other hand, Greece, Montenegro, and Albania improved their position compared to 2020 rankings.

The Visual PROMETHEE software facilitates sensitivity analysis by allowing for changes in the weights of criteria. It provides stability intervals for these weights,

Table 3 Comparison of 2020 and 2023 rankings

Rank	Country	Phi	Rank	Country	Phi
1	Croatia	0.033	1	Croatia	0.031
2	Romania	0.014	2	Albania	0.008
3	Bulgaria	0.002	3	Greece	0.007
4	Serbia	0.002	4	Romania	0.003
5	Greece	0.000	5	Bulgaria	−0.001
6	North Macedonia	−0.004	6	Montenegro	−0.004
7	Bosnia and Herzegovina	−0.008	7	Serbia	−0.011
8	Montenegro	−0.017	8	Bosnia and Herzegovina	−0.015
9	Albania	−0.023	9	North Macedonia	−0.018

indicating that the results remain consistent if the weights fall within these intervals. Table 4 presents the stability intervals for 2020 and 2023.

As shown in Table 4, the smallest range in 2020 is recorded for the Social Capital (SC) criterion, meaning the results are most sensitive to changes in the weight of this criterion. In contrast, the Intellectual Capital (IC) criterion has the largest range, indicating that the ranking results are least sensitive to changes in its weight. A similar analysis for 2023 shows that, once again, the Social Capital (SC) criterion has the smallest range, while the Government Performance (GP) criterion has the largest. Overall, it can be concluded that the results for 2023 are more sensitive to weight changes than those for 2020.

In order to explain obtained results in more detail Visual PROMETHEE software enables usage of different graphical representations and one of the most useful is so-called "rainbow diagram". This diagram gives representation of advantages and disadvantages of each alternative (in this case country). Such diagram for 2020 is presented in Fig. 1.

Figure 1 indicates that Croatia as first-ranked country has advantage in all considered pillars of sustainable competitiveness. Romania has one disadvantage, Bulgaria has two disadvantages, Serbia, Greece, North Macedonia, and Bosnia and Herzegovina have three advantages, while Montenegro and Albania have four disadvantages. It's noteworthy that all Western Balkan nations, with the exception of Serbia,

Table 4 Comparison of stability intervals for 2020 and 2023 rankings

Criteria	Stability interval (2020)	Range	Criteria	Stability interval (2023)	Range
NC	0.1436 – 0.2199	0.0763	NC	0.1891 – 0.2441	0.0550
RI	0.1609 – 0.2624	0.1015	RI	0.1349 – 0.2040	0.0691
SC	0.0886 – 0.1584	0.0698	SC	0.1669 – 0.2109	0.0440
IC	0.2699 – 0.3838	0.1139	IC	0.2003 – 0.2575	0.0572
GP	0.1617 – 0.2556	0.0939	GP	0.1249 – 0.2008	0.0759

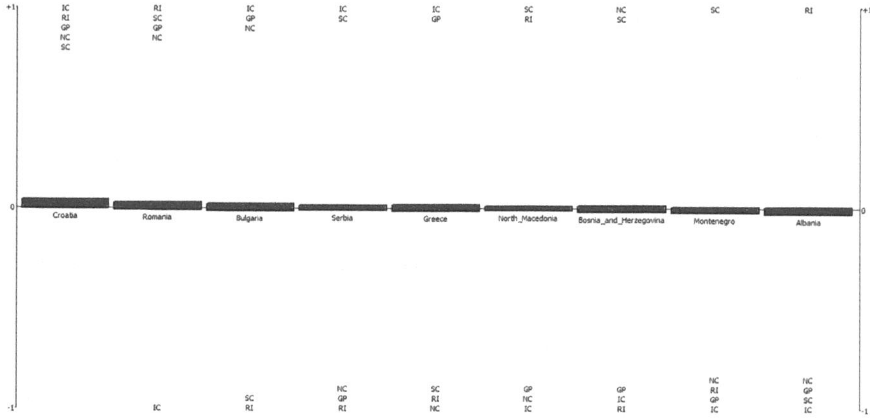

Fig. 1 Rainbow diagram for 2020

were positioned at the lower end of the rankings. Furthermore, these countries exhibited a negative net preference flow, indicating that their disadvantages outweighed their advantages. Weak government performance in these countries, characterized by corruption, bureaucratic inefficiencies, and a lack of transparency and accountability, have hindered effective policy implementation and economic governance. Social capital deficits, including inadequate healthcare systems, limited access to education and social services, and social unrest, have exacerbated the socio-economic impacts of the pandemic and reduced overall resilience. Additionally, resource intensity constraints, such as inefficient resource use and overreliance on non-renewable resources, have impeded economic diversification and sustainable development. Moreover, innovation capital limitations, marked by insufficient investment in R&D and a lack of support for innovation and entrepreneurship, have hindered adaptation and growth in knowledge-based industries.

To explain differences in ranking results disadvantages and advantages of each country in 2023 is presented in rainbow diagram in Fig. 2.

As it is obvious from Fig. 2, Croatia again has advantages in all pillars of sustainable competitiveness. During the period from 2020 to 2023, Croatia introduced several measures aimed at enhancing all pillars of sustainable competitiveness. Firstly, the government implemented policies to promote sustainable tourism and environmental conservation, including initiatives to protect natural habitats, reduce pollution, and promote eco-friendly practices in the tourism sector. These measures contributed to the preservation of Croatia's natural capital and bolstered its attractiveness as a sustainable tourism destination. Secondly, Croatia invested significantly in R&D, particularly in sectors such as renewable energy, green technology, and digital innovation. These investments not only strengthened Croatia's intellectual capital but also positioned the country as a hub for innovation and knowledge-based industries. Thirdly, Croatia implemented social welfare programs aimed at improving access to healthcare, education, and social services, thereby enhancing social capital and

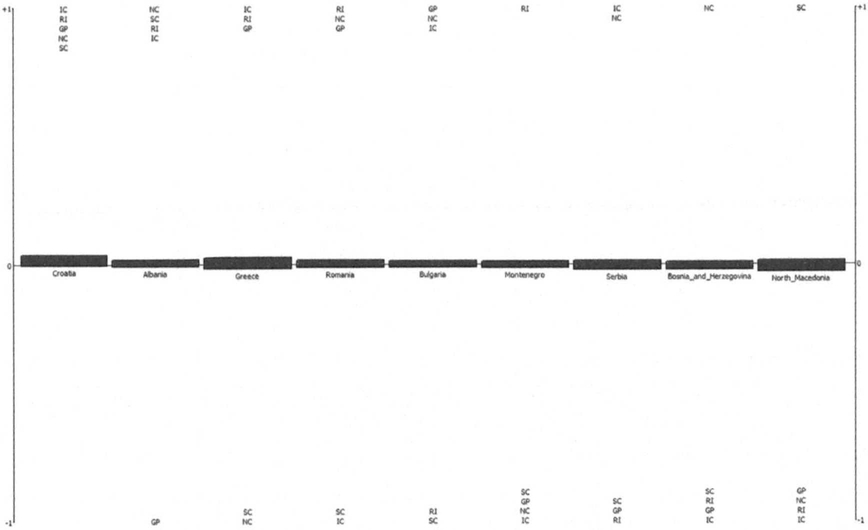

Fig. 2 Rainbow diagram for 2023

fostering greater social cohesion and inclusion. Lastly, Croatia undertook reforms to improve governance efficiency, transparency, and accountability, including measures to streamline bureaucracy, combat corruption, and strengthen institutions. These governance reforms enhanced Croatia's overall business environment and governance performance, contributing to its sustainable competitiveness. Albania, as second-ranked country, has one disadvantage. Greece, Romania, and Bulgaria have two disadvantages. Montenegro, North Macedonia, and Bosnia and Herzegovina have four disadvantages, while Serbia, although it is worse ranked than Montenegro, has three disadvantages.

It is interesting to note that Albania switched its position from the last in 2020 to second in 2023. This result is achieved by introducing several measures aimed at enhancing its sustainable competitiveness across various pillars during the period from 2020 to 2023. Firstly, the government implemented policies to promote environmental conservation and sustainable resource management, including initiatives to protect forests, reduce air and water pollution, and promote renewable energy sources. These measures contributed to the improvement of Albania's natural capital and enhanced its attractiveness for eco-friendly tourism and investment. Secondly, Albania invested in social welfare programs to improve access to healthcare, education, and social services, thereby strengthening social capital and fostering greater social cohesion and inclusivity. Additionally, the government implemented reforms to promote entrepreneurship and innovation, including initiatives to support startups, provide access to funding and mentorship, and foster collaboration between the public and private sectors. Lastly, Albania continued to prioritize resource efficiency and sustainability, implementing measures to promote energy efficiency, reduce waste, and enhance resource productivity.

Albania is replaced at the last position by North Macedonia, which significantly worsened its position compared to other Balkan countries. Governance issues, including corruption and bureaucratic inefficiencies, hindered policy implementation and reform efforts aimed at enhancing sustainable competitiveness. Insufficient investment in research and development, coupled with a lack of support for startups and innovation, hampered the country's ability to foster knowledge-based industries and compete globally. Challenges in natural resource management, such as environmental degradation and inadequate conservation measures, further impacted North Macedonia's attractiveness for investment. Additionally, the shift from resource intensity as an advantage to a disadvantage suggests issues with resource management and efficiency, including wasteful resource use and overreliance on non-renewable resources.

Serbia joined group of last four ranked countries from Western Balkan in 2023. It retained three disadvantages as it has in 2020, but besides GP and RI, SC become considerable disadvantage of this economy. However, this worsening of position is rather result of lagging back and inefficiency in implementing recovery measures in comparing to other Balkan countries.

5 Conclusion

This research has been dedicated to thoroughly assessing sustainable competitiveness among Balkan countries, utilizing data from both the GSCI 2020 and 2023 to compare outcomes amid the pandemic crisis and the most accurate data. Employing a strategic approach, a combination of the Entropy and PROMETHEE methods was adopted within the Multi-Criteria Decision Making (MCDM) framework. Notably, the Entropy method played a pivotal role in objectively assigning weights to criteria. Subsequently, the PROMETHEE method facilitated the ranking of Balkan countries based on these weighted criteria.

The findings from the Entropy method revealed that disparities in innovation capital persisted in 2023, mirroring the challenges observed in 2020 concerning investment in research and development and the support for innovation ecosystems. Conversely, the notable transition from lower disparities in natural capital in 2020 to social capital in 2023 underscores the profound impact of post-pandemic recovery efforts. This shift reflects a strategic pivot towards addressing socio-economic gaps and nurturing societal cohesion post-crisis. According to the results of the PROMETHEE method, Croatia maintained its leading position across both years, while significant fluctuations were observed in the rankings of other countries, highlighting the dynamic nature of sustainable competitiveness. With the majority of Western Balkan nations remaining at the bottom of the rankings, except for Serbia in 2020 and Albania in 2023, it underscores the enduring challenges these economies face in achieving a satisfactory level of sustainable competitiveness.

This paper highlights the crucial necessity of assessing and bolstering sustainable competitiveness within Balkan countries, particularly following the onset of the

COVID-19 pandemic. Through the utilization of the Entropy-based PROMETHEE method, this study offers a methodological contribution by furnishing policymakers with a comprehensive framework to assess and prioritize policy measures across diverse developmental dimensions. Nonetheless, it is essential to acknowledge certain limitations within this research. Firstly, the focus has been solely on Balkan nations, disregarding comparative analyses with countries ranking higher. Future research imperatives entail incorporating nations surpassing the Balkan region, enabling comparative assessments and identifying avenues to enhance sustainable competitiveness. Moreover, a limitation arises from the selection of the multi-criteria analysis method. Subsequent research should incorporate sensitivity analyses or validate results using alternative MCDM methods to validate the accuracy of these findings, as outlined within the scope of this study.

Acknowledgements This work was supported by the Ministry of Science, Technological Development and Innovation of the Republic of Serbia, as part of the financing of scientific research work at the University of Belgrade, Technical Faculty in Bor, according to the contract with registration number 451-03-65/2024-03/200131

References

Adamowicz, M. (2022). Green deal, green growth and green economy as a means of support for attaining the sustainable development goals. *Sustainability, 14*(10), 5901.

Aiginger, K., & Vogel, J. (2015). Competitiveness: From a misleading concept to a strategy supporting beyond GDP goals. *Competitiveness Review, 25*(5), 497–523.

Alidrisi, H. (2021). DEA-Based PROMETHEE II distribution-center productivity model: Evaluation and location strategies formulation. *Applied Sciences, 11*(20), 9567.

Alvino, F., Di Vaio, A., Hassan, R., & Palladino, R. (2021). Intellectual capital and sustainable development: A systematic literature review. *Journal of Intellectual Capital, 22*(1), 76–94.

Ávila, L. V., Leal Filho, W., Brandli, L., Macgregor, C. J., Molthan-Hill, P., Özuyar, P. G., & Moreira, R. M. (2017). Barriers to innovation and sustainability at universities around the world. *Journal of Cleaner Production, 164*, 1268–1278.

Azadfallah, M. (2020). Improving the entropy weighting method performance by using alternative normalisation procedures. *International Journal of Society Systems Science, 12*(3), 231.

Bąk, I., Wawrzyniak, K., & Oesterreich, M. (2022). Competitiveness of the regions of the European Union in a sustainable knowledge-based economy. *Sustainability, 14*(7), 3788.

Balkytė, A., & Tvaronavičienė, M. (2010). Perception of competitiveness in the context of sustainable development: Facets of "sustainable competitiveness." *Journal of Business Economics and Management, 11*(2), 341–365.

Ballet, J., Bazin, D., & Mahieu, F. R. (2020). A policy framework for social sustainability: Social cohesion, equity and safety. *Sustainable Development, 28*(5), 1388–1394.

Bari, P., & Karande, P. (2021). Application of PROMETHEE-GAIA method to priority sequencing rules in a dynamic job shop for single machine. *Materials Today: Proceedings, 46*, 7258–7264.

Behzadian, M., Kazemzadeh, R. B., Albadvi, A., & Aghdasi, M. (2010). PROMETHEE: A comprehensive literature review on methodologies and applications. *European Journal of Operational Research, 200*(1), 198–215.

Biggs, E. M., Duncan, J. M., Atkinson, P. M., & Dash, J. (2013). Plenty of water, not enough strategy: How inadequate accessibility, poor governance and a volatile government can tip the balance against ensuring water security—The case of Nepal. *Environmental Science & Policy, 33*, 388–394.

Bilbao-Terol, A., Arenas-Parra, M., & Onopko-Onopko, V. (2017). Measuring regional sustainable competitiveness: A multi-criteria approach. *Operational Research, 19*(3), 637–660.

Brans, J. P., Vincke, P. H., & Mareschal, B. (1986). How to select and how to rank projects: The PROMETHEE method. *European Journal of Operational Research, 24*(2), 228–238.

Cheba, K., Bąk, I., & Szopik-Depczyńska, K. (2020). Sustainable competitiveness as a new economic category–definition and measurement assessment. *Technological and Economic Development of Economy, 26*(6), 1399–1421.

Çifçi, G., & Sönmez, A. R. (2023). Is sustainability important for returns? *Environment, Development and Sustainability, 25*(12), 15119–15137.

Cowen, T., & Tabarrok, A. (2021). *Modern principles: Macroeconomics.* Worth.

Del-Aguila-Arcentales, S., Alvarez-Risco, A., Jaramillo-Arévalo, M., De-la-Cruz-Diaz, M., & de las Mercedes Anderson-Seminario, M. (2022). Influence of social, environmental and economic Sustainable Development Goals (SDGs) over continuation of entrepreneurship and competitiveness. *Journal of Open Innovation: Technology, Market, and Complexity, 8*(2), 73.

Deng, Y. (2023). Sustainable competitiveness evaluation of regional financial centers with fuzzy number intuitionistic fuzzy TODIM algorithms. *Journal of Intelligent & Fuzzy Systems, 44*(5), 7045–7057.

Despotovic, D., Cvetanovic, S., Nedic, V., & Despotovic, M. (2019). Social aspects of sustainable competitiveness in the selected European countries in the period 2012–2015. *Social Indicators Research, 141*, 841–860.

Doyle, E., & Perez-Alaniz, M. (2017). From the concept to the measurement of sustainable competitiveness: Social and environmental aspects. *Entrepreneurial Business and Economics Review, 5*(4), 35–59.

El-Araby, A., Sabry, I., & El-Assal, A. (2022). A comparative study of using MCDM methods integrated with entropy weight method for evaluating facility location problem. *Operational Research in Engineering Sciences: Theory and Applications, 5*(1), 121–138.

Escandon-Barbosa, D., Urbano-Pulido, D., & Hurtado-Ayala, A. (2019). Exploring the relationship between formal and informal institutions, social capital, and entrepreneurial activity in developing and developed countries. *Sustainability, 11*(2), 550.

Falkowski, K. (2023). Sustainable competitiveness of the visegrad group countries. *Optimum. Economic Studies, 1*(111), 3–19.

Gautam, P., Kamna, K. M., & Jaggi, C. K. (2020). Sustainable production policies under the effect of volume agility, preservation technology and price-reliant demand. *Yugoslav Journal of Operations Research, 30*(3), 307–324.

Groşanu, A., Boţa-Avram, C., Răchişan, P. R., Vesselinov, R., & Tiron-Tudor, A. (2015). The influence of country-level governance on business environment and entrepreneurship: A global perspective. *Amfiteatru Economic Journal, 17*(38), 60–75.

Hsu, L. C. (2013). Investment decision making using a combined factor analysis and entropy-based TOPSIS model. *Journal of Business Economics and Management, 14*(3), 448–466.

Hu, Y. C., Lee, P. C., Chuang, Y. S., & Chiu, Y. J. (2018). Improving the sustainable competitiveness of service quality within air Cargo terminals. *Sustainability, 10*(7), 2319.

Jakovljevic, M., Cerda, A. A., Liu, Y., García, L., Timofeyev, Y., Krstic, K., & Fontanesi, J. (2021). Sustainability challenge of Eastern Europe—Historical legacy, belt and road initiative, population aging and migration. *Sustainability, 13*(19), 11038.

Januškaitė, V., & Užienė, L. (2018). Intellectual capital as a factor of sustainable regional competitiveness. *Sustainability, 10*(12), 4848.

Jati, H., & Dominic, D. D. (2017). A new approach of Indonesian university webometrics ranking using entropy and PROMETHEE II. *Procedia Computer Science, 124*, 444–451.

Jushi, E., Hysa, E., Cela, A., Panait, M., & Voica, M. C. (2021). Financing growth through remittances and foreign direct investment: Evidences from Balkan countries. *Journal of Risk and Financial Management, 14*(3), 117.

Kabir, G., Sadiq, R., & Tesfamariam, S. (2013). A review of multi-criteria decision-making methods for infrastructure management. *Structure and Infrastructure Engineering, Informa UK Limited, 10*(9), 1176–1210.
Karpook, D., Stillebroer, D., & Jaspers, E. (2020). New demands for resilience in real estate: Resilience and adaptability after the COVID-19 pandemic. *Corporate Real Estate Journal, 10*(1), 106–116.
King, R., & Oruc, N. (2018). Editorial introduction: Migration in the Western Balkans—Trends and challenges. *Journal of Balkan and near Eastern Studies, 21*(1), 1–10.
Kolluru, M., & Suresh, V. (2020). A cluster analysis on sustained global competitiveness for European countries. *Economics, 8*(1), 7–22.
Kostakis, I., Paparas, D., & Tsagarakis, K. P. (2023). Disaggregated energy use and socioeconomic sustainability within OECD countries. *Journal of Environmental Management, 334*, Article 117475.
Lahane, S., & Kant, R. (2022). Investigating the sustainable development goals derived due to adoption of circular economy practices. *Waste Management, 143*, 1–14.
Liu, C., Cai, W., Jia, S., Zhang, M., Guo, H., Hu, L., & Jiang, Z. (2018). Emergy-based evaluation and improvement for sustainable manufacturing systems considering resource efficiency and environment performance. *Energy Conversion and Management, 177*, 176–189.
Malaj, V., & de Rubertis, S. (2017). Determinants of migration and the gravity model of migration–application on Western Balkan emigration flows. *Migration Letters, 14*(2), 204–220.
Mamipour, S., Yahoo, M., & Jalalvandi, S. (2019). An empirical analysis of the relationship between the environment, economy, and society: Results of a PCA-VAR model for Iran. *Ecological Indicators, 102*, 760–769.
Mate, D., Novotny, A., & Kovacs, S. (2022). Deep Ranking Analysis by Power Eigenvectors (DRAPE): Linking sustainability and national competitiveness. *Journal of Competitiveness, 14*(1), 80–99.
Melnyk, L. H., Sommer, H., Kubatko, O. V., Rabe, M., & Fedyna, S. M. (2020). The economic and social drivers of renewable energy development in OECD countries. *Problems and Perspectives in Management, 18*(4), 37–48.
Mishchuk, H., Štofková, J., Krol, V., Joshi, O., & Vasa, L. (2022). Social capital factors fostering the sustainable competitiveness of enterprises. *Sustainability, 14*(19), 11905.
Mitreva, M., & Koleva, B. (2021). The upcoming recession due to Covid 19 and its impact on economic growth and the digital transformation in the Balkan region. *Journal of Economics, Special Issue, 6*, 135–144.
Nedić, V., Despotović, D., Cvetanović, S., Djukić, T., & Petrović, D. (2020). Institutional reforms for economic growth in the Western Balkan countries. *Journal of Policy Modeling, 42*(5), 933–952.
Ng, T. H., Lim, Y. S., Lim, Y. Z., Chan, K.-H., & Lye, C. T. (2023). Is economic policy uncertainty detrimental to sustainability? Evidence from Asian countries. *Environment, Development and Sustainability, 26*(8), 1–24.
Nikouei, M. A., Oroujzadeh, M., & Mehdipour-Ataei, S. (2017). The PROMETHEE multiple criteria decision making analysis for selecting the best membrane prepared from sulfonated poly(ether ketone)s and poly(ether sulfone)s for proton exchange membrane fuel cell. *Energy, 119*, 77–85.
Niu, X., Song, Y., & Zhu, H. (2024). Data-Driven decision aids for purchasing battery electric vehicles based on PROMETHEE-II methodology. *IEEE Access, 12*, 27931–27946.
Omri, A., & Mabrouk, N. B. (2020). Good governance for sustainable development goals: Getting ahead of the pack or falling behind? *Environmental Impact Assessment Review, 83*, Article 106388.
Ostovare, M., & Shahraki, M. R. (2019). Evaluation of hotel websites using the multicriteria analysis of PROMETHEE and GAIA: Evidence from the five-star hotels of Mashhad. *Tourism Management Perspectives, 30*, 107–116.
Owusu, E. K., Chan, A. P., & Hosseini, M. R. (2020). Impacts of anti-corruption barriers on the efficacy of anti-corruption measures in infrastructure projects: Implications for sustainable development. *Journal of Cleaner Production, 246*, Article 119078.

Özkaya, G. (2022). Energy consumption trends before and during the Covid-19 pandemic: An entropy-based PROMETHEE analysis. *Current Research in Social Sciences, 8*(1), 1–28.

Petkovski, I., Fedajev, A., & Bazen, J. (2022). Modelling complex relationships between sustainable competitiveness and digitalization. *Journal of Competitiveness, 14*(2), 79–96.

Petreski, M., Petreski, B., Tumanoska, D., Narazani, E., Kazazi, F., Ognjanov, G., Jankovic, I., Mustafa, A. & Kochovska, T. (2017). The size and effects of emigration and remittances in the Western Balkans. A forecasting based on a Delphi process. *Comparative Southeast European Studies, Walter de Gruyter GmbH, 65*(4), 679–695.

Popescu, G., Sima, V., Nica, E., & Gheorghe, I. (2017). Measuring sustainable competitiveness in contemporary economies—Insights from European economy. *Sustainability, 9*(7), 1230.

Porter, M. E., & van der Linde, C. (1995). Toward a new conception of the environment-competitiveness relationship. *Journal of Economic Perspectives, 9*(4), 97–118.

Porter, M. E. (1990). The competitive advantage of nations Harvard business review. *Harvard Business Review, 91*, 1880–1886.

Qazi, A. & Al-Mhdawi, M. K. S. (2024). Exploring the relative importance of sustainable competitiveness pillars. *Journal of Cleaner Production, 443*, 140986.

Qazi, A. (2024). Exploring the impact of global competitiveness pillars on sustainable development. *Environmental Impact Assessment Review, 105*, Article 107404.

Oubahman, L., & Duleba, S. (2021). Review of PROMETHEE method in transportation. *Production Engineering Archives, 27*(1), 69–74.

Shannon, C. E. (1948). A mathematical theory of communication. *The Bell System Technical Journal, 27*(3), 379–423.

Širá, E., Vavrek, R., Kravčáková, I., & Kotulič, R. (2020). Knowledge economy indicators and their impact on the sustainable competitiveness of the EU countries. *Sustainability, 12*(10), 4172.

SolAbility. 2017. The global sustainable competitiveness index 2017 is out! https://solability.com/global-sustainable-competitiveness-index/the-global-sustainable-competitiveness-index-2017-is-out

Song, M., Fisher, R., & Kwoh, Y. (2019). Technological challenges of green innovation and sustainable resource management with large scale data. *Technological Forecasting and Social Change, 144*, 361–368.

Song, Y., & Peng, Y. (2019). A MCDM-Based evaluation approach for imbalanced classification methods in financial risk prediction. *IEEE Access, 7*, 84897–84906.

Škuflić, L., Šokčević, S., & Bašić, M. (2024). Sustainable development and competitiveness: Is there a need for GCI reconstruction? *Economics, 12*(1), 153–173.

Štilić, A., Puška, A., Božanić, D. and Tešić, D. (2023). Assessing the role of institutional reform in enhancing Balkan sustainable competitiveness: An entropy-MARCOS perspective. *Journal of Infrastructure, Policy and Development, 7*(3). https://doi.org/10.24294/jipd.v7i3.2167

Sun, Y., Gao, P., Tian, W., & Guan, W. (2023). Green innovation for resource efficiency and sustainability: Empirical analysis and policy. *Resources Policy, 81*, Article 103369.

Thore, S., & Tarverdyan, R. (2016). The sustainable competitiveness of nations. *Technological Forecasting and Social Change, 106*, 108–114.

Tian, G., Lu, W., Zhang, X., Zhan, M., Dulebenets, M. A., Aleksandrov, A., Fathollahi-Fard, A. M., et al. (2023). A survey of multi-criteria decision-making techniques for green logistics and low-carbon transportation systems. *Environmental Science and Pollution Research, 30*(20), 57279–57301.

Turok, I., & Bailey, N. (2004). Twin track cities? Competitiveness and cohesion in Glasgow and Edinburgh. *Progress in Planning, 62*(3), 135–204.

Vasiljević, M., Fazlollahtabar, H., Stević, Ž., & Vesković, S. (2018). A rough multicriteria approach for evaluation of the supplier criteria in automotive industry. *Decision Making: Applications in Management and Engineering, 1*(1), 82–96.

Velkovska, I., Trenovski, B., & Kozheski, K. (2021). Is there a link between income inequality and economic growth in the Balkans? Testing the Kuznets hypothesis. *Review of Social Policy, 28*(2), 227–238.

Verma, V., Bisht, P., & Joshi, S. (2022). Sustainable supply chain systems of food and beverages SMEs: Analyzing sustainable performance using structured equation modeling. *Journal of Decision Analytics and Intelligent Computing, 2*(1), 53–68.
Xu, H., Ma, C., Lian, J., Xu, K., & Chaima, E. (2018). Urban flooding risk assessment based on an integrated k-means cluster algorithm and improved entropy weight method in the region of Haikou, China. *Journal of Hydrology, 563*, 975–986.
Yang, L., & Zhang, X. (2018). Assessing regional eco-efficiency from the perspective of resource, environmental and economic performance in China: A bootstrapping approach in global data envelopment analysis. *Journal of Cleaner Production, 173*, 100–111.
Yusliza, M. Y., Yong, J. Y., Tanveer, M. I., Ramayah, T., Faezah, J. N., & Muhammad, Z. (2020). A structural model of the impact of green intellectual capital on sustainable performance. *Journal of Cleaner Production, 249*, Article 119334.
Zeneli, V. (2014). Economic development in the Western Balkans: On the road to competitive market economies? *Connections, 13*(4), 53–64.
Ziberi, B., & Alili, M. Z. (2021). Economic growth in the Western Balkans: A panel analysis. *South East European Journal of Economics and Business, 16*(2), 68–81.

Organizational and Industrial Resilience

Building Resilience in the Service Industry: A Study on Nonconformities Typology in Logistics

Olga Snarskė and Birutė Mockevičienė

Abstract In the context of a rapidly evolving business landscape characterized by technological advancements and shifting market dynamics, organizations must prioritize the establishment of comprehensive quality management frameworks and the enhancement of adaptive operational strategies to ensure sustained competitiveness and effective responses to environmental changes. While companies usually assess quality by tracking overall defects, a more thorough examination of nonconformities can help identify specific areas that require management attention. This study reviews and tests potential categories of nonconformities within a logistics service-providing company. This will help organizations proactively identify, rectify, and prevent issues, thereby fortifying their resilience. Research on a logistics company's non-conformance system revealed that the company's resilience is closely linked to its ability to identify patterns of nonconformities, understand their causes, and address them promptly. However, the system's impact on resilience is not immediate and can take up to 2 years as the quality system is analyzed and improved before a reduction in nonconformities becomes noticeable.

Keywords Nonconformities · Defects · Quality · Resilience

Jel Classification Codes L15 · M1 · O3 · O12

1 Introduction

The unique political, economic, technological, environmental, and other challenges of last five years (Narcevičius, 2022) have prompted companies to test and enhance existing methodologies for documenting nonconformities to achieve the highest

O. Snarskė (✉) · B. Mockevičienė
Mykolas Romeris University, Vilnius, Lithuania
e-mail: olgasnarske@gmail.com

B. Mockevičienė
e-mail: birute.mockeviciene@mruni.eu

I. Bartuseviciene et al. (eds.), *Building Economic Resilience*, Contributions to Economics, https://doi.org/10.1007/978-3-031-96428-2_5

possible level of service quality and resilience. The primary existing methodologies involve ISO 9001:2015 international standard, which establishes quality management systems (QMS), based on process model and PDCA (plan-do-check-act) cycle (Fonseca et al., 2021); LEAN methodology, which has been successful in many enterprises (Anuar et al., 2023), aiding in boosting productivity and efficiency; Malcolm Baldrige model, widely used in many organizations in the United States and abroad, covers all key dimensions of total quality management (Mohamed & Yusoff, 2021).

In today's service-oriented economy, where customer satisfaction and operational efficiency are critical, businesses striving to maintain a competitive edge and must understand and manage nonconformities with precision and at the earliest stage possible. By categorizing nonconformities according to established typology and improving operational categories afterward, organizations can effectively address emerging challenges, allocate resources more strategically, and directly impact social progress by fostering a culture of accountability, transparency, and excellence (Ahmady, 2021). Categorizing by type of activity, the most suitable typology is used to best align with specifics of activity. In logistics this might encompass various aspects, such as supply chain management, warehousing, transportation, and service delivery (Vitkus, 2020). Furthermore, continuously refining category's content by upholding fundamental principles of essential typology, it becomes easier to recognize recurring and obscure business patterns and implement preventive measures to mitigate risk of future nonconformities. Ultimately, by improving how nonconformities are managed and resolved in the service industry, a ripple effect of social progress can be achieved through stronger relationships, sustainable practices, and societal benefits (Liu et al., 2023).

Logistics industry is predominantly guided by a typology of nonconformities based on quality management theory. However, practical application of typology and creation of categories can result in uncertainties when determining category content. To manage and optimize classification system for nonconformities, organizations strive to reduce redundancy (Van der Wiele et al., 1997) and enhance efficiency. This natural progression (Rohloff, 2009) and dynamic evolution of operational maturity necessitates continuous oversight and refinement, considering shifting market demands, customer expectations, latest practical methodologies and pliancy. By doing so, organizations can ensure that quality management systems remain pertinent and adept at effectively handling nonconformities while delivering the highest level of service quality.

Additionally, there is a visible connection between quality management and resilience, as analyses show that companies with focus on resilience through QM grow faster because they can race to meet customers' needs when market demand shifts; increase their perfect order rate and customer satisfaction; cut costs and improve cash flow; increase in inventory turns; reduce disruption by building buffers throughout the supply network and invest in advanced analytics to improve planning and forecasting accuracy (Schatteman et al., 2020). This positive interaction can contribute social progress by economic growth, job creation, and overall societal well-being.

Aim of the Article. The aim of this article is to thoroughly investigate the principles of nonconformity typology in practice, focusing on how they can be harnessed to strengthen the resilience of logistics companies in the service industry. By delineating crucial boundaries for defining typology and categorizing nonconformities, this study aims to provide actionable insights that can enhance the effectiveness of various service organizations. The research delves into diverse nonconformity types, proposes adaptive strategies, and underscores the importance of continual monitoring and analysis by emphasizing a systematic approach to nonconformity management. By embracing these insights, companies can foster a culture of quality enhancement, boost customer satisfaction, and fortify their competitive positioning in the dynamic service industry landscape.

2 Theoretical Background

2.1 Enhanced Resilience in Logistics Services Through Quality Management

In today's dynamic and competitive business environment, the logistics industry faces numerous challenges that can impact its operations and overall resilience (Tillement et al., 2009). Quality management practices play a crucial role in enhancing the resilience of logistics services by ensuring efficiency, reliability, and customer satisfaction (Hong et al., 2019) and organizational adaptability. Quality management includes various tools and methods aimed to ensuring services meet both customer expectations (Kryvoruchko et al., 2021) and established standards. This process involves monitoring, analyzing, and refining operational practices to minimize nonconformities and enhance efficiency (Gunasekaran et al., 2004), ensuring seamless service delivery. Continuous quality assessment and gathering customer feedback enable logistics companies to boost service quality and improve customer satisfaction (Le et al., 2020). The pursuit of enhanced resilience in logistics services through quality management encapsulates a multifaceted endeavor that encompasses organizational culture, process optimization, risk mitigation, and technology integration (Xu et al., 2024).

Logistics companies faced significant disruptions during the COVID-19 pandemic, yet the situation also provided an opportunity for them to improve and address emerging challenges. These challenges included infrastructure "bottlenecks," inefficiencies in technical systems, insufficient government support policies, inadequate key performance indicators (KPIs) (Gupta et al., 2018); and reliance on traditional operational methods (Sharma et al., 2011), also had to adapt to increased service volumes and discover successful service quality management models. External challenges such as new technologies, new market entrants, evolving customer expectations, and innovative business models (Zaviša, 2023), alongside internal challenges like skill gaps, employee shortages, high turnover, rising costs of retaining employees and other resources, and fragmented communication, have emerged as the post-pandemic transformation of the logistics sector.

Companies encounter daily challenges that impact quality of logistics services. Purposeful and continuous recording, monitoring, and addressing these challenges lead to greater resilience and learning through experience. Businesses that effectively manage these obstacles achieve higher customer satisfaction and operational efficiency (Küpper et al., 2019), resulting in increased profits—a key objective for any profit-oriented organization. Long-term studies suggest that logistics service providers that do not invest time, money, and expertise in quality improvement (Sandberg & Abrahamsson, 2011), are unlikely to remain competitive. Korzynski highlights that poor quality is the most prominent indicator of logistics process inefficiency (Korzynski & Pacana, 2010), while other authors assert that quality in the logistics sector is unattainable without punctual delivery, clear processes, value for customer, error tracking, flexibility, and reliability (Kilibarda et al., 2020). To help logistics companies better manage quality challenges, various quality management systems (ISO 9001), TQM, LEAN/Agile philosophies, methodologies provide guidance based on establishing standard practices and fostering clear communication (Sıtkı İlkay & Aslan, 2012). Mentioned approaches emphasize continuous improvement (Demir & Bulut, 2018), staying aligned with market trends, applying the latest management practices (Siltori, 2021) and prioritizing customer experience. Furthermore, these approaches advocate for recording nonconformities, categorizing them, and implementing targeted management interventions based on statistical data. Resilience in a company is exemplified by its ability to maintain operational stability, as evidenced by a diminishing non-conformance balance. Therefore, an examination of nonconformities and their fluctuations holds significance for organizations aiming to adopt effective resilience management strategies.

3 The Need for Typology of Nonconformities

In the context of quality management systems, typology as specific, defined groups, provide an adaptive category system that allows classifications based on situations (Bailey, 1994) and individual problem circumstances, considering the organization's needs and field of activity. The need for a typology of nonconformities is essential for organizational efficiency, customer satisfaction, and long-term success, as it enables a systematic approach to problem management and continuous improvement (Borgatti & Foster, 2003). With a structured approach to managing nonconformities, organizations can effectively respond to the challenges they face and improve their performance in the future. A multifaceted typology of nonconformities helps organizations allocate resources more effectively, directing them toward priority areas or solving different types of problems (Buckingham, 2012), and provides the ability to track and analyze trends and statistics (Gulati & Singh, 1998). Proper management of nonconformities allows organizations to respond efficiently to customer inquiries and urgent needs. This enhances overall customer satisfaction (Maidhili & Nithyanandam, 2017), a critical indicator of successful business operations. Proper categorization of nonconformities is also a requirement of external regulation, particularly in the documentation of errors and reporting.

In the field of logistics services, various types of typologies have been developed:

- Vendor; (Fabbe-Costes et al., 2008; Świtała, 2016)
- Entities (Pokrovskaya et al., 2019)
- Logistics activities (urban logistics, last mile delivery, reverse logistics) (Brandão et al., 2022; Carbone et al., 2018; Meza-Peralta et al., 2020; Usama & Ramish, 2020)
- and other typologies (Reinecke et al., 2023)

However, there is limited research on nonconformity typologies in scientific literature.

4 Nonconformity Management and Classification/Typology

Nonconformities represent deviations from established standards or requirements that can hinder service quality, operational efficiency, and overall performance in the service sector (Mabiletsa, 2021). By implementing robust nonconformity management processes and developing a comprehensive classification/typology system, service industry organizations can proactively address and mitigate risks, enhance adaptability, and strengthen their resilience against disruptions. A typology of nonconformities assists an organization in optimizing its operations, reducing time and resource waste, and enhancing operational efficiency and profitability. Companies can establish, monitor, and manage service quality, though scientific literature highlights that quality is a highly subjective concept (Werbińska-Wojciechowska, 2011). To minimize subjectivity, organizations must set quality standards and document deviations. The ability to record nonconformities enables the adoption of flexible and efficient processes to prevent their recurrence (Valmohammadi & Kalantari, 2015). Nonconformities can expose deficiencies in effective process management or the need to improve current systems and procedures (Gadeikis, 2021), creating suitable nonconformity categories help organizations gain a better understanding of sources and causes. This targeted approach can effectively guide problem-solving efforts and process improvements (Mickevičiūtė, 2023).

In general, in literature, nonconformities are defined as any procured products or services from a supplier that are deemed unacceptable during final or technological inspections (Natarajan, 2017), as well as any failure to meet a requirement (Chiarini, 2015). Managing nonconformities involves identifying problems, controlling them, determining their causes, and taking actions to prevent recurrence. Companies can select from a range of tools and methods aimed at recording, enhancing, and refining quality. The most prevalent method for managing quality is the use of a KPI system, which often includes logging complaints, claims, and procedural nonconformities.

Monitoring nonconformities effectively help to achieve quality goals and improve services, making it essential to observe and categorize nonconformities accurately (Claver et al., 2003). Integrating classification and typology practices into resilience-building strategies empowers organizations to anticipate risks, optimize processes, and enhance their ability to adapt to changing circumstances, ultimately leading to sustained success and competitiveness in the service industry landscape (Kubacki, Siemieniako, & Brennan, 2020).

Proper categorization starts with identifying the cause of a nonconformity by examining the quality system's condition at the time of occurrence, directly seeking causes using one or more methods, selecting the most likely cause, and formulating the cause (Shkrobova & Davydov, 2006). The output of this process (the root cause of the nonconformity) serves as input for subsequent phase, which involves devising corrective actions typically focused on eliminating the cause (Ivan & Vyacheslav, 2020). It is crucial to accurately identify and formulate the root cause because further actions in management system hinge on this understanding.

Properly identifying the type of nonconformity enables the most effective approach in line with the stages outlined by the ISO 9001:2015 standard: formulating corrective measures, implementing them, verifying their effectiveness, controlling the process and improving the system (ISO, 2015). Accurately defined types enhance the likelihood of effectively planning and implementing corrective actions with precise execution checks. This lays the groundwork for system improvements without imposing undue burden on employees tasked with identifying causes and implementing corrective actions (Valerievich & Vladimirovma, 2015).

It is essential to recognize that nonconformities can arise from various causes. Some occur under typical market conditions when a company introduces a new product or service (Overstreet et al., 2013), while others stem from service complexity, fluctuating demand, and errors (Hinckley & Barkan, 1995). Errors led to the most manageable nonconformities, which have standardized groups designed to address them, aligned with key quality variables (Krynke & Mielczarek, 2016): material quality, process quality, equipment quality, personnel quality, environmental quality, and measurement quality.

The most common typology focuses on managerial categories:

- People (Man) Service providers are direct participants in the process and have a significant impact on the final quality. Thus, human factors play a vital role in the delivery process, as each delivery scenario is unique and presents different challenges.
- Equipment (Machines) Equipment facilitates service delivery and is a key component of delivery. Various processes have differing requirements, and equipment management should address usage, calibration, and maintenance (Jinab et al., 2022)
- Material. Material forms the foundation of product creation in production. In delivery market, material quality is not typically monitored.
- Method. The precision and rationality of process methods affect process quality, a critical factor in determining product quality. Method-related factors impacting

service quality include adherence to processes, procedures, policies, and technologies.

– Environmental factors. These are external elements influencing service quality. Effective management of environmental factors such as service delivery environment, social context, and managerial surroundings can support the sustained provision of high-quality services (Yingying et al., 2019).

The detailed development of nonconformity categories as described in scientific literature is outlined in Table 1.

Nonconformities can also be categorized by different areas of company's operations, such as transport, facilities, personnel, clients, finance, IT, technology, procedures, policy, software, users, equipment, and environment (Fu & Liu, 2021).

Additionally, there are typology systems that outline potential tactical decisions for organizations in meeting more specific company needs:

- By control object: including service, process, document, or system; (Pacana et al., 2021)
- By recurrence frequency: distinguishing between frequent and rare; (Magomedov Sh.Sh., 2018)
- By detection location: whether in administration, production, other departments, or outside the company's premises; (Zaika et al., 2022)
- By nature of risk: categorizing nonconformities as either related or unrelated to business risk (assessed by impact, frequency, and influence). (Wit, 2014)

In addition to categorizing nonconformities by content, it is essential to classify them by level of importance to facilitate smoother and more efficient identification and resolution. According to Azelia Puteri's research (Puteri & Zagloel, 2022), nonconformities can be classified into three levels: critical, major and minor, which reflect the impact of the nonconformity on the company's processes or overall business. The classification of nonconformities helps assess the broader business impact.

Specific levels of hazardous incidents are linked to a management structure that designates a responsible individual based on quality management practices, such as establishing matrices of responsible personnel. In their work, Yun and Hou emphasize that the importance of nonconformities influences the company's subsequent actions to ensure quality (Yun & Hou, 2016):

– Critical nonconformities. Notify top management; their prompt action is anticipated.
– Major nonconformities. Notify senior managers; their intervention is required.
– Minor nonconformities. Corrective actions are carried out by designated employees.

It is important to recognize that various managerial actions can be linked to the recording of nonconformities. These actions may include conducting additional targeted audits, establishing metrics in the most frequently recorded category, reviewing processes, documenting, creating standards, facilitating supplementary

Table 1 Top nonconformity categories

Author	Variable 1 human resources	Variable 2 Process	Variable 3 Measurement recording	Variable 4	Variable 5 Resources	Variable 6 External factors	Variable 7 Management	Variable 8 Other
Wong et al. (2016)	Human being	Method	Measurement	Equipment	Substance			
Luca et al. (2017)	Staff	Process			Substance	External factors	Management	
Ilie and Ciocoiu (2010)	Staff	Technology		Machinery	Raw materials		Management	Working conditions
Luca (2016)	Staff	Methods	Measurements	Machinery	Material	Environment		
Nascimento-e-Silva et al. (2020)	People	Process		Equipment	Material	Environment	Management	
Krynke and Mielczarek (2016)	Staff	Process	Measurement	Equipment	Substance	Environment		

and periodic communication, managing risks, providing training, collaborating with suppliers, implementing innovations, and carrying out other preventive and corrective actions (Hutchins, 2018).

4.1 *Utilizing Software for Nonconformity Management*

In today's rapidly evolving service industry landscape, the utilization of software solutions has become integral to effective nonconformity management and resilience-building efforts (Cantelmi, 2023). The reduction of nonconformities arising from daily operations is essential for optimizing processes, minimizing workflow disruptions, and thereby enhancing operational efficiency to achieve delivery objectives, improve business profitability, elevate overall customer satisfaction (Mohsen et al., 2019) and grow resilience. To accomplish this, organizations must develop a tool that enables the swift entry and management of nonconformities, facilitating statistical analysis and providing actionable insights (Ju, 2021). One such tool is nonconformity management software, which supports methods, tools, and technologies that synergistically interact within a given process (Afanasjeva, 2007), market in 2016 year could suggest Salesforce, Zogho CRM, HubSpot, Pipedrive, Microsoft Dynamics, SAP, Creation and others.

Application of software for nonconformity management plays a pivotal role in optimizing business processes and enhancing efficiency. Software is designed to achieve high levels of customer satisfaction and responsiveness by enabling organizations to identify more effectively, monitor, analyze, and resolve issues (Berg, 2023) pertaining to quality, process performance, and customer service.

Primary benefit of software for nonconformity management is ability to centralize and organize information of nonconformities (Solutions, 2024), including errors reported by employees and automated system-generated notifications. The software also facilitates the categorization of nonconformities by type or priority (Aghajani et al., 2020), assisting organizations in pinpointing critical nonconformities and taking action to address them. Additionally, the software supports tracking and analyzing process efficiency and identifying long-term trends in nonconformity occurrences (Basso et al., 2020).

For successful utilization of software, it is crucial to have well-configured and deployed systems. In addition, it is important to have a team of well-trained personnel who are capable of effectively utilizing the software and interpreting the resulting data (Srinath & Varghese, 2023). Thus, when investing in software for nonconformity management, organizations must consider not only technological aspects but also organizational culture and human resource efficacy.

5 Methodology

5.1 Selected Case

To achieve the specified objective, a study was conducted to analyze nonconformity data over a predetermined timeframe within a company. The investigation was conducted at a well-established Lithuanian logistics company with over 20 years of experience in the market. The company holds a prominent position within its sector. The company specializes in postal and logistics services and is categorized as a large enterprise due to 650 employees and sales revenue of €64 million in 2022. The company serves both individual consumers (B2C) and businesses (B2B) as its clientele. The organization exhibits high level of innovation, integrating both managerial (LEAN, ISO) and technological advancements into operations. Since company has adopted digital quality management tool, specifically a nonconformity tracking module within its quality management program, it has amassed statistical data on nonconformities related to its activities since 2016.

5.2 Date for Statistical Analysis of Nonconformities

The study utilized nonconformity management data from a parcel delivery company from 2016 to 2022, extracted in.xls format from the company's Quality Management System. The analysis centered on data concerning one-day delays in parcel delivery. The system is accessible to all company employees. Nonconformities are recorded exclusively by staff in transportation and warehousing, customer service, sales, and quality departments. The nonconformity recording system is integrated with employee notification systems, such as email notifications. Employees tasked with completing these assignments were given specific performance indicators (response time, decision-making time, and first-time resolution). These metrics were monitored in real-time. Notably, nonconformities were logged into the system continuously.

The company has implemented a hierarchical system for categorizing nonconformity data. The first hierarchical level comprises quality elements, while the second level pertains to degree of responsibility related to the significance of quality nonconformities. In total, company applies basic categorization that includes nonconformity that could be resolved in managerial tier, on senior management tier, and on top management tier.

The nonconformity monitoring system encompasses the following indicators: the volume of requests created within the system, response time to requests (in minutes), resolution time for requests (in hours), department or warehouse tasked with resolving the request. These indicators are stratified by levels of responsibility, enabling senior managers to track their department's performance and upper management to oversee the company's overall functioning.

This investigation scrutinized nonconformity data within each company-specific category to identify key issues, quantify nonconformities, and assess the prevalence of each category.

For statistical analysis, data from 2016 to 2022 were extracted from the internal nonconformity management system and organized across various dimensions. Collected data was examined using descriptive statistical techniques. The dataset included date of nonconformity creation, type, comments, city, responsible person, position of responsible person, and level of importance.

6 Methods

6.1 *Qualitative Interview*

To gain a comprehensive understanding of the company's processes, the principles underlying the applied quality system, and the dynamics of organizational development, a qualitative study employing qualitative interviews was conducted. The interviews were held in March 2024 and involved five company representatives: sales department coordinator, process and quality coordinator, operations department manager, service department manager, customer support department manager. All interviewers belong to senior and top management, however, depending on nonconformity, they can solve basic managerial nonconformities. The interviews focused on three core aspects: understanding the nonconformity management process, assessing the current situation, and providing recommendations for improving the nonconformity management process. Respondents were asked open-ended questions to elucidate the rationale behind nonconformity category selection, the causes of nonconformities, and strategic quality decisions, with a focus on linking them to nonconformity statistics.

The qualitative interview method facilitated detailed examination of selection of nonconformity types, their significance, and necessity. Qualitative content analysis was employed to investigate types of indicators and quality content. This involved structuring and summarizing research data, characterizing types and categories, and identifying meanings attributed to these types by employees. The interview data were transcribed and subjected to content analysis, with statements classified into subcategories and categories (Table 2).

Table 2 Interview questionnaire

Situational awareness	Describe your perception of the typology of nonconformities. How is it connected with resilience? How would you define this term? What species or categories in the typology of nonconformities would you consider to be the most important or common? Why? How do you classify or categorize nonconformities in your organization or service sector in general? Do you follow specific systems or methodologies for this classification? How do you think nonconformities affect the overall quality of service delivery in the industry? How do they affect customer satisfaction and retention? Can you provide examples of successful initiatives or strategies that have effectively addressed nonconformities while promoting sustainability and social progress within organizations?
Nonconformity management process (prioritization)	How do you prioritize resolving nonconformities in your organization? Are there specific criteria or metrics used to determine the severity or impact of each incident?
Nonconformity management process (technologies)	What role does technology or digitalization play in identifying, monitoring, and addressing nonconformities in the servicсs sector? Are any special tools or software used for this purpose? How do you ensure consistency and accuracy in the classification and categorization of nonconformities in different departments or branches of your organization?
Nonconformity management process (employees)	What role do employees play in identifying and eliminating nonconformities in the service sector? How do you promote a culture of quality and continuous improvement among your colleagues?
Nonconformity management process (communication)	How do you report nonconformities and their resolutions to relevant stakeholders, including customers, regulators, and internal teams? What measures are being taken to ensure transparency and accountability? How do you get information about the state of nonconformities in your organization? What reporting mechanisms do you use to monitor trends and identify areas for improvement?
Improving the nonconformity management process	What challenges or difficulties do you see when applying the typology of nonconformities in your organization or activity? What advantages or benefits do you see in applying the typology of nonconformities? How does it contribute to the effectiveness of the organization's activities? What changes or improvements do you think it would take to make the typology of nonconformities even more effective? How to ensure that a culture of quality and compliance is promoted from top to bottom? What should be done to become more resilient to changes? Based on your expertise, what recommendations would you offer to service industry organizations looking to improve their nonconformity management strategies and enhance their overall resilience in today's dynamic business environment?

7 Findings

7.1 Qualitative Research

Analysis of a Qualitative Interview

To explore the research aspects and clarify ambiguous areas within the study, qualitative interviews were conducted with five employees whose primary responsibilities involve nonconformity management, resolution, and monitoring.

The interviews revealed that employees observed variations in nonconformity management during the pandemic period. They reported an increase in delivery volumes and decrease in the number of nonconformities. Additionally, they attributed effective management of nonconformities to adoption of LEAN methodologies, ISO 9001:2015 implementation, process optimization, and integration of digital tools. According to interviewee, "the digitization of nonconformities allowed us to gain a comprehensive perspective and allocate resources more efficiently." Upon examining the chosen nonconformity management system, which was implemented in 2016, interviewees indicated that the software aligns with employee needs. It is perceived as user-friendly, customer-centric, and deemed to be an appropriate and effective tool. Interviewers agreed that Quality management tool helped company defeat market changes and stay resilient.

Interviewed employees demonstrated knowledge of proper categorization of nonconformities into specific types, including those caused by customers due to systemic or procedural deficiencies; force majeure; nonconformities originating from suppliers or other company personnel; nonconformities attributed to service staff; those related to infrastructure; and nonconformities linked to software. Employees participate in ongoing training and have developed an understanding of the process's value and benefits for the organization and its clients. Software updates and changes are communicated via email, and standardized procedures and policies are considered valuable, fostering continuous improvement and process optimization.

The analysis of nonconformity types revealed that the interviewees noted the successful results of ongoing client engagement efforts, such as clients providing accurate parcel information, which facilitated timely deliveries. Comparable initiatives were implemented with employees involved in sorting—ongoing training, supervision, and structured workflows (hierarchical reporting) led to a reduction in nonconformities related to inaccurate sorting (sorting parcels from the conveyor belt). The decline in nonconformities linked to supplier and employee errors since 2020 is attributed to managing the spread of illnesses during the COVID-19 pandemic and increased managerial involvement in optimizing the parcel distribution process.

While nonconformities arising from service personnel improved during the pandemic, these still require further attention. Respondents identified three main categories within this type: staff shortages, illness, and nonconformity with agreements, stressing the need for targeted focus on these concerns, as they pertain to "courier-related nonconformities—the 'face' of the company." A 55% turnover rate among couriers was reported, and it was noted that employees who remain with the company for more than "four months exhibit greater productivity, higher performance, and positive customer feedback." The respondents acknowledged a positive trend from the pandemic until 2024 (present time) in the infrastructure category due to infrastructure expansion, which had not been previously prioritized. New terminals and parcel lockers reduced delivery delays. The interviewees also mentioned a decline in software-related nonconformities, emphasizing the recruitment of a new information technology director and the assessment and optimization of IT infrastructure.

According to the respondents, the classification of force majeure nonconformities was previously labeled as "Other" in quality management guidelines before software implementation. However, when the software was introduced, the supplier recommended defining it as a type related to nonconformities that did not fall under other categories. This type lacked a clear definition for an extended period, leading to the categorization of all "ambiguous nonconformities." In 2016, additional subcategories were added to include unplanned parcel volumes and weather conditions. The respondents perceived this type as problematic, misleading, and lacking value.

Middle managers reported that categorizing nonconformities based on their importance has proven effective, empowering employees to address issues at their level. However, nonconformities managed by upper-level managers based on their level of importance were noted to have slower resolution rates.

During the interviews, it became evident that employees faced a lack of transparency regarding the overall structured state of company nonconformities. There was an absence of regular meetings or updates in company news about how other departments were reducing or improving nonconformities, common errors within each category, or concerns that not all nonconformities were being captured within the nonconformity management system. Senior managers stated, "When implementing nonconformity typology, challenges and complexities arise—classifying incidents into specific categories can be difficult, particularly when they possess multiple causes or impacts. A significant challenge is training employees to accurately and independently categorize nonconformities."

The interviews underscored that nonconformity management data could be leveraged in the risk assessment process. Nonconformity management is an ongoing, dynamic process that must be continuously updated to reflect market and internal organizational requirements.

8 Enterprise Nonconformity Management Strategy

An analysis of interview responses indicated that the logistics company implemented various measures and methodologies to reduce nonconformities starting in 2016. In that year, the company attained ISO 9001:2015 Quality Management Systems certification and underwent recertification after three years, adhering to the standard until 2022. In 2018, the company's management became acquainted with the LEAN methodology, introducing tools such as an idea submission platform, a key performance indicator system, and a Plan-Do-Check-Act approach. Due to the increasing volume of shipments, the LEAN philosophy was not initially prioritized; however, the company sought to revive its application starting in 2021 through the implementation of meeting systems, improvements to nonconformity recording tools, audit simplification, and the establishment of project groups. Since 2019, the company has adopted digitization and digitalization tools such as Tableau, Power BI, and logistics process-enhancing technologies like GPS, RFID, and NFC and others.

Respondents observed that the study period encompassed several significant disruptions within the company, some of which were officially recognized as crises. These included changes in top-level management, strategic adjustments, new partnerships, high employee turnover, and shifts in the customer portfolio. One of the most impactful external events was the COVID-19 pandemic, which led to a substantial increase in demand for logistics services. Although this surge in demand was beneficial for the business, it also presented considerable challenges for the company's management and the maintenance of sustainable growth.

9 Software Selection

Since 2016, the company has employed software for managing nonconformities; prior to this, the organization utilized nonconformity forms and physically archived them. The software—SalesForce—was chosen from among several vendors, with critical system requirements including global applicability, rapid response times, and the ability to handle substantial volumes of users and information. The selected software is distinguished as a leader in customer relationship management, offering an extensive range of tools designed to streamline customer interactions and improve overall satisfaction. Among its many features, effective customer service is central, with nonconformity typology playing a pivotal role in structuring and efficiently resolving customer issues. The typology of nonconformities within the selected software entails systematic categorization and classification of customer cases or inquiries on the platform, including the creation of distinct nonconformity types, each representing a specific category or nature of issue. Software administrators define various nonconformity types based on different inquiry types or problems typically faced by the organization, such as technical support nonconformities, product or service-related issues, billing inquiries, and other types of inquiries. The organization can establish assignment rules that automatically route incoming nonconformities to the appropriate support teams or agents based on predetermined criteria such as nonconformity type, severity, or location. This ensures that nonconformities are directed to the most qualified personnel.

Nonconformity escalation rules allow the organization to advance cases to higher-level support or management based on specified conditions such as elapsed time or unresolved status. This facilitates timely escalation and resolution of critical issues.

The software enables organizations to create custom workflows for each nonconformity type, delineating specific actions to be undertaken throughout the nonconformity lifecycle. These workflows streamline resolution processes, promoting consistency and adherence to best practices.

Data analysis and insights provided by the nonconformity typology allow organizations to derive meaningful insights into problems and trends. By examining data on various nonconformity types, organizations can identify recurring issues, implement proactive measures, and continuously enhance their products and services.

9.1 *Statistical Survey*

Groups of Nonconformities

During the study, nonconformities associated with agreements recorded in the company's internal system were analyzed. Notably, the volume of shipments has exhibited a consistent upward trend since 2018, averaging approximately thirty-five thousand shipments per day. The incidence of nonconformities reached its highest point in 2019, with an average of ten to eleven nonconformities per day, followed by a steady decline in subsequent periods. It was observed that the COVID-19 pandemic had a pronounced and beneficial impact on the company's operations, as packages turnover doubled between 2020 and 2022 (Fig. 1).

All recorded nonconformities are categorized according to classifications outlined below, as specified in company's ISO 9001:2015 quality management standard, approved by senior management (Table 3).

The categorization of nonconformities according to type is depicted below. The identified types of nonconformities encompass the following categories: customers, created inaccuracies in data provided by (senders and recipients); software, encompassing system errors and updates; suppliers, defined by nonconformities caused by suppliers or other company employees; infrastructure, including issues with

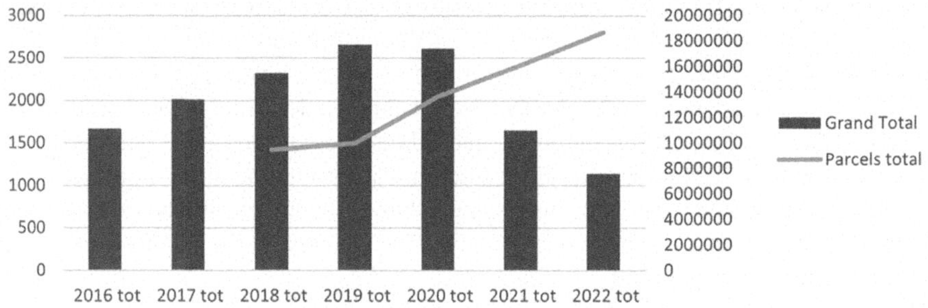

Fig. 1 Dynamics of nonconformities (2016–2022)

Table 3 Categories of nonconformities of the company under investigation

Category of research (according to company's practice)	Description
Customer-induced nonconformities due to systemic/procedural deficiencies	Inaccuracy of customer-provided data
Force majeure	Nonconformities not classified under other categories
Nonconformities caused by suppliers/other company employees	Strikes, illnesses, improper sorting
Nonconformities caused by service personnel	Courier illnesses, absenteeism, nonconformity with agreements
Nonconformities caused by infrastructure	Parcel lockers, terminal equipment, vehicles
Nonconformities caused by software	System errors, updates

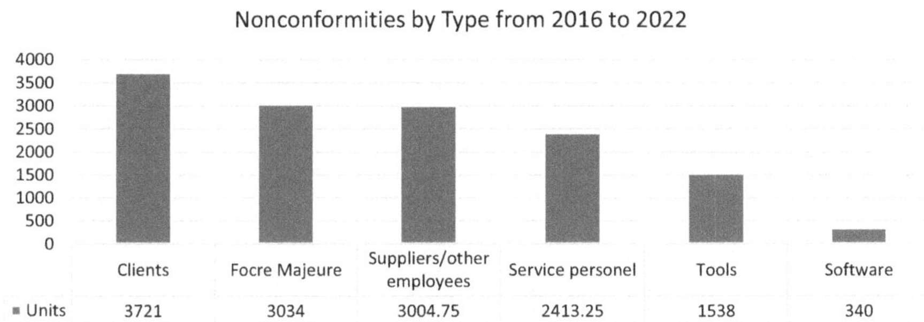

Fig. 2 Nonconformities by type in 2016–2022

parcel lockers, terminal equipment, and vehicles; couriers, involving nonconformities arising from service personnel; and force majeure (Fig. 2).

Statistical data from 2016 to 2022 reveals that the largest share of nonconformities (27%) stemmed from customer errors. Following this, force majeure nonconformities comprised 22% of total nonconformities, and those caused by couriers accounted for 21%, tools-17% of the total, while errors made by other company employees constituted 13%. The software category contributed the smallest share of nonconformities, at 2% of the total.

Preliminary data from the company underscores the prominence of the force majeure category, which was subject to qualitative content analysis. This category does not align with any other categories examined in existing literature (Table 4).

Table 4 Typical nonconformity management process

	Event	Responsible employee	Moment of record occurrence	User responsibility	System
Step 1	Parcel delay exceeding one day	Quality Manager	During report analysis	Assign nonconformity to the relevant warehouse for resolution	Quality Management System's Nonconformity Management Module
Step 2	Parcel delay exceeding one day	Assigned warehouse employee	During report analysis	Resolve nonconformity	Quality Management System's Nonconformity Management Module
Step 3	Parcel delay exceeding one day	Quality Manager	During report analysis	Verify resolution of nonconformity and, if necessary, establish preventive or corrective measures	Quality Management System's Nonconformity Management Module

Nonconformity Management Process

Study examines nonconformities associated with parcel delays for more than one day. The standard nonconformity management process is outlined below.

The table outlines a standard nonconformity management process; however, it should be noted that employees from other departments can also report nonconformities when they receive complaints or claims through various channels, such as company email, phone calls, the customer service department, social media platforms (Facebook, LinkedIn, etc.), or clients visiting the company office. Tasks related to nonconformities are sent to employees' personal email accounts, and nonconformities are reviewed twice a week in departmental meetings to assess progress and address any emerging issues.

To enhance operational efficiency and improve customer satisfaction, the nonconformity management process undergoes regular audits, with suggested enhancements implemented if necessary. Prior to 2016, designated employees recorded nonconformities on paper forms; since then, the company has transitioned to an operational system that enables seamless information sharing among departments, facilitating superior customer service, increased productivity, and more effective use of accumulated data. One of the company's strategic goals is to reduce nonconformities by twenty percent annually; this objective is reassessed quarterly during strategic sessions.

Nonconformity Statistics

This section delves into a deeper analysis of nonconformities. Each type of nonconformity was examined in detail, with the most dominant errors assigned to each type. The table presents the nonconformity categories ranked by the most frequently occurring errors from 2016 to 2022 (Table 5).

Customer-induced nonconformities resulting from systemic or procedural deficiencies have two primary recurring subcategories: improper packaging and inaccurate data provided. A significant shift occurred in 2018 due to errors in provided geocode or contact details, which restricted clients' ability to enter incomplete data. However, this solution was only temporary as customers began to express dissatisfaction and file complaints. Consequently, the number of errors and nonconformities rose again within a year. In recent years, however, these nonconformities have a notable decrease. This improvement can be attributed to a clear understanding of the problem and careful work with clients, including providing email instructions, guidance during packaging, and standardized packaging materials (Fig. 3).

The force majeure category consists of two main recurring subcategories: unexpected increases in parcel volume and adverse weather conditions. The highest incidence of nonconformities was noted during 2019–2020, coinciding with the onset of the COVID-19 pandemic in Lithuania and globally. Graphical analysis juxtaposes nonconformities in this category with trends in parcel volume over time (Fig. 4).

Table 5 Ranking of non-conforming categories

Customer-induced nonconformities	Force Majeure	Nonconformities caused by suppliers/other company employees	Nonconformities caused by service personnel	Nonconformities caused by infrastructure	Nonconformities caused by software
Wrong Packaging (51%)	Unexpected surge in parcel volume (74%)	Inaccurate sorting(54%)	Staff shortage(45%)	Locker unavailability(43%)	Update of A software (64%)
The provided geocode/ contacts are incorrect (48%)	Weather conditions (25%)	Strike (17%)	Illnesses (33%)	Inaccurate sorting due to equipment errors(14%)	Lockers software errors (24%)
		Illnesses (12%)	Nonconformity with agreements (13%)	Parcel locker technical issues (9%)	Update of B software (5%)

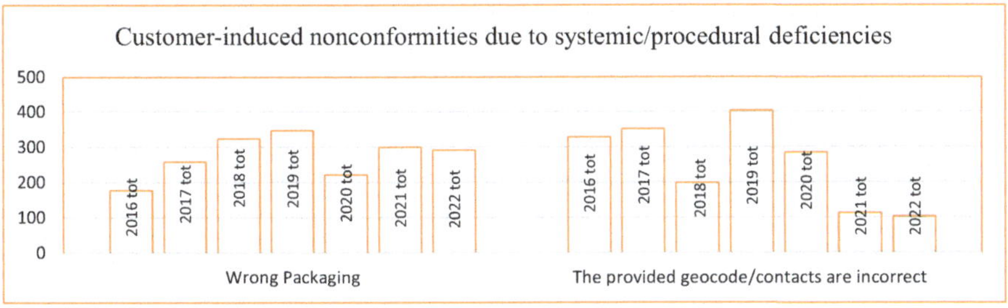

Fig. 3 Customer-induced nonconformities (Typology 1)

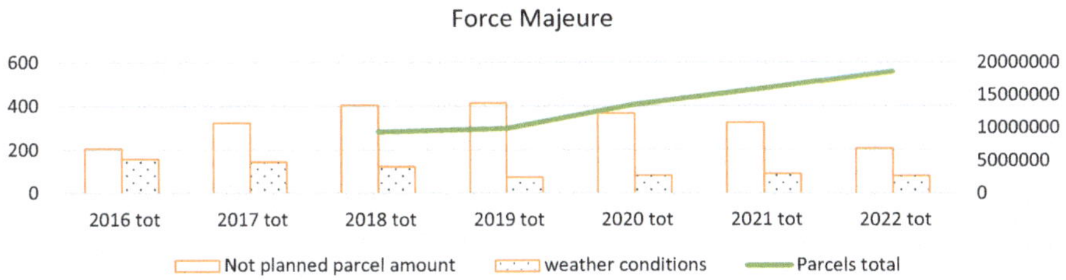

Fig. 4 Force Majeure nonconformities (Typology 2)

The category of nonconformities arising from suppliers or other company employees encompasses three primary recurring subcategories: inaccurate distribution due to employee errors, strikes, and employee illnesses (affecting terminal workers). Nonconformities related to illnesses maintained a consistent level over the years. The company faced several strikes in 2019 and 2020, leading to temporary operational disruptions in specific cities for a few days. Nonconformities related to inaccurate distribution steadily increased until 2020, when the company introduced additional measures for more efficient parcel distribution, including zoning in warehouses and equipping employees with manual scanning devices (Fig. 5).

The category of nonconformities caused by service personnel (couriers, drivers) comprises three main recurring subcategories: employee shortages (excluding

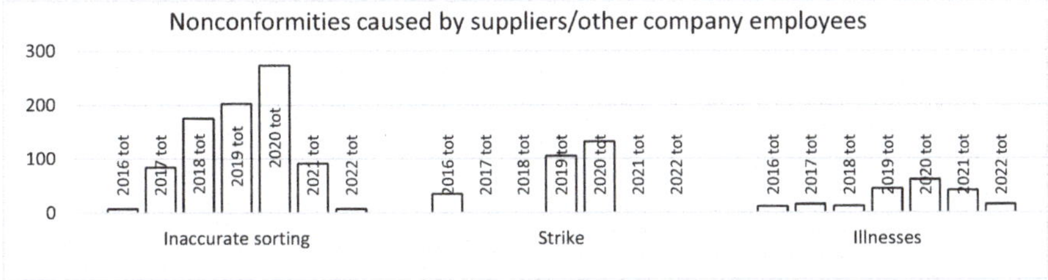

Fig. 5 Nonconformities caused by suppliers/other company employees (Typology 3)

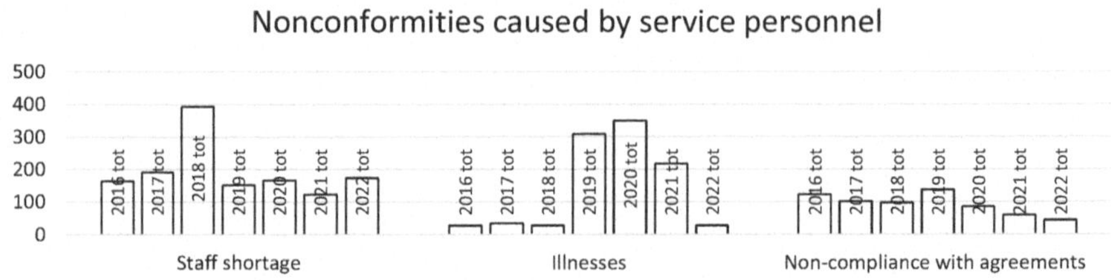

Fig. 6 Nonconformities caused by service personnel (Typology 4)

illnesses), illnesses, and nonconformity with agreements (such as lack of documentation, improper attire, and unprepared vehicles). The most notable change in nonconformities related to employee shortages occurred in 2018, coinciding with an increase in the volume of the company's parcels. The incidence of nonconformities related to illnesses among service personnel rose during the COVID-19 pandemic and only stabilized in 2022 (Fig. 6).

The category of nonconformities related to infrastructure consists of three predominant recurring subcategories: parcel locker occupancy, inaccurate parcel distribution due to equipment errors, and technical issues with parcel lockers. The company invests annually in expanding the parcel locker network; however, newly established customer preferences for "not in hand" delivery options have led to delays. The increase in parcel volume during the pandemic prompted the company to pursue infrastructure expansion, including establishing new sorting centers (e.g., a new parcel locker sorting center in Kaunas and approximately 70 new parcel lockers added each year), optimizing existing processes, and improving systems. Nonconformities caused by inaccurate distribution were effectively managed by the company in 2021 (Fig. 7).

The category of nonconformities due to software comprises three main recurring subcategories: updates to two distinct systems and parcel locker system errors. The company has successfully resolved and eradicated nonconformities associated with parcel locker system errors since 2019. Nonconformities related to system B updates have been limited to fewer than three occurrences annually. The highest incidence

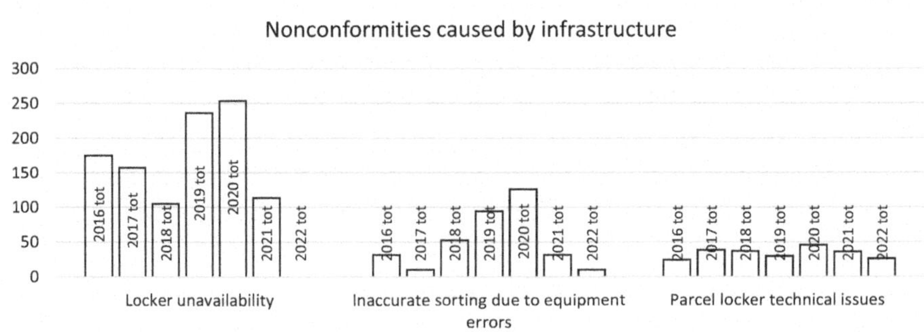

Fig. 7 Nonconformities caused by infrastructure (Typology 5)

of nonconformities stems from system A updates, peaking in 2018 and subsequently showing a downward trend (Fig. 8).

As previously discussed, the company faced several critical periods, one of the most notable being a surge in orders due to the COVID-19 pandemic. Nevertheless, data on nonconformities related to one-day delays showed a reduction in nonconformities during the critical period. The company invested in expanding its infrastructure and enhancing its software. To determine which category of nonconformities was most impacted—customer-induced, force majeure, supplier-induced, service personnel-induced, infrastructure-induced, or software-induced—an analysis was carried out to compare the number of nonconformities in each category in 2016 and 2022 (Fig. 9).

The most significant reduction in nonconformities since 2016 occurred in the infrastructure category, while the smallest decrease was observed in nonconformities related to service personnel.

Analyzing nonconformities by their level of importance—namely, nonconformities related to managerial, middle management, and senior management competence—revealed that 70% of nonconformities in the company are resolved at the managerial level, 21% are escalated to senior management, and only 8% are addressed by top-level executives (Fig. 10).

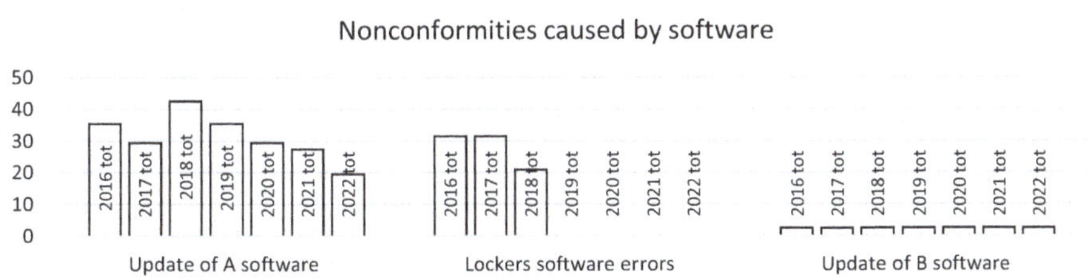

Fig. 8 Nonconformities caused by software (Typology 6)

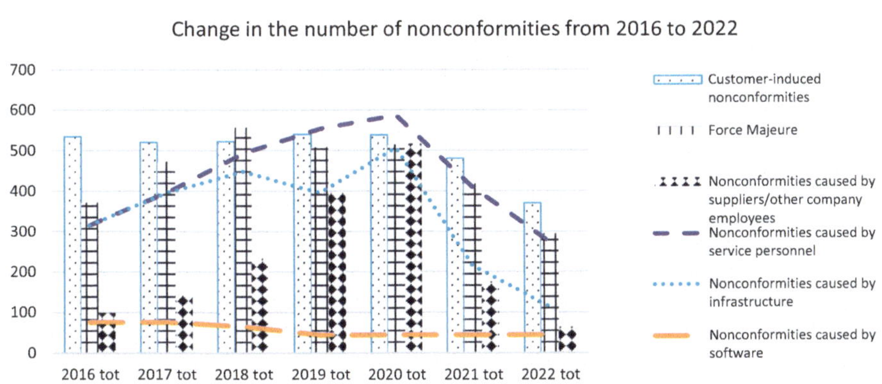

Fig. 9 Change in the number of nonconformities from 2016 to 2022

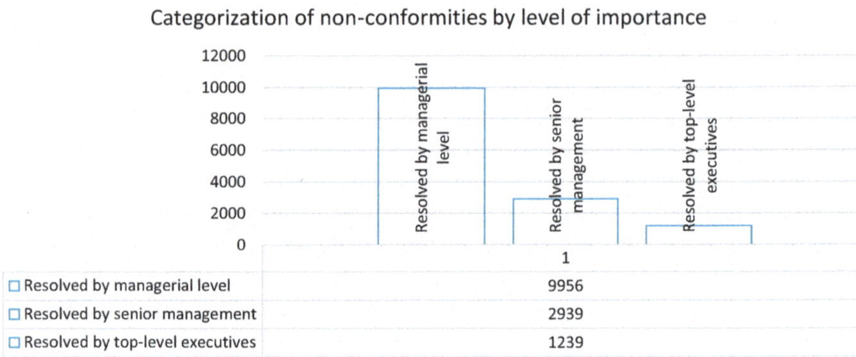

Fig. 10 Categorization of nonconformities by level of importance

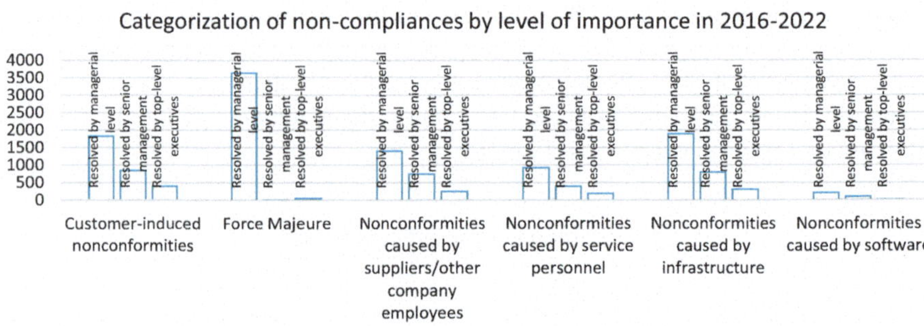

Fig. 11 Categorization of nonconformities by level of importance in 2016–2022

To gain a deeper understanding of nonconformity categories by level, data was analyzed based on the level of importance and the content of the nonconformity formation (Fig. 11).

An analysis of nonconformity categorization based on importance levels and content revealed that 97% of force majeure-type nonconformities were attributed to managerial competence. Nonconformities primarily resolved at the management level included those arising from customer errors, mistakes by suppliers or other employees, and infrastructure issues. Senior management addressed nonconformities related to customers and infrastructure.

Each level is examined in depth to identify patterns and trends (Fig. 12).

A more detailed analysis revealed that managers addressed nonconformities related to customer-generated errors, such as incorrectly specified addresses, contacts, and poorly packaged parcels. During the pandemic, greater attention was given to nonconformities caused by service personnel, such as illnesses and absences from work due to isolation (Fig. 13).

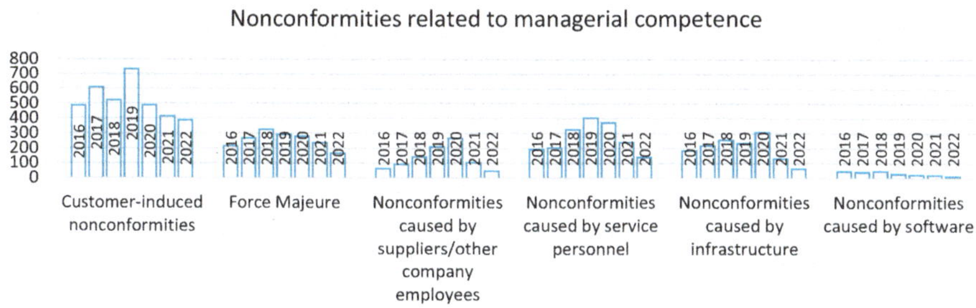

Fig. 12 Nonconformities related to managerial competence

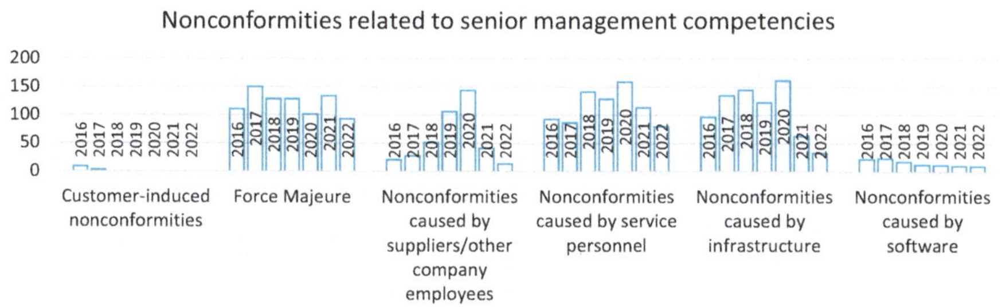

Fig. 13 Nonconformities related to senior management competencies

Second-level nonconformity resolution by senior management is analyzed below.

Senior management competency-related nonconformities were linked to force majeure nonconformities (28%), service personnel-induced nonconformities (27%), and infrastructure-related nonconformities (25%). During the pandemic, senior management had to manage flows by properly allocating resources, resulting in an increase in nonconformities in 2019–2020, primarily related to suppliers and other company employees (Fig. 14).

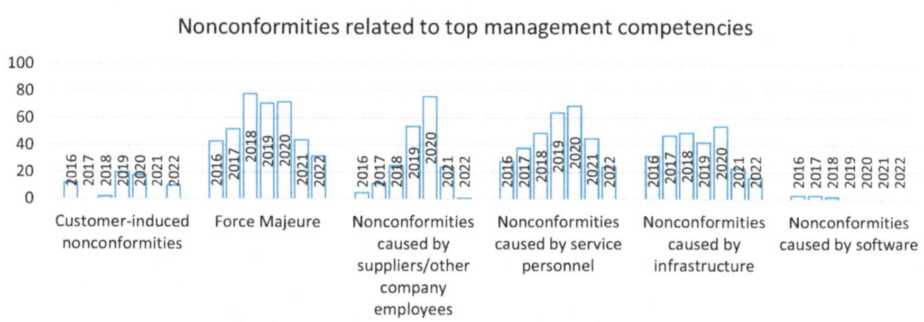

Fig. 14 Nonconformities related to top management competencies

The last level of nonconformity is the top management level, which is not influenced by customer-induced nonconformities or software-related nonconformities. It is notable that higher rates of nonconformities occur during strikes and critical periods such as the pandemic or times of increased volume.

10 Discussion

Within the realm of nonconformity management and classification/typology, exploring the different categories of nonconformities within logistics services offers valuable insights into the intricate operational dynamics essential for building resilience. One particularly intriguing focus lies in the analysis of force majeure nonconformities, uncovering diverse patterns upon closer examination of subcategories. Analysis from the logistics company underscored the significance of force majeure incidents, constituting 22% of all nonconformities during the study period. Upon detailed scrutiny, two distinct subcategories emerged: adverse weather conditions impacting parcel deliveries and sudden spikes in parcel volume. Notably, nonconformity records often lacked detailed information beyond the category, city, and individual responsible, highlighting a key area for improvement in resilience management practices.

Upon analyzing these two subcategories, distinct trends emerged. The increase in parcel volume persisted until 2019, after which it declined. In contrast, the impact of weather conditions remained stable at a consistent level (77–84 instances) (Fig. 15).

A detailed analysis showed that while the volume of parcels increased annually, the number of nonconformities in the force majeure category decreased. Interviews suggest that several factors may have contributed to this trend. First, improvements in training programs played a significant role by focusing on educating employees about how to use this category effectively, what types could be assigned, and providing support to employees through category usage testing and offering examples. Based on employee's responses to improvements in the new recording program, additional "programming rules" were introduced to further automate the system, thereby reducing human errors (Table 6).

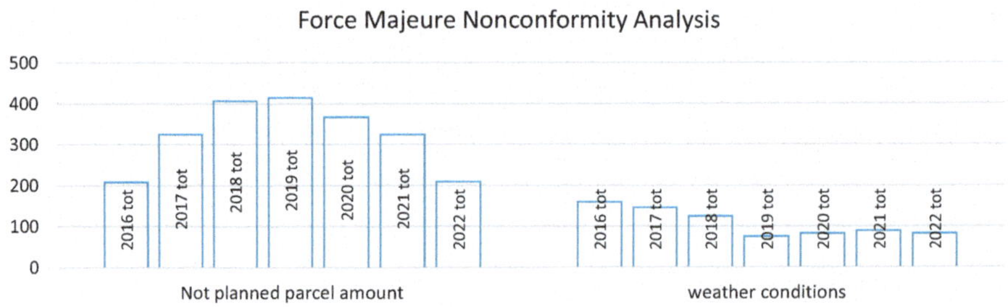

Fig. 15 Analysis of force majeure matches

Table 6 Dynamics of force majeure nonconformities with managerial interventions

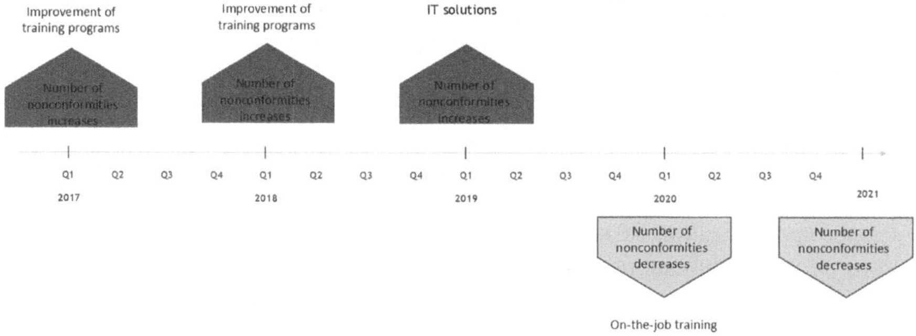

Furthermore, force majeure queries were mainly addressed at the managerial level, with only 2% of issues being escalated to a higher level within the specified timeframe. This finding suggests that rapid and localized managerial interventions are feasible, facilitated by digitalization that has streamlined employees' essential tasks, a goal that has already been achieved.

11 Conclusions

This study aimed to validate the principles of nonconformity typology in practical application and to specify the essential boundaries of typology definitions to improve the management effectiveness and resilience of logistics service companies. The company under analysis faced several significant disruptions from 2016 to 2022, including increased parcel volumes due to the COVID-19 pandemic, turnover at the senior management level, new strategic partnerships, and fluctuations in the customer portfolio. Nevertheless, the company was able to uphold and enhance quality levels through the management of nonconformities.

The company's resilience strategy is based on promptly identifying and analyzing nonconformities. Nonconformities are grouped into six types: customer-induced nonconformities due to systemic or procedural deficiencies, force majeure, supplier—or other company employees—induced nonconformities, service staff-induced nonconformities, infrastructure-induced nonconformities, and software-induced nonconformities. While the occurrence of all types of nonconformities has been decreasing steadily over a two-year period, the uncertainties associated with force majeure nonconformities, caused by large fluctuations in values, are divided into two subcategories: unfavorable weather conditions and unforeseeable increase in parcel volume. The company has put in place specific management measures to address the rising volume of parcels. For example, when the company noticed a sudden uptick in nonconformities, it introduced training and automation processes to better capture instances of non-compliance. These measures have led to a significant decrease in nonconformities over a 2-year period, demonstrating the effectiveness of the resilience strategy.

The study concludes with the following findings:

- Effective IT tools with data entry automation significantly influence nonconformity recording.
- Categorization of nonconformities within the system enables comprehensive data analysis.
- Proper categorization of nonconformities and subsequent managerial interventions positively impact resilience to change.
- Nonconformity categories should be periodically refined based on market and customer demands.
- Novel processes require two years of consistent operations to establish and demonstrate results.

Study Limitations. The quality of logistics services may present certain constraints. Given the rapid evolution of information technology, research results may quickly become outdated due to technological advances and changes in the IT environment. Logistics systems are inherently complex, involving numerous stakeholders, processes, and variables, which complicates isolating the impact of IT on nonconformities due to system interdependence. Establishing a direct causal link between IT utilization and the occurrence of nonconformities may be challenging due to changes in economic conditions.

Further research. Monitoring the service quality system is an important way to identify gaps in a company's resilience. Further research could focus on categorizing nonconformities, creating digital systems to measure resilience levels, and identifying which types of nonconformities are most likely to impact a company, especially in the context of the sudden decrease in demand for services during the post-pandemic period.

References

Afanasjeva, V. (2007). *Programinės įrangos kūrimo projektų kokybės vadyba*. Vilniaus universitetas. https://epublications.vu.lt/object/elaba:1927637/

Aghajani, E., Nagy, C., Linares-vásquez, M., Moreno, L., Bavota, G., Lanza, M., & Shepherd, D. C. (2020). Software documentation: The practitioners' perspective. In *Proceedings of the ACM/IEEE 42nd International Conference on Software Engineering* (pp. 590–601). https://doi.org/10.1145/3377811.3380405

Ahmady, K. (2021). Nonconformity and resistance in Mahabad with focusing on cultural, social, and gender aspects. *EFFLATOUNIA-Multidisciplinary Journal, 5* (2), 2522–2535. ISSN: 1110–8703.

Anuar, A., Othman, N., Sadek, D. M., Hami, N., & Mansor, N. S. (2023). Exploring the challenges and the implementation of lean practices under lean transformation project in Malaysian small and medium enterprises. *Jurnal Pengurusan, 67*, 1–13. https://doi.org/10.17576/pengurusan-2023-67-08

Bailey, K. D. (1994). *Typologies and taxonomies: An introduction to classification techniques*. Sage. ISBN 0803952597, 9780803952591

Basso, V. M., Andrade, B. G., Jacovine, L. A., Silva, E. V., Alves, R. R., R., C. R., & Nardelli, Á. M. (2020). Forest management certification in the Americas: Difficulties in complying with the requirements. *International forestry review, 22(2)*, 169–188. https://doi.org/10.1505/146554820829403478

Berg, H. M. (2023). *Exploring expectations for a non-conformance management system using the design science research framework* (MS thesis, NTNU). ntnuopen.ntnu.nontnuopen.ntnu.no.

Borgatti, S. P., & Foster, P. C. (2003). The network paradigm in organizational research: A review and typology. *Journal of Management, 29*(6), 991–1013. https://doi.org/10.1016/S0149-2063(03)00087-4

Brandão, R., Hosseini, M. R., Macêdo, A. N., & C., A. (2022). Public administration strategies that stimulate reverse logistics within the construction industry: A conceptual typology. *Engineering, Construction and Architectural Management*, 2924–2949. https://doi.org/10.1108/ECAM-07-2020-0547

Buckingham, D. H. (2012). Capturing diversity: A typology of third sector organisations' responses to contracting based on empirical evidence from homelessness services. *Journal of Social Policy, 41*(3), 569–589. https://doi.org/10.1017/S0047279412000086

Cantelmi, R. (2023). *Improving resilience in critical infrastructures through learning from past events*. Sapienza University of Rome, Italy. https://iris.uniroma1.it/retrieve/9c405385-a967-4212-bfe6-e20dcc12aaae/Tesi_dottorato_Cantelmi.pdf

Carbone, V., Rouquet, A., & Roussat, C. (2018). A typology of logistics at work in collaborative consumption. *International Journal of Physical Distribution & Logistics Management*, 570–585. https://doi.org/10.1108/IJPDLM-11-2017-0355

Chiarini, A. (2015). Effect of ISO 9001 non-conformity process on cost of poor quality in capital-intensive sectors. *International Journal of Quality & Reliability Management*, 144–155. https://doi.org/10.1108/IJQRM-03-2013-0041

Claver, E., Tarí, J. J., & Molina, J. F. (2003). Critical factors and results of quality management: An empirical study. *Total Quality Management & Business Excellence*, 91–118. https://doi.org/10.1080/14783360309709

Demir, A., & Bulut, I. (2018). A new model for respected meetings. *Procedia Computer Science*, 1637–1655. https://doi.org/10.1016/j.procs.2018.08.138

Fabbe-Costes, N., Jahre, M., & Roussat, C. (2008). Towards a typology of the roles of logistics service providers as 'supply chain integrators. *Supply Chain Forum An International Journal*, 29–43. https://doi.org/10.1080/16258312.2008.11517197

Fonseca, L., Cardoso, M. C., Pereira, M. T., & Ávila, P. (2021). ISO 9001 certification benefits: A principal component analysis. *FME Transactions, 49*(4), 835–841. https://doi.org/10.5937/fme2104835F

Fu, L., & Liu, M. (2021). How to prepare for the accreditation of calibration and testing laboratories. *Measurement informatization and management*, 59–63.

Gadeikis, L. (2021). *Žmogiškųjų klaidų darbo vietoje analizė remiantis OEE metodu* (Doctoral dissertation, Kauno technologijos universitetas). epubl.ktu.edu.

Gulati, R., & Singh, H. (1998). The architecture of cooperation: Managing coordination costs and appropriation concerns in strategic alliances. *Administrative science quarterly*, 781–814. https://doi.org/10.2307/2393616

Gunasekaran, A., Patel, C., & McGaughey, R. E. (2004). A framework for supply chain performance measurement. *International journal of production economics*, 333–347. https://doi.org/10.1016/j.ijpe.2003.08.003

Gupta, A., Singh, R. K., & Suri, P. K. (2018). Analysis of challenges faced by Indian logistics service providers. *Operations and Supply Chain Management: An International Journal*, 214–225. https://doi.org/10.31387/oscm0350215

Hinckley, C. M., & Barkan, P. (1995). The role of variation, mistakes, and complexity in producing nonconformities. *Journal of Quality Technology, 27(3)*, 242–249. https://doi.org/10.1080/00224065.1995.11979596

Hong, J., Liao, Y., Zhang, Y., & Yu, Z. (2019). The effect of supply chain quality management practices and capabilities on operational and innovation performance: Evidence from Chinese manufacturers. *International Journal of Production Economics, 212*, 227–235. https://doi.org/10.1016/j.ijpe.2019.01.036

Hutchins, G. (2018). *SO 31000: 2018 enterprise risk management.* ISBN 1732554579.

ISO. (2015). *State standard ISO 9001-2015. Quality management systems. Requirements.* Standartinform Publ.

Ilie, G., & Ciocoiu, C. N. (2010). Application of fishbone diagram to determine the risk of an event with multiple causes. *Knowledge Management Research & Practice*, 1–20. eISSN2067-2462.

Ivan, G., & Vyacheslav, B. (2020). Features of 8D methodology application. *Science without borders*, 65–69. https://nauka-bez-granic.ru/№-5-45-2020/5-45-2020/.

Jinab, D., Maa, D., Zhanga, Y., Yanga, B., Wanga, D., & Guoab, L. (2022). Introduction of '5M1E' mode of quality management in chemical analysis laboratory of special equipment. *Proceedings of the 2022 International Conference on Creative Industry and Knowledge Economy (CIKE 2022)* (pp. 1–4). Atlantis Press. https://doi.org/10.2991/aebmr.k.220404.001

Ju, Y. H. (2021). Integration quality, value co-creation and resilience in logistics service supply chains: moderating role of digital technology. *Industrial Management & Data Systems, 121*, 364–380. ISSN: 0263-5577.

Kilibarda, M., Andrejic, M., & Popovic, V. (2020). Research in logistics service quality: A systematic literature review. *Transport, 35.2*, 224–235. https://doi.org/10.3846/transport.2019.11388

Korzynski, M., & Pacana, A. (2010). Centreless burnishing and influence of its parameters on machining effects. *Journal of Materials Processing Technology*, 1217-1223. https://doi.org/10.1016/j.jmatprotec.2010.03.008

Krynke, M., & Mielczarek, K. (2016). Problems concerning product quality enhancement. *Production Engineering Archives*, 17–20. e-ISSN: 2353-7779.

Kryvoruchko, O., Dmytriiev, I., Poyasnik, G., Shevchenko, I., & Levchenko, I. (2021). Transport and logistics services as a component of the transport complex and their quality management. *Problems and prospects of development of the road transport complex: financing, management, innovation, quality, safety--integrated approach*, 42–62. https://doi.org/10.15587/978-617-7319-45-9.ch4

Kubacki, K., Siemieniako, D., & Brennan, L. (2020). Building positive resilience through vulnerability analysis. *Journal of Social Marketing 10.4, 10*(4), 471–488. https://doi.org/10.1108/JSOCM-09-2019-0142

Küpper, D., Knizek, C., Ryeson, D., & Noecker, J. (2019). *Quality 4.0 takes more than technology*. Retrieved from https://www.bcg.com/publications/2019/quality-4.0-takes-more-than-technology

Le, D. N., Nguyen, H. T., & Truong, P. H. (2020). Port logistics service quality and customer satisfaction: Empirical evidence from Vietnam. *The Asian Journal of Shipping and Logistics*, 89–103. https://doi.org/10.1016/j.ajsl.2019.10.003

Liu, W., Li, J., & Zhou, J. (2023). Organizational non-conformity in an emerging economy: Exploring the non-adoption of credit rating in China. *Asia Pacific Journal of Management*, 1–37. https://doi.org/10.1007/s10490-023-09918-0

Luca, L. (2016). A study on quality analysis measuring process. *Fiabilitate si Durabilitate—Fiability & Durability No 2/ 2016 Editura "Academica Brâncuşi", Târgu Jiu, ISSN 1844 – 640X*, 68–72. ISSN 1844 – 640X.

Luca, L., Pasare, M., & Stancioiu, A. (2017). Study to determine a new model of the Ishikawa diagram for quality improvement. *Fiabilitate si Durabilitate - Fiability & Durability No 1/ Editura "Academica Brâncuşi", Târgu Jiu, ISSN 1844 – 640X*, 250–254. ISSN 1844 – 640X.

Mabiletsa, V. H. (2021). *Reducing non-conformance from foundry products through supplier quality management.* Cape Peninsula University of Technology. https://etd.cput.ac.za/handle/20.500.11838/3406

Magomedov Sh.Sh., B. G. (2018). *Product quality management.* Kyiv.

Maidhili, S., & Nithyanandam, K. (2017). External audit and non conformance. *International Journal of Library Science and Research*, 35–38. ISSN(P): 2250-2351; ISSN(E): 2321-0079.

Meza-Peralta, K., Gonzalez-Feliu, J., Montoya-Torres, J. R., & Khodadad-Saryazdi, A. (2020). A unified typology of urban logistics spaces as interfaces for freight transport: A systematic literature review. *Supply Chain Forum: An International Journal*, 274–289. https://doi.org/10.1080/16258312.2020.1801107

Mickevičiūtė, L. (2023). *Kaizen "veiklos principų taikymas tobulinant kokybės valdymo sistemą biotechnologijų sektoriuje* (Doctoral Dissertation, Vilniaus Gedimino technikos universitetas). https://etalpykla.vilniustech.lt/handle/123456789/107911

Mohamed, Z., & Yusoff, M. S. A. (2021). Malcolm Baldrige approach in University management: An importance—Performance Matrix Analysis (IPMA). *Asian Journal of University Education (AJUE), 17*(2), 273–283. https://doi.org/10.24191/ajue.v17i2.13408

Mohsen, O., Mohamed, Y., & Al-Hussein, M. (2019). Data analytics application for non-conformance reports in a cabinet manufacturing facility. *Modular and Offsite Construction (MOC) Summit Proceedings*, (pp. 341–348). https://doi.org/10.29173/mocs112

Narcevičius, M. (2022). Tiekimo grandinės valdymo iššūkiai. *Jaunasis mokslininkas 2022: konferencijos straipsnių rinkinys= Young scientist 2022: conference proceedings* (pp. 119–126. https://hdl.handle.net/20.500.12259/247855). Kaunas: Vytauto Didžiojo universitetas.

Nascimento-e-Silva, D., Valente, S. B., Simões, C. D., Soares, M. L., & Pereira, D. R. (2020). Variables that affect the product quality: A study in an electronic industry of the Manaus industrial Pole, Brazil. *IOSR Journal of Business and Management (IOSR-JBM)*, 31–37. https://doi.org/10.2139/ssrn.3456114

Natarajan, D. (2017). *ISO 9001 Quality Management Systems.* Springer International Publishing. ISBN978-3-319-54382-6.

Overstreet, R. E., Hazen, B. T., Byrd, T. A., & Hall, D. J. (2013). Innovativeness in the motor carrier industry. *International Journal of Logistics Research and Applications: A Leading Journal of Supply Chain Management*, 367–379. https://doi.org/10.1080/13675567.2013.833597

Pacana, A., Czerniawska, K., & Dwornicka, R. (2021). Analysis of quality control efficiency in the automotive. *Transportation Research Procedia*, 691–698. https://doi.org/10.1016/j.trpro.2021.07.037

Pokrovskaya, O., Fedorenko, R., & Khramtsova, E. (2019). Study of the typology of logistic entities using functional and logistic approach. *Global Challenges and Prospects of the Modern Economic Development, vol 57. European Proceedings of Social and Behavioural Sciences*, 91–101. https://doi.org/10.15405/epsbs.2019.03.10

Puteri, A., & Zagloel, T. Y. (2022). Design of supplier quality monitoring system considering nonconformity level in electronics manufacturing. *Proceedings of the International Conference on Industrial Engineering and Operations Management Nsukka, Nigeria, 5 - 7 April, 2022* (pp. 884–896). IEOM Society International. https://doi.org/10.46254/AF03.20220168

Reinecke, P. C., Wrona, T., Rückert, N., & Fischer, K. (2023). A typology of the collaboration willingness of carriers in hinterland logistics. *International Journal of Physical Distribution & Logistics Management*, 967–984. https://doi.org/10.1108/IJPDLM-07-2022-0216

Rohloff, M. (2009). Case study and maturity model for business process management implementation. *Business Process Management: 7th International Conference* (pp. 128–142). Springer. https://doi.org/10.1007/978-3-642-03848-8_10

Sandberg, E., & Abrahamsson, M. (2011). Logistics capabilities for sustainable competitive advantage. *International Journal of Logistics Research and Applications*, 61–75. https://doi.org/10.1080/13675567.2010.551110

Schatteman, O., Woodhouse, D., & Terino, J. (2020). *Supply chain lessons from Covid-19: Time to refocus on resilience.* BIAN Company. https://www.bain.com/

Sharma, S., Panda, B., Mahapatra, S. S., & Sahu, S. K. (2011). Analysis of barriers for reverse logistics: An Indian perspective. *International Journal of Modeling and Optimization, 1*(2), 101–106. https://doi.org/10.7763/IJMO.2011.V1.18

Shkrobova, V., & Davydov, V. (2006). *Research of errors in determining the causes of inconformity as a factor of increasing product quality.* Pacific National University, ISSN 2310-757X.

Siltori, P. F. (2021). Analysis of ISO 9001 certification benefits in Brazilian companies. *Total Quality Management & Business Excellence*, 1614–1632. https://doi.org/10.1080/14783363.2020.1756246

Sıtkı İlkay, M., & Aslan., E. (2012). The effect of the ISO 9001 quality management system on the performance of SMEs. *International Journal of Quality & Reliability Management 29.7*, 753–778. ISSN: 0265–671X.

Solutions, I. (2024). *ISO tracker*. Retrieved from https://www.isotracker.com: https://www.isotracker.com/products/non-conformance-management-software/

Srinath, P., & Varghese, K. (2023). Identifying and analysing the root causes of quality non-conformance in construction project baseline schedules. *Journal of The Institution of Engineers (India): Series A*, 397–416. https://doi.org/10.1007/s40030-023-00713-0

Świtała, M. (2016). Typology of logistics service providers according to the level of innovativeness. *Handel Wewnętrzny*, 317–333. ISSN0438-5403.

Tillement, S., Cholez, C., & Reverdy., T. (2009). Assessing organizational resilience: an interactionist approach. *M@n@gement, 12*, 230–264. https://doi.org/10.3917/mana.124.0230

Usama, M., & Ramish, A. (2020). Towards a sustainable reverse logistics framework/typologies based on Radio Frequency Identification (RFID). *Operations and Supply Chain Management: an International Journal, 13.3*, 222–232. https://doi.org/10.31387/oscm0420264

Valerievich, V. E., & Vladimirovma, G. A. (2015). Methods 8D as an innovative solutions to the problems associated with the quality of the production process. *Economics and Management of innovative technologies*, https://ekonomika.snauka.ru/2015/08/9629

Valmohammadi, C., & Kalantari, M. (2015). The moderating effect of motivations on the relationship between obtaining ISO 9001 certification and organizational performance. *The TQM Journal*, 503–518. https://doi.org/10.1108/TQM-05-2014-0042

Van der Wiele, A., Dale, B. G., & Williams, A. R. (1997). ISO 9000 series registration to total quality management: the transformation journey. *International Journal of Quality Science*, 236–252. https://doi.org/10.1108/13598539710192601

Vitkus, E. (2020). *Veiksnių skatinančių išmaniųjų technologijų taikymui logistikos paslaugas teikiančiose įmonėse vertinimas* (Doctoral Dissertation, Mykolo Romerio universitetas). https://talpykla.elaba.lt/elaba-fedora/objects/elaba:64444695/datastreams/MAIN/content.

Werbińska-Wojciechowska, S. (2011). On logistics service quality evaluation—Case study. *Logistics and Transport*, 45–56. ISSN: 1734-2015.

Wit, M. (2014). *Exploring the nature of nonconformities: The development of a procedure that classifies construction project nonconformities into risks and non-risks.* University of Twente. https://essay.utwente.nl/66452/

Wit, M. (2014). *Exploring the nature of nonconformities: The development of a procedure that classifies construction project nonconformities into risks and non-risks.* University of Twente. https://essay.utwente.nl/66452/

Xu, H., Zheng, H., Sun, D., Wang, M., & Ye, C. (2024). An integrated framework for enablers in supply chain resilience: Model development and analysis. *IEEE Access*, 42490–42508. https://doi.org/10.1109/ACCESS.2024.3379212

Yingying, S., Lianjuan, H., Jianan, W., & Huimin, W. (2019). Quantum-behaved RS-PSO-LSSVM method for quality prediction in parts production processes. *Concurrency and Computation: Practice and Experience*, e5522. https://doi.org/10.1002/cpe.5522

Yun, C. Z., & Hou, T. B. (2016). PC-based system for benchmarking quality management via ISO 9000 auditing. *Benchmarking for Quality Management & Technology*, 213–220. ISSN: 1351–3036.

Zaika, I., Smolentsev, V., & Fedulov, Y. (2022). *Systematic management of quality and environmental aspects.*

Zaviša, Ž. (2023). Sumanios technologijos ir jų naudojimo galimybės logistikoje. *20-osios jaunųjų mokslininkų konferencijos straipsnių rinkinys*, 168–173. ISSN 2335-7940.

Aligning Management and Employee Perspectives: A Key to Organizational Resilience in Uncertain Times

Ilona Bartuseviciene

Abstract Previous studies have revealed that organizational resilience can be characterized by their intrinsic ability to maintain and regain a dynamically stable state, enabling them to successfully continue their activities after various shocks or function effectively in an environment of continuing threats. Scholars also highlight the prominence of employee engagement, trust, and commitment to strengthening organizational capacity. However, empirical evidence demonstrates that organizational resilience development patterns are commonly explored from the managerial level rather than the employee viewpoint. Consequently, this research aims to analyze the extent to which perceptions regarding the levels of organizational resilience are perceived equivalently from the standpoint of both management and employees. By gathering the data from 591 respondents and applying the structural equation modelling technique, this study elucidated that different dimensions of organizational resilience are positively interconnected in both groups and that perceptions regarding organizational resilience are similar (CMIN = 3.010; CFI = 0.924; TLI = 0.904 and RMSEA = 0.0041). Meanwhile, exogenous effects confirmed no direct effect of network dimension on change-ready & learning in the group of managers. In this group, we only confirmed the direct effects of the network on leadership & culture as well as leadership & culture to change-ready & learning.

Keywords Organizational resilience · Bounce-back · Bounce-forward · Employees · Managers · Model · Uncertainty

JEL Classification D81 · D23 · D83 · C51

I. Bartuseviciene (✉)
Mykolas Romeris University, Vilnius, Lithuania
e-mail: ilona.bartuseviciene@mruni.eu

I. Bartuseviciene et al. (eds.), *Building Economic Resilience*, Contributions to Economics, https://doi.org/10.1007/978-3-031-96428-2_6

1 Introduction

Preparing for uncertainty has become crucial in the past few years as organizations have faced unexpected threats, such as COVID-19, geopolitical issues, energy crises, etc. Due to the fast-changing economic, social, and technological environment, organizational resilience has become a vital object of study. Most researchers distinguish organizational resilience as the ability to appropriately adapt and recover from unusual situations that emerge in the daily field of knowledge and experience. Resilient organizations are also characterized by their intrinsic ability to maintain and regain a dynamically stable state, enabling them to successfully continue their activities after various shocks or function effectively in an environment of continuing threats (Wiig & Fahlbruch, 2019). A resilient system can withstand complex situations and return to its pre-crisis state. Nevertheless, organizations can use the experience gained from shocks as a driving force, thus strengthening the organization further (Pashapour et al., 2019).

Analyzing organizational resilience, it is crucial to become aware of this phenomenon's strategic nature, which must be heightened within all levels of the organization, incorporating managers and employees. Individual-level actions are crucial in the organizational ability to build resilience and become vital in managing uncertainties as they become inevitable (Al-Atwi et al., 2021). Employee engagement leads directly to participation, transparency, trust, and commitment to change, as it is associated with effective communication, leadership, situational awareness, and responsive, proactive posture. Employee engagement enhances problem-focused and emotion-focused coping, which boosts organizational resilience (Liang & Cao, 2021). However, many organizational resilience studies explore the phenomenon exclusively amongst the management/upper seniority level (Filimonau et al., 2020; Gonçalves et al., 2019; Pashapour et al., 2019). Even if the data is collected within various positions, including general staff and middle and senior management, no in-depth analysis benchmarking the perceptions of organizational resilience amongst employees and managers is being analyzed (Chen et al., 2021).

To address the abovementioned limitation, this research provides an overview of organizational resilience from management and employee perspectives. Since we believe that everyone in the organization must understand and engage in activities that reinforce organizational resilience, we aim to identify organizational resilience structure and use it to explore managers' and employees' perceptions of organizational resilience assessment patterns.

First, this study confirms the dimensional structure of organizational resilience assessment. Second, it examines the interrelations between organizational resilience dimensions, i.e., leadership and culture, networks, and change-ready and learning. Third, it delves into organizational resilience from management and employee perspectives. This approach will provide evidence-based knowledge about organizational resilience patterns within different positions and perspectives. Furthermore, the ability to benchmark the results will determine critical gaps recognized differently amongst managers and employees.

This paper is structured as follows: Sect. 2 explores theoretical insights into organizational resilience phenomena, followed by two hypotheses; Sect. 3 introduces the methodology of this study; Sect. 4 examines and interprets the results; Sect. 5 delves into the discussion, and Sect. 6 concludes the paper.

2 Theoretical Background and Hypotheses

The notion of organizational resilience is understood as an attribute that deals with uncertainty and ambiguity and refers to the organizational robustness and ability to prepare (Pashapour et al., 2019; Ramezani & Camarinha-Matos, 2020; Russo & Ciancarini, 2016), adaptiveness to the new conditions after the crisis (Al-Atwi et al., 2021; Bento et al., 2021; Saad & Elshaer, 2020; Sharma et al., 2020) and ability to use the experience accumulated during the crises to gain a competitive advantage (Ruiz-Martin et al., 2018; Altenberg, 2020; Duchek, 2020; Chen et al., 2021; Petersen et al., 2020; Ruiz-Martin et al., 2018). It delves into an organization's ability to manage the leadership & culture, and networks that cultivate the organization's ability to bounce back, i.e., to return to the state before the crisis (Bento et al., 2021; Cantu et al., 2021; Fang et al., 2020; Klimek et al., 2019; Morgan et al., 2019; Sharma et al., 2020; Teixeira & Werther, 2013).

However, other researchers argue that after the crises, organizations never go back to the usual routine and are impelled to excel in their equilibrium and adapt to the new normal (Al-Ghattas & Marjanovic, 2021; Fasey et al., 2021; Hynes et al., 2020; Liu & Tong, 2020; Tortorella et al., 2021; Wong et al., 2019). This ability can be prospered by an organization's commitment to constant learning and eagerness for change. Moreover, both stages are strongly interconnected. Organizational ability to bounce forward cannot be achieved without a successful bounce back and shall be treated as a prerequisite to a successful bounce forward. Supportive evidence indicating positive links between bounce-back and bounce-forward, as well as the interrelation between leadership & culture, networks, and change-ready & learning dimensions, has been identified in research by Bartuseviciene et al. (2022).

Cantu et al. (2021) examined resilience through the five High-Reliability Organizations (HROs) highlighted by Weick and Sutcliffe (2015), where HROs were identified as being capable of anticipating, controlling, and reversing unavoidable events at the moment of occurrence, enabling them to be taken for granted as inevitable phenomena. Nonetheless, Anderson et al. (2021) identify organization resilience as the momentum that goes beyond capacities and can instead be seen as a philosophy for how organizations can manage and face surprises, complexities, and uncertainties in responsible and proactive ways, often even before crises occur. This approach inevitably requires the active involvement of everyone in the organization, regardless of position and seniority. Employee resilience has been a research objective in many studies (Liang & Cao, 2021). Resilient employees successfully deal with the change and setbacks in their work environment, and to which they adapt quickly and successfully. In addition, "learning organizations foster individual resilient capability to adapt to change, which boosts employees' confidence to get involved in the business and display proactive work behavior" (Malik, 2022, p. 12). This evidence-based finding is paramount in today's rapidly changing environment since it addresses the importance of employee adaptiveness and learning and disregards required adjustment to chaotic challenges. Engaged, proactively postured, well-aware, and informed employees contribute to their work performance, organizational commitment, and creativity (Caniëls & Hatak, 2022; Suparna et al., 2024). Since organizational resilience is recognized as a capability that might be developed over time, the importance of leadership has become more vital than ever. Depending on the leadership ability, employee motivation and engagement might increase or decrease, positively or negatively affecting organizational resilience.

Many authors recognize robustness as fundamental momentum for organizational resilience to develop (Pashapour et al., 2019; Ramezani & Camarinha-Matos, 2020; Ruiz-Martin et al., 2018). Robustness provides the conditions for organizations to ensure stability and sustain shocks during turbulent times. Although robustness is considered a prerequisite to organizational resilience, the connection between those two properties is rather complicated. Robustness concerns stability, whereas resilience deals with dynamic stability, i.e., constant transformation and learning, also called transformative resilience, which can be achieved by cementing the organization's preparation, absorption, recovery, and adaptation phases. Further, supporting evidence suggested that the ability to return to the routine, adapt to a changing environment, and overcome dynamic events is insufficient for organizations to thrive. Instead, it becomes necessary for organizations to enhance the learning phase, which allows for growth by constantly learning from oneself and gaining unique experiences (Dahal et al., 2023; Lichtman et al., 2018; Russo & Ciancarini, 2016). Malik (2022) argues that transformative learning organizations cultivate individual resilient capabilities to adapt to change. It also improves employee confidence as long as employees sense that their work is valued and appreciated, are included in decision-making processes, and are well aware of the situation.

Organizational resilience cannot be cultivated without full staff engagement, i.e., senior, upper, and lower management employees. Hence, exploring and assessing organizational resilience from management and employee perspectives becomes vital. We aim to determine organizational resilience by examining endogenous and exogenous dependencies amongst its dimensions. Secondly, we want to examine the behaviours of two groups, i.e., managers and employees. Based on our previous research and the aim of this study, we hypothesize that:

- **Hypothesis 1 (H1).** There exists an interrelation between organizational resilience dimensions, i.e., (a) leadership & culture, (b) networks, and (c) change-ready & learning in the management and employee groups.
- **Hypothesis 2 (H2).** Organizations' managers distinct/perceive/recognize organizational resilience dimensions similar to the rest of the employees.

3 Methodology

3.1 Measurement Instrument

This study applied the dimensional structure of organizational resilience proposed by Brown et al. (2017), i.e., Resilience Benchmark Tool RBT-53. Organizational resilience is assessed through a three-dimensional prism, i.e., (1) leadership & culture; (2) networks; (3) change-ready & learning. RBT-53 includes 13 indicators that are explored by 53 questions. Whitman et al. (2013) developed a shorter version of RBT-53, i.e., RBT-13, which sustains the same 13 indicators suggested by Brown et al. (2017). However, each indicator is presented only by one question and is user-friendlier from the respondent's perspective. BRT-13 validity was proven by Gonçalves et al. (2019). Our study applied the dimensional structure of organizational resilience suggested by Brown et al. (2017) with questions proposed by Whitman et al. (2013) and Gonçalves et al. (2019) in RBT-13 (see Table 1).

Following Brown et al.'s latest update (2017), an 8-point Likert scale has been used, with eight representing strong agreement and one representing strong disagreement.

Further, we test theoretical hypotheses by applying structural equation modelling (SEM). This method has been extensively practiced in various organizational resilience assessment studies (Filimonau et al., 2020; Gonçalves et al., 2019; Melián-Alzola et al., 2020; Saad & Elshaer, 2020; Sobaih et al., 2021; Wong et al., 2020). Following Fan et al. (2016), we consider the model a good fit if at least two fit indices support that. In this analysis, we used the ratio between chi-squared and degree of

Table 1 The structure of the organizational resilience measurement instrument

Organizational resilience dimensions	Indicator distribution in the original BRT-53	Indicator abbreviation
Leadership & culture L&C	Innovation and creativity	L&C1
	Leadership	L&C2
	Decision making	L&C3
	Situation awareness	L&C4
	Staff Engagement	L&C5
Networks N	Effective partnerships	N1
	Leveraging knowledge	N2
	Breaking silos	N3
	Internal resources	N4
Change-ready & learning CR&L	Unity of purpose	CR&L1
	Proactive posture	CR&L2
	Planning strategies	CR&L3
	Stress testing plans	CR&L3

freedom, i.e., χ^2/df (CMIN/DF), Comparative Fit Index (CFI), Tucker–Lewis coefficient (TLI), and Root Mean Square Error of Approximation (RMSEA) to assess model's goodness of fit. The values below 3.0 for CMIN/DF, higher than 0.90 for CFI and TLI, and lower than 0.08 for RMSEA indicate a good fit. *p*-Values below 0.05 were considered to be indicating a good fit to be statistically significant.

3.2 Data Collection and Sample Characteristics

This study intends to identify the organizational resilience framework by exploring the interrelations between organizational resilience dimensions. First, we question whether endogenous relationships associate dimensions with each other. Moreover, we delve into exogenous links amongst dimensions to examine whether they can be independent variables. Second, we discuss organizational resilience assessment patterns rendered by organization managers and nonmanagers.

This study adopts a quantitative methodology, which is generally considered a more reliable and objective method and is often used by various scholars to assess organizations' resilience (Alayed, 2019; Brown et al., 2017; Gonçalves et al., 2019; McManus et al., 2007; Santoro et al., 2018; Sobaih et al., 2021; Zumente & Lāce, 2020).

Data was collected in private and public organizations in Lithuania. The survey was conducted by analyzing data collected using a stratified random sample design. Organizations were divided into homogeneous groups according to the number of employees: (1) micro organizations (up to 9 employees), (2) small organizations (10–49 employees), (3) medium-sized organizations (50–250 employees), and (4) large organizations (over 250 employees). The selection of the organizations was carried out using the database of organizations operating in Lithuania. On June 15, 2021, 250 519 organizations were operating in Lithuania. Organizations in each group have been selected using a random number generator. According to official statistics of the Lithuanian Department of Statistics, quotas were allocated to 4 groups of organizations: (1) micro organizations (83% of the total sample), (2) small organizations (12% of the total sample), (3) medium-sized organizations (4% of the total sample), (4) large organizations (1% of the total sample). Quotas were completed by interviewing the managers of organizations or corresponding positions with a managerial function (further –manager) and nonmanagers (further– employees).

As mentioned, in this study, we used an already validated questionnaire proposed by Whitman et al. (2013) and Gonçalves et al. (2019), which professional interpreters carefully translated into the Lithuanian language. In addition, a pilot study was conducted to determine whether the respondents understood the questionnaire well by sending it to twenty randomly selected respondents. We have received 13 responses, which accounted for a response rate of 65%. There were no significant discrepancies or misinterpretations of the questionnaire. Therefore, we have made no adoptions to its original version. The response rate of 65% during the pilot study gave us the knowledge to disseminate the questionnaire to no less than 700 organizations to ensure the required minimum number of respondents to the survey. 95% of data reliability (with a maximum statistical error of 5% of the survey results) was used to determine the minimum number of respondents to the survey, i.e., 384. The data was collected from the period of August to October 2021. Four hundred thirty-four organizations participated in the study with 591 responses, i.e., 434 (73.4%) organization managers and 157 (26.6%) employees. Most of the organizations included in the survey have been operating in the field for more than six years, i.e., 13.4% have been working in the area for 6–10 years, 38.2%—11–20 years, 44.9% have been in the area for more than 21 years. Only 3.4% of organizations have been in the area for up to five years. Depending on the information available about the organizations, they were contacted by e-mail or phone (Table 2).

4 Data Analysis

4.1 Descriptive Statistics

Statistical analysis revealed that organizational resilience levels differ amongst organizations depending on the sector they represent, their size, years spent in the field, etc. The highest average scores of overall organizational resilience have been demonstrated amongst the category of local government organizations, i.e., 7.23 (SD = 0.89). On the contrary, organizations representing the central government account for the lowest average score of organizational resilience, i.e., 5.60 (SD = 1.39).

The averages of leadership & culture and change-ready & learning dimensions are similar. However, the averages of the network dimension have been considerably lower than the other two. Charitable trust and privately held LLCs assess their network dimension respectfully 4.20 (SD = 1.2) and 4.96 (SD = 1.41); the highest averages in network dimension have been demonstrated by local government and government-owned organizations, respectfully 7.10 (SD = 1.09) and 5.99 (SD = 1.36) (see Fig. 1).

Medium-sized organizations that employ 50–25 employees reported the highest results of organizational resilience. On the contrary, large organizations that employ more than 250 employees demonstrate the lowest results, with an average score of 5.91 (SD = 1.23). Analysis of the results amongst different organizational resilience dimensions revealed that micro organizations (up to 10 employees) rank the highest in leadership & culture, i.e., 6.67 (SD = 1.03), and change-ready & learning, i.e., 6.74 (SD = 1.13). However, this category has also demonstrated the lowest results in network dimension, i.e., 5.03 (SD = 1.44) (see Fig. 2). It could be explained by the fact that smaller organizations tend to be more flexible and more ready to adapt to new conditions in the short run. However, smaller organizations usually do not invest enough resources to boost their robustness. Therefore, it might be challenging to sustain resilience in the long run.

Table 2 Descriptive analysis of the sample

Sector	Frequency	Percent
Professional. Scientific. Technical. Administrative and Supportive Services	76	17.5
Retail trade and Accommodation	51	11.8
Wholesale trade	45	10.4
Construction	42	9.7
Arts. Recreation. and Other Services	38	8.8
Manufacturing	36	8.3
Health care and Social Assistance	29	6.7
Rental. Hiring and Real Estate Services	20	4.6
Education and Training	18	4.1
Information. Media and Telecommunications	15	3.5
Agriculture. Forestry. Fishing	13	3.0
Transport. Postal and Warehousing	13	3.0
Financial and Insurance Services	12	2.8
Public Administration and Safety	9	2.1
Mining	7	1.6
Electricity. Gas. Water and Waste services	7	1.6
Other	3	0.7
Total	434	100.0
The gender of the respondents	**Frequency**	**Percent**
Female	310	52.5
Male	281	47.5
Total	591	100.00
Type	**Frequency**	**Percent**
Privately held LLC	282	65.0
Individual proprietorship	69	15.9
Association	23	5.3
Public institution	23	5.3
Publicly listed LLC	11	2.5
Government-owned organization	10	2.3
Cooperative	5	1.2
Local government	4	0.9
Partnership	2	0.5
Central Government	2	0.5
Other	2	0.5
Charitable trust	1	0.2
Total	434	100.0

(continued)

Table 2 (continued)

The education level of the respondents	Frequency	Percent
Higher (university: master's degree or equivalent)	256	43.3
Higher (university: bachelor) college)	170	28.8
College	57	9.6
Higher (technical)	48	8.1
Middle	25	4.3
Professional (special secondary)	19	3.2
Graduate (doctor of science)	16	2.7
Total	591	100

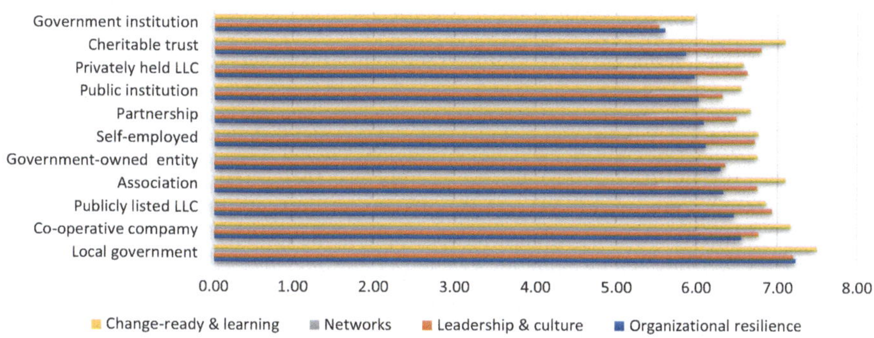

Fig. 1 Organizational resilience assessment

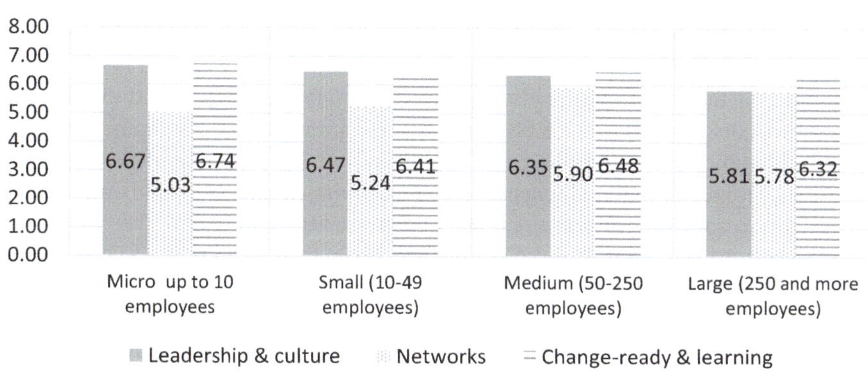

Fig. 2 Organizational resilience by the size of an organization

Organizations operating in the field for less than a year are the most resilient. The average overall resilience score in this category is 7.08 (SD = 1.01). The lowest resilience score has been found amongst the organizations operating in the field for

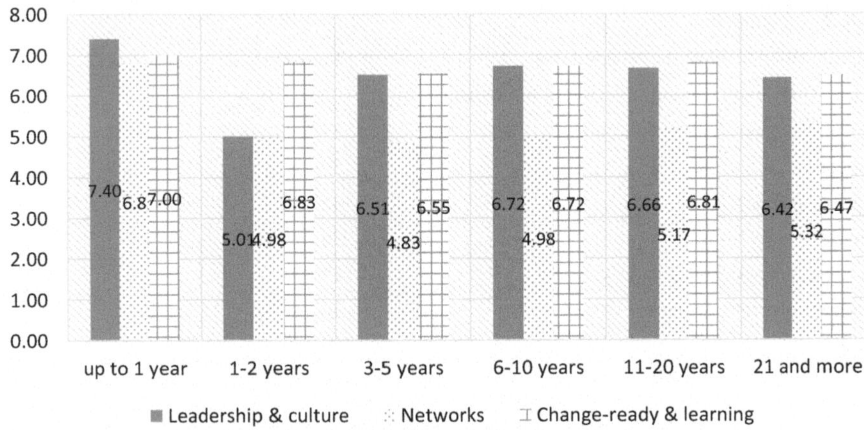

Fig. 3 Organizational resilience by the year's organization is operating in the field

1–2 years, i.e., 5.42 (SD = 1.03). The older organizations are, the more resilient they become, respectfully 3–5 years—5.88 (SD = 1.06), 6–10 years—6.05 (SD = 1.06), and 11–20 years—6.12 (SD = 1.02). However, there is a slight decrease in the average score amongst the organizations operating in the field for more than 21 years, i.e., 6.01 (SD = 1.06). The results also revealed similar averages amongst different dimensions of organizational resilience (see Fig. 3).

The average score of organizational resilience in different sectors varied from 5.10 to 6.82. The highest results were demonstrated in financial and insurance services, i.e., 6.82 (SD = 0.7), information, media, and telecommunications, 6.49 (SD = 0.7), and health care and social assistance, 6.44 (SD = 092). The lowest performance was revealed amongst mining, i.e., 5.10 (SD = 0.7), manufacturing, 5.77 (SD = 1.02), and construction, 5.77 (SD = 1.17) (See Fig. 4).

Analysis of organizational resilience results amongst managers and employees showed little discrepancy, i.e., 6.08 (SD = 0.98) amongst the managers and 5.96 (SD = 1.21) amongst the employees. In addition, we have examined the averages of different organizational resilience dimensions amongst managers and employees, i.e., leadership and culture, networks, and change-ready and learning (see Fig. 5).

The average leadership & culture assessed by managers is 6.72 (SD = 0.95), compared to 6.04 (SD = 1.46) evaluated by the employees. 30% of managers strongly agree that their staff is rewarded for thinking outside the box, compared to 18% of employees. Also, 58% of managers strongly agree that they can make tough decisions quickly, compared to only 29% of employees. 40% of the managers strongly agree that they are mindful of how the crisis could affect them, and only 29% of employees think the same. Only 24% of employees strongly agree that managers actively listen to the problems, compared to 45% of the managers. Results reveal a slight discrepancy in how leadership & culture have been assessed amongst the managers and employees. This could be explained by the subjectivity factor, which is inevitable during the data

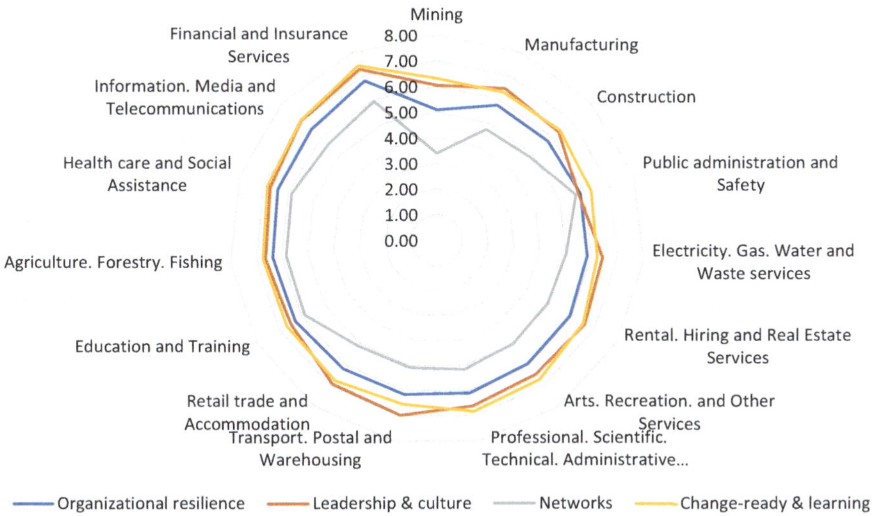

Fig. 4 Organizational resilience by sector

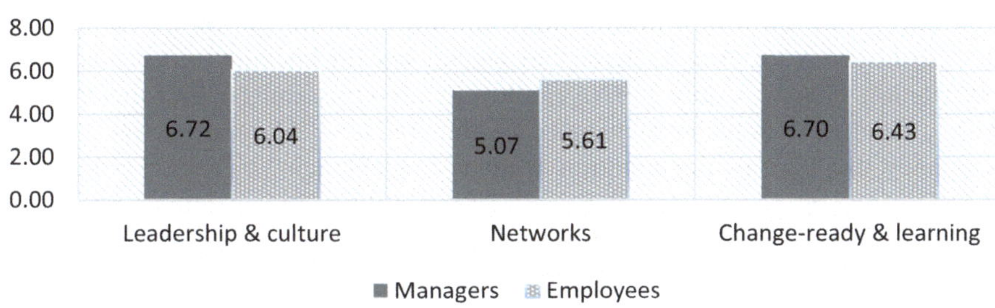

Fig. 5 Organizational resilience assessment by managers and employees

collection process using the survey method. However, a slight discrepancy could also demonstrate the lack of leadership from the top management.

The average scores of the network dimension are the lowest compared to the other dimensions amongst managers and employees, respectively 5.07 (SD = 1.45) and 5.61 (SD = 1.38) (see fig. 5). Only 19% of the managers and 18% of employees strongly agree that they are building relationships with the organizations they might have to work within a crisis. Nevertheless, only 12% of the managers and 15% of employees strongly agree that their organization maintains sufficient resources to absorb unexpected changes, compared to 10% of managers and 3% of employees who strongly disagree with this statement. In addition, 32% of managers and 11% of employees strongly disagree that emergency plans must be practiced and tested to be effective. This momentum is essential for organizational readiness for unexpected threats. However, results show that organizations, especially their managers, do not consider it crucial. The lowest averages of the importance of emergency plan practice in the organization have been declared in the mining, i.e., 1.00 (SD = 1.01), retail trade and accommodation—3.04 (SD = 1.77), manufacturing—3.16 (SD = 2.09), rental and real state sectors—3.30 (SD = 2.09). On the contrary, the highest average scores are demonstrated in public administration at 5.16 (SD = 2.24), education and training at 4.76 (2.29), and health care and social assistance sectors at 4.63 (SD = 2.39).

The change-ready & learning dimension is influential and significant for organizational bounce-forward. It deals with the organization's ability to use the lessons learned during the crisis and enhances its ability to alter its equilibrium and adapt to the new normal (Floetgen et al., 2021). The results have revealed that organizations from the financial and insurance service sector scored the highest in change-ready & learning averages, i.e., 7.48 (SD = 0.61), followed by the information, media, and telecommunications sector—7.05 (SD = 0.68), health care and social assistance—6.88 (SD = 0.94). Lower results have been confirmed in the public administration and safety industry—6.25 (SD = 1.35), wholesale and trade—6.31 (SD = 1.25), and manufacturing—6.33 (SD = 1.12). A little discrepancy has been discovered within organizations with various years of experience in the industry, i.e., the average range of change-ready & learning varies from 7.00 (up to 1 year of experience) to 6.47 (more than 21 of experience). To assess change-ready & learning, the respondents were asked if they knew how to respond to unexpected problems. 50% of managers and 54% of employees strongly agree they would have the knowledge needed during the disruption. However, only 55% of employees strongly agree or agree that there is a sense of teamwork in their organizations, compared to 73% of the managers. Such discrepancy should draw the attention of upper management since solid collaboration and teamwork are considered critical areas in building organizational resilience (Chaudhary et al., 2019; Franken et al., 2021). The lowest average score has been indicated amongst organizations in public administration and safety, i.e., 5.66 (SD = 2.22), electricity, gas, water, and waste service—6.00 (SD = 1.and 48), education, and training—6.37 (SD = 1.70). Respondents from financial and insurance feel more positively about a sense of teamwork in their organizations, i.e., 7.57 (SD = 0.65), also information, media, and telecommunication—7.15 (SD = 0.87), retail trade—7.02 (SD = 1.46).

To sum up, the level of organizational resilience differs amongst organizations in terms of different characteristics such as industry, size, years spent in the field, etc. Organizations operating in the field for less than a year tend to be more resilient than those in the area for over twenty years. Also, medium-sized organizations demonstrate the highest average rates of overall organizational resilience. On the contrary, large organizations are the least resilient. The highest results of organizational resilience were encountered in the financial and insurance sectors, information, media, telecommunications, and healthcare sectors, and the lowest—were in mining, manufacturing, and construction services. Minor discrepancies were discovered by analyzing the differences in organizational resilience within different dimensions amongst the managers and the employees. However, the overall assessment of organizational resilience amongst these two groups has not been significantly different.

4.2 Research Findings

Firstly, we applied the CFA method to confirm the structure of organizational resilience. Kaiser–Meyer–Olkin (KMO) measure of sampling adequacy was 0.895, i.e., greater than 0.6. Since KMO examines how factors explain each other, it supports that the questionnaire used to collect our data was valid at a 99% significance level. Thus, the sample was considered adequate for the factor analysis. The Chi-Square of Bartlett's sphere test was 2508.506 with 78 degrees of freedom and a *p*-Value <0.001.

The application of principal component analysis (PCA) extracted three components with a cumulative variance contribution rate of 56.851% (see Table 3). The first component, leadership, and culture, explained 25.3% of the total variance, the second, networks, 20.1%, and the third, change-ready and learning, 11.5%.

5 Hypothesis Testing

Hypothesis 1 (H1) There exists an interrelation between organizational resilience dimensions, i.e., (a) leadership & culture, (b) networks, and (c) change-ready & learning in the management and employee groups.

After CFA, which suggested the structure of organizational resilience (see Table 3), we applied SEM to test our hypotheses. It analyses whether the theoretical structural relationships between the dimensions are empirically meaningful. We used SEM separately in groups of organizations' managers and employees. Two models explaining the interrelations amongst the different sizes of organizational resilience have been identified and evaluated (Table 4).

The results of Model 1 recognize that all three organizational resilience dimensions have endogenous positive associations with each other. The model goodness of fit was evaluated based on the following indices: CMIN = 3.010; CFI = 0.924; TLI = 0.904 and RMSEA = 0.0041; *p*-Values less than 0.05 (see Table 5). *p*-Values in both groups, i.e., managers and employees, are less than 0.05, indicating the significance at the 1% level (see Table 5). Therefore, we accept Model 1 as a good fit model that recognizes positive endogenous relationships amongst all three dimensions (see Table 4).

Model 2 analyzed the *exogenous effects* of organizational resilience dimensions in groups of managers and employees. The Model goodness of fit was evaluated based on the following indices: CMIN = 3.010; CFI = 0.924; TLI = 0.904 and RMSEA = 0.0041; *p*-Values less than 0.05 have been estimated only in the group of employees. However, SEM results in the management group recognized that only the leadership & culture dimensions are positively associated with change-ready & learning. The network dimension directly affects leadership & culture; thus, there is no direct effect on change-ready & learning (see Table 5). Therefore, we reject

Table 3 Rotated component matrix

Rotated Component Matrix			
	Components		
	Leadership & culture	Networks	Change-ready & learning
L&C1—Innovation and creativity 14.3	0.674		
L&C2—Leadership 9.5	0.589		
L&C3—Decision making 13.2	0.559		
L&C4—Situation awarenes 11.4	0.545		
L&C5—Planning strategies 21.4	0.512		
N1—Effective partnerships 15.3		0.697	
N2—Proactive posture 20.3		0.697	
N3—Unity of purpose 19.2		0.668	
N4—Internal resources 18.2		0.614	
N5—Stress testing plans 26.1		0.531	
CR&L1—Staff engagement 10.2			0.743
CR&L2—Breaking silos 17.2			0.710
CR&L3—Leveraging knowledge 16.1			0.422

Extraction Method Principal component analysis
Rotation Method Varimax with Kaiser normalization
[a]Rotation converged in 8 iterations

Model 2 as a good fit model that explains the exogenous effects of the network to change-ready & learning from a management perspective.

Based on these results, we accept H1 and conclude that all three dimensions ***have endogenous effects*** *on themselves, i.e., all the dimensions—(a) leadership & culture, (b) networks, (c) change-ready & learning are associated with each other in both groups, i.e., managers and employees.* ***Exogenous effects*** *exist amongst organizational resilience dimensions in the employee group only; therefore, we will not continue examining the patterns of exogenous effects within those two groups further in this study.*

Hypothesis 2 (H2) Organizations' managers distinct/perceive/recognize organizational resilience dimensions similar to the rest of the employees.

Table 4 Organizational resilience models

Models/ Indices	CMIN/DF	CFI	TITLE	RMSEA	Model description	Model Fit
A value indicating a good fit	<3.0	>0.9	>0.9	<0.08	–	–
Model 1	3.010	0.924	0.904	0.041	All three dimensions have endogenous effects on themselves	Accepted
Model 2	3.010	0.924	0.904	0.041	All three dimensions have exogenous effects on each other	Accept partially

We will continue the comparison of the perceptions about organizational resilience dimensions amongst the managers and employees, examining interrelations in Model 1. It has been identified as a good fit model that explains the interrelations amongst the dimensions in both groups by recognizing positive endogenous relationships amongst three dimensions, i.e., (a) leadership & culture, (b) networks, (c) change-ready & learning (see Fig. 6).

Minor discrepancies occur benchmarking the correlations amongst the dimensions in both groups, except for the correlations amongst change-ready & learning and network. The strength of correlations between those two dimensions in the management groups is average. Meanwhile, the employee group estimated strong correlations between these two dimensions (see Table 6).

Analysis of the results revealed strong effects of leadership & culture dimensions on variables such as situation awareness (0.9), decision-making (0.722), and leadership (0.813) in the employee group. Thus, the management group identified the medium-size effect of leadership & culture on situation awareness (0.715). The network dimension has a medium-sized effect on the unity of purpose indicator (0.839) in the employee group. Meanwhile, medium-size effects on the unity of purpose dimension (0.795) and proactive posture (0.774) have been recognized in the management group. Change-ready & learning dimension has below medium size effects on staff engagement, breaking silos, and leveraging knowledge indicators in both groups (see Table 7).

Based on the results, we accept H2, which hypothesizes that organizational managers perceive organizational resilience dimensions similar to employees. Although we have observed minor discrepancies between these two groups, they

Table 5 Statistical significance of organizational resilience structure model

Dimensions/Indicators	Link	Dimensions	Model 1		Model 2	
			Managers	Employees	Managers	Employees
			Accepted		Accept partially	
L&C	<---	N			0.541*** (0.062)	1.147*** (0.171)
CR&L	<---	L&C			0.782*** (0.105)	0.203*** (0.046)
CR&L	<---	N				0.171 $p-$ 0.004
Situation awareness	<---	L&C	1.000	1.000	0.004 (0.057)	1.000
Planning strategies	<---	L&C	1.044*** (0.088)	0.512*** (0.062)	1.044*** (0.088)	0.512*** (0.062)
Decision making	<---	L&C	0.553*** (0.059)	0.676*** (0.063)	0.553 *** (0.059)	0.676 *** (0.063)
Leadership	<---	L&C	0.845*** (0.078)	0.960*** (0.073)	0.845*** (0.078)	0.960*** (0.073)
Innovation and creativity	<---	L&C	1.048*** (0.116)	0.816*** (0.086)	1.048*** (0.116)	0.816*** (0.089)
Internal resources	<---	N	1.000	1.000	1.000	1.000
Stress testing plans	<---	N	0.724*** (0.114)	1.204*** (0.192)	0.724*** (0.114)	1.204*** (0.192)
Unity of purpose	<---	N	1.217*** (0.114)	1.316*** (0.167)	1.217*** (0.114)	1.316*** (0.167)
Proactive posture	<---	N	1.324*** (0.125)	1.024*** (0.150)	1.324*** (0.125)	1.024*** (0.150)
Effective partnerships	<---	N	0.924*** (0.123)	1.188*** (0.172)	0.924*** (0.123)	1.188*** (0.172)
Staff engagement	<---	CR&L	1.000	1,000	1.000	1.000
Breaking silos	<---	CR&L	1.238*** (0.137)	2.898*** (0.571)	1.238*** (0.137)	2.898*** (0.571)
Leveraging knowledge	<---	CR&L	1.452*** (0.146)	1.962*** (0.399)	1.452*** (0.146)	1.962*** (0.399)

*** indicates significance at a 1% level

are insignificant and bring similar trends in organizational resilience assessment to light.

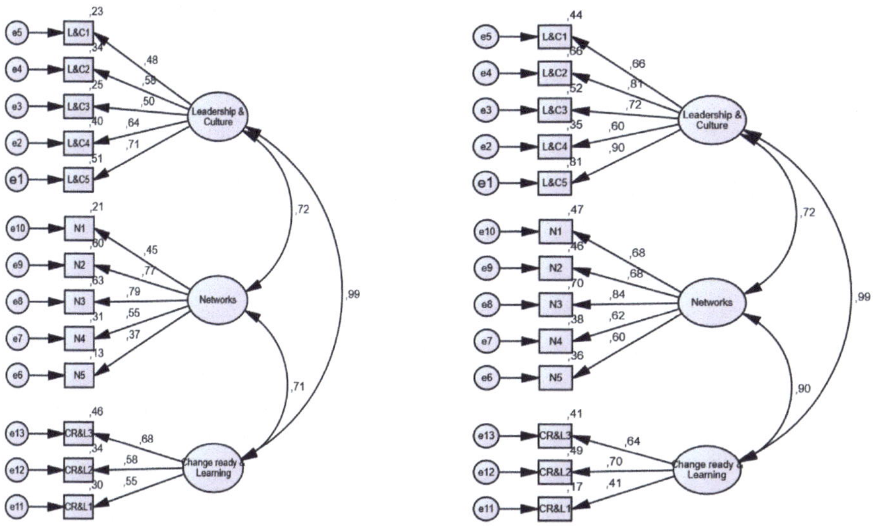

Fig. 6 Interrelation between organizational resilience dimensions in the managers (left) and employee (right) groups

Table 6 Correlation analysis

Dimensions	Links	Dimensions	Management Group	Employee group
			Estimates	
Leadership & culture	< − >	Network	0.716	0.720
Change-ready & learning	< − >	Leadership & culture	0.991	0.994
Change-ready & learning	< − >	Network	0.712	0.900

6 Conclusions

Firstly, this study confirms organizational resilience structure, which consists of three dimensions, i.e., (a) leadership & culture, (b) networks, and (c) change-ready & learning. Secondly, we examine the interrelations amongst the dimensions, and thirdly, we delve into organizational resilience assessment benchmarks amongst the managers and employees. This study revealed that organizational resilience dimensions have endogenous effects on each other and are statistically significant in both groups. Correlation analysis demonstrated a positive relationship between leadership & culture and change-ready & learning amongst managers and employees. Both groups have observed high correlations between leadership & culture, and network.

Table 7 Standardized regression weights between the management and employee groups

Indicators	Link	Abbreviations	Estimate	
			Managers	Employees
Situation awareness	<---	L&C	**0.715**	**0.900**
Planning strategies	<---	L&C	0.636	0.595
Decision making	<---	L&C	0.496	**0.722**
Leadership	<---	L&C	0.583	**0.813**
Innovation and creativity	<---	L&C	0.480	0.662
Internal resources	<---	N	0.553	0.619
Unity of purpose	<---	N	**0.795**	**0.839**
Proactive posture	<---	N	**0.774**	0.675
Effective partnerships	<---	N	0.454	0.682
Stress testing plans	<---	N	0.367	0.604
Staff engagement	<---	CR&L	0.547	0.412
Breaking silos	<---	CR&L	0.581	0.698
Leveraging knowledge	<---	CR&L	0.680	0.640

Meanwhile, insignificant discrepancies have been identified by analyzing correlations between change-ready & learning and network dimensions. A very high correlation has been observed in the employee group, followed by a high correlation in the management group. Results also revealed that the increase of leadership & culture dimension by one standard deviation would have a strong size effect on employee situation awareness and leadership, followed by a medium effect on management situation awareness and employee decision-making. An increase in network dimensions would strongly affect the unity of purpose in both groups and a proactive posture in the management group. The increase of change-ready & learning dimensions by one standard deviation would have a medium size effect on all the indicators, i.e., staff engagement, breaking silos, and leveraging knowledge in both groups. Based on the results, we argue that organizational resilience is perceived similarly in both groups, and no significant discrepancies have been identified.

Analysis of the exogenous effects amongst the dimensions revealed statistical significance dimensions. Therefore, we argue that positive exogenous effects exist amongst all three dimensions of the employee group. However, the data in the management group did not support this model. The results revealed that the network dimension only directly affects the leadership & culture dimension, thus no direct effect on change-ready & learning. For this reason, this study did not further examine benchmarking of exogenous effects within dimensions amongst management and employee groups.

7 Theoretical and Practical Implications

7.1 Theoretical Implications

The growing prominence of organizational resilience studies outlines its importance amongst various scholars. In this study, we confirmed the structure of organizational resilience that has already been recognized by other researchers (Brown et al., 2017; Gonçalves et al., 2019; Whitman et al., 2013). Nevertheless, we explored exogenous and endogenous effects amongst organizational resilience dimensions in two groups, i.e., managers and employees. Study results revealed that all three dimensions have positive endogenous effects on each other. These findings contribute to the scientific literature on organizational resilience by confirming the structure of organizational resilience, which other scholars have already explored. The results show that different dimensions of organizational resilience are positively associated in both groups and that perceptions regarding organizational resilience are similar. Meanwhile, exogenous effects confirmed no direct effect of network dimension on change-ready & learning in the group of managers. In this group, we only witnessed the direct effects of the network on leadership & culture as well as leadership & culture to change-ready & learning.

7.2 Practical Implications

This study recognized the differences and similarities in the perceptions amongst managers and employees about organizational resilience. The results confirmed very strong and strong correlations amongst all three dimensions of organizational resilience in both groups. It also identified no significant difference in how both groups assessed and perceived organizational resilience. This result is essential from a management perspective as it provides evidence-based statements about recognizing the importance of organizational resilience amongst employees. Enhancement of organization resilience dimensions would significantly impact employee situation awareness, leadership, unity of purpose, and decision-making, followed by a lower impact on the rest of the indicators. This result is meaningful, supporting the (Malik, 2022) study, where he argues about the imperative of employee ability to deal with change and setbacks in their work performance and the competence to adapt quickly and successfully.

References

Al-Atwi, A. A., Amankwah-Amoah, J., & Khan, Z. (2021). Micro-foundations of organizational design and sustainability: The mediating role of learning ambidexterity. *International Business Review, 30*(1), Article 101656. https://doi.org/10.1016/j.ibusrev.2019.101656

Altenberg, P. (2020). Improving economic resilience through trade—Should we rely on our own supply? (Report No. 51). National Board of Trade Sweden.

Alayed, S. (2019). The impact of strategic human resource management on organizational resilience: An empirical study on hospitals. *Business: Theory and Practice, 20*, 179–186. https://doi.org/10.3846/btp.2019.17

Al-Ghattas, H., & Marjanovic, O. (2021). *Business analytics capabilities for organisational resilience*. https://doi.org/10.24251/HICSS.2021.026

Anderson, B., Poeschel, F., & Ruhs, M. (2021). Rethinking labor migration: Covid-19, essential work, and systemic resilience. *Comparative Migration Studies, 9*(1). https://doi.org/10.1186/s40878-021-00252-2

Bartuseviciene, I., Butkus, M., & Schiuma, G. (2022). Modelling organizational resilience structure: Insights to assess resilience integrating bounce-back and bounce-forward. *European Journal of Innovation Management, 27*(1), 153–169. https://doi.org/10.1108/EJIM-04-2022-0180

Bento, F., Garotti, L., & Mercado, M. P. (2021). Organizational resilience in the oil and gas industry: A scoping review. *Safety Science, 133*, Article 105036. https://doi.org/10.1016/j.ssci.2020.105036

Brown, C., Seville, E., & Vargo, J. (2017). Measuring the organizational resilience of critical infrastructure providers: A New Zealand case study. *International Journal of Critical Infrastructure Protection, 18*, 37–49. https://doi.org/10.1016/j.ijcip.2017.05.002

Caniëls, M. C. J., & Hatak, I. (2022). Employee resilience: Considering both the social and economic sides of leader-follower exchanges in conjunction with the dark side of followers' personalities. *The International Journal of Human Resource Management, 33*(2), 297–328. https://doi.org/10.1080/09585192.2019.1695648

Cantu, J., Tolk, J., Fritts, S., & Gharehyakheh, A. (2021). Interventions and measurements of highly reliable/resilient organization implementations: A literature review. *Applied Ergonomics, 90*, Article 103241. https://doi.org/10.1016/j.apergo.2020.103241

Chaudhary, M., McCarty, J., Shah, S., Hashmi, Z., Caterson, E., Goldberg, S., Goolsby, C., Haider, A., & Goralnick, E. (2019). Building community resilience: A scalable model for hemorrhage-control training at a mass gathering site, using the RE-AIM framework. *SURGERY, 165*(4), 795–801. https://doi.org/10.1016/j.surg.2018.10.001

Chen, R., Xie, Y., & Liu, Y. (2021). Defining, conceptualizing, and measuring organizational resilience: A multiple case study. *Sustainability, 13*(5), 2517. https://doi.org/10.3390/su13052517

Dahal, R. K., Ghimire, B., Karki, D., & Joshi, S. P. (2023). Elevating job search effectiveness: The significance of self-directed learning and self-control. *Intellectual Economics, 17*(2), Article 2. https://doi.org/10.13165/IE-23-17-2-08

Duchek, S. (2020). Organizational resilience: A capability-based conceptualization. *Abstract Business Research, 13*(1), 215–246. https://doi.org/10.1007/s40685-019-0085-7

Fan, Y., Chen, J., Shirkey, G., John, R., Wu, S. R., Park, H., & Shao, C. (2016). Applications of structural equation modeling (SEM) in ecological studies: An updated review. *Ecological Processes, 5*(1), 19. https://doi.org/10.1186/s13717-016-0063-3

Fang, S. (Echo), Prayag, G., Ozanne, L. K., & de Vries, H. (2020). Psychological capital, coping mechanisms, and organizational resilience: Insights from the 2016 Kaikoura earthquake, New Zealand. *Tourism Management Perspectives, 34*, 100637. https://doi.org/10.1016/j.tmp.2020.100637

Fasey, K. J., Sarkar, M., Wagstaff, C. R. D., & Johnston, J. (2021). Defining and characterizing organizational resilience in elite sport. *Psychology of Sport and Exercise, 52*, Article 101834. https://doi.org/10.1016/j.psychsport.2020.101834

Filimonau, V., Derqui, B., & Matute, J. (2020). The COVID-19 pandemic and organizational commitment of senior hotel managers. *International Journal of Hospitality Management, 91*, Article 102659. https://doi.org/10.1016/j.ijhm.2020.102659

Floetgen, R. J., Strauss, J., Weking, J., Hein, A., Urmetzer, F., Böhm, M., & Krcmar, H. (2021). Introducing platform ecosystem resilience: Leveraging mobility platforms and their ecosystems for the new normal during COVID-19. *European Journal of Information Systems, 30*(3), 304–321. https://doi.org/10.1080/0960085X.2021.1884009

Franken, E., Plimmer, G., Malinen, S., Bryson, J., & Berman, E. (2021). Building people up growth-oriented leadership in the public sector. *Australian Journal of Public Administration, 80*(4), 661–689. https://doi.org/10.1111/1467-8500.12520

Gonçalves, L., Navarro, J. B., & Sala, R. (2019). Spanish validation of the benchmark resilience tool (short-form version) to evaluate organizational resilience. *Safety Science, 111*, 94–101. https://doi.org/10.1016/j.ssci.2018.09.015

Hynes, W., Trump, B., Love, P., & Linkov, I. (2020). Bouncing forward: A resilience approach to dealing with COVID-19 and future systemic shocks. *Environment Systems and Decisions, 40*(2), 174–184. https://doi.org/10.1007/s10669-020-09776-x

Klimek, P., Varga, J., Jovanovic, A. S., & Székely, Z. (2019). Quantitative resilience assessment in emergency response reveals how organizations trade efficiency for redundancy. *Safety Science, 113*, 404–414. https://doi.org/10.1016/j.ssci.2018.12.017

Lee, A. (Stephenson). (n.d.). *Benchmark resilience: A study of the resilience of organizations in the Auckland region.* Retrieved May 21, 2021, from https://www.academia.edu/226115/Benchmark_Resilience_A_study_of_the_resilience_of_organisations_in_the_Auckland_Region

Liang, F., & Cao, L. (2021). Linking employee resilience with organizational resilience: The roles of coping mechanism and managerial resilience. *Psychology Research and Behavior Management, 14*, 1063–1075. https://doi.org/10.2147/PRBM.S318632

Lichtman, M., Vondal, M. T., Clancy, T. C., & Reed, J. H. (2018). Antifragile Communications. In *IEEE Systems Journal* (Vol. 12, Issue 1, pp. 659–670). IEEE-INST Electrical Electronics Engineers INC. https://doi.org/10.1109/JSYST.2016.2517164

Liu, J., & Tong, E. (2020). The relation between official whatsapp-distributed covid-19 news exposure and psychological symptoms: Cross-Sectional survey study. *Journal of Medical Internet Research, 22*(9). https://doi.org/10.2196/22142

Malik, P. (2022). Measuring the impact of learning organization on proactive work behavior: Mediating role of employee resilience. *Asia-Pacific Journal of Business Administration, ahead-of-print*(ahead-of-print). https://doi.org/10.1108/APJBA-10-2020-0379

McManus, S., Seville, E., Brunsdon, D., & Vargo, J. (2007). *Resilience management: A framework for assessing and improving the resilience of organisations.*

Melián-Alzola, L., Fernández-Monroy, M., & Hidalgo-Peñate, M. (2020). Hotels in contexts of uncertainty: Measuring organizational resilience. *Tourism Management Perspectives, 36*, Article 100747. https://doi.org/10.1016/j.tmp.2020.100747

Morgan, K. H., Libby, N. E., Weaver, A. K., & Cai, C. (2019). Development of an early warning resilience survey for healthcare organizations. *Heliyon, 5*(10), Article e02670. https://doi.org/10.1016/j.heliyon.2019.e02670

Pashapour, S., Bozorgi-Amiri, A., Azadeh, A., Ghaderi, S. F., & Keramati, A. (2019). Performance optimization of organizations considering economic resilience factors under uncertainty: A case study of a petrochemical plant. *Journal of Cleaner Production, 231*, 1526–1541. https://doi.org/10.1016/j.jclepro.2019.05.171

Petersen, L., Lange, D., & Theocharidou, M. (2020). Who cares what it means? Practical reasons for using the word resilience with critical infrastructure operators. *Reliability Engineering & System Safety, 199* Article 106872. https://doi.org/10.1016/j.ress.2020.106872

Ramezani, J., & Camarinha-Matos, L. M. (2020). Approaches for resilience and antifragility in collaborative business ecosystems. *Technological Forecasting and Social Change, 151*, Article 119846. https://doi.org/10.1016/j.techfore.2019.119846

Ruiz-Martin, C., Lopez-Paredes, A., & Wainer, G. (2018). What we know and do not know about organizational resilience. *International Journal of Production Management and Engineering, 6*, 11. https://doi.org/10.4995/ijpme.2018.7898

Russo, D., & Ciancarini, P. (2016). A Proposal for an Antifragile software Manifesto | Elsevier enhanced reader. *Procedia Computer Science, 83*(2016), 982–987. https://doi.org/10.1016/j.procs.2016.04.196

Saad, S. K., & Elshaer, I. A. (2020). Justice and trust's role in employees' resilience and business' continuity: Evidence from Egypt. *Tourism Management Perspectives, 35*, Article 100712. https://doi.org/10.1016/j.tmp.2020.100712

Santoro, G., Bertoldi, B., Giachino, C., & Candelo, E. (2018). Exploring the relationship between entrepreneurial resilience and success: The moderating role of stakeholders' engagement. *Journal of Business Research*, 119. https://doi.org/10.1016/j.jbusres.2018.11.052

Sharma, A., Rangarajan, D., & Paesbrugghe, B. (2020). Increasing resilience by creating an adaptive salesforce. *Industrial Marketing Management, 88*, 238–246. https://doi.org/10.1016/j.indmarman.2020.05.023

Sobaih, A. E. E., Elshaer, I., Hasanein, A. M., & Abdelaziz, A. S. (2021). Responses to COVID-19: The role of performance in the relationship between small hospitality enterprises' resilience and sustainable tourism development. *International Journal of Hospitality Management, 94*, Article 102824. https://doi.org/10.1016/j.ijhm.2020.102824

Suparna, G., Kot, M., Dacko-Pikiewicz, Z., Riana, I. G., Rihayana, I. G., & Arsha, I. M. R. M. (2024). Cultivating creativity: Strategies for enhancing innovative behavior in small and medium enterprises. *Intellectual Economics, 18*(2), Article 2. https://doi.org/10.13165/IE-24-18-2-09

de Teixeira, E., & O., & Werther, W. B. (2013). Resilience: Continuous renewal of competitive advantages. *Business Horizons, 56*(3), 333–342. https://doi.org/10.1016/j.bushor.2013.01.009

Tortorella, G. L., Saurin, T. A., Fogliatto, F. S., Rosa, V. M., Tonetto, L. M., & Magrabi, F. (2021). Impacts of healthcare 4.0 digital technologies on the resilience of hospitals. *Technological Forecasting and Social Change, 166*, 120666. https://doi.org/10.1016/j.techfore.2021.120666

Weick, K. E., & Sutcliffe, K. M. (2015). *Managing the unexpected: Sustained performance in a complex world* (3rd ed.). Wiley.

Whitman, Z., Kachali, H., Roger, D., Vargo, J., & Seville, E. (2013). Short-form version of the Benchmark Resilience Tool (BRT-53). *Measuring Business Excellence, 17*(3), 3–14. https://doi.org/10.1108/MBE-05-2012-0030

Wiig, S., & Fahlbruch, B. (Eds.). (2019). *Exploring resilience: A scientific journey from practice to theory.* Springer International Publishing. https://doi.org/10.1007/978-3-030-03189-3

Wong, C. W. Y., Lirn, T.-C., Yang, C.-C., & Shang, K.-C. (2020). Supply chain and external conditions under which supply chain resilience pays: An organizational information processing theorization. *International Journal of Production Economics, 226*, Article 107610. https://doi.org/10.1016/j.ijpe.2019.107610

Wong, G., Luttrell, C., Loft, L., Yang, A., Pham, T., Naito, D., Assembe-Mvondo, S., & Brockhaus, M. (2019). Narratives in REDD plus benefit sharing: Examining evidence within and beyond the forest sector. *Climate Policy, 19*(8), 1038–1051. https://doi.org/10.1080/14693062.2019.1618786

Zumente, I., & Lāce, N. (2020). Does diversity drive non-financial reporting: Evidence from the Baltic States. *Intellectual Economics, 14*(2), Article 2. https://doi.org/10.13165/IE-20-14-2-04

Digital Indicators for Evaluation of the Organizational Development: American and Finnish Methodologies

Lidija Kraujalienė and Alytis Gruodis

Abstract The lack of systematic organizational development (OD) methodologies and their limited application led to low productivity. Combining "systemic development" methods could help managers improve their management and leadership skills. Unfortunately, two created systematic development practices have spread in North America (C. Argyris and D. Schön's Harvard Business School practice "Action Science") and developed quite different operational performance instruments in Scandinavia. Therefore, there is a need for research on effective OD methods that can unify the measures, considering the developed management context. This research aims to develop a set of digital indicators for the evaluation of OD at enterprises using artificial neural networks. Quantitative estimation of indicators is planned to be carried out using Artificial Neural Network (ANN) system tools, which will more effectively replace previously widely used decision support systems based on comparative analysis. The competence of leadership and management of human resources in organizations contributes to the resilience capability that helps rapidly adapt to continuously changing business environments and maintain the competition in markets. The research will identify clusters of indicators and the most significant groups of indicators, based on which OD evaluation model will be created. The set of indicators will be digitalized for usage in artificial neural networks. This research presents the determination of clusters of digital quantitative parameters in known OD methodologies to evaluate OD and increase the productivity of organizations. Digital evaluation requires modern AI methods. An innovative intersection for classifying sets of indicators of OD methodologies is presented. Research results will provide leaders with digital indicators to evaluate OD and contribute to building leadership capacity in any country.

Keywords Evaluation · Organizational development · Indicators · Artificial neural networks

L. Kraujalienė (✉) · A. Gruodis
Institute of Economics and Management, Faculty of Public Governance and Business, Mykolas Romeris University, Vilnius, Lithuania
e-mail: Lidija.Kraujaliene@mruni.eu

A. Gruodis
e-mail: Alytis.Gruodis@mruni.eu

I. Bartuseviciene et al. (eds.), *Building Economic Resilience*, Contributions to Economics, https://doi.org/10.1007/978-3-031-96428-2_7

Jel Classification Code M12 · M54 · C45

1 Introduction

Lithuania is not reaching the business performance results compared to the average level of the European Union (EU) and America. Statistics and rankings show a demand to improve the management and leadership skills of heads of organizations. Considering the leaders in talent rankings and the world's most famous organizational development (OD) methodologies, two direct countries, America and Finland, were selected for the research. Thus, the research aims to analyze the most prominent OD practices in America and Finland and identify unique digital indicators to evaluate OD for the research selected Action Science methodology from America's scientific world (based on action learning practices) and Finnish methodology from European Scandinavian world (based on consensus principle). The issue is that many new scientific productions are coming into the public's view. However, new knowledge should be evaluated time after time with meta-theories that have been created, tested, and practically verified in organizations. This problem could be solved using Artificial Neural Network (ANN) integration into the evaluation process.

The novelty of this research is the intersection of management and computer sciences, which provides new interdisciplinary knowledge on the issue of productive management and organization development for leaders. Research results will bring added value and innovative cuts (projections) in the classification of OD techniques.

The competence of leadership and management of human resources in organizations contributes to the resilience capability that helps rapidly adapt to continuously changing business environments and maintain market competition. Successful leaders should be able to make quick decisions for complicated risk management. It helps to maintain the resilience of an organization successfully. The main goal of the Chief Executive Officer (CEO) is to keep the organization competitive and create a strong enterprise to respond to the outside world with various unexpected changes and competitive games. There is a need to choose the most appropriate methodology for how leaders should work with teams and teams with leaders. Therefore, OD methodologies used in organizations are actual to consider. A strong leader must know how to respond effectively to external disturbances. Organizational resilience refers to the ability of organizations not only to anticipate but also to cope with and benefit from unexpected disruptive changes. However, it helps companies survive, grow, and thrive. Moreover, as strategic tools, digital technologies are an engine of resilience in organizations under difficult external competitive and environmental conditions. Therefore, digital tools have become increasingly necessary for organizations to improve competitiveness and performance (Garrido-Moreno et al., 2024).

This research aims to identify the new applicable set of unique digital indicators for evaluating the organization's OD using artificial neural networks. That would also positively influence Lithuanian business performance results (productivity). The novelty of the idea is the determination of a digital quantitative set (clusters) of parameters (indicators) from prominent American and Finland OD methodologies to estimate OD for high productivity impact. A large number of system input parameters could not be estimated as dominant. Due to weak correlations between socially and hierarchically related indicators, modern artificial intelligence (AI) system approach is necessary for digital estimation. The primary research question could be formulated as follows. Is it possible to relate the digital numeric indicators (representing the quality of methodology) and the semantic context of items (words, be-words, etc.) to the semantic behavior?

This work is aimed:

(a) to carry out the theoretical analysis of the prominent action theories of organizational development in America and Europe and identify a set of indicators, clustering them for evaluation of OD;
(b) to identify unique digital numeric indicators for evaluating organizational development (OD);
(c) to train clusters of indicators/parameters and digitalize them with an artificial neural network;
(d) to estimate indicators in clusters with the most significant influence on OD in the enterprise..

2 Literature Review

2.1 Analysis of the Organizational Development (OD) Problem

Labor productivity in Lithuania is lower than the EU average (in 2022—productivity decreased by 3.3% compared to the EU average (OECD, 2022). Productivity is the most important indicator of the country's economic progress and is determined by education, experience, and competencies. How to increase productivity? Leaders should improve management and leadership skills and use systematic development methodologies to increase the satisfaction and motivation of employees in the organization. Only 10% of employees in Lithuania are highly motivated compared to the EU average of 17% (OECD, 2021). We often hear from general managers of organizations that the most well-known countries with excellent business results are America and Finland (in Europe). Let us analyze these countries from this perspective.

Global Talent Competitiveness Index 2023 shows that the leaders are America at—TOP3 and Finland is on TOP6 (INSEAD, 2023). In Global Skills Report 2023, the United States was learning accounting (99%), marketing (74%), and sales (70%) the most, while Finland—71% of business skills in Europe (Coursera, 2023). In 2022, only 15% of job places applied systematic OD methodology, equaling only a 1/2 of the average of OECD countries (OECD, 2021). In Lithuania in 2022, even 22% of managers had low leadership skills compared to the OECD average—of 15% (OECD, 2021); by European Innovation Scoreboard 2023, Lithuania is still in the group of moderate innovators while Finland is in the TOP 3 (European Commission, 2023); OECD Lithuania lacks awareness of the importance of management and leadership skills (OECD, 2021). The formal education in Lithuania is not strong, learning programs—are insufficient, and high-performance work practices such as teamwork, training, development, and performance management—are only 15%: half of the OECD average (OECD, 2021).

Publications from the Clarivate Analytics Web of Science and Scopus databases related to effective leadership and management approaches represent a powerful teaching tool when two topics, OD, American Action Science (abbreviation AM) and Finnish case OD (FIN), are presented in comparison form.

2.2 *Organizational Development (OD) Approach: American* "Action Science" *Leadership and Management Methodology*

The most prominent OD methodology in the world is Action Science (meta-theory), developed by C. Argyris and D. Schön during 50 years of research in the field of organizational learning and leadership development (Bolman, 2021; Olhager, 2024). Argyris worked at the Harvard Business School. He gave insights into how organizations can adapt to personalities and their needs, make strong relationships, use emphasis on adaptive problem-solving, observation, reflection, and action, fostering a culture of continuous improvement (Choain & Malzy, 2019; Raaijmakers et al., 2018; Stoyanov, 2018). "Theory of action" can help organizations plan and implement change effectively (Luechtefeld, 2005), provide knowledge for transformation, facilitation, improving team dynamics (Moreno-Poyato et al., 2023), use double-loop learning (Hammond, 2013), identify actions for entrepreneurship, progress, and test predictions (Frese & Gielnik, 2023). Action learning is a systematic thinking strategy (Young et al., 2021) used by NASA, Rotary International (Volz-Peacock et al., 2016), Coca-Cola (Marquardt, 2016), American Airlines (Harris & Gokcekus, 2000), Toyota Motor (Fuchs, 2007), The United Nations (Echezona et al., 2017), MOOG (Schwartz, 2024), Walt Disney (Horan, 2007), etc. The action theory approach considers attitude, perceived norms, and behavioral control as key determinants of a human's intention to perform a behavior of interest (Dong et al., 2024; Zandee & Coghlan, 2024).

American Action Science methodology is based on the central organizational core values: transparency, curiosity, internal commitment, informed choice, accountability, and compassion (Raaijmakers et al., 2018) and solving the same problems in different spheres of companies. However, the following are several practical examples. Toyota Motor Company used Action Science to improve its sales process. The company found that its sales agents often needed to catch up on important information about customers. To remedy this, Toyota introduced a new sales training program that emphasizes understanding customer needs (Harris & Gokcekus, 2000; Bolman, 2021). The Action Science OD methodology helped American Airlines deal with organizational communication and management culture challenges and improve cooperation. The management team learned to make decisions effectively, communicate properly, and encourage employees to openly and honestly discuss problems without hiding mistakes or fears. This contributed to a smoother and more efficient collaboration between the American Airlines management board and employees. Also, the AM methodology helped solve conflicts constructively: it encouraged analyzing problems instead of looking for someone's blame. Also, the company resolved the non-sharing of information and created an environment where you can safely express your opinions and trust each other. The methodology helped managers better understand the needs of employees and implement changes. This has led to continuous organizational growth and operational efficiency improvement (Marquardt, 2016; Bolman, 2021). Action Science methodology helped the Coca-Cola company solve communication, culture, and decision-making challenges. Using Action Science, the company improved internal communication between managers and employees at different structural levels, encouraged openness and constructive discussions, learned to solve conflicts and problems when there are different points of view, employees began to talk more freely about their ideas and problems, and increased trust and cooperation. The company has employees from different cultures, and Action Science helped engage employees in achieving the company's goals. Decision-making is enhanced by the concept that it should be based on data and open discussion rather than emotions or hierarchical barriers. This has helped Coca-Cola build a stronger team and more efficient processes and continuously maintain competitiveness in the global market (Volz-Peacock et al., 2016; Bolman, 2021).

2.3 Organizational Development (OD) Approach: Finnish Leadership and Management Concept

Scandinavia is known for using progressive and collaborative approaches for organizational development, including transformation, problem-solving, and high employee engagement through collaboration activity, coaching and feedback from leaders on the side, and self-managed teams for high-performance results. One author mentioned the importance of organizational, processual, contextual, and relational facilitation in multi-professional collaboration as essential for delivering effective and comprehensive services. Sufficient time must be distributed during the regular day at work to share feedback and reflections and engage in mutual learning (Sørensen et al., 2018). Cooperation is related to management cultures and how different interests are considered, starting from the beginning and continuing throughout the process. The emerging paradigm highlights a collaborative approach to great process management (Laukka et al., 2021). In group decision-making and negotiations, we can use such interaction modes as inquiry and advocacy. The authors found that smiles were specific to the inquiry mode when emotional empathy predicted expressiveness. Interaction modes can influence group interaction: when influencing one's emotional state, it is reflected in a group decision (Leppänen et al., 2018).

A case analysis was performed in a business school in Finland for teamwork evaluation. Results showed that the game environment is appropriate for collaborative work. It promotes students for self-reflection and evaluation of individual team roles, highlights the importance of information sharing in teamwork, and evaluation of team results (Riivari et al., 2021). The model for proper use of micro-level behavioral, interactional, informal, and accessible-to-all aspects was suggested to construct learning organization as a framework for improvement. Alternatively, to recruit a human–computer approach and interact to support empathy (Jumisko-Pyykkö et al., 2021; Törmänen et al., 2022). The work-family practices as human socially responsible resource management practice is necessary in Finnish context. The complex interconnectedness is important of organisations and individuals as well (Heikkinen et al., 2021).

Finland's management style is based on consensus-seeking negotiation and discussion (Laukka et al., 2021; Koskinen & Lämsä, 2017). Uljens and Ylimaki (2017) accented an idea of educational leadership, which generally focused on organizational conditions and expectations for managing and leading activities. Finland has a strong educational system for leadership development and practices (Polterovich, 2022; Geeraerts et al., 2015; Heikkinen et al., 2021). However, many approaches have been raised to leadership development, e.g., separately used coaching (Tuppurainen, 2020), action learning (McGuire et al., 2013), and mentoring in the Scandinavian Airlines System (SAS) company (Walton, 1998). Action learning, coaching, and mentoring OD methodologies were used in Nokia (Ropponen, 2008), Finnair (Hawkins, 2018), Neste (Baird et al., 1994), and SAS (Walton, 1998). By applying coaching practices, the Finnair company has solved the leadership skills of managers, employee engagement, and efficiency issues. Managers learn how to communicate more effectively with employees, motivate them (increase their involvement), communicate openly, build trust, collaborate, and understand their strengths and weaknesses as managers understand the goals. Coaching helped Finnair employees and managers better adapt to changes in the company, overcome and manage related stresses and, find creative solutions, anticipate personal and professional growth of employees, thus increasing the efficiency of the company's operations (McGuire et al., 2013). Meanwhile, mentoring and action science theories helped Nestle solve problems related to leadership development, communication, innovation, employee engagement, and decision-making efficiency, allowing the company to grow and strengthen its position in the competitive market. Mentoring helped encourage senior managers to share their experiences with younger managers (Walton, 1998). Coaching, mentoring, and action science theories helped the SAS company to improve leadership skills, promote innovation and organizational change, increase employee engagement, improve communication and teamwork, and make decision-making processes (Heikkinen et al., 2021). Consensus theory is based on reaching an agreement among all interested parties rather than imposing decisions from above. Thus, consensus theory helped SAS company to improve decision-making processes, involve employees in key strategic and operational decisions by empowering them to participate in discussions and make suggestions, encourage open discussion and compromise, involve employees in the planning and implementation of the organization, change from the very beginning (Heikkinen et al., 2021; Törmänen et al., 2022; Jumisko-Pyykkö et al, 2021).

Comparative analysis of consensus and Action Science theories shows that both methodologies focus on better decision-making and more effective collaboration in organizations, but they differ in their approach and methodologies. Compared to Action Science, Consensus theory has some weaknesses, described in several References Törmänen et al., (2022), Jumisko-Pyykkö et al., (2021), Stoyanov (2018) and Young et al. (2021).

1. Speed of decision-making (a slow process often leads to consensus-seeking until all interested parties agree) can be an obstacle to quick decision-making if the circumstances require it. Meanwhile, the theory of action science focuses on quick reflection and learning from actions and facts, striving for efficiency so decisions can be made more quickly, even if not completely unanimously.
2. Lack of effectiveness (when many participants or opinions are very different, consensus can become complicated and ineffective in encouraging the implementation of actions.) Meanwhile, action science theory is focused on action and continuous learning from actions, even if there is no ideal solution. Action science emphasizes the analysis of facts and data and learning from mistakes to achieve faster decision-making, even if the process is imperfect.
3. Avoiding conflicts. Consensus often seeks to avoid conflict, leading to compromises that could be more efficient and beneficial in the long run. This means that teams can make better decisions to maintain harmony. The theory of Action Science promotes the open resolution of conflicts and tensions because it believes that the analysis and deep discussion of these differences can lead to more advanced solutions.
4. Lack of data utilization and analysis. Consensus is usually based on discussion and opinion but may need more solid data and evidence-based decision-making. Therefore, decisions may be based on emotions or personal preferences rather than objective data. However, the Action Science methodology strongly focuses on factual analysis and learning from data and experience. Action Science emphasizes that decisions must be made based on objective analysis and facts, which helps to make more accurate and valid decisions.
5. The goal of unanimity. The principle of consensus requires that decisions be made unanimously or at least by a broad majority. This can be difficult in organizations with a high diversity of opinion, leading to stagnation or unnecessary compromises to avoid disagreement. Moreover, Action Science's methodology is based on the premise that everyone must be willing to question and learn rather than seeking total agreement. It allows you to act and improve the process by learning from mistakes, even if the opinions of all participants do not agree.
6. Risk of groupthink. Consensus-seeking can lead to "groupthink," where group members tend to make decisions to avoid conflict, even if the decisions are not

optimal. This way, individual opinions can be ignored. Meanwhile, action science theory encourages constant challenge of the status quo and critical analysis of all decisions. The methodology encourages challenges and deeper analysis of problems, making groupthink less likely.

7. Loss of individual votes. While the pursuit of consensus in principle involves everyone, stronger personalities may dominate the final discussion, while quieter participants may be overlooked or choose to acquiesce simply because of peer pressure. However, Action Science actively encourages the participation and expression of opinion by all participants by hearing the views and reflections of each participant.

In summary, American and Finnish management and leadership approaches can be stated that while consensus theory is valuable for organizations seeking to maintain democracy and team harmony, it has shortcomings when it comes to decision-making speed, efficiency, and conflict-solving. Action Science can theoretically be a more effective methodology for responding quickly to challenges, analyzing problems, and learning from mistakes.

An interesting fact is that nowadays, there are many other management and leadership approaches on the wave of "fashion" that are not based on any scientific evidence but are popular among users who are not familiar with "really working" and science-based methodologies—for example, Basque method—collective transformation program. The Basque method is a more practice-tested model and was not directly developed based on scientific research. The Basque method is a proven model that grew out of the need to address regional/community social responsibility and economic issues. The method has been developed and improved over a long period. The main principle is cooperative management, where employees are also owners. Research shows that cooperatives can increase employee motivation (because they are involved in decision-making), loyalty, and productivity because employees feel more engaged and committed to achieving goals. The Basque method also emphasizes a long-term approach and social responsibility, thus contributing to the sustainability policy in the organization. Thus, in the practical example of Mondragon, fostering continuous learning and innovation is critical in keeping an organization competitive (Pillado-Arbide, 2024; Voigt & von der Oelsnitz, 2024). Another popular program is Neuro-Linguistic Programming (NLP)—psychological therapy and communication theory that posits that it is possible to improve human behavior, thinking, and emotions by manipulating brain (neuro) processes, language (linguistics), and internal "programming" patterns. NLP was developed as a methodology to understand how people structure their thoughts, feelings, and language. NLP is based on subjectivity because it states that people's thinking and behavior depend on internal processes, e.g., the use of senses (sight, hearing, smell, taste, touch) and speech. NLP tries to change these internal structures through manipulation. The NLP method assumes that it is possible to learn by observing and modeling the behavior of successful people. It is claimed that if we imitate successful people's ways of thinking, speaking, and acting, we will experience similar successes. Sensory techniques (such as color, volume, and size) are also used, which change the emotions associated with specific memories or beliefs and, at the same time, the images, sounds, and sensations in the memory. NLP focuses on body language attraction, which helps build interpersonal relationships by mirroring body language, tone, or words to build trust and better communication (Deshwal et al., 2024), (Ochilova, 2024). NLP techniques are not research-based and empirically validated, and solid data on their effectiveness is lacking. NLP's claims about the interaction between the brain, language, and behavior are exaggerated and do not create long-term sustainable benefits.

At the end of Sect. 2, American Action Science and Finnish management and leadership approaches were identified for this paper, which is a limitation of this research. Action Science methodology was proven by 50 years of research, and moreover, this is a systematic approach, while others are not, with less evidence about efficiency. Methods like Basque or NLP are not science-based approaches, especially the latter one, which needs to be proven by data.

Action Science or Finnish methodologies for management and leadership work best in democratic cultures that encourage open communication. However, this methodology may not be effective in countries like Russia or North Korea.

3 Methods for Evaluation of Organizational Development (OD)

To estimate the Organizational Development (OD) two approaches are possible: traditional as well as innovative. We will describe both because some ideas are presented in overlapped manner. In both cases, it is necessary to describe the current state together with the perspective of growing potential, to estimate potential or possible obstacles to development and fields needing improvement. In all cases, long-term goals are necessary.

3.1 The Most Used Techniques for Evaluation so Far

An expert can perform the strategic goal—valuation of company activities, based on one of two methodologies (Action Science (AM) or Finish case (FIN)). In both cases, several tactical actions are necessary.

1. Definition of objectives and scope which areas of the organization will be assessed, such as specific departments, processes etc.
2. Collecting relevant date from surveys, interviews, observations, archives etc. It helps to understand the organization's current state and historical trends.
3. Analyze of data allows evaluating the leadership (including hierarchy, roles, and responsibilities), and management (identifying inefficiencies, redundancies, and areas for improvement).

4. Generation of the actions plans or recommendations for improvement (related to the resources, responsibilities, changes, etc.).

This method of organizational assessment requires extensive knowledge of the OD subject. Generally, the assessment results must be reported after a manual step-by-step examination using different methodologies and methods. A low-skilled expert can use a popular or best-advertised pseudo-methodology instead of two globally known and recognized technologies (Action Science (AM) or Finish case (FIN)). To help the expert, it is always necessary to use new theoretical methods, which must be compared with previous, already-recognized ones. Qualitative descriptive methodology evaluation is widely known as a classic method after university studies. Its disadvantage is that it is difficult to objectively define transitional stages, which are always subject to negotiation/dispute. Applying digital indicators lets you switch to a new methodology evaluation system immediately.

3.2 Proposed Novel Method for Evaluation Using AI Tool

Quantitative estimation of OD methodologies could be done using a digital approach using Artificial Intelligence (AI) systems tools. Previous research works applied primitive decision support systems or methods of comparative analysis. Only methods of artificial neural networks are suitable for developing a cluster of quantitative digitalized indicators.

Artificial Neural Networks (ANNs) represent the central realization of predictions in decision-making processes. ANNs allow learning complex patterns and relationships from large, weakly correlated data sets of different types. The ANN's adaptability to complex parameters is well known due to the network's possibility to generalize new, unknown data of different types. Feed-forward neural networks (FNNs) are suitable for such purposes (Gruodis, 2023a).

Next, the methodology step by step is presented; firstly, the literature review should be conducted, and the indicators for the evaluation of organizational development (OD) in Action Science (AM) and Finish case (FIN) should be identified. Secondly, three significant articles representing the Actions Science (AM) and Finish case (FIN) behavior were selected. Thirdly, a qualified expert in the field of understanding both methodologies should be found, and he/she should use his/her knowledge to set the cluster of indicators for the evaluation of OD. Fourthly, the same expert will be used to estimate the indicators in clusters with the most significant influence on OD in the enterprise: to create sets of words (keywords) extracted from selected articles separately that represent the behavior of a method (AM or FIN). Fifthly, ANN should be applied in the framework of programmed package VALLUM01 (Gruodis, 2023b) to digitalize identified indicators. Sixthly, integrate a selected set of clusters of indicators for training in the program VALLUM01—to monitor model performance if the training process determines the successful predictions of an expert. Seventh, the simulation (validation) is performed, and the results are obtained if the simulation gives satisfactory results.

3.3 Artificial Neural Network (ANN) as AI Tool for Evaluation in Linguistics

Generally, many problems (related to the usage of human–computer interfaces in linguistics, organization of computer-mediated education systems, and obtaining the prediction of mental disorders and physical diseases in medicine) could be solved using natural language processing (NLP) methods, including different realizations of ANNs. Several approaches for solving the training neural language models (NLMs) are presented by Xiao et al. (2017). Sagae describes the principles of language-specific information designed by experts (Sagae, 2021) used to examine the child's language. Statistical approach related to the usage of Zipf law is also suitable due to the universality of ranking (Būdienė & Gruodis, 2016) and the possibility of using the dictionary approach (Būdienė et al., 2012).

Feed-forward neural networks (FNN) are helpful for semantic analysis (Ponti & Korhonen, 2017) and for any analysis of text items via the Principal Component Analysis (PCA) (Aras et al., 2022). Several techniques, such as neural network-based speech synthesis (Wu et al., 2016), could be realized using various ANNs: FNN, mixture density neural network, recurrent neural network (RNN), and long short-term memory (LSTM) RNN. Interpretable feed-forward neural network (IFFNN) helps achieve high classification performance and interpretability for item detection (Li et al., 2022).

FNN-based algorithms are helpful for speech-emotion recognition systems (Gavrilescu & Vizireanu, 2019). Schematically, a three-layer system is capable of linguistic tasks: the first layer for evaluation of speech features, the second layer for classification scores obtained from the first level, and the third layer must be organized according to rule-based classifiers (Gavrilescu & Vizireanu, 2019). Several novel systems, such as linguistic fuzzy neural networks (LFNN) (Chien & Juang, 2024), are helpful in systematizing and estimating chaotic and stochastic data extracted from the environment. Chong et al. (2015) proposed using FNN to improve the term-distance term-occurrence (TDTO) language model for obtaining information about n-grams. FNN expressed higher quality for generalization property than other conventional methods.

4 Framework for Artificial Neural Network (Ann) Simulation

4.1 Data Preparation

Firstly, data should be gathered. Data preparation starts with identifying unique digital numeric indicators for evaluating organizational development (OD). Theoretical analysis of the prominent action theories of OD in America and Europe allows us to estimate the indicators in clusters that have the most significant influence on OD in the enterprise. Data preparation requires the job of a qualified expert in the field of understanding both mentioned methodologies. Initially, a set of keywords (items representing the first or second methodology) was created using manual analysis; see Table 1. The sample was selected due to the broadest and most precise publications related to organizational development based on American and Finnish approaches. We have selected three articles, RolNo ∈ (0, 1, 2,) representing the behavior of Actions Science (AM) (Argyris, 1994; Friedman et al., 2009; Luechtefeld, 2005) and three articles, RolNo ∈ (3, 4, 5) representing the Finish case (FIN) (Haavisto & Linge, 2022; Puumala & Maiche, 2021; Larison, 2022).

Firstly, creating sets of words extracted from a current article that represents the method's behavior (AM or FIN) was necessary. According to the expert's decision (we suppose that the expert expresses excellent experience in knowing OD theory!), the mentioned sets of items (called keywords)—grammatically correct words were created for each article separately—See Table 1. Signs of punctuation were removed, and decapitalization of items was provided. To present the input layer for ANN containing unique items for input, six sets were related to the new one (012,345-kw.txt) and ranked using the a-z routine—see Table 2.

$$\begin{gathered}0-\text{kw.txt}+1-\text{kw.txt}+2-\text{kw.txt}+3-\text{kw.txt}\\+4-\text{kw.txt}+5-\text{kw.txt}\rightarrow 012345-\text{kw.txt}\end{gathered}$$

The list of the final set (containing 92 unique items) is presented in Table 3.

Secondly, sets of all items—grammatically correct words were created for each article separately. Signs of punctuation were removed, and decapitalization of items was provided. For each item labeled as x, the frequency of occurrence f_x in the article was calculated, Eq. 1:

$$f_x = \frac{N_x}{N_{tot}} \tag{1}$$

where N_x is the number of items in the current article, and N_{tot} is the number of items in the current article. For the ANN input layer, we have included the frequencies f_x

Table 1 Extraction of items as keywords that correspond to the essence of the OD methodology according to expert decision. Scientific articles represent two methods: Action Science (AM) and Finish case (FIN)

Method	RolNo	Source	File name	Keywords without ranking and ordering
AM	0	Luechtefeld (2005)	0-kw.txt	Action; actions; change; behavior; management; initiative; organizational; managers; effective; learning; values; reaction; question; advocate; culture; reason; result; reflect; team; dialogue; participation; reasoning; participation; transform; performance; inquiry
	1	Argyris (1994)	1-kw.txt	Learning; management; managers; behavior; action; business; reason; supervisors; commitment; communication; organizational; issues; question; questions; threat; leaders; group; initiative; reflect; avoid; strategy; loyal; truth; culture; satisfaction; feelings; conversation; blame; motives; psychological; thinking; caring; embarrassment; values; contribution; manipulation
	2	Friedman et al. (2009)	2-kw.txt	Action; behavior; executives; change; learning; inquiry; practical; conditions; organizational; critical; relationship; beliefs; thinking; trust; blame; meta-theory; effectiveness; processes; cognitive; reflection; co-creating; psychology
FIN	3	Haavisto & Linge (2022)	3-kw.txt	Crisis; communication; leaders; internal; leadership; managers; sensemaking; COVID; effective; trust; organizations; transparent; Finland; hotels; restaurants; openness; consensus; conflict; cooperation

(continued)

Table 1 (continued)

	4	Puumala & Maiche, (2021)	4-kw.txt	Community; urban; consensus; relation; Finland; culture; negotiation; belonging; interaction; diversity; communication; norms; habits; values; thinking; behavior
	5	Larison (2022)	5-kw.txt	Scientific; narrative; students; argumentation; consensus; knowledge; actions; contextual; interaction; conflict; inquiry

Table 2 Input layer of ANN consisting of D0-D91 units

Method	RolNo	Source	File name	Parameter	Interval	
					Xmin	Xmax
AM	0	Luechtefeld (2005)	012,345-kw.txt	D0-D91, Keywords – Items, see Table 3	0.000	0.020
	1	Argyris (1994)				
	2	Friedman et al. (2009)				
FIN	3	Haavisto & Linge (2022)				
	4	Puumala & Maiche (2021)				
	5	Larison (2022)				

Table 3 Keywords—items according to expert decision extracted from scientific articles representing different methods: Action Science, AM (Argyris, 1994; Friedman et al., 2009; Luechtefeld, 2005), and Finish case, FIN (Haavisto & Linge, 2022; Puumala & Maiche, 2021; Larison, 2022). The input layer of ANN is constructed as the set of D0-D91 parameters

Keywords—92 items in ordered form (a-z)
action actions advocate argumentation avoid behavior beliefs belonging blame
business caring change co-creating cognitive commitment communication community conditions
conflict consensus contextual contribution conversation cooperation covid crisis critical
culture dialogue diversity effective effectiveness embarrassment executives feelings Finland
group habits hotels initiative inquiry interaction internal issues knowledge
leaders leadership learning loyal management managers manipulation meta-theory motives
narrative negotiation norms openness organizational organizations participation performance practical
processes psychological question questions reaction reason reasons reasoning reflect
reflection relation relationship restaurants result satisfaction scientific sensemaking strategy
students supervisors team thinking threat transform transparent trust truth
urban values

(normalization interval (0; 0.02)) as parameters of D0-D91 corresponding to the items presented in the keyword list—see Table 3.

Also, a joint set of all unique items used in six articles (see Table 2) was prepared and ranked. Figure 1 represents the ranked distribution of all items used in six articles: (Luechtefeld, 2005), (Argyris, 1994), (Friedman et al., 2009), (Haavisto & Linge, 2022), (Puumala & Maiche, 2021), (Larison, 2022) according to Zipf law. Keywords presented in Table 3 are placed on the tail of Zipfian distribution. The central part of keywords characterized by ranking index presented in the interval (24; 800) corresponds to Zipfian distribution when exponent $\gamma \approx 1$. The last part (ranking index is presented in the intervals (800; 3000)) corresponds to Lotka distribution when exponent $\gamma \approx 2$ (see Ref. [53]). It allows us to conclude that rare words (so-called dictionary words, $\gamma \approx 2$) and common ones ($\gamma \approx 1$) with a strictly defined semantic meaning were included in the examination.

Finally, values of frequencies of the ranked keywords were used in FNN as an input layer for training and validation purposes.

Table 4 lists ANN output parameters related to the article quality indicators typical for both systems: AM and FIN. Two indicators (E4, Presence of Action Science, and E12, Presence of Consensus) are key indicators for the final evaluation of AM methodology (E4 = 1) and FIN methodology (E12 = 1), respectively. All indicators.

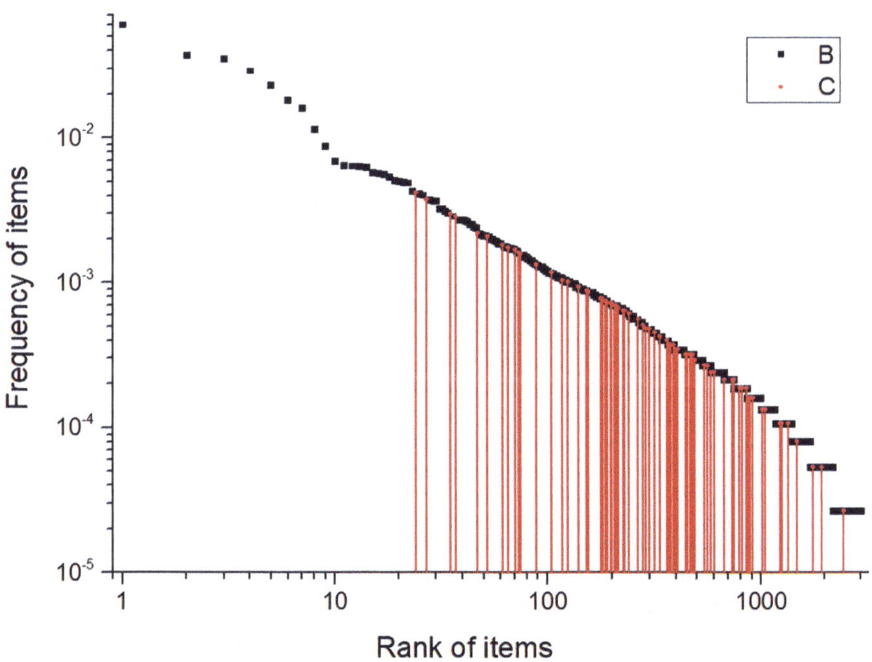

Fig. 1 Ranked distribution of all items used in six articles: (Luechtefeld, 2005; Argyris, 1994; Friedman et al., 2009; Haavisto & Linge, 2022; Puumala & Maiche, 2021; Larison, 2022) according to Zipf law. Positions of selected 92 keywords (Table 3) are depicted in red

Table 4 The output layer of ANN consisting of 17 units representing E0-E16 expert-established indicators/parameters for different methods: Action Science, AM: (Argyris, 1994; Friedman et al., 2009; Luechtefeld, 2005); Finish case, FIN: (Haavisto & Linge, 2022; Puumala & Maiche, 2021; Larison, 2022)

Method	Cluster	Index	Parameter	Indicator	Interval	
					Xmin	XMax
AM, FIN	1	6	*E0*	Increasing of personal efficiency and organizational results	0.000	1.000
AM, FIN	1	5	*E1*	Mentoring skills for leader	0.000	1.000
AM, FIN	1	4	*E2*	Coaching skills for leader	0.000	1.000
AM	1	3	*E3*	Facilitation skills for leader	0.000	1.000
AM	1	0	*E4*	Presence of Action Science	0.000	1.000
AM, FIN	2	1	*E5*	Efficient work in a group	0.000	1.000
AM	2	2	*E6*	Mature mindset & Productive behavior	0.000	1.000
AM	2	7	*E7*	Effective discussions technique	0.000	1.000
AM, FIN	2	8	*E8*	Decision-making and individual empowerment	0.000	1.000
AM, FIN	2	9	*E9*	Difficult talks (conversation) plus effective feedback	0.000	1.000
AM	2	10	*E10*	Double-loop learning	0.000	1.000
AM, FIN	2	11	*E11*	Problem solving and change management	0.000	1.000
FIN	3	12	*E12*	Presence of Consensus	0.000	1.000
FIN	3	13	*E13*	Consensus (negotiations and discussions)	0.000	1.000
AM, FIN	3	14	*E14*	a la Action Science theory principles (behavior, norms, thinking, argumentation…)	0.000	1.000
FIN	3	15	*E15*	Communication	0.000	1.000
FIN	3	16	*E16*	Transparent behavior (trust building, openness)	0.000	1.000

E0-E16 are presented in three clusters. The real value of the indicator in the range (0;1) was established by an expert to evaluate the category of behavior presented as a parameter. Indicators were clustered in this way. There are three categories of clusters. Because Action Science American methodology is systematic, two clusters were identified: leader competence and high-performing teams (dynamic groups). In the Finnish case, because it was not identified as a systematic methodology for organizational development, indicators are used in the following form: partially the same as in AM methodologies, but they are decentralized from one usable model. Thus, indicators in the Finnish case were grouped in one cluster.

For AM methodology, the first cluster is related to the features of group leader (E0, Increasing of personal efficiency and organizational results; E1, Mentoring skills for leader; E2, Coaching skills for leader; E3, Facilitation skills for leader), and second cluster is related to the group behavior (E5, Efficient work in a group; E6, Mature mindset & Productive behavior; E7, Effective discussions technique; E8, Decision-making and individual empowerment; E9, Difficult talks (conversation) plus effective feedback; E10, Double-loop learning).

The first cluster of indicators for a leader shows that it is critically important to learn coaching practices, implement them for a team, and educate lower-level managers on the mentioned method for their teams. The top-level leader should demonstrate the example of the best behavior, which, as a rule, is copied by other leaders. The mentoring method is suitable for new incomers in the organization, as it helps them to stick to the company's culture and rules. To increase personal efficiency, it is relevant to understand yourself as a leader and learn how to work with people in a group (team). The second cluster of indicators is important for productive work in a team, explaining mature mindset principles and suggesting practical discussions during meetings and methods for decision-making. It is essential to know how to provide feedback for your team members, how to prepare and organize it, and how to lead difficult discussions with employees. Action Science methodology explains people's behavior in one or another scenario and suggests ways to stand with cooperation in a group activity.

Then, for FIN methodology, the third cluster was formed (E13, Consensus (negotiations and discussions); E14, a la Action Science theory principles (behavior, norms, thinking, argumentation…); E15, Communication; E16, Transparent behavior (trust building, openness)). While searching for Finnish OD methodology, it was identified that Finland had not created a systematic OD methodology. Companies name like that when they use some Finnish cultural elements because the literature analysis shows that Finnish companies use separate indicators or a complex of several indicators without using science-based methodologies like Action Science. Anyway, literature analysis showed that the main principles used in the Finnish case were Consensus, Transparent Behavior, and Communication. Without clusterization (when data of different types are presented in a chaotic manner), the network might not converge in the training regime, leading to poor performance. This type of clusterization (two clusters for AM, one for FIN) allows us to receive satisfied training results.

The practical context for applying indicators mentioned in Table 4 is the following. In practice, according to the indicators of the Action Science methodology, it is possible to measure the level of organizational learning, management, teamwork efficiency, personal development, and leadership. According to Action Science theory, managers learn through deep reflection on their actions. By measuring the development activities of your organization according to the American methodology, you can optimize processes, improve action planning, etc. By using the indicators (components) mentioned, managers or leaders of organizations can identify the obstacles to the organization's development and provide a strategy for eliminating gaps. The systematic methodology of Action Science distinguishes what organizational development processes exist in the organization and how to carry them out effectively to increase personal and organizational efficiency and profitability. For example, if decision-making is delayed or complicated, the reasons are analyzed, and the quality of decision-making is improved. This can avoid repeated mistakes. The reasons are explained if the problem is communication and a new culture is cultivated. Companies that use the basis of Action Science theory permanently learn how to solve complex problems, drive change, communicate effectively, promote innovation, adjust their actions, manage conflicts, and gain a deeper understanding of their assumptions and beliefs (Ponti & Korhonen, 2017), (Aras et al., 2022), (Bolman, 2021), (Raaijmakers et al, 2018), (Stoyanov, 2018), (Young et al., 2021). In the Finnish case, the practical application of identified indicators, including the principle of consensus, is used in practice to monitor organizational performance, decision-making quality, and inclusion in teamwork. These indicators help organizations formulate effective strategies, consider the needs of employees, and contribute to the organization's long-term growth. Indicators help managers identify areas for improvement and implement effective strategies that drive innovation, improve the work environment, increase employee engagement, and ensure organizational sustainability (Stoyanov, 2018; Young et al., 2021; Heikkinen et al., 2021; Törmänen et al., 2022; Jumisko-Pyykkö et al., 2021).

4.2 Artificial Neural Network: Several Routines of Simulation

Figure 2 represents the general scheme of ANN in the framework of programmed package VALLUM01 (Gruodis, 2023b) described previously in Refs. Matijošius et al., (2024a), Matijošius et al., (2024a). The VALLUM01 package (created using the JAVA Eclipse framework) contains a graphical, user-friendly interface for input, output, and control. For ANNs, two typical JAVA classes (Sonawane, 2024) were used: Matrix and Neural_Network. As an S-shaped function, a sigmoidal function was used:

$$\sigma(x) = \frac{1}{1 + e^{-x}} \tag{2}$$

Normalization/denormalization plugins were used to convert/deconvert any real value (pink) from the requested interval into the (0; 1) interval.

For ANN using the nonlinear sigmoidal function, input and output values must only be presented in the intervals (0;1). Due to that, for all actual values, the interval of distribution ($X_{\mathrm{MIN};}\ X_{\mathrm{MAX}}$) was established initially (see Tables 2 and 4). Plugins of data conversion recalculate the actual input values X_{i} ($i = 0; D$) and output values Y_{j} ($j = 0; E$) to corresponding fuzzy logic values XX_{i}, YY_{j} in the forward or backward

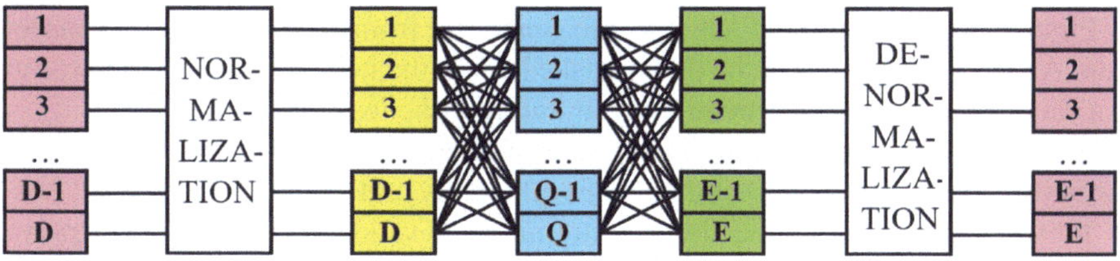

Fig. 2 Feedforward neural network (FNN). Input layer, number of units D = 92 (yellow); single hidden layer, number of perceptrons Q = 2,000 (blue); output layer, number of units E = 17 (green). Normalization/denormalization plugins were used for conversion/deconversion of any real value (pink) from the requested interval into (0; 1) interval. Flow from left to right

direction according to the Eqs. (3) or (4) respectively:

$$XX_i = \frac{X_i - X_{MIN}}{X_{MAX} - X_{MIN}} \tag{3}$$

$$X_i = X_{MIN} + XX_i(X_{MAX} - X_{MIN}) \tag{4}$$

The central part of Fig. 2 represents the realization of a Feedforward neural network (FFN). Table 4 presents the parameters of ANN. ANN was used in two regimes: training and validation.

5 Results of Estimation of Two Organizational Development (OD) Methodologies: American and Finnish

Data describing the two opposite OD representatives were developed using the FNN tool. Table 4 represents the main parameters of ANN simulations. The selected ANN model was realized using the usual architecture: FNN containing a single hidden layer. The hyperparameters of ANN describe the features of architecture: the amount of input layer, output layer, and hidden layer.

5.1 Training Regime of ANN for Predicting the Indicators Representing the Sets of AM&FIN Methodologies

For FNN, a training regime is necessary for learning generalization and parameter optimization. Analyzing training progress, it is possible to estimate two features: avoiding overfitting and the efficiency of ANN architecture and training regime.

Firstly, through training, FNN learns to generalize from the training data to unseen data. ANN convergence can be distinguished when the network's weights converge to a set of values that correspond to a minimum of the loss function.

Secondly, a training regime is essential for ensuring that an FNN converges correctly (effective learning) and operates efficiently and stably.

Table 5 represents the procedures for training and validation of ANNs. The previously described data set 012,345-kw.txt (containing six events) was used for training and validation. Figure 3 represents the evolution of the ANN training. The main parameter of the training quality—Total Network Error, *TNE* could be calculated using Eq. 5

$$TNE^2 = \frac{1}{E}\sum_{i=1}^{E}\left(X_i^{current} - Target_i^{fix}\right)^2 \tag{5}$$

The training procedure involves adjusting the weights and biases of the FNN to minimize the *TNE* between the FNN's predictions $X_i^{current}$ and the actual target values

Table 5 Parameters of ANN simulations

No	Behavior or parameter	Name or value
1	Realization of ANN	Feedforward Neural Network (FNN)
2	Package name	*VALLUM01* (Gruodis, 2023b)
3	Architecture of ANN	FNN containing single hidden layer
4	Nonlinear function	Sigmoid
5	Input layer	Number of units D = 92
6	Hidden layer	Number of perceptrons Q = 2,000
7	Output layer	Number of units E = 17
8	Learning rate	0.01
9	Training interval	Number of epochs until 50,000
10	Training until escape	Number of epochs 39,234
11	Escape parameter for end of training	$TNE^2 < 1*10^{-9}$
12	Training amount	Number of events 6 = (3 + 3)
13	Validation amount	Number of events 6 = (3 + 3)

Table 6 The procedure of training and validation of ANNs. Input layer, $D = 92$; output layer, $E = 17$, amount of perceptrons in the single hidden layer Q, learning rate 0.01

Project	Q	Routine	Training				Validation	
			File	Events	Epochs	TNE^2	File	Events
AM02	2000	*T10*	012,345-kw.txt	6	39,234	$8.23*10^{-10}$		
AM02	2000	*T10*					012,345-kw.txt	6

$Target_i^{fix}$ (fixed from the start to the end of training). The distribution of TNE^2 on the number of training epochs allows us to estimate the criteria of ANN convergence or divergence. This optimization is crucial for the FNN to learn the underlying patterns for accurate predictions. TNE^2 dependence on epoch's number is presented in log–log form because parameters are presented in large intervals (four orders at horizontal scale, eight orders at vertical). Training routine was requested for 50,000 epochs but was interrupted after 39,234 epochs because the escape parameter was distinguished:

$$TNE^2 = 8.23 * 10^{-10} < 1 * 10^{-9}. \tag{6}$$

We can estimate the training process as very successful because the convergence criterion was exceeded after a low number of training epochs, which is sufficient.

The profile of the decreasing curve presented in Fig. 3 allows us to estimate the absence of overfitting (absence of significant increase of *TNE* parameter per two orders and more). Several traditional techniques (to avoid overfitting), such as regularization, dropout, and cross-validation, needed to be revised. FNN's ability to fit the training data is well-balanced. The absence of overfitting and the related decrease in TNE2 value allows us to conclude that a stable model is achieved. The architecture of ANN is satisfied (FNN containing a single hidden layer). Selected

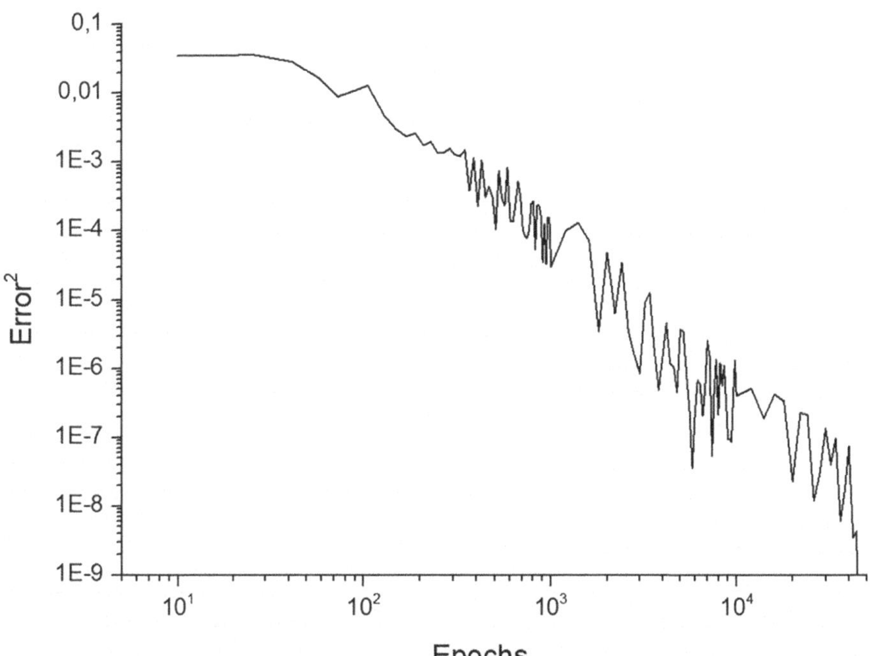

Fig. 3 TNE2 dependence on epochs number. Evolution of the ANN training. Number of events, 6. Number of epochs, 39,234

hyperparameters (number of perceptrons $Q = 2{,}000$ in the hidden layer; learning rate 0.01; the number of units $D = 92$ in the input layer; the number of units $E = 17$ in the output layer, see Table 4) should be treated as parameters close to the best ANN configuration. The efficiency of the training process allows us to conclude that the training regime is well-designed.

5.2 Validation Regime for Indicators Representing the Set of AM&FIN Methodologies

For FNNs, a validation regime is necessary for several important reasons: monitoring model performance and calibrating confidence.

Generally, the training process determines the successful predictions, and this feature could be established from training dynamics. However, when relatively large values of TNE are distinguished (convergence is present but not expected, not satisfied), FNN's prediction may need to reflect its performance on training data accurately. A validation set allows for monitoring how well the FNN generalizes to training data.

For small datasets, when two opposite data sets are present (in our case, AM-FIN), two-fold cross-validation is often used, where the data is split into k subsets. FNN was trained using data from AM and FIN representatives, and a validation routine was provided separately for AM and FIN representatives.

Figure 4 represents the distribution of the key parameters as E4 and E12 on RolNo of the requested article (see Table 1). E4 represents the presence of Action Science, and E12 represents the presence of Consensus.

The consensus method is not the best choice to solve the organizational issues of the organization because, first, it takes much time to get the interests of all interested parties to agree on a standard solution. It becomes a problem when decisions need to be made with immediate urgency and prompt action. On the other hand, when there are many stakeholders and interests, it is difficult to reach a compromise solution; when there are many different opinions and own (personal) priorities, it becomes impossible to ensure that all parties will be satisfied and not disappointed about the final decision. In consensus management, there must be a strong leader who does not allow others to dominate in discussions because the process of finding a compromise can turn into uncontrollable chaos, and the best decision (proper for an organization) may not be made.

For example, the Action Science (AM) methodology suggests methods that use majority voting to decide using a specific decision-making scale. Considering the new trends, a transformational or generative leadership style can be adopted to change the company's decision-making culture.

Comparison of expert-established values (E4 and E12, expert values) and ANN-validated values (E4* and E12*, simulated values) allows us to conclude the high precision of simulations. Pure switching of AM-FIN behavior, RolNo $\in$ (0, 1, 2)

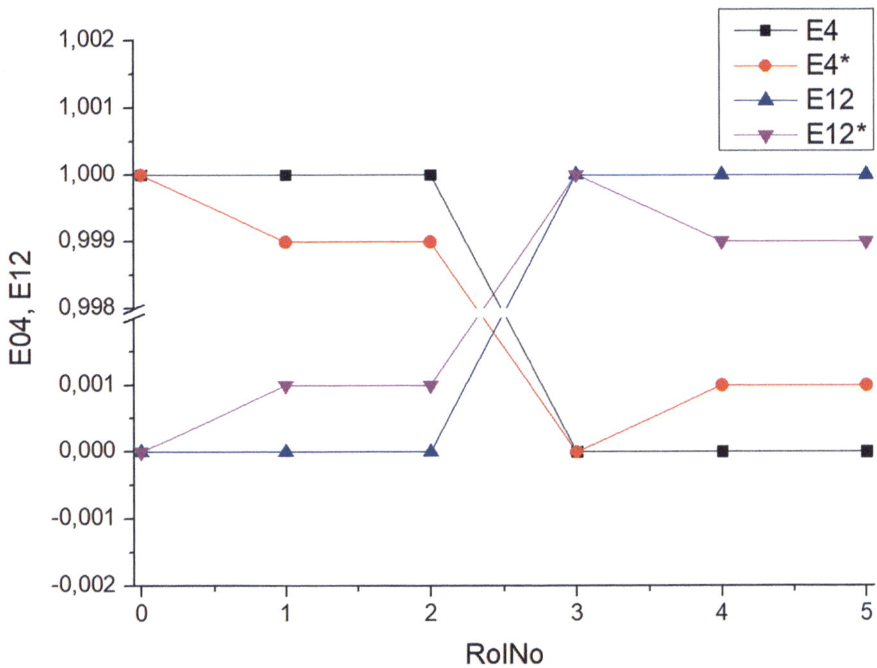

Fig. 4 Distribution of parameters on RolNo of the requested article (see Table 1). Action Science, AM, RolNo ∈ (0, 1, 2), (Argyris, 1994; Friedman et al., 2009; Luechtefeld, 2005); Finish case, FIN, RolNo ∈ (3, 4, 5), (Haavisto & Linge, 2022; Puumala & Maiche, 2021; Larison, 2022). Presence of Action Science, E4 (expert value), E4* (simulated value) and Presence of Consensus, E12 (expert value), E12* (simulated value)

and RolNo ∈ (3, 4, 5) without intermediate values were realized in the form of 1 → 0 (AM to FIN) and 0 → 1 (FIN to AM). We can conclude that the behavior of AM using E4 and E12 indicators is fulfilled nearly 100% without any influence of another (FIN), and vice versa with the FIN case.

Figure 5 represents distributions of simulated values of several indicators characteristic of AM only or FIN only. Differences between expert-established values and ANN-predicted values are negligible (less than 0.005) and are not depicted for simplicity. Left part of Fig. 5 is devoted to the parameters typical for AM only, RolNo ∈ (0, 1, 2): Facilitation skills for leader, E3*; Mature mindset & Productive behavior, E6*; Effective discussions technique, E7*; Double-loop learning, E10*. It helps to improve the activities and processes of the organization every time to follow the path of continuous improvement and innovation. Facilitation abilities are also important for management activities. The facilitation concept is based on evidence and context information as a tool to serve teams to make changes and implement innovations, helping to understand what and how. Usually, a practical discussion should be heard by participants in a meeting (which is very rare in real life) when the organizer can highlight the sense of every participant and make a summary at the end. During

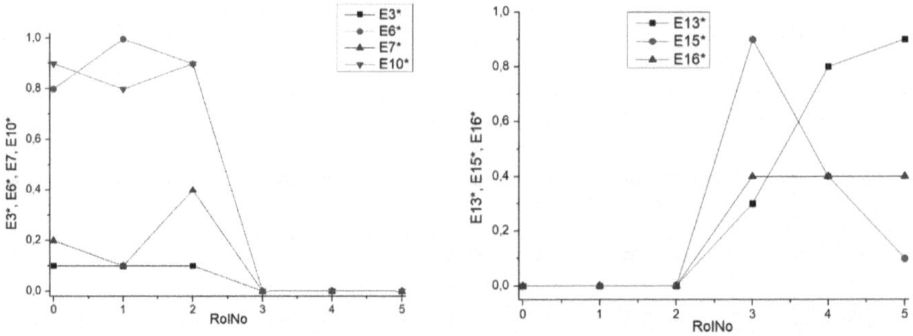

Facilitation skills for leader, E3 (simulated value); Mature mindset & Productive behaviour, E6* (simulated value); Effective discussions technique, E7* (simulated value); Double-loop learning, E10* (simulated value).*
Parameters typical for AM only, RolNo (0, 1, 2)), (Luechtefeld, 2005), (Argyris, 1994), (Friedman et al., 2009).

Consensus (negotiations and discussions), E13 (simulated value); Communication, E15* (simulated value); Transparent behaviour (trust building, openness), E16* (simulated value).*
Parameters typical for FIN only, RolNo (3, 4, 5), (Haavisto et al., 2022), (Puumala et al., 2021), (Larison, 2022).

Fig. 5 Distribution of parameters on RolNo of requested article, see Table 1

discussions, it is essential to get all related information. Double-loop learning (DLL) is important for organizational learning from each other. This method is used to learn from mistakes (for example, to share information after project activities, etc.), which helps to solve problems more effectively for the next time, as well as to evaluate and improve the existing legislation, processes, and goals of the organization.

The presence of simulated parameters at position RolNo ∈ (0, 1, 2) and zero parameters at position RolNo ∈ (3, 4, 5) shows the high separation accuracy between two sets of parameters. The right part of Fig. 5 is devoted to the parameters typical for FIN only (RolNo 3, 4, 5): Consensus (negotiations and discussions), E13*; Communication, E15*; Transparent behavior (trust building, openness), E16*. The presence of simulated parameters at position RolNo ∈ (3, 4, 5) and zero parameters at position RolNo ∈ (0, 1, 2) shows high separation accuracy between two sets of parameters.

Figure 6 represents distributions of simulated values of several common indicators for AM and FIN. Differences between expert-established values and ANN-predicted values are negligible (less than 0.005), and they are not shown for simplicity. This means that the ANN simulation gives exact results (a coincidence of nearly 100%). In that case, parameter RolNo∈ (0, 1, 2, 3, 4, 5) is common parameter. Eight parameters characterize the AM as well FIN methods in a chaotic manner: Increasing of personal efficiency and organizational results, E0*; Mentoring skills for leader, E1*; Coaching skills for leader, E2*; Decision-making and individual empowerment, E8*; Efficient work in a group, E5*; Difficult talks (conversation) plus effective feedback, E9*; Problem solving and change management, E11*; a la Action Science theory principles (behavior, norms, thinking, argumentation…), E14*.

In summary, a validation regime is essential for assessing and ensuring the generalization capability of FNN. After the validation procedure, we ensure that the selected model (see Table 4) works fine and could be titled the near-to-the-best model.

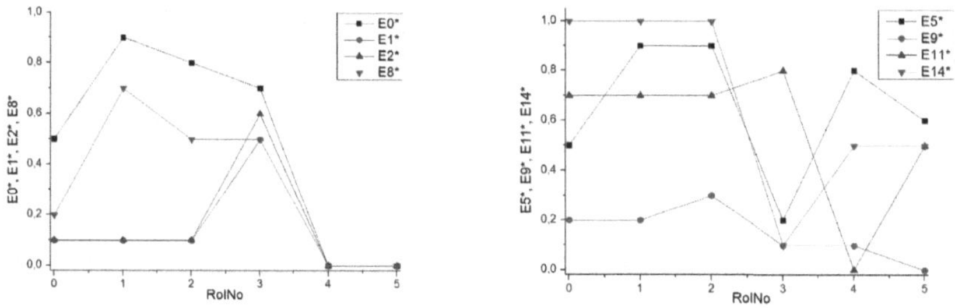

Increasing of personal efficiency and organizational results, E0 (simulated value); Mentoring skills for leader, E1* (simulated value); Coaching skills for leader, E2* (simulated value); Decision making and individual empowerment, E8* (simulated value).*

Efficient work in a group, E5 (simulated value); Difficult talks (conversation) plus effective feedback, E9* (simulated value); Problem solving and change management, E11* (simulated value); a la Action Science theory principles (behaviour, norms, thinking, argumentation...), E14* (simulated value).*

Fig. 6 Distribution of parameters on RolNo of the requested article (see Table 1). Parameters. AM (Action Science), RolNo ∈ (0, 1, 2), (Argyris, 1994; Friedman et al., 2009; Luechtefeld, 2005). FIN (Finnish case), RolNo ∈ (3, 4, 5), (Haavisto & Linge, 2022; Puumala & Maiche, 2021; Larison, 2022)

6 Conclusion

Research results will bring added value to social sciences as innovative cut (projection) in classification of indicators of American and Finnish OD techniques and opposite them. The new applicable and practical set of digitalized indicators for evaluation of OD of the organization on the intersection of computer sciences were created. These results would make positive influence also on Lithuanian business performance results (productivity). The research will bring practical value for organizations' leaders providing the set of indicators for digital tool to evaluate OD of organization. This set of indicators can be adapted for any country willing to evaluate OD level. Important effect will be reached by contribution and raising up the leadership and management competences for executives. The research question formulated in the introduction could be answered positively, because using Artificial Intelligence tools, it is possible to establish a well-connected relationship between the linguistic content of the analyzed articles and digital numerical indicators (denoting the quality of the methodology). Direct correlations (without ANNs) are elusive because the abundance of verbal information prevents direct correspondences.

Analysis of OD in the framework of American Action Science methodology (AM) and Finnish case (FIN) was conducted to identify the set of digital indicators for qualitative evaluation of OD. Presented set of indicators was validated using comparative critical analysis. Identified set of indicators will be integrated into the model for evaluation of OD in the future study. Digitalized indicators will be integrated into the for evaluation of OD model in the next research. Meanwhile, this research is valuable to create the model for evaluation of OD for executives. Digital technologies as strategic tool is contributing to maintain the resilience in organizations under difficult external competitive environment. Therefore, these days digital tools become more and more important for organizations serving as competitiveness and performance tool.

A new ANN-based OD quality estimation method using a Feed-forward Neural Network (FNN) was developed, designed, and validated. Using six peer-reviewed scientific articles representing the highest performance of the respective methodology (AM or FIN), we created an FNN input interface (based on frequencies of the requested keyword values) and an FNN output interface (based on values of expert-defined metrics).

A set of numerical indicators will be integrated into the OD assessment model. There are several topics where until now only qualitative and not quantitative evaluation prevailed, such as industrial planning, advertising industry, fashion industry, etc. This study is valuable in developing a model for evaluating managerial OD.

FNN training using the expert obtained data was successful, and network convergence was achieved as fully satisfied. Differences between expert-established values and FNN predicted values are negligible (less 0.005), and simulation using ANN gives very precise result (coincidence near 100%).

Limitations of the study are related to the choice of indicators (keywords and key-phrases). The use of keywords as meaningful units must be validated and cross-validated using different methodological sources.

Created model of estimation of OD indicators at enterprises using ANNs can be applied for critical review of theories useful for enterprise management performance in different framework. Latter model is important for executives of the enterprises, business owners and shareholders to evaluate the status quo of the organizational development level in the enterprises, and to estimate actions for exact indicators improvement to increase the efficiency of the overall organization, as well as to improve the management skills of managers within organization.

Acknowledgements Lidija Kraujalienė acknowledges the funding from Research Council of Lithuania (LMTLT), agreement No: S-PD-24-111.

Abbreviations

AI	Artificial Intelligence
AM	American Action Science
ANN	Artificial Neural Network
CEO	Chief Executive Officer
FIN	Finish case
FNN	Feed-Forward Neural Network
IFNN	Interpretable FNN
LFNN	Linguistic Fuzzy Neural Network
LSTM	Long Short-Term Memory
NLP	Natural Language Processing
OECD	Organization for Economic Cooperation and Development

OD	Organizational Development
PCA	Principal Component Analysis
RNN	Recurrent Neural Network
SAS	Scandinavian Airlines System
TDTO	Term-Distance Term-Occurrence
TNE	Total Network Error

References

Aras, A. C., Öztürk, C. E. & Koç, A. (2022). *Feedforward neural network based case prediction in Turkish Higher Courts - 2022 30th signal processing and communications applications conference (SIU), Safranbolu, Turkey, 2022* (pp. 1–4). https://doi.org/10.1109/SIU55565.2022.9864970

Argyris, C. (1994). Good communication that blocks learning -. *Harvard Business Review, 94401*(1994), 78–85.

Baird, L., Briscoe, J., Tuden, L., & Rosansky, L. M. H. (1994). World class executive development. *People and Strategy, 17*(1), 1.

Bolman, L. (2021). Argyris, Chris: The Iconoclast. In D. B. Szabla (Eds.), *The Palgrave handbook of organizational change thinkers*. Palgrave Macmillan. https://doi.org/10.1007/978-3-030-38324-4_29

Būdienė, G. & Gruodis, A. (2012). Zipf and Related Scaling Laws. 2. Literature Overview of Applications in Linguistics – *Innovative Infotechnologies for Science, Business and Education*, ISSN 2029- 1035 – 1(12) 17–26.

Būdienė, G. & Gruodis, A. (2016). Zipf and related scaling laws. 3. Literature overview of multidisciplinary applications (from informational aspects to energetic aspects) – *Innovative Infotechnologies for Science, Business and Education*, ISSN 2029–1035 – 2(21) 12–19.

Chien, L.-H., & Juang, J.-G. (2024). Application of linguistic fuzzy neural network to landing control - *Advances in Mechanical Engineering, 16*(1), 1–10 https://doi.org/10.1177/16878132241227115

Choain, L., & Malzy, T. (2019). Leading change through your creative class. *Journal of Organizational Change Management, 32*(3), 377–384. https://doi.org/10.1108/JOCM-04-2017-0118

Chong, T. Y., Banchs, R. E., Chang, E. S. & Li, H. (2015). *TDTO language modeling with feed-forward neural networks - INTERSPEECH 2015 September 6–10, 2015, Dresden, Germany* (pp. 1458–1462). https://doi.org/10.21437/Interspeech.2015-348

Coursera. (2023). Global skills report. https://www.coursera.org/skills-reports/global

Deshwal, V., Arora, S., & Batta, K. (2024). Application of neuro-linguistic programming techniques in organizational leadership. In *Improving service quality and customer engagement with marketing intelligence* (pp. 293–307). IGI Global. https://doi.org/10.4018/979-8-3693-6813-8.ch013

Dong, C., Zhang, Y., & Ao, S. (2024). How to engage employees in corporate social responsibility? Exploring corporate social responsibility communication effects through the reasoned action approach. *Management Communication Quarterly, 38*(1), 27–59. https://doi.org/10.1177/08933189231161621

Echezona, R. I., Momoh, R. I. & Afegbua, I. S. (2017). Enabling action research and action learning to enhance capacity and empowerment across SDGs dimensions and targets. https://library.ifla.org/id/eprint/1749/1/220-echezona-en.pdf

European Commission. (2023). *European innovation scoreboard.* Luxembourg: Publications Office of the European Union. https://op.europa.eu/en/web/eu-law-and-publications/publication-detail/-/publication/04797497-25de-11ee-a2d3-01aa75ed71a1

Frese, M., & Gielnik, M. M. (2023). The psychology of entrepreneurship: Action and process. *Annual Review of Organizational Psychology and Organizational Behavior, 10*, 137–164. https://doi.org/10.1146/annurev-orgpsych-120920-055646

Friedman, V., J. & Rogers, T. (2009). There is nothing so theoretical as good action research *7*(1) 31–47. https://doi.org/10.1177/1476750308099596

Fuchs, B. (2007). Learning from Toyota: How action learning can foster competitive advantage in new product development (NPD). *Action Learning: Research and Practice, 4*(1), 25–43. https://doi.org/10.1080/14767330701231446

Garrido-Moreno, A., Martín-Rojas, R., & García-Morales, V. J. (2024). The key role of innovation and organizational resilience in improving business performance: A mixed-methods approach. *International Journal of Information Management, 77*, Article 102777. https://doi.org/10.1016/j.ijinfomgt.2024.102777

Gavrilescu, M. & Vizireanu, N. (2019). Feedforward neural network-based architecture for predicting emotions from speech. *Data, 4,* 101. https://doi.org/10.3390/data4030101

Geeraerts, K., Tynjälä, P., Heikkinen, H. L., Markkanen, I., Pennanen, M., & Gijbels, D. (2015). Peer-group mentoring as a tool for teacher development. *European Journal of Teacher Education, 38*(3), 358–377. https://doi.org/10.1080/02619768.2014.983068

Gruodis, A. (2023a). Realizations of the artificial neural network for process modeling. overview of current implementations. *Applied Business: Issues & Solutions, 2*(2023), 22–27. ISSN 2783–6967. https://doi.org/10.57005/ab.2023.2.3

Gruodis, A. (2023b). *VALLUM01.* Advanced tool for implementation of artificial neural network containing tabular interface for input/output 2023.

Haavisto, V. E., & Linge, T. T. (2022). Internal crisis communication and Nordic leadership: The importance of transparent and participative communication in times of crisis. *Scandinavian Journal of Hospitality and Tourism, 22*(4–5), 331–356. https://doi.org/10.1080/15022250.2022.2123038

Hammond, R. D. (2013). Reflections on recursion and the evolution of learning. *Kybernetes, 42*(9/10), 1396–1403. https://doi.org/10.1108/K-11-2012-0103

Harris, C., & Gokcekus, O. (2000). *Learning in Action: A Guide to Putting the Learning Organization to Work.* https://doi.org/10.5465/ame.2000.4474573

Hawkins, P. (Ed.). (2018). *Leadership team coaching in practice: Case studies on developing high-performing teams.* Kogan Page Publishers.

Heikkinen, S., Lämsä, A. M., & Niemistö, C. (2021). Work–family practices and complexity of their usage: A discourse analysis towards socially responsible human resource management. *Journal of Business Ethics, 171*, 815–831. https://doi.org/10.1007/s10551-020-04458-9

Horan, J. (2007). Business driven action learning: A powerful tool for building world-class entrepreneurial business leaders. *Organization Development Journal, 25*(3), P75.

INSEAD. (2023). *The global talent competitiveness index 2023: What a difference ten years make what to expect for the next decade.* Fontainebleau, France. https://www.insead.edu/system/files/2023-11/gtci-2023-report.pdf

Jumisko-Pyykkö, S., Viita-Aho, T., Tiilikainen, E. & Saarinen, E. (2021, June). Towards systems intelligent approach in empathic design. In *Proceedings of the 24th international academic Mindtrek conference* (pp. 197–209). https://doi.org/10.1145/3464327.3464370

Koskinen, S., & Lämsä, A. M. (2017). Development of trust in the CEO-chair relationship. *Baltic Journal of Management, 12*(3), 274–291. https://doi.org/10.1108/BJM-02-2017-0029

Larison, K. D. (2022). Argumentation and scientific consensus-building: Using the nonfiction narrative to generate contextual understanding. *Teaching in Higher Education, 27*(1), 130–139. https://doi.org/10.1080/13562517.2021.1965569

Laukka, V., Katko, T. S., Peltonen, L., & Juuti, R. (2021). *Creating Collaboration for Contentious Projects on Managed Aquifer Recharge: Two Cases from Finland.* https://doi.org/10.1007/s10040-021-02334-y

Leppänen, I., Hämäläinen, R. P., Saarinen, E., & Viinikainen, M. (2018). Intrapersonal emotional responses to the inquiry and advocacy modes of interaction: A psychophysiological study. *Group Decision and Negotiation, 27*, 933–948. https://doi.org/10.1007/s10726-018-9584-8

Li, M. Q., Fung, B. C. M. & Abusitta A. (2022). On the effectiveness of interpretable feedforward neural network. In *2022 international joint conference on neural networks (IJCNN), Padua, Italy, 2022* (pp. 1–8). https://doi.org/10.1109/IJCNN55064.2022.9892343

Luechtefeld, R. (2005). A "theory of action" perspective on effective organizational change. https://doi.org/10.1109/IEMC.2005.1559106

McGuire, J. B., Palus, C. J., Warrick, D. D. & Mueller, J. (2013). Toward interdependent leadership culture: Transformation in KONE Americas. Lessons in.

Marquardt, M. J. (2016). Action learning around the world. In *Action learning in practice* (pp. 325–337). Routledge. ISBN 9781409418412

Matijošius, J., Rimkus, A., & Gruodis, A. (2024a). Validation challenges in data for different diesel engine performance regimes utilising HVO fuel: A study on the application of artificial neural networks for emissions prediction. *Machines, 12*, 279. https://doi.org/10.3390/machines12040279

Matijošius, J., Rimkus, A., & Gruodis, A. (2024b). Validation of ecology and energy parameters of diesel exhausts using different fuel mixtures, consisting of hydrogenated vegetable oil and diesel fuels, presented at real market: Approaches using artificial neural network for large-scale predictions. *Machines, 12*, 353. https://doi.org/10.3390/machines12060353

Moreno-Poyato, A. R., Subias-Miquel, M., Tolosa-Merlos, D., Ventosa-Ruiz, A., Pérez-Toribio, A., El Abidi, K., & Puig-Llobet, M. (2023). A systematic review on the use of action research methods in mental health nursing care. *Journal of Advanced Nursing, 79*(1), 372–384. https://doi.org/10.1111/jan.15463

Ochilova, V. R. (2024). Neuro-linguistic programming is an extensive and complex technique. *Progress Annals: Journal of Progressive Research, 2*(6), 11–13.

OECD. (2021). *OECD Skills strategy Lithuania: Assessment and recommendations.* OECD Publishing, Paris. https://doi.org/10.1787/14deb088-en

OECD. (2022). OECD economic surveys: Lithuania 2022. *OECD Publishing, Paris.* https://doi.org/10.1787/0829329f-en

Olhager, J. (2024). Action research as a meta-methodology: insights from an operations development project. *Production Planning & Control*, 1–11. https://doi.org/10.1080/09537287.2024.2380367

Pillado-Arbide, L. (2024). Developing relationships between corporations and startups through public-private collaboration: A Basque case study. https://hdl.handle.net/20.500.11984/6626

Polterovich, V. M. (2022). Competition, collaboration, and life satisfaction part 1. The seven of European leaders. *Ekonomicheskie i Sotsialnye Peremeny*, 15(2), 31–43.

Ponti, E. A. & Korhonen, A. (2017). Event-related features in feedforward neural networks contribute to identifying causal relations in discourse. In *Proceedings of the 2nd workshop on linking models of lexical, sentential and discourse-level semantics* (pp. 25–30). Valencia.

Puumala, E., & Maïche, K. (2021). 'Whether you like it or not, this is the future!': Everyday negotiations of the community's boundary in urban space. *Citizenship Studies, 25*(6), 808–824. https://doi.org/10.1080/13621025.2021.1968718

Raaijmakers, S., Bleijenbergh, I., Fokkinga, B., & Visser, M. (2018). The gender subtext of organizational learning. *The Learning Organization, 25*(1), 19–28. https://doi.org/10.1108/TLO-05-2017-0048

Riivari, E., Kivijärvi, M., & Lämsä, A. M. (2021). Learning teamwork through a computer game: For the sake of performance or collaborative learning? *Educational Technology Research and Development, 69*, 1753–1771. https://doi.org/10.1007/s11423-021-10009-4

Ropponen, T. (2008). The Nokia story of using action learning. *Action Learning: Research and Practice, 5*(2), 161–165. https://doi.org/10.1080/14767330802185822

Sagae, K. (2021). Tracking child language development with neural network language model -. *Frontiers in Psychology, 12*(2021), Article 674402. https://doi.org/10.3389/fpsyg.2021.674402
Schwartz, R. (2024). Why mutual learning brings about leadership team success - https://schwarzassociates.com/why-mutual-learning-brings-about-leadership-team-success/, accessed 11 Jun 2024.
Sonawane, S. (2024) Understanding and implementing neural networks in java from scratch - towards data science. Available online: https://towardsdatascience.com/understanding-and-implementing-neural-networks-in-java-from-scratch-61421bb6352c (Retrieved 24 April 2024).
Sørensen, M., Stenberg, U. & Garnweidner-Holme, L. (2018). A scoping review of facilitators of multi-professional collaboration in primary care. *International journal of integrated care*, 18(3). https://doi.org/10.5334/ijic.3959
Stoyanov, S. (2018). *An analysis of Chris Argyris's integrating the individual and the organization.* CRC Press.
Törmänen, J., Hämäläinen, R. P., & Saarinen, E. (2022). On the systems intelligence of a learning organization: Introducing a new measure. *Human Resource Development Quarterly, 33*(3), 249–272. https://doi.org/10.1002/hrdq.21455
Tuppurainen, R. (2020). Success factors of global implementation of asset management (Master's thesis).
Uljens, M., & Ylimaki, R. M. (2017). *Bridging educational leadership, curriculum theory and Didaktik: Non-affirmative theory of education.* Springer Nature. https://doi.org/10.1007/978-3-319-58650-2
Voigt, L., & von der Oelsnitz, D. (2024). A framework of HRM in cooperatives: A systematic literature review and future research agenda. *Journal of Co-Operative Organization and Management, 12*(1), Article 100232. https://doi.org/10.1016/j.jcom.2024.100232
Volz-Peacock, M., Carson, B., & Marquardt, M. (2016). Action learning and leadership development. *Advances in Developing Human Resources, 18*(3), 318–333. https://doi.org/10.1177/1523422316645884
Walton, J. (1998). Mentoring in mainland Europe and the republic of Ireland.
Wu, Z., Watts, O., & King, S. (2016, Merlin 2016). An open source neural network speech synthesis system. In *9th ISCA speech synthesis workshop (2016)* (pp 218–223).
Xiao, T., Zhu, J., Liu, T., & Zhang C. (2017) Fast parallel training of neural language models. In *Proceedings of the twenty-sixth international joint conference on artificial intelligence (IJCAI-17)*
Young, T. L., Carter-Edwards, L., Frerichs, L., Green, M. A., Hassmiller-Lich, K., Quarles, E., & Corbie-Smith, G. (2021). Action learning cohort series: An innovative community-engaged approach for translating research into practice. *Health Promotion Practice, 22*(1), 63–71. https://doi.org/10.1177/1524839919858592
Zandee, D. P., & Coghlan, D. (2024). Action research for impact in addressing the grand challenges. *Strategic Organization.* 14761270241270913. https://doi.org/10.1177/14761270241270913

Lidija Kraujalienė —design of the concept of presented idea, literature review, model constructing, analysis and evaluation of data: establishing of indicator sets and item sets. AG—ANN simulations, graphical representations. Both authors discussed the results, wrote the manuscript, and approved the final manuscript.

Sustainability and Environmental Governance

Sustainability in the Packaging Industry. A Small Step for One—A Huge Contribution to the Economy

Ewelina Idziak

Abstract The problem that the chapter tries to solve is the lack of support in the packaging industry for taking the first step towards innovations in sustainability. As a result will be examined sustainable practices adopted by companies in the packaging industry as innovations in packaging materials, design, production processes, recycling, and waste management as the main areas of changes. It will be analyzed showing the costs and benefits associated with implementing sustainable packaging solutions and the effect (IRR, NPV). The research is focused on two selected,real case-study companies, both working in the packaging sector and doing similar innovations in production processes. The research was conducted by a literature review, desk research, and case study analysis of financial documents and business plans. Based on those analyzed case-studies with the IRR indicator at the end of the project's period and without subsidy was planned at the level of IRR = 4.68% and IRR = 30.27%. It is worth encouraging companies to multiply sustainability activities by showing those examples. The smaller company showed significantly higher project effectiveness on NPV and IRR. This may be an area for further examining whether the size of the company has an influence on effectiveness in sustainable projects.

Keywords Sustainability · Packaging industry · Practices · Economic effect

Jel Classification Codes O12 · O33 · Q01

E. Idziak (✉)
Kazimierz Wielki University, Bydgoszcz, Poland
e-mail: ewelina.idziak@ukw.edu.pl

Azerbaijan State University of Economics, Baku, Azerbaijan

Vilniaus Kolegija—Higher Education Institution, Vilnius, Lithuania

I. Bartuseviciene et al. (eds.), *Building Economic Resilience*, Contributions to Economics, https://doi.org/10.1007/978-3-031-96428-2_8

1 Introduction

The packaging industry is a vital component of modern society and the global economy with an influence across multiple domains. Its importance stems from various factors, each highlighting its indispensable role in contemporary life, just for example: product protection, branding and marketing, sustainability and environmental impact, supply chain efficiency, regulatory compliance and safety, product differentiation and innovation and economic contribution and many more. To establish the general background of the sustainability in packaging industry it is not enough to write that it is an important issue and in the past decade many researchers and practitioners focused on this subject.

Firstly, packaging acts as a crucial shield for products, safeguarding them from damage, spoilage, contamination, and breakage during storage and transportation. The effectiveness of the packaging industry help products to reach consumers in good condition. Moreover the way of the packaging (nice and safe wrap, colors, quality) also create the branding of the company. That is why, innovative designs and strategic messaging could be a powerful tool for brand communication targeted the right group of the customers, because it conveys product information and influences consumer perceptions for further purchasing decisions. It also seems that nowadays the packaging industry is instrumental in driving sustainability and environmental initiatives as it is connected with all the spheres of production and consumption in the economy. Some activities are now important not to leave significant footprints to the environment, for example: recycling programs, sustainable materials, waste reduction, which are reshaping the industry landscape, heading to a more eco-friendly approach. In the field of supply chain it is emphasizes some important activities improving efficiency as: streamlining logistics operations, optimizing storage space, reducing costs of materials. All those activities are planned for getting higher operational efficiency. The next important area for the packaging industry is also legal framework that varies from country to country even in the same continent. Because so many aspects of consumer's everyday life, the packaging industry is one of the pioneer in adapting new solutions and technologies like: innovative materials, designs, and technologies, which is always challenging. We cannot forget about the significant role of the packaging industry as an important employer provider for the economy. The importance of the packaging industry also might be proved by statistics providing insight into the importance of the packaging industry. The total market value of packaging materials worldwide reached nearly 896 billion U.S. dollars in 2022. It is forecast that this global market value will increase considerably, reaching approximately 1.15 trillion U.S. dollars by 2030 across all regions. The Asia–Pacific region is expected to lead the market, with a contribution of roughly 289 billion U.S. dollars in 2022 and an estimated 392 billion U.S. dollars in 2030 (Garside, 2024). The packaging industry comprises various segments including rigid packaging (e.g., bottles, cans, containers), flexible packaging (e.g., bags, pouches, wraps), paper and cardboard packaging, metal packaging, glass packaging, and others. The global food and beverage industry is expected to experience significant growth in the coming years, which will further increase the demand for packaging materials. These materials are commonly used to package unprepared and prepared food items, as well as bulk food items such as cereals and grains. The increasing global demand for frozen meat products, canned seafood, and ready-to-eat meals is also expected to contribute to the growth of the packaging materials industry (Extrapolate, 2023).

It is observed that from one hand the growth of the packaging industry is driven by rising demand for packed products, but on the other hand it is seen that customers starts to be more aware about sustainability and eco-friendly solutions. The answer from the packing industry come very quickly by the intensification of the projects that should change the processes into more friendly to the environment by for example the adoption of biodegradable materials for packaging, which naturally decompose over time and present fewer ecological risks. There is the variety of new solutions starting from bio-plastics to compostable packaging, and other alternatives. It is also more frequently raised idea of the "minimalism in packaging" by such activities as: using less superfluous materials, simplified packaging designs and minimizing unnecessary layers (as it is demonstrated in the case studies in this paper). Governments and regulatory bodies are also implementing policies to promote sustainable packaging practices by rewarding with for example grants or preferential financing. It is observed also, that advancements in technology are driving innovation in the packaging industry, with developments such as smart packaging, active packaging, quick-drying and harmless paints and varnishes, and intelligent labeling gaining traction. These innovations aim to enhance product safety, extend shelf-life, and improve consumer engagement. McKinsey & Company in 2023 launched a survey across 11 countries to explore consumers' attitudes towards sustainable packaging, which covers a statistically significant sample size across 66% of global GDP and 50% of the global population, as well as across demographics in each of the 11 countries. Responses from more than 11,500 consumers reveal three main findings. First, across all countries, hygiene and shelf-life top the list of factors important in consumers' purchasing decisions. Second, on the environmental impact of product packaging, consumer concerns related to ocean litter are most evident in Europe, Japan, and the United States. Meanwhile, consumers in other Asian countries and Latin America seem most concerned about other forms of pollution. And finally, consumers around the world have different opinions on what type of packaging is most sustainable. Feber emphasizes that the packaging industry is expected to tailor their approaches to respond to more aware consumers (Feber, 2023).

The legal aspects were rised also by many authors (Beitzen-Heineke, Kroon and Vrijens, Grimes-Casey, Martínez-Sala and many more). Beitzen-Heineke rises that stricter laws and regulations about the amount of packaging waste generated across the supply chain could encourage the adoption of reusable packaging (Beitzen-Heineke et al., 2017). Especially, Camps-Posino et al. (2021) suggest that policy should strongly support the transition from single-use to reusable packaging systems as a must. On the other hand also, many authors agreed that environmental laws should insist on reduction of the packaging waste, also with legislation increasing producer responsibility to reduce the use of packaging (Grimes-Casey et al., 2007;

Kroon & Vrijens, 1995; Martínez-Sala et al., 2009). Some authors suggest connection between wastes and taxes. Also, Lisińska-Kuśnierz suggests that the legislation should be enacted alongside tax reliefs to drive research and increase producer responsibility and should focus on the development of new technology, materials, and packaging techniques, allowing companies to utilize newer waste management processes (Lisińska-Kuśnierz, 2001). EURACTIV reports that E.U. new regulations aim to cut packaging by 15% by 2040 while restricting single-use plastic packaging for sauces like mayonnaise and cosmetics. The law, which will take effect in 2026, also contains an interim 5% reduction target for 2030 as well as product-specific restrictions (Keating, 2024).

In the past decades, much research has focused on sustainability in the packaging industry. Those research areas are characterized from the scientific perspective in the part of this paper dedicated to literature review, but it should be noted that due to the ongoing phase of increasing interest in the topic of sustainability in the packaging industry, there is still a number of uncertainties and gaps between business practice and scientific evidence.

Therefore, to establish the niche for this research, it seems to be important to join together a theoretical framework with practical case studies to assess the economic effect of selected activities. Chosen case studies have received positive opinions from one of the Polish government agencies supporting entrepreneurship and innovation. This agency is an independent public institution in Poland that supports and promotes entrepreneurship and innovation.

2 Literature Review

The paper contributes to the literature dealing with sustainability in the packaging industry. This research is directly related to the impact of activities aimed at sustainability in the packaging sector. The literature review begins by surveying extant literature to discern prevailing theories, methodologies, and empirical findings, providing a foundational understanding of the research domain. Based on Scopus base filtering analysis, the filter was used: "TITLE-ABS-KEY (sustainability AND in AND packaging AND industry)". Readily discernible, is that this scientific inquiry into the sustainability in packaging returns information about highly increasing numbers of scientific papers in this area. Figure 1 shows the number of papers by year registered in Scopus base for sustainability in packaging.

A dynamically increasing number of published papers can be observed. In the period 1995–2023, the total number of papers were 1222, whereas during the last 10 years were published 995 papers and last 3 years it is the strongest dynamics by publishing 689 papers. Deepening the analysis of countries' activity in sustainability in the packaging industry. It is seen that the most active country in the subject of sustainability in the packaging industry is the United States. Scientists from this country published 187 papers noted in Scopus base in the period 1995–2023 about sustainability in the packaging industry. Then, very active are also scientists from

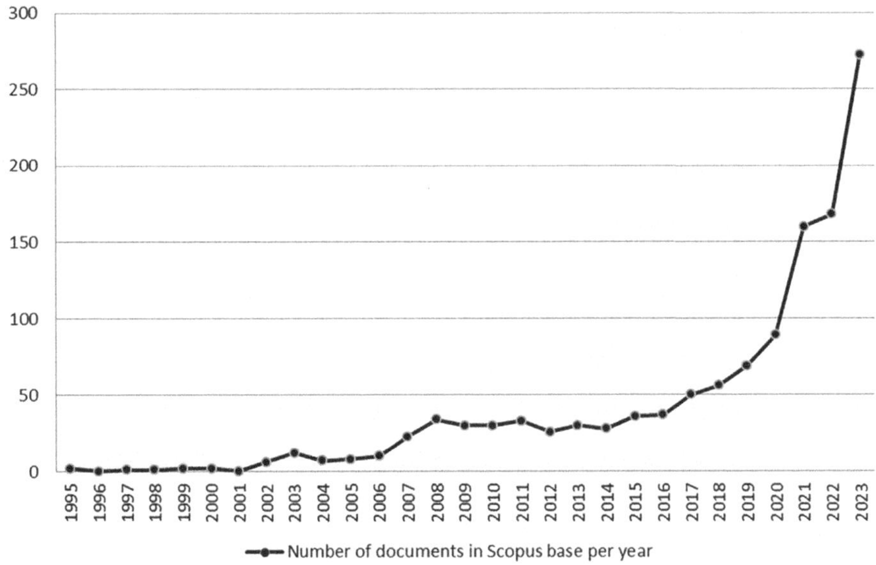

Fig. 1 Number of papers for sustainability in packaging by year (*Source* own study)

India (166 papers) and then in order: Italy, United Kingdom, China, Spain, Brazil, Portugal, Germany, and France, what is presented on Fig. 2.

In terms of the type of papers published, there is a clear predominance of articles, constituting 49.6% of papers recorded in the Scopus database in the field of sustainability in packaging. Significance share have also such forms of publication as review (16.7%), book chapter (13.3%), and conference paper (12.8%). The other forms of publication like books, conferences, reviews, short surveys and others, have only a few percent share per each, which is presented on Fig. 3.

For the current scientific trends identification it is needed to focus on the main areas for which published papers. Main areas mostly address: the environmental impacts of current packaging practices in the industry, how sustainable packaging solutions can reduce the industry's carbon footprint, the economic benefits of adopting sustainable packaging practices, and the role of technology in advancing sustainability in the packaging industry. Starting from a wide perspective, it is worth consistently calling the conclusions of research in the main selected areas:

- environmental impacts of current packaging practices;
- reducing the carbon footprint with sustainable packaging;
- economic benefits of sustainable packaging;
- role of technology in advancing sustainability.

Environmental impacts of current packaging practices often manifest themselves in raising issues such as negative environmental impacts, largest plastic share footprint, and advantages of flexible packaging but also in the context of economic mechanical recycling. Kaestener et al. points out that packaging protects products, keeps

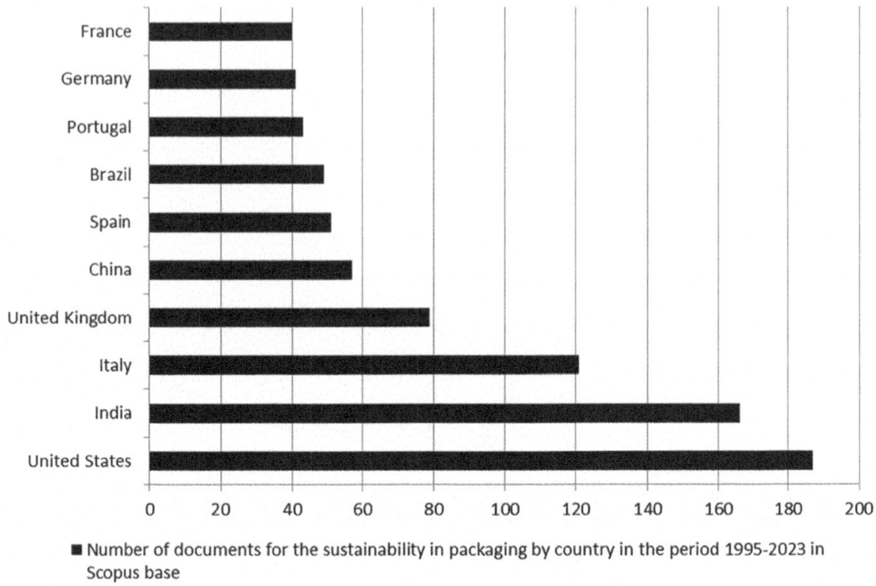

Fig. 2 Number of papers for the sustainability in packaging by country in the period 1995–2023 in Scopus base (*Source* own study)

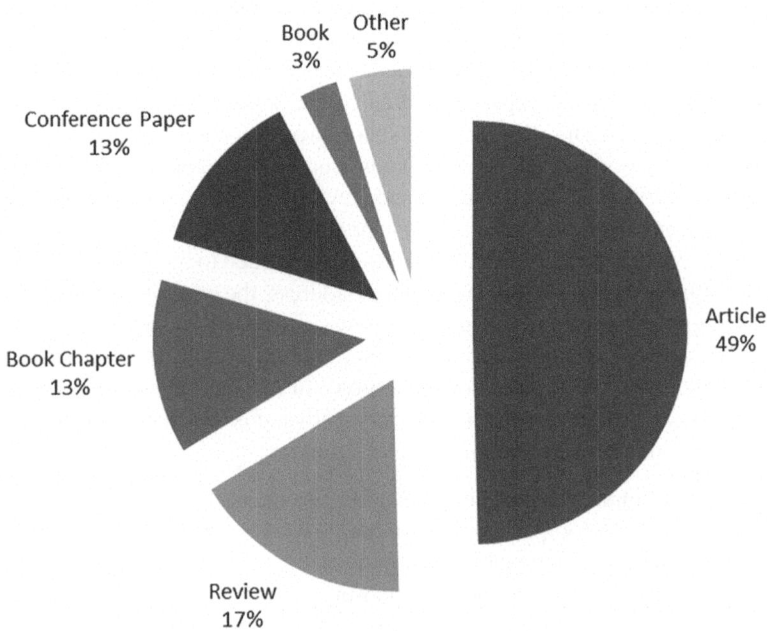

Fig. 3 Papers share by type on sustainability in packaging from 1995 to 2023: A Scopus database study (*Source* own study)

their value, and reduces waste. This is especially crucial in domains with perishable goods such as food, medicine or cosmetics. On the other hand, conventional packaging solutions yield negative environmental impacts. In the EU, the largest share of plastics is used for packaging, causing a corresponding footprint. The application of sustainable strategies to packaging should help to reduce carbon dioxide emissions and promote the development of sustainable consumption. In this paper, a review is conducted on research that brings together circular economy, and packaging design. In addition to the current standards of conventional packaging, packaging alternatives are presented, which are categorized according to the R-strategies Refuse, Reduce, Reuse, and Recycle (Kaestner et al., 2023). Also, Rajesh and Subhashini raised the importance of packaging is when items are shipped around the world, which in recent years has been on a daily basis. At the same time, the large number of companies transporting goods from factories to warehouses and then to retailers, as well as the enormous online orders placed daily, there is a massive amount of plastic waste such as Styrofoam, cardboard, and paper that are utilized in the process. However, sustainable packaging is a boon to this problem. The manufacturing process of such packaging materials also tends to be more efficient, further minimizing resources needed and reducing the negative impact that the business has on the environment. Sustainable packaging is produced in an environmentally friendly manner through the use and reuse of biodegradable and recyclable materials and is considered energy efficient (Rajesh & Subhashini, 2021). To be more energy efficient is nowadays crucial from the cost perspective. Cooper underlines that flexible packaging (low use of materials and energy, low carbon footprint and GHG emissions, and reduction in food waste) is still under attack by environmental groups because of the difficulty of economic mechanical recycling, so it presently mostly ends up in landfills. In contrast, the food, packaging, and recycling industries are responding strongly to this attack with programs to educate consumers on sustainability advantages and to obviate landfilling by developing: Improved collection, identification, marking and sorting methods Economic new recycling and recovery methods, including delamination and dissolution processes and conversion to energy, liquid fuels and downstream chemicals New materials and package designs Implementation of these various potential routes will depend on local and national logistical, economic, social and political situations, not just technological factors (Cooper, 2017).

Reducing the carbon footprint with sustainable packaging is the second most frequently raised topic for research on an interdisciplinary level. Usually, reducing the carbon footprint is connected in research with R-strategies, recycled and biodegradable materials, environmentally friendly manner, minimizing resources and reducing the negative impact, obviating landfilling, and developing new recycling and recovery methods. All those aspects were raised together with the environmental impact of current packaging practices by Kaestener et al., Rajesh and Subhashini, and Cooper (Cooper, 2017; Kaestner et al., 2023; Rajesh & Subhashini, 2021).

The economic benefits of sustainable packaging also have garnered significant attention and scrutiny in contemporary scholarly discourse. In this research area are important: economic viability for both consumers and manufacturers, ensuring a cleaner environment for future generations, consumer behavior as under consideration is if consumers are willing to pay more for products offered in "eco-friendly" packaging, indicating a potential market advantage for companies adopting sustainable packaging practices. Singh et al., have shared their understanding of "Sustainability" a term that is often referred to as development that meets the needs of the present without compromising the ability of future generations to meet their own needs. Some of the current drivers for sustainable packaging include customer and consumer demands, legislation, and recent international reports and policies. Even in this global economic downturn, consumers are being reported to be willing to pay more for less as related to products offered in "eco-friendly" packaging. In addition, they have become more tuned to only getting products that they want fast and directly from their phones and mobile devices from any region in the world, getting confirmation of the financial transaction, a guarantee of the delivery process, and receiving the product or products from various sources at their doorsteps. This is the biggest trend and change in both logistical and sustainable packaging challenges where transportation costs, delivery in high populations, green packaging, use of new drones, and fuel-efficient delivery vans are the trend. This paper provides a perspective on the challenges and trends in these areas that are closely related to the final product delivery where you require consumer satisfaction, low costs, environmentally friendly materials, no damage to the environment, and being able to face criticism on social media. This paper also wants to avoid "Green-washing", a term commonly used to indicate false promotion or exaggeration of the "greenness" of packaging is reported to be plentiful in the packaging industry as marketers try to take advantage of consumers' vulnerabilities associated with environmental stewardship (Singh et al., 2019). Also, Roy has emphasized, that a range of global practices is visible in various business operations, including designing, manufacturing, storage, and distribution. This paper has focused on some of the innovative and sustainable packaging practices adopted by companies in New Zealand and other parts of the world to improve operational efficiency and environmental sustainability towards better profits and corporate social responsibility. The literature review indicates that while there is an appetite for changes in the packaging materials towards sustainability, users or shoppers are still not fully prepared to pay for such changes. There are many examples of sustainable packaging practices undertaken by companies, researchers, and innovators worldwide. However, it may not be pragmatic to do away with all the plastic packaging from every product because consumers still want to enjoy the packaging's convenience. So, while people might be shocked to see the frequent imagery of wildlife crippled or killed by discarded packaging not every consumer is putting the planet's health ahead of their fresh choice of produce. The challenge ultimately lies with the food and other industries to innovate their packaging to ensure they are biodegradable, recyclable, sustainable, and affordable. Fortunately, the changing consumers' awareness of sustainable packaging and perceived readiness to accept some of the costs provide significant optimism (Roy, 2022).

The importance of technology in advancing sustainability is still increasing, especially since we are in a period of a changing economy—changing by unexpected phenomena, rapidly changing technology, new reality and new approaches and generations, and many more. Technology plays a fundamental role in shaping the future of the packaging industry, particularly in advancing sustainability trends and topics. In this matter Berg, examine sustainability trends and topics that will create a better packaging industry, using some insights from Berg's work with DS Smith's North America Packaging and Paper division. They have claimed, that innovative technologies such as nanotechnology and biotechnology are driving the growth of smart packages that encompass food shelf-life while maintaining and monitoring their safety and environmental impact. Also, enabling technologies, when properly used, may provide a solution to the balance between sustainability and consumer demands, particularly in the context of biodegradable, recyclable, and affordable packaging (Berg, 2023).

Shortly concluding, the environmental impacts of current packaging practices in the industry are substantial, with conventional packaging solutions contributing to a significant carbon footprint. However, sustainable packaging solutions offer a promising avenue for reducing this footprint, with economic benefits for both consumers and manufacturers. Technology plays a crucial role in advancing sustainability in the packaging industry, offering innovative solutions to balance environmental sustainability and consumer demands. That is why, at this stage is important to connect theory, acts of law, and regulations with practical experience resulting straight from business practice. It is the subject of the next parts of this paper.

3 Methodology

This study employs a couple of methods to investigate the sustainability in packaging case study, selected companies both from the scientific and practical perspective. The main purpose of this study is to examine selected sustainable practices, which reveal various sustainable practices and initiatives adopted by case study companies from the packaging industry as innovations in packaging materials, design, production processes, recycling, and waste management. The assessment of economic effects for those companies also will be analyzed showing the costs and benefits associated with implementing sustainable packaging solutions in those two companies.

Firstly, desk research and literature review were realized to establish a general background and niche for the topic. The niche is the lack of practical examples for sustainable improvements in packaging companies. The scientific background was connected with two practical examples. In the next step, data was collected in a number of secondary data reports, to have an understanding of the background and compare it with the literature research. As the workout for this part was prepared the list of areas as the framework for practical analysis. The areas for the examination of sustainable practices were chosen: innovations in packaging materials, design, production processes, recycling, and waste management.

Then, a crucial step was done in the process of selecting positively assessed projects by one of the Polish government agencies supporting entrepreneurship and innovation. Companies were selected by the following criteria:

- company from the packaging industry;
- the project connected with sustainable improvements in the production process;
- positive, formal decision about the financing for the project from Polish government agencies supporting entrepreneurship and innovation.

Filtering in the base of Polish government agencies supporting entrepreneurship and innovation was used as the method for selecting companies. Two companies were selected by those criteria. As the indicators constitute economic impact IRR and NPV were chosen. The purpose of choosing targeted companies exactly from the packaging industry and exactly planning innovations in packaging production technology was done according to the subject of this research paper.

Those two companies from the packaging industry have applied for funding the new technology for packaging production. Because of the sensitive data, the analysis will be done anonymously using the names: Company 1 and Company 2.

For **Company 1**, the main goal of the investment was to implement the production of innovative low-migration packaging (especially for food) on a national scale, protected with a special varnish coating ensuring increased protection of the print against abrasion, scratches, and damage during technological processes in the printing house and when packing products on automatic packaging lines. The implementation of the project is the result of previously planned and completed R&D works.

For **Company 2**, the main goal of the investment is to implement the production of innovative commercial and advertising prints protected on a national scale with a dispersion varnish with a gloss and scratch resistance comparable to UV varnish. The implementation of the project is the result of previously planned and completed R&D works. Research work was crucial in the development of new products. As a result, a modification of the dispersion varnish recipe used in offset printing technology was developed to refine and protect the surface of commercial and advertising prints. The implementation of innovative products into company 2 will have a significant impact on improving the condition of the natural environment, because the use of dispersion varnish, which will replace previously used protection and refining techniques, such as UV varnish or foils, will result in these products having a minimal impact on the environment. The use of dispersion varnish will also translate into a reduction in energy demand (the drying process of such varnish generates approximately 55% less electrical energy consumption compared to the UV varnish drying process and 35 to 48% less electrical energy consumption compared to the lamination process) and to reduce the amount of waste generated in the printing process.[1]

Project applications, financial documents like profit and loss statements, balance sheets, cash flows, and business plans were analyzed.

[1] Data about efficiency improvements comes from case study applications and business plans.

Then, the study-case methodology was used to analyze exact examples for in-depth investigation, mainly by comparison analysis, and financial indicators analysis.

The issue of the gap or differences between theory and practice is still unresolved neither by regulations nor by practice, so the paper contributes to this area. In the next step, quantitative and descriptive methodology was used, to analyze data and make conclusions. Visualization methods (charts, tables, schemes) were used to make complex conclusions clear.

The assessment **criteria** for the selected sustainable practices in case study companies have been adopted as positive or negative depending on whether the project has properly proven activities related to a given category. The assessment focuses on the evaluation criteria used in a competition for financing sustainability and innovation activities used by Polish government agencies supporting entrepreneurship and innovation. By using these criteria and evaluations, the methodology ensures a structured, transparent assessment of sustainable practices, linking theoretical research with real-world business applications.

Standard criteria for NPV and IRR were adopted. IRR decision rule was used:

- if IRR > Required Rate of Return (or cost of capital): The project is considered acceptable as it promises a return greater than the required rate;
- if IRR = Required Rate of Return: The project breaks even in terms of return;
- if IRR < Required Rate of Return: The project is not financially attractive, as it promises a lower return than the cost of capital.

The interest rate on 10-year treasury bills can be taken as a reference point. According to the Ministry of Finance in Poland, in (2024), the average interest rate for 10-year treasury bonds in Poland, known as EDO bonds (indexed to inflation), is around 6.75% during the first year. After the first year, the interest rate is adjusted annually, based on the inflation rate plus a fixed margin of 1.25% (Gov.pl, 2024).

Also, standard criteria were used for NPV assessment. NPV Decision Rule was applied:

- if NPV > 0: The project is considered profitable as it is expected to generate more value than the cost;
- if NPV = 0: The project is expected to break even;
- if NPV < 0: The project is not considered financially viable.

Standard principles for assessing financial ratios generally used in the financial analysis of enterprises were also applied.

4 Results

The results part of this paper is intentionally divided into two sections. First, dedicated to the examination of various sustainable practices and initiatives adopted by companies in the packaging industry as innovations in packaging materials, design, production processes, recycling, and waste management. The second section is dedicated to the assessment of economic effects. Based on chosen case companies will be shown: the costs and benefits associated with implementing sustainable packaging solutions, profitability, liability structure and debt service ratios, liquidity ratios, and asset turnover ratios.

4.1 Sustainable Practices

Companies work out sustainable practices in many ways according to their needs, resources, possibilities, research findings, and others. In literature and business practice there are many ways and influences to work with sustainability for example: material science advances, sustainability considerations as environmentally friendly alternatives, barrier properties, functional packaging, nanotechnology applications, consumer perception and behavior, regulatory compliance, life cycle assessment, industry trends and market dynamics, future directions and many others. For the purposes of this study, the focus was only on the following areas: innovations in packaging materials, design, production processes, recycling, and waste management. Figure 4 shows selected activities as an examples of sustainable practices.

According to Scopus base, the most cited papers about innovations in packaging materials are connected with: food packaging based on polymer nanomaterials—729 times cited (Silvestre et al., 2011), cellulose nano-materials in water treatment technologies—564 times cited (Carpenter et al., 2015) and also about sustainable supplier selection and order lot-sizing: An integrated multi-objective decision-making process—302 times cited (Azadnia et al., 2015).

It is also crucial to understand the significant role of design because innovative packaging design can impact sustainability in the packaging industry by optimizing material usage, reducing packaging waste, and enhancing recyclability. Designing packaging with lightweight materials, efficient shapes, and minimalistic designs can decrease the environmental footprint associated with production, transportation, and disposal. Additionally, incorporating sustainable design principles such as material reduction, use of renewable resources, and consideration of end-of-life options can contribute to overall sustainability efforts.

The production process in the packaging industry is special, because of playing an essential role for environmental impact of packaging materials. By adopting eco-friendly manufacturing practices, the packaging industry may help prevent environment against damages. In this case, one of the most significant activities are: minimizing water usage, utilizing energy-efficient machinery, recycling, renewable energy sources, or closed-loop recycling systems that may reduce greenhouse effect and resource consumption and sustainability.

Nowadays, also particular important place is dedicated to waste management as the mitygant of environmental impact of packaging industry, as implementation of waste reduction strategies, such as reuse, source reduction and composting, can minimize the amount of packaging waste generated and alleviate pressure on landfill

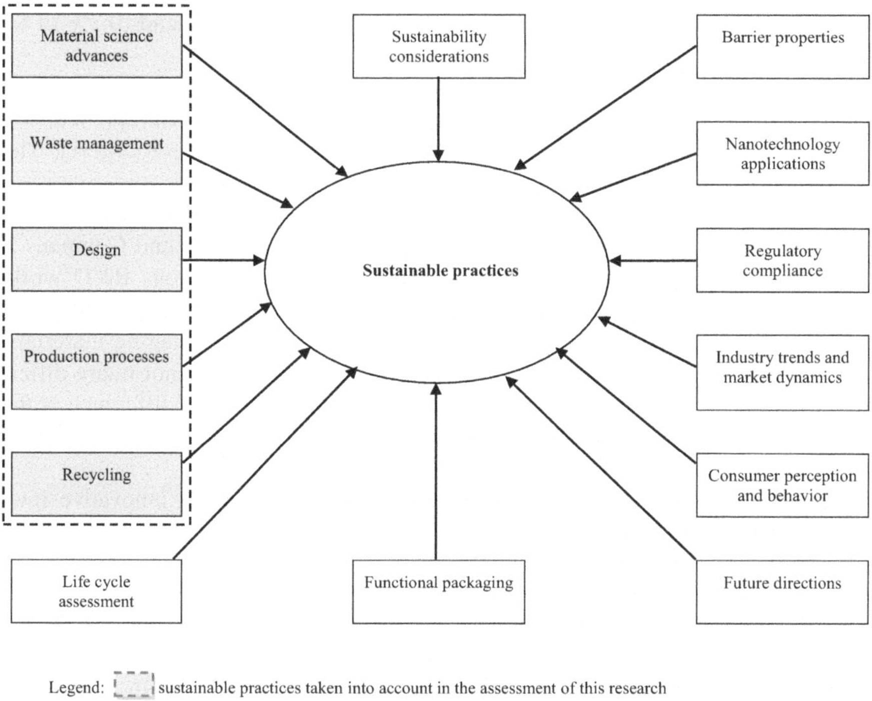

Fig. 4 Only chosen examples of sustainable practices in the packaging industry (*Legend* sustainable practices taken into account in the assessment of this research. *Source* own study based on: Azadnia et al., 2015; Carpenter et al., 2015; Silvestre et al., 2011)

capacity. Especially, investing in advanced waste management technologies, such as waste-to-energy facilities or anaerobic digestion may help to recover the energy and resources from packaging waste, at the same time promoting sustainability.

For the practical case studies assessment, certain areas were chosen to compare activities of the two case study companies, for example: design, production processes, recycling, and waste management practices. Two selected case study companies are from Poland and they work in the packaging industry. Company 1 is a medium-sized company, whereas Company 2 is small company. According to definition,[2] a small company is an enterprise that employs from 10 to 50 employees. The company's total annual balance sheet and/or turnover must not exceed EUR 10 million. According to the latest data for 2020, small companies in Poland constitute 2.4% of all enterprises and there are 52.7 thousand of them. While a medium-sized company is an enterprise that employs from 50 to 250 employees. The turnover of an average company does not exceed EUR 50 million, and the annual balance sheet does not exceed EUR 43

[2] Annex I to Commission Regulation (EU) No 651/2014 of 17 June 2014 declaring certain categories of aid compatible with the internal market in application of Articles 107 and 108 of the Treaty.

million. There are 15.2 thousand medium-sized companies in Poland (0.7% of all companies).

The assessment was done by criteria of the competition in which case study companies applied to one of the Polish government agencies supporting entrepreneurship and innovation for financing and also by selected for this research criteria. The assessment in both areas is presented in Table 1.

The assessment of sustainable practices in the case study companies reveals several positive aspects across various criteria. Both Company 1 and Company 2 exhibit positive evaluations in key areas such as purpose, previous R&D work, effect, eco-effect, business effects, enterprise size, tasks, compliance with horizontal EU policies, eco-innovations, strategy, innovations in packaging materials, design, production processes, and waste management. There are not many differences between the analyzed companies. The only one significant difference is the enterprise size, because Company 1 is the medium size, and Company 2 is the small size.

Company 1 demonstrates a positive outlook in implementing innovative low-migration packaging production on a national scale, as well as in introducing new recipes and improving the natural environment by reducing cardboard waste. Additionally, Company 1 shows a commitment to business growth through diversification, acquiring new customers, and entering new markets.

Similarly, Company 2 displays positive initiatives in implementing innovative commercial and advertising prints protected with dispersion varnish, enhancing its competitive position and increasing sales revenues. Both companies exhibit a medium to small enterprise size, demonstrating adaptability and scalability in their sustainability efforts.

However, both companies receive negative evaluations regarding recycling, as there is no specific information provided about activities connected with recycling. This indicates a potential area for improvement in their sustainability practices. Recycling wasn't the criteria in the competition for financing sustainability and innovative activities.

In conclusion, the table highlights the commendable efforts of the casestudy companies in adopting sustainable practices across various aspects of their operations. While there are areas of strength, such as innovation, eco-effect, and business growth, there is also room for enhancement, particularly in terms of incorporating recycling initiatives into their sustainability strategies.

4.2 Economic Effect

The section is dedicated to the assessment of economic effect for the case study companies. Economic effect refer to the effects that a particular action, policy, or event has on the economy of an individual, company, region, country or even globally. Economic importance can manifest in various forms, influencing factors such as employment, income, economic growth, productivity, trade, investment patterns,

Table 1 The assessment of sustainable practices in case study companies

Project evaluation criteria in the competition for financing sustainability and innovative activities				
Criteria	Company 1—explanation	Company 1—evaluation	Company 2—explanation	Company 2—evaluation
Purpose	Implementation of innovative low-migration packaging production, particularly for food, (national scale). This packaging is protected by a special varnish coating to ensure enhanced print protection against abrasion, scratches, damage during technological processes in the printing house, when on automatic packaging lines	POSITIVE	Implementation of the production of innovative commercial and advertising prints protected with dispersion varnish with a gloss and scratch resistance comparable to UV varnish	POSITIVE
Previous R&D work	YES	POSITIVE	YES	POSITIVE
Effect	New recipe	POSITIVE	Modification of the dispersion varnish recipe used in offset printing technology	POSITIVE
ECO effect	Improve the state of the natural environment by reducing the amount of cardboard waste generated during packaging production and product packaging	POSITIVE	The use of dispersion varnish, which will replace previously used protection and refinement techniques, such as UV varnish or foil, will ensure that these products have a minimal impact on the environment	POSITIVE

(continued)

Table 1 (continued)

Project evaluation criteria in the competition for financing sustainability and innovative activities				
Criteria	Company 1—explanation	Company 1—evaluation	Company 2—explanation	Company 2—evaluation
Business effects	–introducing new, innovative products to the Company's offer that have not been offered on the market before; –increasing the competitive position of the company by diversifying the range of products offered; –acquiring new customers; –entering new markets;	POSITIVE	–introducing new, innovative products to the Company's offer, not previously offered on the market, for example commercial and advertising prints protected with dispersion varnish with a gloss and scratch resistance comparable to UV varnish; –increasing the competitive position of the company by diversifying the range of products offered; –increase in sales revenues; –acquiring new customers; –entering new markets;	POSITIVE
Enterprise size	Medium	POSITIVE	Small	POSITIVE
Tasks	–purchase and installation of machines; –hiring a new employee; –launching the production of innovative packaging printed with low-migration inks protected with a special varnish coating ensuring increased protection of the print against scratches, abrasion and related damages;	POSITIVE	–purchase and installation of the machine; –hiring a new employee; –introducing a new product to the market;	POSITIVE
Compliance of the project with horizontal EU policies	–horizontal equality principles; –the principle of equality between women and men; –the principle of sustainable development; –compliance with 6R principles or other environmental principles;	POSITIVE	–horizontal equality principles; –the principle of equality between women and men; –the principle of sustainable development; –compliance with 6R principles or other environmental principles;	POSITIVE

(continued)

Table 1 (continued)

Project evaluation criteria in the competition for financing sustainability and innovative activities				
Criteria	Company 1—explanation	Company 1—evaluation	Company 2—explanation	Company 2—evaluation
Eco-innovations	YES—implementation	POSITIVE	YES—implementation	POSITIVE
Strategy	–implementation of innovative low-migration packaging production;	POSITIVE	–implementation of innovative production technologies; –optimization of production processes; –improving the quality of products/services; –expanding cooperation with research units and conducting own R&D work; –reducing the negative impact on the natural environment; –increasing share in the domestic market and acquiring new foreign markets; –increase in sales revenues;	POSITIVE
Selected criteria for the purpose of the research				
Innovations in packaging materials	–innovative low migration packaging; –special varnish coating;	POSITIVE	protected with dispersion varnish with a gloss and scratch resistance comparable to UV varnish	POSITIVE
Design	–optimizing material usage; –reducing packaging waste;	POSITIVE	optimizing material usage; –reducing packaging waste;	POSITIVE
Production processes	–innovative low-migration packaging production	POSITIVE	–production of innovative commercial and advertising prints protected with dispersion varnish	POSITIVE
Recycling	No specific information about recycling activities	NEGATIVE	No specific information about recycling activities	NEGATIVE
Waste management	–reducing packaging waste;	POSITIVE	–reducing packaging waste;	POSITIVE

Source own study

and overall welfare and many more. What's more, economic effect assessments are crucial for informing decision-making processes at multiple levels, from local development projects to national policy initiatives and international trade agreements. By understanding the economic implications of different actions, policymakers can design more effective policies, businesses can make informed investment decisions, and communities can anticipate and manage potential changes in their economic landscape. Additionally, economic effect analysis helps stakeholders identify opportunities for growth, mitigate risks, and promote sustainable development. Based on the chosen case companies, the costs and benefits, as well as the Internal Rate of Return (IRR) and Net Present Value (NPV) associated with implementing sustainable packaging solutions as declared by the company, will be presented. Data are presented in Euro (EUR). Firstly, for each company it is presented the general financial positions with the planned grant and costs (Table 2). Then it is presented the benefits and the effect of the project realization with and without the grant (Tables 3 and 4).

Table 2 presents the general financial positions of Company 1 over the period from 2023 to 2034, along with the planned grant and costs in thousand EUR. In the initial years, particularly from 2023 to 2028, the company reports zero revenue and operating costs, indicating a period of setup or initial investment with no operational activities. However, from 2025 onwards, there is a notable increase in revenue, reaching 4,523 thousand EUR in 2026 and gradually rising to 5,560 thousand EUR by 2033. This suggests a successful transition from the setup phase to operational profitability. Operating costs also begin to appear from 2026 onwards, indicating the commencement of business operations. The inclusion of amortization and capital expenditure reflects investments in assets and infrastructure necessary for business activities, particularly in 2025 with a significant capital expenditure of 8,382 thousand EUR. The planned grant, introduced in 2025, contributes to the financial position of

Table 2 General financial positions for Company 1's project in thousand EUR

Year	Revenue	Operating costs (excluding depreciation)	Amortization	Capital expenditure (design)	Grant	Change in working capital	Discount rate	Discount factor
2025	0	0	129	8,382	4,191	0	4.00%	0.9246
2026	4,523	3,222	1,173	0	0	−987	4.00%	0.8890
2027	4,660	3,315	1,173	0	0	−26	4.00%	0.8548
2028	4,796	3,407	1,173	0	0	−26	4.00%	0.8219
2029	4,939	3,503	1,173	0	0	−34	4.00%	0.7903
2030	5,089	3,604	1,173	0	0	−42	4.00%	0.7599
2031	5,240	3,706	1,173	0	0	−43	4.00%	0.7307
2032	5,396	3,811	1,146	0	0	−31	4.00%	0.7026
2033	5,560	3,921	67	0	0	−38	4.00%	0.6756

Source own study

Table 3 Benefits and efficiency of the Company's 1 project without subsidies

Option without subsidies [Implementation of innovation] Year	Free cash flow (FCF) [net of subsidies]	Accumulated free cash flow (FCF) [net of grants]	Discounted cash flow (FCF) [without grants]	Cumulative discounted cash flow (FCF)—NPV [without subsidies]	IRR [without subsidy]
2025	−8,382	−8,382	−7,750	0	n/d
2026	314	−8,068	280	−7,470	−96.25%
2027	1,319	−6,749	1,128	−6,343	−58.41%
2028	1,363	−5,386	1,120	−5,222	−34.43%
2029	1,403	−3,983	1,108	−4,114	−19.51%
2030	1,444	−2,539	1,097	−3,017	−9.85%
2031	1,491	−1,048	1,090	−1,927	−3.31%
2032	1,555	507	1,092	−835	1.33%
2033	1,600	2,107	1,081	246	4.68%

Source own study

Table 4 Benefits and efficiency of the Company's 1 project with subsidies

Variant with subsidies [Innovation Implementation module] Year	Free cash flow (FCF)	Accumulated free cash flow (FCF)	Discounted cash flow (FCF)	Cumulative discounted cash flow (FCF)—NPV	IRR
2025	−4,191	−4,191	−3,875	0	n/d
2026	314	−3,877	280	−3,595	−92.50%
2027	1,319	−2,557	1,128	−2,468	−40.02%
2028	1,363	−1,194	1,120	−1,347	−13.14%
2029	1,403	208	1,108	−239	1.71%
2030	1,444	1,652	1,097	858	10.51%
2031	1,491	3,144	1,090	1,948	16.06%
2032	1,555	4,698	1,092	3,040	19.75%
2033	1,600	6,299	1,081	4,122	22.25%

Source own study

the company, offsetting a portion of the capital expenditure and potentially supporting sustainable packaging initiatives. The change in working capital fluctuates over the years, occasionally showing negative values, which may indicate efficient management of working capital or adjustments in operational activities. Discounting future cash flows using a discount rate of 4.00% provides the present value of future cash flows, reflected in the discount factor. This analysis facilitates the evaluation of the financial viability of the company's investments and operations over the specified period. Overall, the data suggests a phased approach to financial planning and investment, with an emphasis on sustainability and long-term profitability. The presence of revenue generation from 2026 onwards, along with careful management of costs and investments, indicates a positive outlook for Company 1's financial performance and its ability to implement sustainable packaging solutions effectively. Tables 3 and 4 present the efficiency of the project in two dimensions: without and with the grant.

The table outlines the benefits and efficiency of Company 1's project without subsidies, focusing on the implementation of innovation over the period from 2025 to 2033. Initially, the absence of free cash flow in first years suggests a period of investment without immediate returns, typical during the setup or early stages of a project. However, starting from 2025, there is a significant negative free cash flow of −8,382 thousand EUR, indicating substantial investment or expenditure, likely associated with the implementation of innovation. As the project progresses, free cash flow gradually improves, becoming positive from 2026 onwards. This positive trend reflects the project's maturation and the generation of returns on investment. Generally, when the cumulative discounted cash flow (FCF) demonstrates the project's overall financial performance, considering the time value of money, the internal rate of return (IRR), is a critical metric for investment appraisal, indicates the project's efficiency in generating returns. IRR starts to be positive from the 2032 year (+1.33%) and in the 2033 year is 4.68%. The data shows that while the project initially incurs significant costs, it gradually becomes financially sustainable, generating positive cash flows with positive NPV from 2033 year (+246.000 EUR). It is observed, that the IRR, although negative in the early years, steadily improves, indicating increasing efficiency and profitability of the project over time. This analysis underscores the long-term viability and potential profitability of Company 1's project without subsidies, supporting the case for continued investment in innovation and sustainable practices. The next step is to analyze how the project may perform with the grant. Table 4 presents the benefits and efficiency of the project with the grant.

Table 4 outlines the benefits and efficiency of Company 1's project with subsidies, specifically focusing on the implementation of the Innovation Implementation module over the period from 2023 to 2034. Similar to the analysis without subsidies, the initial years of 2023 and 2024 exhibit zero free cash flow, indicating a period of investment without immediate returns. However, from 2025 onwards, there is a noticeable improvement in financial performance compared to the scenario without subsidies. In 2025, the negative free cash flow is −4,191 thousand EUR, which is significantly less than the corresponding value without subsidies (−8,382 thousand EUR). This reduction in negative cash flow suggests that the subsidies provided have helped alleviate some of the financial burden associated with implementing innovation. As the project progresses, free cash flow becomes positive from 2026 onwards, with the accumulated free cash flow showing a similar trend. To make quick characteristic, it is good to understand that the discounted cash flow, calculated by discounting future cash flows with an appropriate discount rate, demonstrates the project's net present value (NPV) over time. Also important to know it that the cumulative discounted cash flow (FCF)—NPV indicates the project's overall financial performance, considering the time value of money and the influence of subsidies. In next step, to make a comparison to the scenario without subsidies, the cumulative discounted cash flow—NPV shows a more favorable trajectory, informing that subsidies contribute positively to the project's financial effects. It is seen that the NPV is positive from the 2030 year (+858.000 EUR). The explanation for the internal rate of return (IRR) is, that IRR reflects the project's efficiency in generating returns, with the percentages indicating the rate of return relative to the cost of capital according to the general understanding. It is also observed that the IRR values, although initially negative, gradually improve over time, indicating increasing efficiency and profitability of the project with subsidies. IRR is positive from the 2029 year (+1.71%) and finally in 2033 is 22.25%. Overall, the data suggests that subsidies play a crucial role in the financial performance and efficiency of Company 1's project. By reducing the initial financial burden and improving cash flow dynamics, subsidies contribute to the project's long-term sustainability and profitability, highlighting the importance of government support in promoting innovation and sustainable practices within the business sector.

The analysis of Company 2's project also starts from general financial positions, which are presented in Table 5.

Table 5 provides an overview of the general financial positions for Company 2's project, denominated in thousand EUR, spanning from the year 2023 to 2034. The table delineates revenue, operating costs (excluding depreciation), amortization, capital expenditure (design), grant, change in working capital, discount rate, and discount factor. In the initial years, particularly 2023 and 2024, Company 2 reports no revenue, indicating a period of setup or preparatory activities. Subsequently, from 2025 onwards, there will be a notable increase in revenue, signifying the commencement of operational activities and revenue-generating operations. For the assessment of the project it is important to verify couple of typical financial areas. For example, operating costs (without depreciation) usually are compared with revenue, to show fluctuations of the revenue trends. Moreover, the inclusion of amortization and capital expenditure in this case demonstrates investments made by Company 2 into its project. The grant (as external financial support) is observed in 2024. This is significant for the project's financial position. Another important area to analyze are cash flows using in this case the discount rate of 4.00%. It provides the present value of future cash flows, reflected in the discount factor. The data presented in Table 5 show the financial trajectory of Company 2's project, highlighting revenue generation, operational costs, investment activities, external financial support, and working capital management.

Table 6 and Table 7 present the benefits and efficiency of the project in two dimensions: without and with the grant. Table 6 provides an analysis of the efficiency of Company 2's project without subsidies. In the initial years, the project shows negative free cash flow, as it is an initial investment phase with no returns so far. However, from 2025, the project begins to generate positive free cash flow, heading to operational profitability. Similarly to Company 1, the discounted cash flow without grants provides insights into the present value of future cash flows,

Table 5 General financial positions for Company 2's project in thousand EUR

Year	Revenue	Operating costs (excluding depreciation)	Amortization	Capital expenditure (design)	Grant	Change in working capital	Discount rate	Discount factor
2024	0.00	0.00	28.22	2,411.56	1,446.89	0.00	4.00%	0.96
2025	2,002.67	1,176.89	337.56	0.00	0.00	−360.22	4.00%	0.92
2026	2,015.56	1,184.67	337.56	0.00	0.00	6.44	4.00%	0.89
2027	2,116.22	1,242.67	337.56	0.00	0.00	−8.44	4.00%	0.85
2028	2,216.89	1,301.11	337.56	0.00	0.00	−6.67	4.00%	0.82
2029	2,317.56	1,359.78	337.56	0.00	0.00	−7.78	4.00%	0.79
2030	2,418.22	1,414.86	337.56	0.00	0.00	−5.78	4.00%	0.76
2031	2,518.89	1,476.44	337.56	0.00	0.00	−4.89	4.00%	0.73
2032	2,619.56	1,535.11	92.0	0.00	0.00	−3.33	4.00%	0.70
2033	2,720.22	1,593.78	0.00	0.00	0.00	−4.22	4.00%	0.68

Source own study

while the cumulative discounted cash flow—NPV is positive from the 2028 year (342.890 EUR) and finally in 2033 is 4.125.560 EUR. The IRR values, although initially negative, steadily improve over time, indicating increasing efficiency and profitability of the project. IRR is positive in 2028 (+9.56%) and in 2033 is +30.27%. Overall, the data in Table 6 highlights the financial trajectory of Company 2's project without subsidies, showcasing the initial investment phase followed by operational profitability and positive cash flow generation. The analysis underscores the project's financial viability and potential for long-term sustainability, despite the absence of external financial support.

The next step is to analyze how the project may perform with the grant. Table 7 presents the benefits and efficiency of the project with the grant.

Table 7 provides a comprehensive analysis of the benefits and efficiency of Company 2's project with subsidies, focusing on the implementation of the Innovation Implementation module. Initially, the table indicates zero free cash flow in 2023, reflecting a period of investment or setup with no immediate financial returns. Subsequently, in 2024, the project incurs negative free cash flow, indicating an initial investment phase exceeding revenue generation. However, from 2025 onwards, the project begins to generate positive free cash flow, signifying operational profitability and the positive influence of subsidies. The accumulated free cash flow demonstrates a gradual increase over time, reflecting the project's cumulative financial performance. Discounted cash flow calculations provide insights into the present value of future cash flows, considering the time value of money and the impact of subsidies. NPV is positive in 2026 (+247.330 EUR) and in 2033 is +5.516.890 EUR. The IRR values, particularly from 2026 onwards, demonstrate a highly positive trend,

Table 6 Benefits and efficiency of the Company's 2 project without subsidies

Option without subsidies [Implementation of innovation]	Free cash flow (FCF) [net of subsidies]	Accumulated free cash flow (FCF) [net of grants]	Discounted cash flow (FCF) [without grants]	Cumulative discounted cash flow (FCF)—NPV [without subsidies]	IRR [without subsidy]
2024	−2,411.56	−2,411.56	−2,318.89	0.00	n/d
2025	465.56	−1,946.00	430.44	−1,888.44	−80.69%
2026	837.33	−1,108.67	744.44	−1,144.00	−30.64%
2027	865.11	−243.56	739.56	−404.44	−4.73%
2028	909.11	665.56	747.33	342.89	9.56%
2029	950.00	1,615.56	750.89	1,093.78	17.92%
2030	994.44	2,610.00	755.78	1,849.56	23.11%
2031	1,037.56	3,647.56	758.22	2,607.78	26.47%
2032	1,081.11	4,728.67	759.56	3,367.33	28.73%
2033	1,122.22	5,850.89	758.22	4,125.56	30.27%

Source own study

Table 7 Benefits and efficiency of the Company's 2 project with subsidies

Variant with a subsidy [Innovation Implementation module]	Free cash flow (FCF)	Accumulated free cash flow (FCF)	Discounted cash flow (FCF)	Cumulative discounted cash flow (FCF)—NPV	IRR
2024	−964.67	−964.67	−927.56	0.00	n/d
2025	465.56	−499.11	430.44	−497.11	−51.74%
2026	837.33	338.22	744.44	247.33	20.37%
2027	865.11	1,203.33	739.56	986.89	47.92%
2028	909.11	2,112.44	747.33	1,734.22	60.25%
2029	950.00	3,062.44	750.89	2,485.11	66.28%
2030	994.44	4,056.89	755.78	3,240.89	69.43%
2031	1,037.56	5,094.44	758.22	3,999.11	71.16%
2032	1,081.11	6,175.56	759.56	4,758.67	72.12%
2033	1,122.22	7,297.78	758.22	5,516.89	72.68%

Source own study

indicating increasing efficiency and profitability of the project with subsidies. IRR for 2026 is positive (+20.37%) and in 2033 is +72.68%, which confirms a highly effective project. Overall, the data in Table 7 underscores the financial viability and efficiency of Company 2's project with subsidies. The positive free cash flow generation, cumulative financial performance, and increasing IRR values highlight the project's ability to generate sustainable returns and achieve long-term financial success with the support of subsidies.

The interest rate on 10-year treasury bills can be taken as a reference point. According to the Ministry of Finance in Poland, in 2024, the average interest rate for 10-year treasury bonds in Poland, known as EDO bonds (indexed to inflation), is around 6.75% during the first year. After the first year, the interest rate is adjusted annually, based on the inflation rate plus a fixed margin of 1.25% (Gov.pl, 2024).

It is useful also to present the comparison of the costs of the projects for both companies. Figure 5 presents the sustainable project's cost comparison between Company 1 and Company 2 in % by type.

From a financial perspective, Company 2 exhibits a higher dependency on external funding (60%) compared to Company 1. This can have implications for risk exposure and financial sustainability. Heavy reliance on external funding may cause risks associated with changes in policy, grant availability, or market conditions. On the other hand, Company 1 shows a more diversified approach, using a mix of private funds, own resources, and loans, which might provide it with greater control over its financial operations and decision-making. The absence of own funds for Company 2 raises questions about the company's liquidity, but the company confirmed the positive decision to receive financing through a bank promise. This comparative analysis shows that case study companies have chosen different financial strategies

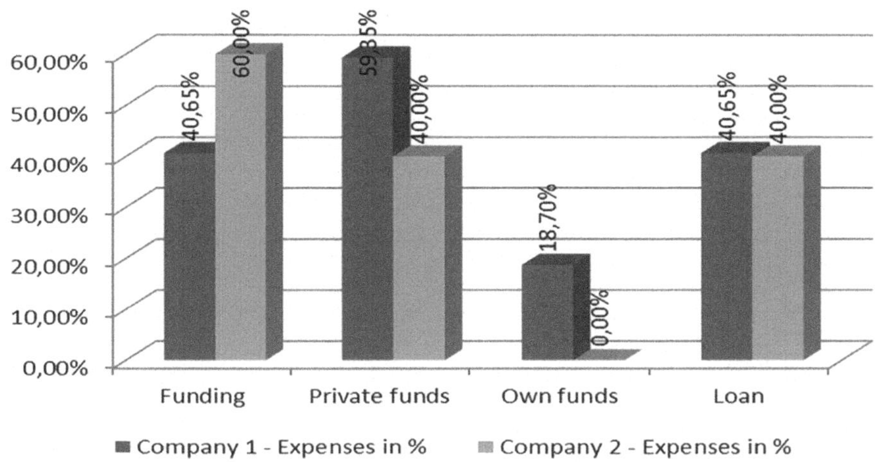

Fig. 5 Project's costs comparison by type (in %) (*Source* own study)

in their sustainability projects. The Company 1 chooses a more balanced structure between external and internal financing, while Company 2 depends more on external funding and loans. This may have an impact on the future long-term success of the projects at the end of this processes.

Figure 6 provides a detailed financial information of both case study companies' historical and projected performance in selected ratios groups as: profitability, liquidity, and asset turnover rate in the period from 2019 to 2033. The comparison of the financial indicators for Company 1 and Company 2 present different trends in profitability, liquidity, asset turnover, and liability structures during the project implementation. Analyzing profitability ratios it is worth noticing that Company 1 show a stable and increasing trend in Return on Sales, with a peak of 19.44% in 2033. However, its Net Profitability and Return on Assets show a declining trend from 2024, indicating that while sales are increasing, the overall profitability and efficiency of assets are slowing down. Company 2, in contrast, shows a more volatily in profitability, with a lower moments in Return on Sales and Net Profitability in 2022 and 2023, but followed by a significant recovery by 2033 in the end. Return on Assets in Company 2 remains notably higher than in Company 1 in the earlier years but starts to converge as both companies approach 2033.

Taking into account liability structure and debt service ratios, Company 1 demonstrates stronger debt management, as indicated by its consistently low and decreasing debt ratio, which drops to 4% by 2033. The equity share ratio improves steadily, reflecting reduced reliance on external financing and greater self-sufficiency. Company 2, however, experiences fluctuations in its debt ratio, with a significant increase in 2024 (61%) before decreasing to 4% by 2033. This could indicate periods of high financial leverage, possibly due to investments in the project. Despite this, Company 2 maintains high coverage of fixed assets with permanent capital, suggesting strong capital management despite the variability in debt levels.

Company 1															
Assessment of indicators for total activity to date, combined with the planned implementation of the project.	**2019**	**2020**	**2021**	**2022**	**2023**	**2024**	**2025**	**2026**	**2027**	**2028**	**2029**	**2030**	**2031**	**2032**	**2033**
I. Profitability indicators															
1. Return on Sales	12,83%	14,58%	15,22%	12,70%	15,37%	15,67%	15,58%	13,11%	13,50%	13,87%	14,24%	15,42%	15,89%	16,29%	19,44%
2. Net profitability	14,13%	17,38%	13,99%	10,95%	12,82%	13,06%	12,76%	11,74%	12,15%	12,55%	12,93%	13,97%	14,07%	14,36%	15,74%
3. Return on Assets	17,82%	24,60%	19,87%	19,21%	18,55%	16,23%	10,88%	9,63%	9,53%	9,41%	9,26%	9,51%	9,09%	8,82%	8,99%
II. Liability structure and debt service ratios															
1. equity share ratio	66%	79%	62%	78%	81%	85%	68%	73%	78%	83%	87%	90%	93%	95%	96%
2. coverage of fixed assets with permanent capital	147%	184%	135%	186%	250%	323%	231%	279%	343%	429%	553%	713%	948%	1334%	1537%
3. debt ratio	34%	21%	38%	22%	19%	15%	32%	27%	22%	17%	13%	10%	7%	5%	4%
4. debt service ratio	171,8	737,5	247,4	71,7	bd.	bd.	38,5	7,6	8,4	9,2	10,1	11,3	12,3	13,2	758,1
III. Liquidity ratios															
1. current liquidity	2,1	5,8	1,7	3,8	5,0	6,5	6,6	7,9	9,2	10,5	11,9	13,3	14,7	19,5	21,5
2. quick ratio	1,3	3,8	0,8	1,8	3,4	4,9	5,2	6,5	7,8	9,1	10,5	11,8	13,2	17,7	19,6
IV. Asset turnover rates															
1. inventory rotation cycle	62	52	73	69	61	61	65	59	60	60	60	61	61	61	64
2. receivable turnover cycle	58	53	46	50	51	48	47	49	48	48	48	48	48	48	48
3. liabilities rotation cycle	13	17	21	11	17	18	19	17	17	17	17	17	17	17	18

Company2															
Assessment of indicators for total activity to date, combined with the planned implementation of the project.	**2019**	**2020**	**2021**	**2022**	**2023**	**2024**	**2025**	**2026**	**2027**	**2028**	**2029**	**2030**	**2031**	**2032**	**2033**
I. Profitability indicators															
1. Return on Sales	17,64%	18,09%	18,66%	8,96%	8,95%	8,69%	9,15%	9,41%	10,28%	11,06%	11,79%	12,82%	13,54%	20,75%	21,60%
2. Net profitability	21,24%	24,11%	31,26%	13,11%	10,38%	9,84%	13,35%	13,76%	14,59%	15,35%	16,06%	17,00%	17,59%	20,14%	20,64%
3. Return on Assets	65,67%	43,11%	69,36%	39,60%	26,09%	8,92%	12,14%	11,99%	12,32%	12,48%	12,49%	12,58%	12,34%	12,64%	11,70%
II. Liability structure and debt service ratios															
1. equity share ratio	67%	68%	76%	73%	84%	39%	49%	58%	67%	76%	83%	90%	95%	96%	96%
2. coverage of fixed assets with permanent capital	286%	325%	515%	530%	860%	159%	195%	246%	326%	462%	738%	1489%	11540%	20817%	23665%
3. debt ratio	33%	32%	24%	27%	16%	61%	51%	42%	33%	24%	17%	10%	5%	4%	4%
4. debt service ratio	bd.	bd.	bd.	bd.	bd.	16,9	5,5	5,9	6,6	7,3	8,1	9,1	10,3	bd.	bd.
III. Liquidity ratios															
1. current liquidity	3,7	2,5	5,0	4,1	8,5	5,7	7,3	9,2	10,9	12,7	14,5	16,7	29,6	32,8	35,7
2. quick ratio	3,7	2,5	4,4	4,1	8,1	5,5	6,9	8,8	10,5	12,4	14,2	16,3	29,1	32,2	35,1
IV. Asset turnover rates															
1. inventory rotation cycle	0	0	18	0	6	8	12	10	11	11	11	11	12	13	13
2. receivable turnover cycle	69	77	85	73	76	79	74	73	73	72	71	71	70	69	69
3. liabilities rotation cycle	15	16	21	20	17	18	18	18	18	19	19	20	20	22	23

Fig. 6 Assessment of indicators for total activity to date, combined with the planned implementation of the project (*Source* own study based on projects' data)

Company 1 steadily improves its liquidity position, with both current liquidity and quick ratio surpassing about 20 by 2033. This trend reflects increasing cash reserves and short-term asset availability, ensuring the company's ability to meet short-term obligations.

Company 2 shows similar trends in liquidity, but with more pronounced fluctuations, particularly between 2023 and 2024. Its liquidity ratios spike in later years, indicating a more aggressive accumulation of liquid assets compared to Company 1. By 2033, both companies display strong liquidity, with Company 2 having a slightly higher ratio than Company 1.

Going to asset turnover rates it is worth to notice, that Company 1 maintains relatively stable inventory rotation cycles and receivable turnover cycles throughout the period, indicating consistent management of its resources. Its liabilities rotation cycle also remains steady, with no significant changes. Company 2 shows some irregularities, particularly in the inventory rotation cycle, which varies significantly in earlier years before stabilizing around 13 by 2033. This may reflect initial challenges in managing inventory, possibly linked to changes in production processes. However, receivable turnover remains steady and comparable to Company 1's performance.

Overall, both companies are on positive trajectories, but with differing approaches and challenges. Company 1 displays more stability across all indicators, particularly in profitability and asset management, which may provide it with a competitive advantage in the long term. On the other hand, Company 2 shows higher initial volatility but recovers strongly, especially in terms of liquidity and profitability. The fluctuations in Company 2's debt and liquidity ratios may suggest that it is more reliant on external financing for growth, but its overall financial health improves significantly by 2033.

The comparative analysis highlights the strengths and weaknesses of both companies, providing valuable insights for stakeholders. Company 1 may be better positioned for steady, sustainable growth, while Company 2 appears more dynamic but with potential risks associated with financial leverage and asset management in earlier years.

5 Conclusion

The findings of this study clearly show that combining theory background, and current trends with the practical examination of various sustainable practices and initiatives adopted by companies in those two case study companies from the packaging industry with the assessment of economic effect could bring benefit by showing good business practices towards building solutions to the development of sustainability. The two presented examples of projects from the companies working in the packaging industry are characterized by good and very good economic efficiency. Those positively assessed projects have shown a wide range of activities supporting sustainability with positive grading. In the case of those two enterprises, extensive activity in the field of sustainability also goes hand in hand with economic efficiency.

Moreover, it seems that submitting a competitive application for project financing significantly supports the objective and efficient structuring of the project and motivates to supplement sustainability activities with additional activities and compliance assessed in the projects, which makes these projects very well prepared for implementation with a good plan for effective performance. Linking pro-sustainability activities with financial effectiveness also helps to awareness and the role of projects among the company's management. That is why, analyzed case studies might be examples of good practices of sustainability activities.

Both theory and practice show a clear increase in interest in the topic of sustainability. Therefore, the topic is important from a scientific point of view, in order to structure the scientific background for this issue. However, from a practical point of view, it is also important due to the popularization of the measurability of the effect of sustainability activities and the economic effect at least. It seems that the best effect could be realized by joining those two areas together for sustainability development.

In this matter, also practical aspect of activities multiplication seems to bring significant benefits. Based only on those two analyzed case studies with the IRR indicator at the end of the project's period and without subsidy was planned at the level of IRR = 4.68% and IRR = 30.27%. It is worth encouraging companies to multiply sustainability activities.

Interestingly, the smaller company showed higher project effectiveness. This may be an area for further, in-depth research. It would be worth examining in the future whether the size of the company influences the effective implementations of sustainability projects.

The comparison of costs and financial indicators between Company 1 and Company 2 reveals distinct approaches to financing, debt management, and operational efficiency, offering important insights into the sustainability of their projects.

From a cost perspective, Company 2 relies more heavily on external funding (60%), which exposes it to risks associated with changing market conditions, policy shifts, and grant availability. In contrast, Company 1 adopts a more balanced financial strategy, incorporating private funds, own resources, and loans, providing it with greater control over financial operations and decision-making. Company 1's diversified funding approach suggests better long-term stability, whereas Company 2's higher external dependency raises concerns about liquidity, despite securing financing through a bank promise.

In terms of profitability, Company 1 demonstrates stable and increasing Return on Sales, peaking at 19.44% by 2033, but its Net Profitability and Return on Assets show a slight decline starting in 2024. This indicates that while the company is experiencing sales growth, its overall efficiency and profitability are expected to slow. Conversely, Company 2 exhibits more volatility in profitability, with a sharp decline in Return on Sales and Net Profitability in 2022–2023, followed by recovery by 2033. Its Return on Assets remains higher than Company 1's in earlier years but gradually converges by 2033.

Debt management also differentiates the two companies. Company 1 presents a lower debt ratio, dropping to 4% by 2033, and also a rising equity share ratio in the period of the project. On the other hand Company 2, predict fluctuations in its debt ratio (with a peak in 2024–61%), what may be connected with capital management through high coverage of fixed assets by permanent (stable) capital. This may suggests periods of high financial leverage in Company 2, because of significant investments in its projects.

Liquidity is next important area where the case study companies diverse. Both examples show increasing liquidity ratios, but Company 1 present a steady improvement, around 20 by 2033, while Company 2 predict more fluctuations once again. However, Company 2 finally get higher levels of liquid assets, what may reflect a more aggressive strategy in next years.

Eventually, asset turnover rates show that Company 1 keep stable inventory and receivable turnover cycles, indicating consistent management of resources, whereas Company 2 experiences variability in inventory rotation cycle before stabilization at the end. This may suggest changes in managing inventories, because of changing process of the production.

In conclusion, Company 1 presents a more stable financial plan, favoring long-term, sustainable growth with controlled risk exposure and steady improvements in profitability, liquidity, and debt management. On the other hand, Company 2, seems to be more dynamic and going for higher short-term gains, with higher risks associated with financial volatility and external funds. Both companies show potential for success, but the strategies they choose may carry different implications for their long-term financial sustainability.

Both analyzed projects did not take into account the element of recycling in their business plan, but this should be indicated as an area for improvement in the future.

The new reality teaches that sustainability is the right direction from many points of view. This study was limited by the access to the data and just two examples, but it seems it could be an inspiration for researchers and practitioners as well.

References

Azadnia, A. H., Saman, M. Z. M., & Wong, K. Y. (2015). Sustainable supplier selection and order lot-sizing: An integrated multi-objective decision-making process. *International Journal of Production Research, 53*(2), 383–408.

Beitzen-Heineke, E. F., Balta-Ozkan, N. & Reefke, H. (2017). The prospects of zero-packaging grocery stores to improve the social and environmental impacts of the food supply chain. Journal of Cleaner Production, *140*(2017), 1528–1541. https://doi.org/10.1016/j.jclepro.2016.09.227 (Accessed 05 May 2024).

Berg, A. (2023) Little things mean a lot. Package printing. Volume 70, Issue 4. Available at: https://www.scopus.com/record/display.uri?eid=2-s2.0-85168115556&origin=resultslist&sort=plf-f&src=s&sid=3bd8738a2e19189b2210babb79e61e97&sot=b&sdt=sisr&s=TITLE-ABS-KEY%28Little+things+mean+a+lot%29&sl=74&sessionSearchId=3bd8738a2e19189b2210babb79e61e97&relpos=0 (Accessed 05 May 2024).

Camps-Posino, L., Batlle-Bayer, L., Bala, A., Song, G., Qian, H., Aldaco, R., Xifré, R., & Fullana-i-Palmer, P. (2021). Potential climate benefits of reusable packaging in food delivery services.

A Chinese case study. *Science of The Total Environment, 794*(2021), Article 148570. https://doi.org/10.1016/j.scitotenv.2021.148570 (Accessed 05 May 2024).
Carpenter, A. W., De Lannoy, C.-F., & Wiesner, M. R. (2015). Cellulose nanomaterials in water treatment technologies. *Environmental Science and TechnologyOpen AccessVolume, 49*(9), 5277–5287.
Cooper, T. A. (2017). The end-of-life challenge for flexible packaging: Multilayer films, barrier structures and pouches. *AIMCAL R2R Conference USA 2017—Roll 2 Roll Web Coating and Finishing with SPE's FlexPackCon*. https://www.scopus.com/record/display.uri?eid=2-s2.0-85055342139&origin=scopusAI (Accessed 05 May 2024).
European Union. Annex I to Commission Regulation (EU) No 651/2014 of 17 June 2014 declaring certain categories of aid compatible with the internal market in application of Articles 107 and 108 of the treaty.
Extrapolate. (2023) Global packaging materials market (2023–2030). https://www.extrapolate.com/chemicals-and-advanced-materials/packaging-materials-market/87428 (Accessed 09 May 2024).
Feber, D. et al. (2023) *Sustainability in packaging 2023: Inside the minds of global consumers*. McKinsey & Company. Available at: https://www.mckinsey.com/industries/packaging-and-paper/our-insights/sustainability-in-packaging-2023-inside-the-minds-of-global-consumers/ (Accessed 09 May 2024).
Garside, M. (2024). Statista. Global packaging material market value 2020–2030, by region. https://www.statista.com/statistics/1422303/global-packaging-material-market-value/ (Accessed 10 May 2024).
Gebrezgabher, S. A., Meuwissen, M. P., Prins, B. A., & Oude Lansink, A. G. (2010). Economic analysis of anaerobic digestion-A case of Green power biogas plant in the Netherlands. *NJAS—Wageningen Journal of Life Sciences, 57*(2), 109–115. https://doi.org/10.1016/j.njas.2009.07.006 (Accessed 25 September 2024)
Ghisellini, P., Cialani, C., & Ulgiati, S. (2016). A review on circular economy: The expected transition to a balanced interplay of environmental and economic systems. *Journal of Cleaner Production, 114*, 11–32. https://doi.org/10.1016/j.jclepro.2015.09.007 (Accessed 25 September 2024).
Grimes-Casey, H. G., Seager, T. P., Theis, T. L., & Powers, S. E. (2007). A game theory framework for cooperative management of refillable and disposable bottle lifecycles. *Journal of Cleaner Production, 15*(17), 1618–1627. https://doi.org/10.1016/j.jclepro.2006.08.007 (Accessed 05 May 2024).
Han, J.-W. Ruiz-Garcia, L., Qian, J. P., & Yang, X. T. (2018, July). Food packaging: A comprehensive review and future trends. *Comprehensive Reviews in Food Science and Food Safety, 17*(4), 860–877.
Ishrat, M., et al. (2018). Novel food packaging technologies: Innovations and future prospective. *Journal of the Saudi Society of Agricultural Sciences, Open Access, 17*(4), 454–462. https://doi.org/10.1016/j.jssas.2016.11.003(Accessed:25.09.2024)
Kaestner, L. et al. (2023) Sustainable circular packaging design: A systematic literature review on strategies and applications in the cosmetic industry. *Proceedings of the Design Society, 3*, 3265–3274. https://www.scopus.com/record/display.uri?eid=2-s2.0-85165447042&origin=scopusAI (Accessed 05 May 2024).
Keating, D. (2024) New packaging rules set to become law despite commission objections. EURACTIV. https://www.euractiv.com/section/energy-environment/news/new-packaging-rules-set-to-become-law-despite-commission-objections/ (Accessed 05 May 2024).
Kroon, L., & Vrijens, G. (1995). Returnable containers: An example of reverse logistics. *International Journal of Physical Distribution & Logistics Management, 25*(2), 56–68. https://doi.org/10.1108/09600039510083934 (Accessed 05 May 2024).
Lisińska-Kuśnierz, M. (2001). The range of pro-ecological activities concerning packaging in Poland against the background of the European Union (EU): Pro-ecological activities in Poland

packag. *Packaging Technology and Science, 14*(6), 275–279. https://doi.org/10.1002/pts.558 (Accessed 05 May 2024).

Martínez-Sala, A. S., Egea-López, E., García-Sánchez, F., & Garcia-Haro, J. (2009). Tracking of returnable packaging and transport units with active RFID in the grocery supply chain. *Computers in Industry, 60*(3), 161–171. https://doi.org/10.1016/j.compind.2008.12.003 (Accessed 05 May 2024).

Mendonca, M. C., Durães, A. F. S., dos Santos, A. D. A., Matos, L. C., Mascarenhas, A. R. P., Scatolino, M. V., Martins, C. C. N., Damásio, R. A. P., Muguet, M. C. S., Tonoli, G. H. D. (2024). Natural rubber, cellulose micro/nanofibrils and carnauba wax: renewable and low-cost coatings improving the barrier properties in papers. *Springer Nature. Cellulose.* https://doi.org/10.1007/s10570-024-06162-7

Ministry of Finance in Poland. (2024). https://www.gov.pl/web/finanse/biezaca-oferta2 (Accessed 25.09.2024).

Paul Singh, S., Smith, K. D., Singh, J., & Rutledge, N. (2019). Packaging and logistics sustainability for the 21st century. *21st IAPRI World Conference on Packaging 2018—Packaging: Driving a Sustainable Future.* https://www.scopus.com/record/display.uri?eid=2-s2.0-85064987169&origin=scopusAI (Accessed 05 May 2024).

Rajesh, P., & Subhashini, V. (2021) Sustainable packaging from waste material: A review on innovative solutions for cleaner environment. *Environmental Science and Engineering 2021.* https://www.scopus.com/record/display.uri?eid=2-s2.0-85104145528&origin=scopusAI (Accessed 05 May 2024).

Roy, R. N. (2022). Sustainable packaging practices across various sectors: Some innovative initiatives under the spotlight. *Operations and Supply Chain Management.* https://www.scopus.com/record/display.uri?eid=2-s2.0-85149943638&origin=scopusAI (Accessed 05 May 2024).

Rundh, B. (2009). Packaging design: Creating competitive advantage with product packaging. *British Food Journal, 111*(9), 988–1002. https://doi.org/10.1108/00070700910992880(Accessed:25.09.2024)

Silvestre, C., Duraccio, D., & Cimmino, S. (2011). Food packaging based on polymer nanomaterials. *Progress in Polymer Science, 36*(12), 1766–1782. https://www.scopus.com/record/display.uri?eid=2-s2.0-80055084025&origin=resultslist&sort=cp-f&src=s&sid=ca93d058b0f9b8a74b3acca366cf374d&sot=b&sdt=b&s=TITLE-ABS-KEY%28sustainability+in+packaging+industry%29&sl=30&sessionSearchId=ca93d058b0f9b8a74b3acca366cf374d&relpos=2 (Accessed 05 May 2024).

Singh, A. K. Itkor, P., Lee, M., Choi, S., & Lee, Y. S. (2024). Advancing sustainable molded packaging: Integrating silica aerogel into recycled paper pulp for the fabrication of thermally and mechanically stable superhydrophobic composites. *Industrial Crops and Products, 22*(2), Article number 119649. https://doi.org/10.1016/j.indcrop.2024.119649 (Accessed 25 September 2024).

Advancing Sustainable Development in Central and Eastern Europe: The Interplay of Environment, Energy, and Economy

Petar Mitić and Aleksandar Zdravković

Abstract Renewable energy is of central importance for global sustainable development. While the interaction between conventional energy sources and pollutant emissions in developing countries has already been extensively researched, there is still considerable research potential regarding the impact of electricity generated from renewable sources on development. The Central and Eastern European (CEE) countries are characterized by a strong dependence on energy-intensive industrial processes, for which they have to ensure a stable and cost-effective energy supply. The future of a cost-efficient energy supply depends on the integration of renewables into the energy mix. The main objective of this paper is to investigate and quantify the complex relationship between CO_2 emissions and electricity generated from renewables in 15 CEE countries from 1995 to 2021. Therefore, the model used in this paper establishes a comprehensive relationship between CO_2 emissions and renewable electricity generation, considering other relevant variables such as final electricity consumption growth, GDP per capita growth, inflation rate, human development index, and trade openness. The empirical model was then estimated using various panel methods tailored to the specific data characteristics in order to obtain precise and consistent results. These methods include Fixed Effects, Generalized Least Squares, Panel-Corrected Standard Errors, Arellano Bond, and System Generalized Method of Moments. The results support the relationship between CO_2 emissions growth rates and electricity generated from renewables. The results show that a 1 percentage point increase in electricity generated from renewables growth reduces CO_2 emissions in CEE countries in a range of 0.07 to 0.11 percentage points. The model also shows that a 1 percentage point increase in growth of final electricity consumption accelerates growth of CO_2 emissions by approximately 0.51 percentage points. Furthermore, a 1 percentage point increase in GDP per capita growth corresponds to a significant increase in growth of CO_2 emissions, ranging from 0.48 to 0.73 percentage points. In addition, a 1 percentage point increase in the inflation rate

P. Mitić (✉) · A. Zdravković
Institute of Economic Sciences, Belgrade, Serbia
e-mail: petar.mitic@ien.bg.ac.rs

A. Zdravković
e-mail: aleksandar.zdravkovic@ien.bg.ac.rs

I. Bartuseviciene et al. (eds.), *Building Economic Resilience*, Contributions to Economics, https://doi.org/10.1007/978-3-031-96428-2_9

is associated with a small but statistically significant increase in CO_2 emissions of about 0.0002 percentage points. The human development index and trade openness are not statistically significant. The research results underline the positive impact of increasing renewable electricity generation on green development in CEE countries, which is crucial for reducing carbon emissions in the region. Despite the potential for increased use of renewable energy in CEE economies, they face technical, economic, and social challenges in generating electricity from renewables. Therefore, public policies need to incentivize investment in renewable energy projects. The implementation of appropriate policy measures and institutional frameworks, such as public–private partnerships and fiscal incentives, is crucial to promote greater use and production of renewable energy in these countries and to drive the modernization of the power sector.

Keywords Electricity generated from renewables · Energy use · CO_2 emissions · Environment · Sustainable development · Economic growth · Central and Eastern Europe

1 Introduction

The increase in CO_2 concentrations is primarily due to the burning of fossil fuels to generate energy. Fossil fuels, such as oil and coal, contain carbon compounds that have been sequestered by plants over millions of years through photosynthesis. Remarkably, this carbon is reintroduced into the atmosphere within a significantly shortened time frame of just a few centuries (NOAA, 2024). In the second half of the twentieth century, annual emissions from fossil fuel combustion increased steadily, from about 11 billion tons of CO_2 per year in the 1960s to an estimated 36.6 billion tons in 2023, as reported by Friedlingstein et al. (2023).

Significant global efforts are needed to mitigate climate change and reduce rising carbon emissions. Renewable energy sources can reduce the use of fossil fuels for energy production and thus reduce carbon emissions resulting from their combustion (Voumik et al., 2023). Furthermore, increasing energy efficiency can significantly reduce the overall demand for energy and the harmful emissions generated by the production of that energy. Introducing more detailed regulations and protocols and encouraging industries to adopt cleaner technologies and practices can also help reduce emissions, as well as promoting international cooperation and implementing global agreements to combat climate change, such as the Paris Agreement.

Central and Eastern Europe (CEE) has certain specific considerations and challenges that make it significantly different from the rest of Europe. Thus, the CEE countries have a specific energy profile based on high dependence on fossil fuels for the production of electricity (Jonek-Kowalska, 2022). In addition, most of these countries share a post-communist legacy, primarily reflected in outdated industrial practices and infrastructure (Ćetković & Buzogány, 2019). This presents prominent obstacles to the implementation of sustainable energy solutions and makes any significant reduction of harmful emissions difficult. However, it is necessary to point out that there are still economic and technological differences between CEE countries that require adapted approaches to reducing emissions, regardless of the somewhat shared socio-economic-historical context. International cooperation and financial support are vital to support CEE countries in their transition to a low-carbon economy.

Therefore, the scientific motivation for studying the interactions between economy, environment, energy, and society emerges from their crucial importance, as their interactions and balance are pivotal for a better future for all. Today, this is more important than ever, as we live in a post-pandemic era characterized by global socio-political uncertainties such as the Russia-Ukraine and Israel-Palestine conflicts. This analysis is necessary for the promotion of an environmentally balanced and resource-conscious CEE.

This paper examines the relationship between CO_2 emissions, electricity generated from renewables, final electricity consumption, GDP per capita, inflation, human development index (HDI), and trade openness in 15 CEE countries over the period 1995–2021. The 15 countries were selected based exclusively on the data availability, and they are Albania, Bulgaria, Croatia, the Czech Republic, Estonia, Hungary, Latvia, Lithuania, North Macedonia, Poland, Romania, Serbia, Slovakia, Slovenia, and Ukraine. By analyzing economic, environmental, energy and social factors, the study aims to provide a comprehensive understanding of their complex dynamics in the CEE region. Moreover, the analysis uses a robust methodological framework that includes residual tests and five panel models: Fixed Effects, Generalized Least Squares, Panel-Corrected Standard Errors, Arellano Bond, and System Generalized Method of Moments. The robustness of the results is increased by providing insights from this multi-method approach.

By examining CO_2 emissions, electricity generated from renewables, final electricity consumption, and key economic and social indicators such as GDP per capita, inflation, trade openness, and HDI, this paper promotes sustainability in the CEE region while providing empirical evidence useful for policymaking. It offers nuanced insights into regional dynamics, fills gaps in the literature, strengthens academic and policy discourse, and highlights the major role of effective governance.

The remainder of this paper is organized as follows. Section 2 provides a detailed literature review, while Sect. 3 outlines the data and methodology used. Section 4 presents the main results and Sect. 5 contains a detailed discussion. Finally, Sect. 6 provides concluding remarks about the paper.

2 Literature Review

The relationships that exist between energy, the economy, the environment, and other aspects of sustainability and well-being are largely based on different theoretical frameworks, among which we single out the Environmental Kuznets Curve (EKC) and the Energy-Economy-Environment Nexus (3E). According to Dinda (2004),

EKC "...is the assertion that environmental quality deteriorates in the early stage of economic development/growth and improves in the later stage as an economy develops. In other words, environmental pressure increases faster than income in the early stage of development and slows down relative to GDP growth at higher income levels" (Dinda, 2004, p. 432). The 3E Nexus highlights the importance of the interdependence of energy, economy and environment, and illustrates how changes in one aspect affect others (Chen, 2016). These and similar theories provide a theoretical rationale and basis for understanding today's complex relationships, with the ultimate goal of achieving the most sustainable outcomes possible.

A large number of studies have been carried out within the framework of the aforementioned and other theories. All of them point to significant connections between CO_2 emissions, electricity consumption from renewables and various economic, energy, and well-being indicators. For example, Balsalobre-Lorente et al. (2018) conclude that electricity consumption from renewables, natural resources, and energy innovation have improved environmental quality in Germany, France, Italy, Spain and the UK. Similarly, Bélaïd and Zrelli (2019) indicated bidirectional causality between non-renewable electricity consumption and CO_2 emissions in Mediterranean countries. They also state that reliance on non-renewable sources affects the quality of the environment. In the EU, Simionescu et al. (2019) observed a positive effect of GDP per capita on the share of electricity consumption from renewables. In their study, Luxembourg is the only exception. Mentel et al. (2022) demonstrated that electricity generated from renewables significantly reduces CO_2 emissions in Sub-Saharan Africa, while Khan et al. (2024) demonstrated the effectiveness of renewable electricity in reducing CO_2 emissions in 133 countries worldwide.

In addition to renewables, several studies have examined total electricity consumption to provide a broader perspective. Anastacio (2017) analyzed Canada, the United States, and Mexico and found a long-term unidirectional causal relationship from energy consumption to economic growth and CO_2 emissions. In contrast, Gyamerah and Gil-Alaña (2023) reported that electricity consumption and economic growth in West and Central Africa have a positive effect on CO_2 emissions, but do not Granger- cause them. Rahman (2020) examined the relationships between electricity consumption, economic growth, and globalization in the 10 countries with the highest electricity consumption and concluded that these factors contribute significantly to long-term CO_2 emissions.

Inflation has also become an important variable in environmental economics. AlShafeey and Saleh Saleh (2024) examined the relationship between inflation and GHG emissions in the US, EU, and China and found that GHG emissions in the EU decline sharply when the inflation rate exceeds 7.5%. In Southeast Asia, Nguyen (2022) found that tourism revenue and CO_2 emissions have a positive impact on inflation, while GDP and energy consumption have a negative impact on it in five developing countries. Shpak et al. (2022) illustrated the role of inflation as a macroeconomic factor influencing CO_2 emissions in the US and Asia–Pacific, while Jin et al. (2024) found a significant negative effect of inflation on CO_2 emissions in the BRICS countries.

Composite indexes like HDI are often used to assess a wide range of socio-economic impacts and well-being. Thus Akbar et al. (2020) examined the relationship between HDI, health care costs and CO_2 emissions in OECD countries and indicated that there is a positive bidirectional causality between health care expenditures and HDI. However, there is bidirectional causality between CO_2 emissions and HDI in Germany, Japan, the UK, and the US, and unidirectional causality from CO_2 emissions to HDI in Canada, China, Brazil, and France (Sezgin et al., 2021).

Trade openness is also a factor that the professional literature has indicated has an impact on the quality of the environment. Li and Haneklaus (2022) concluded that trade openness affects the increase of CO_2 emissions in the G7 countries, while Galvan et al. (2022) analyzed this impact more deeply and concluded that trade has a stronger impact on emissions in upper-middle-income countries, such as Singapore and the United States, than in countries with lower income levels, such as Latin American countries. Additional confirmation of this influence is provided by Ansari et al. (2020), who point to unidirectional causality from trade openness to CO_2 emissions in the USA, Canada, Iran and France, suggesting that in the long run, less trade activity could result in lower emissions.

Although the CEE countries have not been overly interesting from the point of view of empirical research on the interdependence of the economy, energy, and the environment, there are still certain studies that are useful to refer to. Thus, Simionescu (2021) examined the EKC and the RKC (renewable energy environmental Kuznets curve) hypothesis in CEE countries over a period of two decades (1990–2019). Her results show that there is an inverse N-shaped relationship between GDP and GHG emissions. Furthermore, Fedajev et al. (2023) analyzed the impact of electricity infrastructure inferiority on GDP and industrial value-added in the CEE countries, highlighting renewable energy sources as a key aspect that must be worked on in this region with the aim of achieving sustainability. Mitić et al. (2024) analyzed the causal relationship concerning industry value-added and CO_2 emissions in CEE and emphasized the long-run relationship between industry development and CO_2 emissions.

Majewska and Gierałtowska (2022) took a slightly altered approach and focused on the relationship between CO_2 emissions and prosperity measures, including GDP and HDI, in CEE countries. Despite the fact that their results were somewhat inconclusive, they pointed out that the main generator of harmful emissions was energy consumption per capita, while renewable energy was a factor that served to mitigate emissions. Finally, Manta et al. (2020) examined the relationship between CO_2 emissions, energy consumption, economic growth, and financial development in 10 CEE countries from 2000 to 2017. The results indicate that energy consumption and harmful emissions do not have a long-term impact on economic growth, but that financial development affects the growth of emissions and energy consumption.

It is certain that the current professional and scientific literature provides significant insights into the complex relationships between the economy, energy, well-being and the environment, which shape our everyday lives. Theoretical frameworks, such as the EKC and the 3E Nexus, have been validated in numerous countries and regions. And by analyzing a large number of literature units, it can be concluded that renewable energy is extremely important for the reduction of CO_2 emissions. This is consistent with the energy-sustainability trade-offs discussed in the 3E Nexus model. However, the global reality and rapid changes to which we all must adapt further complicate the picture and require consideration of a larger number of variables. This is particularly important when considering regional and global circumstances, as national and regional differences in, for example, financial development, inflation, and trade openness lead to relationships that are not always fully captured by these established frameworks. Consequently, the results in terms of policy measures also clearly indicate that more sophisticated theoretical models that consider these trade-offs are necessary in developing countries and regions, such as CEE.

In order to adequately draw inferences, it is necessary to note that the mixed results of different countries and regions indicate that only those policies that take into account specific developmental and environmental circumstances will be successful in the future. This study seeks to improve understanding of these complex phenomena by examining the specificities of the CEE region and examining how policy interventions can promote sustainability in line with the global goals of achieving net-zero growth.

3 Data and Methodology

3.1 Data

This study examines the impact of electricity generated from renewables on CO_2 emissions in the period from 1995 to 2021. The observation period of 27 years was chosen based on the availability of data. Additional explanatory variables were included in the model to improve its robustness. Those variables include final electricity consumption, GDP per capita, inflation rate, HDI, and trade openness.

The CO_2 emissions data in tons per capita are taken from the Global Carbon Atlas (2023), which originally collected and aggregated data from Friedlingstein et al. (2022), Andrew and Peters (2022), Peters et al. (2011), and the United Nations (2019). Electricity generated from renewables and HDI were taken from Our World in Data (2023), final electricity consumption from Eurostat (2023), while data on GDP per capita, inflation rate, and trade openness were taken from the World Bank (2023). Table 1 shows a systematized description of all variables used in this study.

CO_2 emissions are the most frequently used indicator of environmental degradation in scientific literature (Acheampong & Opoku, 2023; Asongu & Odhiambo, 2019; Mamun et al., 2014; Zheng et al., 2019). As with environmental degradation, scientific literature often uses GDP per capita as an indicator of economic growth (Acheampong & Opoku, 2023; Galvan et al., 2022; Mitić et al., 2017; Petrović-Ranđelović et al., 2019; Rahman, 2020).

Electricity generated from renewables is an indicator of the dependence of a certain country or region on renewable energy sources when creating electricity.

Table 1 Variable description

Variable	Abbreviation	Scale	Source
CO_2 emissions	CO_2	Tons per capita growth	Global Carbon Atlas (2023)
Electricity generated from renewables	ELER	% of total electricity generation	Our World in Data (2023)
Final electricity consumption	ELEF	Growth in %	Eurostat (2023)
GDP per capita	GDP	Growth in %	The World Bank (2023)
Inflation	INF	%	The World Bank (2023)
Human development index	HDI	Score from 0 to 1	Our World in Data (2023)
Trade openness	TO	% of GDP	The World Bank (2023)

Source Authors' calculation

In other words, it shows the share of renewable sources (such as wind, solar, hydro, geothermal, and biomass) in electricity production. Electricity generated from renewables is also an indicator of the energy transition, the efficiency of energy policies and resistance to the volatility of the energy market, but it is also used to indicate whether countries use renewable sources to meet the increased demand for energy (Khan et al., 2024; Balsalobre-Lorente et al., 2018; Simionescu et al., 2019).

Putting renewable sources aside for a second, electricity consumption, as a broader indicator, is often a variable that is analyzed in scientific and professional research, as shown in studies such as those by Gyamerah and Gil-Alaña (2023), Rahman (2020), and Rodrigues et al. (2020). It refers to the total amount of electricity consumed by households, businesses, and industry in a certain area. Research into the production and consumption of electricity from renewable and non-renewable sources allows for a more refined and nuanced understanding of how the use of energy and the sources from which it is obtained affect the quality of the environment. This distinction is essential because renewable energy sources lead to lower emissions compared to non-renewable sources, such as coal, oil, and natural gas. Understanding the clear dynamics of the contribution to harmful emissions also provides insight to policymakers who want to reduce emissions while providing enough energy for the adequate functioning of the economy.

From a strictly economic perspective, the inflation rate is an important indicator of economic stability and as such is often used in scientific research (Jin et al., 2024; AlShafeey & Saleh Saleh, 2024; Fedajev et al., 2023). The inflation rate affects all actors in the market - consumers, businesses, investors, policymakers, financial markets, and the overall economic reality in general. Adding inflation to the model along with GDP per capita illustrates how changes in economic performance and purchasing power contribute to CO_2 emissions.

Moreover, the use of variables that describe certain complex, or more "comprehensive" phenomena, such as HDI (Akbar et al., 2020; Sezgin et al., 2021; Bieth,

2021), is not uncommon. The HDI is an indicator of human well-being and development, and its inclusion in the model provides a robust measure of development that includes aspects such as health, education, and happiness.

Trade openness is a variable that quantifies integration into the global economy. In other words, trade openness is a proxy for the commitment of a certain country or region to open markets, free trade, and economic cooperation, and as it is one of the most significant indicators in the era of globalization, it is a frequently used variable in research (Ansari et al., 2020; Dauda et al., 2021; Li & Haneklaus, 2022). Trade openness has a significant role in promoting economic development, strengthening competitiveness and promoting sustainability. However, trade openness is an unpredictable variable that can have both positive and negative effects on CO_2 emissions. Although it can facilitate the transfer of clean technologies and the adoption of sustainable practices, it can also lead to carbon leakage and the import of carbon-intensive goods.

In the context of research of the CEE region, all the aforementioned variables were selected based on their importance in achieving a sustainable future. CO_2 emissions serve as a basic indicator of environmental degradation, which is crucial for understanding the environmental impact of economic activities. Similarly, GDP per capita provides an indication of economic growth. In addition, electricity generation from renewable sources and final electricity consumption provide a nuanced perspective on energy use patterns and their impact on CO_2 emissions, which is especially significant given the shift to renewable energy sources. The inflation rate and trade openness reflect the economic factors that influence carbon emissions, while comprehensive indices such as the HDI provide holistic measures of human well-being that are critical to understanding socio-economic dynamics in the region.

3.2 Methodology

The empirical methodology comprises three steps. First, we specified the econometrical panel model that puts CO_2 emission in relation to the set of our key explanatory variables. Second, we examined the characteristics of model residuals to get insight into possible estimation issues. Eventually, we estimated the empirical model using several panel estimators with respect to the characteristics of our data to ensure the reliability of estimates.

The specified panel regression model reads as:

$$\begin{aligned} CO2_{it} =& \beta_0 CO2_{it-1} + \beta_1 ELER_{it} + \beta_2 ELEF_{it} + \beta_3 GDP_{it} \\ &+ \beta_4 INF_{it} + \beta_5 HDI_{it} + \beta_6 TO_{it} + \nu_i + \tau_t + u_{it}; \\ &i = 1, \ldots N, t = 1, \ldots \end{aligned}$$

where $CO2_{it}$ is a growth rate in CO_2 per capita emissions (%); $ELER_{it}$ is a change in share of a country's electricity generation that comes from renewable energy sources (percentage point); $ELEF_{it}$ is a growth rate in electricity final consumption (%); GDP_{it} is a real GDP per capita growth rate (%); INF_{it} is an inflation rate (%); HDI_{it} is the human development index (index number); TO_{it} is a change in trade openness (percentage point); ν_i is a country-specific effect; τ_t is an time-specific effect; u_{it} is a random disturbance.

Second, we examine the characteristics of model residuals to figure out a proper estimation approach. It is common knowledge that OLS-based estimators require IID distributed errors and exogeneous regressors to provide reliable estimates. In the case of panel data modeling, it is typically assumed that model errors are composite, i.e., that model errors can be decomposed into individual effects that capture time-invariant specifics of the panel units ν_i, time effects that captures common shocks τ_t and random disturbances u_{it} that follows IID process. However, when macroeconomic data are modeled, the assumption on IID distributed disturbances is arguably too strong. Therefore, we started with the most general set of assumptions that model error is composite and model disturbances are heteroskedastic, autocorrelated, and cross-sectionally dependent and then tested each of these assumptions.

A proper estimation of the panel model, when OLS assumptions on residuals are not valid, is a challenging task since all panel estimators proposed in the literature have some pros and cons. When individual effects are present within the model error, the benchmark estimator is an OLS-based fixed effects estimator (FE OLS). The major advantage of the FE OLS estimator is that it produces a consistent estimate of regression coefficients as long as model disturbances are not correlated to the regressors, even in cases where individual effects are correlated with regressors (Wooldridge, 2002). The alternative LS-based estimator to FE is the Feasible Generalized Least Square estimator (FGLS), which also produced estimates of residuals robust to heteroskedasticity and autocorrelation. In case that residuals are also cross-sectionally dependent, the Panel-Corrected Standard Errors (PCSE) estimator improves the reliability of estimates through additional correction (Beck & Katz, 1995).

The main shortcoming of the FE OLS estimator is possible endogeneity issues in the estimation of dynamic panel models when the first lag of the dependent variable is included in the model, which undermines the reliability of the estimates; this issue is known as Nickel bias (Nickell, 1981). However, Nickel bias turns out to be considerable only in cases of "short" panels, i.e., panels in which the T dimension of the panel is very small; increasing T reduces the bias of OLS estimates. Since our model is specified in dynamic form, we anyway considered GMM-based estimators as an alternative to LS-based estimators to get insight into the reliability of LS-based estimates. More specifically, we use Difference (Arellano & Bond, 1991) DIF GMM and System (Arellano & Bover, 1995; Blundell & Bond, 1998) SYS GMM estimators in addition to FE OLS and FGLS.

4 Results

The residual tests performed for the regression model provide crucial insights into the properties of the data. The results, summarized in Table 2, show significant findings regarding heteroskedasticity, autocorrelation, and cross-sectional dependency in the residuals.

The Modified Wald test indicates that the residual variances are not equal across observations, indicating the presence of heteroskedasticity in the data. The Wooldridge test for first-order autocorrelation indicates a rejection of the null hypothesis at a 10% significance level. This implies that there is evidence of first-order autocorrelation in the residuals, which can lead to biased and inefficient estimates. The Breusch-Pagan LM test for cross-sectional dependency strongly rejects the null hypothesis, indicating the residuals are cross-sectionally correlated. This correlation between the units could affect the consistency and efficiency of the model. The Pesaran test for cross-sectional dependency also strongly rejects the null hypothesis and thus confirms a significant cross-sectional dependence in the residuals. This indicates that the residuals are correlated across different cross-sectional units.

Since the results of individual tests indicate that the panel model exhibits heteroskedasticity, first-order autocorrelation and cross-sectional dependency, the empirical model was subjected to careful estimation using a range of panel estimators carefully selected to ensure the derivation of accurate and reliable results. Using Fixed Effects (FE), Generalized Least Squares (FGLS), Panel-Corrected Standard Errors (PCSE), Difference GMM (DIF GMM), and System GMM (SYS GMM) estimators, the analysis aimed to capture the complex dynamics of the data. This comprehensive approach allowed for a nuanced examination of the relationships under investigation, yielding valuable insights into the complex interplay of variables. The results are presented in Table 3.

The results offer insightful implications for the dynamics between different factors and the growth of CO_2 emissions in CEE countries. The estimated overall explanatory power of the model based on the R-squared, which is available only in the case of FE

Table 2 Residual tests

Test	Null hypothesis	Statistics
Heteroskedasticity (Modified Wald)	All residual variances are equal	$\chi^2(14) = 1381.00$***
Autocorrelation (Wooldridge)	Residuals are not first-order autocorrelated	F(1,13) = 3.640*
CSD dependency Breusch-Pagan LM	Residuals are not cross-sectionally correlated	$\chi^2(91) = 151.471$***
CSD dependency Pesaran	Residuals are not cross-sectionally correlated	z = 3.490***

Source Authors' calculation. *Note* *** indicates a 1% significance level, ** indicates a 5% significance level, and * indicates a 10% significance level

Table 3 Estimation results

	FE OLS	FGLS	PCSE	DIF GMM	SYS GMM
CO_2(-1)	–0.1014 (0.0872)	–0.1021** (0.0461)	–0.0954 (0.0692)	–0.0991* (0.0521)	–0.1040** (0.0464)
ELER	–0.1005** (0.0371)	–0.0694*** (0.0136)	–0.1030*** (0.0210)	–0.1145*** (0.0291)	–0.1143*** (0.0288)
ELEF	0.5034*** (0.0475)	0.5341*** (0.0640)	0.4913*** (0.0816)	0.5061*** (0.0871)	0.5058*** (0.0862)
GDP	0.6692*** (0.1588)	0.4808*** (0.0914)	0.6916*** (0.1378)	0.7333*** (0.1159)	0.7313*** (0.1173)
INF	0.0002*** (0.0000)	0.0001** (0.0001)	0.0002*** (0.0001)	0.0002*** (0.0000)	0.0002*** (0.0000)
HDI	–0.2376 (0.4935)	–0.3900 (0.3330)	–0.5726 (0.4789)	0.2168 (0.5331)	0.2600 (0.4674)
TO	0.0006 (0.0006)	–0.0000 (0.0004)	0.0007 (0.0006)	0.0003 (0.0006)	0.0003 (0.0006)
No. of obs	375	375	375	375	375
R^2	0.49	–	0.54	–	–

Source Authors' calculation. Note: *** indicates a 1% significance level, ** indicates a 5% significance level, and * indicates a 10% significance level; Country-specific and time-specific effects included in each estimation. Hansen test of overidentifying restrictions in both DIF GMM and SYS GMM indicate validity of instruments

OLS and PCSE estimates, ranges from 49 to 55%, thus indicating that variations in explanatory variables predict about half of the variations in CO_2 emissions. Although there is no threshold to deem explanatory power sufficient, an R-squared between 10 and 50% is deemed acceptable in social science research if some or most of the explanatory variables are statistically significant, while high values of R-squared may be caused by spurious causation or multi-collinearity among the explanatory variables (Ozili, 2023). Considering that five of seven regressors exhibit statistically significant impact on CO_2 emissions, estimated values of R-squared close to 50% clearly suggest significant and systematic nature of relationship between variables.

When it comes to the relations between specific explanatory variables and CO_2 emissions, the results indicate that a 1 percentage point increase in renewable electricity generation growth leads to a notable reduction in CO_2 emissions growth, ranging from 0.07 to 0.11 percentage points in the different estimation models. This underlines the significant role of renewable energy in reducing CO_2 emissions. Conversely, the analysis shows that a 1 percentage point increase in the growth of final electricity consumption leads to a considerable acceleration in the growth of CO_2 emissions, namely by around 0.51 percentage points. This illustrates how electricity consumption affects CO_2 emissions, highlighting the need for energy consumption to be sustainable. This study also indicates that there is a strong correlation between economic growth and the increase in CO_2 emissions. When GDP per capita increases by 1 percentage point, it leads to an increase in CO_2 emissions ranging from 0.48 to

0.73 percentage points. The results also indicate that the inflation rate has a statistically significant (although very small) impact on the increase in CO_2 emissions. When the inflation rate increases by 1 percentage point, it leads to an increase in CO_2 emissions by 0.00002 percentage points. Although the effect of inflation on CO_2 emissions can be considered minor, or even negligible, we cannot ignore it due to statistical significance. The fact that inflation affects CO_2 emissions additionally confirms that there is an extremely complex interaction between macroeconomic stability factors and the effect that macroeconomic (monetary) policy has on the environment. Although somewhat counterintuitive, the results also indicate that HDI and trade openness do not have a statistically significant impact on CO_2 emissions in the CEE region, in this observation period.

5 Discussion

The results of this study highlight the urgent need for investments in renewable energy to reduce CO_2 emissions in CEE countries. This also applies to sustainable energy consumption practices. The reduction in CO_2 emissions growth associated with renewable electricity generation (0.07 to 0.11 percentage points per 1% increase) indicates the key role of renewable energy sources in the transition to a low-carbon economy. This is consistent with the existing professional and scientific literature, which indicates that renewable energy is the basis of reducing carbon emissions (Khan et al., 2024). Furthermore, Mentel et al. (2022) pointed out the resilience of renewable energy sources to price volatility, which further contributes to their importance. Creating a (more) favorable regulatory framework and incentives (subsidies, tax breaks, feed-in tariffs and green bonds) to reduce investment barriers and promote the application of renewable technologies should be a priority focus of policymakers in CEE countries. In this way, decarbonization of the energy sector can be achieved, attracting capital from the private sector, and contributing to long-term climate goals.

The CO_2 emissions growth due to the increase in final electricity consumption (0.49 to 0.53 percentage points per 1% increase) confirms that urgent measures are necessary to further improve energy efficiency. This was also confirmed in the work of Simionescu et al. (2019), where it was emphasized that it is most cost-effective to improve energy efficiency in order to reduce emissions. Policymakers need to work further to introduce and further develop regulations that encourage the use of energy-efficient devices, modernize insulation standards for buildings and other construction facilities, and improve public transportation systems to reduce electricity demand. These sets of measures should be accompanied by various tax incentives and other financial support programs for households and businesses that invest in energy-saving technologies and practices. In addition, industries should be motivated to adopt energy-efficient practices through energy audits and stricter consumption standards. Companies should be motivated to invest in research and development, as this is one of the most important ways to develop innovative energy storage and grid integration technologies to ensure that renewable sources can reliably deliver electricity to consumers. In accordance with the findings presented by Balsalobre-Lorente et al. (2018), the importance of reducing dependence on fossil fuels is crucial, and CEE countries should consider integrating more nuclear, geothermal, and biomass sources into their energy strategies.

The relationship between GDP per capita growth and CO_2 emissions increase (0.48 to 0.73 percentage points per 1% increase) clearly demonstrates the relationship between economic growth and environmental degradation. This result for the CEE countries indicates that this region is facing the same phenomenon that is present at the global level, which is a general concern regarding the sustainability of economic growth if only economic indicators are observed. Policymakers should prioritize green growth strategies that balance economic growth and environmental sustainability as the only path that can ensure sustainability for generations to come. These strategies should emphasize resource efficiency and innovation and focus on investing in clean technologies and promoting circular economy principles. In line with the European Commission's recommendations, green financial instruments, such as sustainability-linked loans, can incentivize the uptake of decarbonization technologies. From a managerial perspective, companies can play a key role to support green transition by implementing environmental management systems (EMS), such as ISO 14001.

The statistically significant impact of inflation on the growth of CO_2 emissions (0.0002 percentage points per 1% increase), although small, brings an intriguing insight that must be taken into consideration. This result highlights the need to also consider the environmental consequences of monetary and fiscal policy interventions aimed at addressing inflation. Central banks in CEE countries, especially those outside the EU monetary system, could further work to consider an inflation target that includes the widest range of environmental objectives. This is not unknown in the literature either, because, for example, Nguyen (2022) emphasized the importance of integrating green goals into economic policy. Macroeconomic decision makers could also work to encourage investment in sustainable infrastructure and clean technologies as part of their broader efforts to achieve price stability and environmental sustainability. From a strictly fiscal perspective, policymakers should give tax breaks to companies that invest in energy-efficient technologies or charge higher taxes to carbon-intensive industries, as suggested by AlShafeey and Saleh Saleh (2024). Such fiscal measures would ensure that inflation control is aligned with environmental goals, which would ultimately lead to a sustainable and resilient economic structure.

Finally, there is no statistically significant impact of HDI and trade openness on CO_2 emissions in CEE countries. This result is in opposition to the majority of professional and scientific literature that links higher levels of human development and trade liberalization with environmental degradation (Sezgin et al., 2021). However, this still highlights the need for tailored policies that are predominantly focused on energy structures. Policymakers should consider sector specific strategies that target the most carbon-intensive activities, rather than broad-based measures that may not address the nuances of regional economies.

Ansari, M. A., et al. (2020). Does trade openness affects global carbon dioxide emissions: Evidence from the top CO_2 emitters. *Management of Environmental Quality, 31*(1), 32–53. https://doi.org/10.1108/MEQ-12-2018-0205

Asongu, S. A., & Odhiambo, N. M. (2019). Governance, CO_2 emissions and inclusive human development in sub-Saharan Africa. *Energy Exploration & Exploitation, 38*(1), 18–36. https://doi.org/10.1177/0144598719835594

Balsalobre-Lorente, D., et al. (2018). How economic growth, renewable electricity and natural resources contribute to CO_2 emissions? *Energy Policy, 113*, 356–367. https://doi.org/10.1016/j.enpol.2017.10.050

Beck, N., & Katz, J. (1995). What to do (and not to do) with time-series cross-section data. *American Political Science Review, 89*, 634–647. https://doi.org/10.2307/2082979

Bélaïd, F., & Zrelli, M. H. (2019). Renewable and non-renewable electricity consumption, environmental degradation and economic development: Evidence from Mediterranean countries. *Energy Policy, 133*, Article 110929. https://doi.org/10.1016/j.enpol.2019.110929

Bieth, R. C. E. (2021). The influence of gross domestic product and human development index on CO_2 emissions. *Journal of Physics: Conference Series, 1808*, Article 012034. https://doi.org/10.1088/1742-6596/1808/1/012034

Blundell, R. W., & Bond, S. (1998). Initial conditions and moment restrictions in dynamic panel data models. *Journal of Econometrics, 87*, 115–143. https://doi.org/10.1016/S0304-4076(98)00009-8

Chen, B. (2016). Energy, ecology and environment: A nexus perspective. *Energy, Ecology and Environment, 1*, 1–2. https://doi.org/10.1007/s40974-016-0017-8

Ćetković, S., & Buzogány, A. (2019). The political economy of EU climate and energy policies in Central and Eastern Europe revisited: Shifting coalitions and prospects for clean energy transitions. *Politics and Governance, 7*(1), 124–138. https://doi.org/10.17645/pag.v7i1.1786

Dauda, L., et al. (2021). Innovation, trade openness and CO_2 emissions in selected countries in Africa. *Journal of Cleaner Production, 281*, Article 125143. https://doi.org/10.1016/j.jclepro.2020.125143

Dinda, S. (2004). Environmental Kuznets curve hypothesis: A survey. *Ecological Economics, 49*, 431–455. https://doi.org/10.1016/j.ecolecon.2004.02.011

Eurostat. (2023). Supply, transformation and consumption of electricity. https://ec.europa.eu/eurostat/databrowser/view/nrg_cb_e__custom_9320579/default/table?lang=en

Fedajev, A., et al. (2023). Driving industrial and economic growth in Central and Eastern Europe: The role of electricity infrastructure and renewable energy. *Utilities Policy, 85*, 101683. https://doi.org/10.1016/j.jup.2023.101683

Friedlingstein, P., et al. (2022). Global carbon budget 2022. *Earth System Science Data, 14*(11), 4811–4900. https://doi.org/10.5194/essd-14-4811-2022

Friedlingstein, P., et al. (2023). Global carbon budget 2023. *Earth System Science Data, 15*(12), 5301–5369. https://doi.org/10.5194/essd-15-5301-2023

Galvan, L. P. C., et al. (2022). The nexus between CO_2 emission, economic growth, trade openness: Evidences from middle-income trap countries. *Frontiers in Environmental Science, 10*, Article 938776. https://doi.org/10.3389/fenvs.2022.938776

Global Carbon Atlas. (2023). CO_2 Emissions. https://globalcarbonatlas.org/emissions/carbon-emissions/

Gyamerah, S. A., & Gil-Alaña, L. A. (2023). A multivariate causality analysis of CO_2 emission, electricity consumption, and economic growth: Evidence from Western and Central Africa. *Heliyon, 9*(1), Article e12858. https://doi.org/10.1016/j.heliyon.2023.e12858

Jin, X., et al. (2024). How do inflation rate and energy alternatives influence environmental quality? *A BRICS Analysis. Energy Strategy Reviews, 53*, Article 101369. https://doi.org/10.1016/j.esr.2024.101369

Jonek-Kowalska, I. (2022). Multi-criteria evaluation of the effectiveness of energy policy in Central and Eastern European countries in a long-term perspective. *Energy Strategy Reviews, 44*, Article 100973. https://doi.org/10.1016/j.esr.2022.100973

Khan, A., et al. (2024). Efficacy of CO_2 emission reduction strategies by countries pursuing energy efficiency, nuclear power, and renewable electricity. *Energy, 300*, Article 131418. https://doi.org/10.1016/j.energy.2024.131418

Li, B., & Haneklaus, N. (2022). Reducing CO_2 emissions in G7 countries: The role of clean energy consumption, trade openness and urbanization. *Energy Reports, 8*, 704–713. https://doi.org/10.1016/j.egyr.2022.01.238

Majewska, A., & Gierałtowska, U. (2022). Impact of economic affluence on CO_2 emissions in CEE countries. *Energies, 15*(1), 322. https://doi.org/10.3390/en15010322

Mamun, A., et al. (2014). Regional differences in the dynamic linkage between CO_2 emissions, sectoral output and economic growth. *Renewable and Sustainable Energy Reviews, 38*, 1–11. https://doi.org/10.1016/j.rser.2014.05.091

Manta, A. G., et al. (2020). The nexus between carbon emissions, energy use, economic growth and financial development: Evidence from Central and Eastern European countries. *Sustainability, 12*(18), 7747. https://doi.org/10.3390/su12187747

Mentel, U., et al. (2022). Industrialization and CO_2 emissions in Sub-Saharan Africa: The mitigating role of renewable electricity. *Energies, 15*(3), 946. https://doi.org/10.3390/en15030946

Mitić, P., et al. (2017). A cointegration analysis of real GDP and CO_2 emissions in transitional countries. *Sustainability, 9*(4), 568. https://doi.org/10.3390/su9040568

Mitić, P., et al. (2024). Fostering green transition in Central and Eastern Europe: Carbon dioxide emissions, industrialization, financial development, and electricity nexus. *Technological and Economic Development of Economy, 30*, 1009–1036. https://doi.org/10.3846/tede.2024.20630

Nguyen, A. T. (2022). The relationship between tourism receipt, economic growth, inflation, energy consumption, and carbon dioxide emissions: Evidence in Southeast Asia. *e-Review of Tourism Research, 19*(1), 54–88.

Nickell, S. (1981). Biases in dynamic models with fixed effects. *Econometrica, 49*(6), 1417–1426.

NOAA. (2024). Climate change: Atmospheric carbon dioxide. https://www.climate.gov/news-features/understandingclimate/climate-change-atmospheric-carbondioxide#:~:text=Since%20the%20middle%20of%20the,the%20Global%20Carbon%20Budget%202023

Our World in Data. (2023). Our World in Data. https://ourworldindata.org/

Ozili, P. (2023). The acceptable R-square in empirical modelling for social science research. *MPRA* Paper No. 115769. https://mpra.ub.uni-muenchen.de/115769/1/MPRA_paper_115769.pdf

Peters, G. P., et al. (2011). Growth in emission transfers via international trade from 1990 to 2008. *Proceedings of the National Academy of Sciences of the United States of America, 108*(21), 8903–8908. https://doi.org/10.1073/pnas.1006388108

Petrović-Ranđelović, M., et al. (2019). Economic growth and carbon emissions: Evidence from CIVETS countries. *Applied Economics, 52*(16), 1806–1815. https://doi.org/10.1080/00036846.2019.1679343

Rahman, M. M. (2020). Environmental degradation: The role of electricity consumption, economic growth and globalisation. *Journal of Environmental Management, 253*, Article 109742. https://doi.org/10.1016/j.jenvman.2019.109742

Rodrigues, J. F. D., et al. (2020). Drivers of CO_2 emissions from electricity generation in the European Union 2000–2015. *Renewable and Sustainable Energy Reviews, 133*, Article 110104. https://doi.org/10.1016/j.rser.2020.110104

Sezgin, F. H., et al. (2021). Do environmental stringency policies and human development reduce CO_2 emissions? Evidence from G7 and BRICS economies. *International Journal of Environmental Research and Public Health, 18*(13), 6727. https://doi.org/10.3390/ijerph18136727

Shpak, N., et al. (2022). CO_2 Emissions and macroeconomic indicators: Analysis of the most polluted regions in the world. *Energies, 15*(8), 2928. https://doi.org/10.3390/en15082928

Simionescu, M., et al. (2019). Renewable energy in the electricity sector and GDP per capita in the European Union. *Energies, 12*(13), 2520. https://doi.org/10.3390/en12132520

Simionescu, M. (2021). Revised environmental Kuznets Curve in CEE countries. Evidence from panel threshold models for economic sectors. *Environmental Science and Pollution Research, 28*(43), 60881–60899. https://doi.org/10.1007/s11356-021-14905-3

The World Bank. (2023). World Bank Open Data. https://data.worldbank.org/

United Nations. (2019). World Population Prospects: The 2019 Revision. United Nations Population Division. https://esa.un.org/unpd/wpp/

Voumik, L. C., et al. (2023). CO_2 emissions from renewable and non-renewable electricity generation sources in the G7 countries: Static and dynamic panel assessment. *Energies, 16*(3), 1044. https://doi.org/10.3390/en16031044

Wooldridge, J. M. (2002). *Econometric analysis of cross section and panel data.* MIT Press.

Zheng, J., et al. (2019). Regional development and carbon emissions in China. *Energy Economics, 81*, 25–36. https://doi.org/10.1016/j.eneco.2019.03.003

EU Membership and Institutional Governance in Advancing Climate Change Mitigation: A Comparative Analysis of the Balkan Economies

Eirini Triarchi, Dimitrios Kolias, and Efstratios Kypriotelis

Abstract The urgent challenge of climate change, driven by human activities, necessitates a coordinated international response to mitigate its impacts and advance towards a sustainable future. The political and institutional frameworks within countries significantly influence the effectiveness of climate policies, as evidenced by variations in annual CO_2 emissions. Studies indicate that democracies with strong public involvement and governance are more adept at enacting efficient environmental measures. However, authoritarian regimes favoring rapid policy execution may deprioritize environmental goals for political stability, impeding holistic climate mitigation efforts. In this context, the role of our audience, consisting of academic researchers, policymakers, and environmentalists, is crucial in understanding and addressing these challenges. This study examines the impact of institutional governance, European Union (EU) membership and the level of economic development on climate change mitigation. By drawing on data from the V-Dem database and World Governance Indicators (WGI), encompassing 10 Balkan countries, divided into EU members, Bulgaria, Croatia, Greece, Romania, Slovenia, and non-EU members Albania, Bosnia and Herzegovina (BiH), North Macedonia, Montenegro, Serbia, this research probes the impact of political and institutional factors on CO_2 emissions from 1998 to 2022. Additionally, by integrating the Environmental Kuznets Curve (EVC) hypothesis, the correlation between economic growth and environmental degradation is elucidated. This study uses Inverse Probability Weighting (IPW) regression in the context of estimating the Average Treatment Effect (ATE) to evaluate the differences in CO_2 emissions depending on whether a Balkan country is part of the European Union) or not. Through a comprehensive review of existing literature, this study uncovers notable disparities in CO_2 emission patterns and the effectiveness of environmental

E. Triarchi (✉) · E. Kypriotelis
Department of Accounting and Finance, University of Ioannina, Ioannina, Greece
e-mail: etriarhi@uoi.gr

E. Kypriotelis
e-mail: kypriot@uoi.gr

D. Kolias
School of Social Sciences, Hellenic Open University, Patras, Greece
e-mail: std525794@ac.eap.gr

I. Bartuseviciene et al. (eds.), *Building Economic Resilience*, Contributions to Economics, https://doi.org/10.1007/978-3-031-96428-2_10

policies between EU and non-EU Balkan nations. Empirical evidence supports the proposition that EU membership is pivotal in bolstering climate mitigation efforts through policy frameworks and improvements in governance quality. The amalgamation of empirical findings and literature review suggests that EU membership impacts Balkan countries' climate change mitigation strategies, with EU members demonstrating substantial strides in CO_2 emission reduction. This study emphasizes the importance of institutional governance and environmental policy implementation in tackling climate change. It demonstrates how EU integration encourages stricter regulations in Balkan states and calls for detailed research on policy interventions and outcomes. The paper offers insights into the effect of EU membership and political and institutional backgrounds on climate resilience, which is valuable for policymakers and scholars of the field.

Keywords Institutional Governance · EU membership · Balkan economies · Climate change · CO_2 emissions · Environmental Kuznets Curve

Jel Classification Code F55 · 013 · 017

1 Introduction

Mitigating climate change is one of the most pervasive challenges of the century and requires the international community to act. Global action requires intergovernmental collaboration to produce effective policies that reduce the impact of climate change on the planet's sustainable development. The effectiveness of climate policies is strongly influenced by political and institutional structures within states, as evidenced by variations in annual CO_2 emissions. Research has shown that democracies with strong public engagement and high-quality governance are generally more successful in implementing effective climate actions. Conversely, the centralized decision-making processes in authoritarian regimes, while capable of rapid policy implementation, often prioritize political stability over environmental considerations, which risks undermining overall climate change mitigation strategies.

Quantitative studies have indicated that national political systems impact emission levels. However, differences in emissions might be influenced by factors beyond the degree of democracy, potentially including stages of economic development as conceptualized in the Environmental Kuznets Curve (EKC) hypothesis (Clulow, 2019; Eren, 2022). The existing literature also identifies distinct differences in CO_2 emission trends and the effectiveness of environmental policies in the EU and non-EU Balkan states. Shkurti (2019) notes the high CO_2 intensity of electricity generation in non-EU Balkan countries, mainly due to dependence on lignite, a situation that stands in stark contrast to the diversified energy portfolios and stricter environmental regulations seen in EU Member States. Ali et al. (2022) provide a comprehensive analysis of the interaction between GDP per capita, CO_2 emissions, and Combustible Energy and Waste Consumption (CEWC) in the Balkans. Their findings reveal a significant positive impact of CEWC on economic growth, alongside a notable negative influence of CO_2 emissions on environmental quality, highlighting the intricate balance these countries face between fostering economic development and ensuring environmental sustainability. In light of the research conducted by Knez et al. (2022), it is evident that Croatia, as a member of the European Union (EU), has already begun integrating climate change mitigation policies and practices. In contrast, the remaining countries of the Western Balkans (WB)—Bosnia and Herzegovina, Montenegro, Albania, and the Republic of North Macedonia—are in various stages of formulating and adopting necessary regulations and strategies to confront climate change effectively. Despite these efforts, the implementation of targeted climate actions remains relatively subdued across the region. This sluggish progress is primarily attributed to the limited economic resources, insufficient investments, and a cautious approach by policy-makers prioritizing maintaining social stability over the urgent need for environmental reforms. On the other hand, through its policy frameworks that provoke improvements in the quality of governance in its member states, the EU positively influences action against climate change.

This study aims to discover the influence of EU membership, the effect of the political and institutional backgrounds, and economic development on climate resilience in the Balkan countries. Using data from the V-Dem database and World Bank, it assesses the quality of governance and democratic practices across 10 Balkan nations, categorized into EU members (Bulgaria, Croatia, Greece, Romania, Slovenia) and non-EU members (Albania, Bosnia and Herzegovina, Montenegro, North Macedonia, Serbia), also known as Western Balkans (WB), for the period 1988–2022. This research also incorporates the EKC hypothesis to investigate the relationship between economic growth and environmental degradation. To our knowledge, no prior study has incorporated these factors to assess their impact on climate change in this region, especially by distinguishing the two groups above countries. This focus on the Balkans, a unique region regarding the political, institutional, economic and environmental issues that it experiences, adds a new dimension to the discourse on climate resilience, which has traditionally been explored in broader or different regional contexts.

The amalgamation of empirical findings and literature review suggests that EU membership significantly influences the climate mitigation strategies employed by Balkan countries, with EU members showing more strident progress in reducing CO_2 emissions. This analysis highlights the critical role of institutional governance and the implementation of effective environmental policies in addressing climate change challenges. It underlines the benefits of EU integration in promoting more stringent environmental regulations and policies among Balkan states, advocating for further targeted research to elucidate the specific policy interventions and their environmental impacts. Policymakers, scholars, and students in the field will benefit from this paper since it provides a nuanced understanding of the impact of EU membership on advancing environmental sustainability.

The rest of the study is structured as follows: Section two provides the theoretical background by reviewing the literature on the relationship between political systems, institutional governance, economic growth, and climate change. Section three includes the empirical analysis, and section four provides conclusions.

2 The Theoretical Background

This section presents the study's main concepts and synthesizes empirical findings from existing research on the relationship between institutional governance, economic growth, European membership, and climate change.

2.1 Institutional Governance and Climate Change

A country's institutional environment comprises a set of formal and informal institutions, laws and regulations, governance mechanisms, enforcement procedures, and societal norms and values, influencing a country's operational landscape (North, 1990). The political institutions refer to the regime type, the architecture of national policy-making, and the judicial framework (Mudambi & Navarra, 2002). Institutions can be seen as the underlying framework that supports a country's development, manifest in various forms, including political stability, regulatory quality, government effectiveness, voice and accountability, rule of law and control of corruption (Kaufmann et al., 2011). Even when societies have identical institutional frameworks, the outcomes they produce can differ significantly (Mudambi & Navarra, 2002).

The way these institutions are governed emerges as a critical determinant in the performance of the state. Hence, the quality of institutional governance plays a pivotal role in achieving the desired goals of sustainable development. Notably, a large number of local and national policy measures exist in many countries to reduce CO_2 emissions and deliver wider sustainable benefits but are not always taken up due to several factors, some of them related to the political regime and the country's quality of institutional governance (Lah, 2017). The term governance incorporates features of political systems like democratic and electoral systems, the division of powers and citizens' rights, and technocratic public sector management elements, such as regulatory systems, service provision and tax administration. In literature, definitions of governance reflect a normative bias favoring democratic structures, processes and practices, commonly referring to these as "good governance" (Frazer et al., 2022). In the 1990s, the World Bank first introduced the term "good governance" as the effective implementation of the state's capacity to deliver essential public goods and services in which countries can advance their development goals (Kaufmann et al., 2011). Notably, there are three governance areas, each comprising two dimensions. The first area refers to the process by which governments are selected, monitored and replaced, including the dimensions of voice and accountability, and political stability & the absence of Violence/Terrorism; the second area is the capacity of the government to effectively formulate and implement sound policies measured by the dimensions of government effectiveness and regulatory quality. Finally, the third concerns the respect of citizens and the state for the institutions that govern economic and social interactions among them with the dimensions of the rule of law and control of corruption Kaufmann et al. (2011, p. 222).

The prevailing political system significantly shapes societal preferences, thereby influencing the pace at which environmental policies are introduced into the political discourse of the state (Lægreid & Povitkina, 2018). Environmental policies are designed to promote the well-being of individuals across the political spectrum; however, the methodologies employed in decision-making vary. International collaboration and the free flow of information, hallmarks of democratic states, support establishing efficient and inclusive environmental policies (Kneuer, 2012). In liberal democracies, citizens are granted the freedom and even urged to undertake actions against climate change and to voice criticism regarding the indifference or inadequacy of the authorities (Lindvall, 2021, p. 9). A consensus democracy provides institutions that foster political stability and create better environmental policies over the long term (Lah, 2017, p. 5). Consequently, an enhanced level of democracy within the state could lead to a more substantial reduction in environmental degradation. On the contrary, states governed by authoritarian regimes, marked by the leadership of either a single ruler or a non-democratically elected elite, and might exhibit a more limited temporal perspective regarding environmental policy. Such governance structures often prioritize maintaining immediate political stability at the expense of enduring environmental sustainability (Congleton, 1992; Fredriksson & Neumayer, 2013). Beeson (2016) posits that authoritarian regimes may effectively address climate change, supported by Jahanger et al. (2021), who found that in a globalized context, democracy tends to exacerbate emissions, in contrast to autocratic regimes. Gilley (2012) introduces the notion of authoritarian environmentalism, suggesting that such regimes' centralized authority and tight control over policy processes, albeit at the cost of personal freedoms, enable more productive environmental strategies. Thus, the country's governance significantly influences its environmental outcomes.

The correlation between democracy and environmental protection should not be viewed unidimensionally. While democracy positively affects climate change mitigation, the effect on policy outcomes regarding emission levels and trends can be ambiguous (Battig & Bernauer, 2009; Wurster, 2013). Current research underscores that democratic systems are more effective in climate change mitigation by incorporating a more significant number of mechanisms and critical factors into their analyses (Bernauer & Koubi, 2009; Clulow, 2019; Fredriksson & Neumayer, 2013; Kim et al., 2019; Lægreid and Povitkina, 2018; Lv, 2017; Povitkina, 2018; Sinha et al., 2021; Von Stein, 2022; You et al., 2020). Factors such as civil liberties, the type of democracy, the justice system, and groups of interest play a nuanced role in shaping environmental outcomes. Sinha et al. (2021) proved that an empowered rule of law and access to justice can reduce carbon dioxide emissions and increase environmental quality in democracies. Clulow (2019) points out that democratization has uneven effects across countries, with the type of electoral system emerging as a determinant of the impact of democratization on national emissions. Von Stein (2022) included electoral accountability, the protection of civil liberties, and political constraints as determinants of the relationship between political institutions and the environment. Electoral accountability improves environmental outcomes when citizens acknowledge environmental protection as a policy objective, while civil liberties protections' and environmentalism depend on which actors in society hold power; limited evidence is available to support that political constraints are preventing climate change (Von Stein, 2022, p. 353). Fredriksson and Neumayer (2013) highlight the importance of democratic capital. Higher levels of democratic capital stock, such as the stock of the historical experience of constraints on the executive, are associated with more stringent climate change policies (Fredriksson & Neumayer, 2013, p. 18). Corruption is another crucial factor, as democracies with low corruption rates tend to emit less CO_2, while highly corrupted democracies do not differ significantly from autocracies in emission patterns (Lægreid & Povitkina, 2018; Povitkina, 2018). Kim et al. (2019) use a combination of five democratic features, election system, civil liberties, government function, political participation, and political culture, with a country's income to assess the environmental impact of democracy in high-income and low-income countries. A strong positive correlation between environmental quality and the five democratic indices exists in high-income countries. In contrast, this correlation becomes less pronounced in low-income countries, where the government function maintains its strength (Kim et al., 2019, p. 12).

Some studies underscore the importance of solid institutional frameworks in environmental policy efficacy. Muhammad and Long (2021) examine how specific institutional factors beyond the political regime influence carbon emissions, focusing on variations by country income levels. Political stability, control of corruption, and the rule of law are crucial for reducing carbon emissions and effectively addressing climate change. Güney (2017) study also examines institutional factors such as the protection of property rights, the effective operation of the legal system, the rule of law, participation, accountability, transparency, respect for human rights, and tolerance for differences. These governance components create a variable that can mitigate the severe damage caused by our present use of natural resources (Güney, 2017, p. 17). Contemporary research in the field focuses on the importance and effects of institutions' governance quality on countries' sustainable development. Omri and Ben Mabrouk's (2020) study on 20 MENA economies finds that enhanced institutional governance aids in mitigating carbon emissions' adverse effects on economic growth, human development, and the exacerbation of emissions by economic growth, thus facilitating sustainable development. Similarly, Hussain and Dogan's (2021) research in BRICS countries concludes that high institutional quality plays a crucial role in curbing environmental degradation. Tamazian and Rao (2010) identify that in transitional economies, robust policy frameworks and institutional structures are essential for improving environmental quality and achieving long-term advantages from greenhouse gas emission reductions. Lau et al. (2014) further outline the critical role of strong domestic institutional frameworks in managing CO_2 emissions throughout the development process. Azam et al. (2021) present a controversial view on the role of institutional governance, arguing that in their study of lower-middle-income and middle-income countries, institutional factors actually exacerbate environmental pollution. They suggest that this could be due to the focus of varying democratic systems on industrial development, which prioritizes the interests of substantial constituencies, leading to increased local and global pollution levels.

2.2 *Economic Growth and Climate Change*

The debates regarding the effect of the political environment on environmental outcomes and economic growth on environmental degradation are becoming more intertwined. Empirical analysis of the correlation between the last two has yielded ambiguous findings. On this basis, many scholars use the Environmental Kuznets Curve (EKC) hypothesis, based on the original Kuznets curve, which examines the relationship between economic growth and income distribution (Kuznets, 1955), to draw out robust results. The environmental Kuznets curve states that an inverted U-shaped relationship exists between economic growth, as depicted by GDP per capita, and CO_2 emissions. Hannesson (2022) noted that a country's economic status predominantly affects the amount of CO_2 emitted. Low- or middle-income countries appear to have experienced increasing emissions since 1990, while high-income countries seem to have seen a downslope trend. Kacprzyk and Kuchta (2020) corroborated the EKC's effectiveness in their study by using nighttime light imagery as a proxy for a country's development status while also suggesting a lower threshold for CO_2 reduction. Zhang (2021) found the association between CO_2 emissions and real GDP per capita to be N-shaped in the long term, which places a spotlight on the contrasting roles of urbanization and energy consumption. Pata (2018) found that the EKC is supported in the instance of Turkey since economic growth, among other factors, has a positive effect on the country's emissions. Htike et al. (2022) suggest that the EKC can be applied to specific industry sectors, which present varying income level turning points. Bilgili et al. (2016) showed that renewable energy consumption negatively impacts emissions within the EKC model. These studies' findings outline a complex and multifaceted relationship and intervals between economic growth and environmental impact, as evidenced by carbon dioxide emissions, with results varying across countries, time periods, and methodologies. Ahmad et al. (2021) examine the impact of innovation shocks on environmental quality in OECD economies, using data from 1990 to 2014. The study considers factors like foreign direct investment (FDI), exports (EXP), renewable energy consumption (REC), and GDP per capita. The results indicate that positive innovation shocks enhance environmental quality by reducing CO2 emissions, while negative shocks have the opposite effect. This supports both the Environmental Kuznets Curve (EKC) and the Pollution Halo Hypothesis (PHH) in the economies of the sample. The study emphasizes the positive role of renewable energy consumption in improving environmental quality and suggests using innovation shocks as a policy tool for better environmental policies. Akram et al. (2020) explores the impact of energy efficiency and renewable energy on reducing CO2 emissions in developing countries from 1990 to 2014. This research incorporates energy efficiency's role in the Environmental Kuznets Curve (EKC) hypothesis, which has been previously overlooked. The study finds that energy efficiency consistently reduces CO_2 emissions across all quantiles analyzed, with the most substantial effects noted at the highest emission levels (90th quantile). Renewable energy also contributes to reducing CO_2 emissions, showing significant effects, especially at the lower emission quantiles (10th quantile). Moreover, they argue that GDP increases CO_2 emissions, with the effect intensifying at higher income levels. Conversely, the squared GDP term strongly mitigates emissions at upper quantiles, supporting the EKC hypothesis in these countries.

There are studies supporting that in countries where initial economic growth correlates to an increase in CO_2 emissions, a trend which peaks and reverses when a high enough income is achieved, enabled by stable and well-established democratic institutions (Bättig & Bernauer, 2009; Bernauer & Koubi, 2009; Eren, 2022; Lv, 2017; Sinha et al., 2021; You et al., 2020). Bättig and Bernauer (2009) established that in full democracies, higher income levels are required to reverse the EKC trend. The EKC hypothesis and its implications have been the subject of rigorous research in the past decade, the findings of which are very diverse. Lv (2017) and You et al. (2020) regard income as a decisive factor in explaining the ambiguous outcomes of democratization on a country's CO2 emissions. It appears that democratization is initially detrimental to the environment, and only after a certain threshold of economic growth, it becomes beneficial, thus supporting the EKC hypothesis (Lv, 2017). Generally, countries where strong and stable democratic institutions reside seem to be more willing to implement robust environmental protection policies, while in less, or non, democratic countries, income inequality correlates to increased CO_2 emissions (You et al., 2020). Through empirical analysis, Sinha et al. (2021) concluded that the turning point in the relationship between emissions and income is significantly higher. As a result, autocracies tend to emit more CO_2 per unit change in income than democracies. Eren (2022) finds that democratization will initially lead to lower emission levels, while in the long run, it may delay the trend reversal in the Kuznets curve, thus increasing democracies' environmental cost of growth. The non-agreement of the varying outcomes can be attributed to the causality relationships between variables. Higher levels of democracy can stimulate economic growth, adherence to the rule of law, control of corruption, etc., but in the case of nations whose economies turn on fossil fuels, higher development levels do lead to further environmental degradation (Eren, 2022, p. 71,456).

2.3 EU Membership and Climate Change

EU is recognized as a global leader in climate action due to its most advanced climate policy framework among leading international players. The development of

EU climate policy is extensively recorded, starting with initial efforts in the 1980s and 1990s, followed by the systematic advancement and fortification of a more comprehensive policy framework in the 2000s and particularly in the 2010s with the Europe 2020 Strategy, followed up by the European Green Deal (EGD) strategy in 2019 (Brodny & Tutak, 2023; Oberthür & von Homeyer, 2023). The EGD strategy operates as a roadmap for the key policies and measures needed to transform the EU into an inclusive and prosperous society featuring a modern, resource-efficient and competitive economy, where the target of net-zero greenhouse gas emissions by 2050 and the decoupling of economic growth from resource use will be attained (Cifuentes-Faura, 2022; European Commission, 2019). Achieving climate neutrality is acknowledged to impose considerable costs on both social and economic levels. At the heart of these efforts is the principle of transition or transformation, aimed at connecting the present legal and policy framework with the envisioned status of the Union's economic position in 2050 as a global frontrunner (Sikora, 2021).

The formal institutions of the EU support its member states' climate change and energy policies. One of the primary goals of EU environmental policies is to enhance the environmental sustainability of the economies within its member states. The integration of the climate law into the EU legal framework, as officially proclaimed in the Lisbon Treaty, represents a significant alignment with major international legal milestones, including the Paris Agreement, the United Nations 2030 Agenda and the Sustainable Development Goals (SDGs) (Sikora, 2021, p. 683). The European Commission (EC) introduces a significant number of legal acts, indicating a high commitment at the EU institutional level and in terms of implementation efficiency required from member states. The EDG's ambitious goals demanded unparalleled participation from public and private investors, civil society and every EU citizen.

The Europeanisation in the Balkans, the study's target group of countries, is framed by adopting the EU rules and standards that promote regional cooperation and environmental policies. Notably, the EU acts through various mechanisms, including the enlargement process, the adoption of EU standards and the promotion of institutional reforms. For the EU enlargement process in non-EU countries as the WB ones, that are candidates for more than 18 years, scholars criticize the delays and underscore the impact of the "enlargement fatigue" on the uptake and implementation of EU policies (Economides, 2020; O'Brennan, 2014). However, the EU keeps the WB's European perspective alive but demands that the adoption and implementation of EU accession reforms be expedited so that WB countries can join the EU by the set deadline. Dabrowski and Myachenkova (2018) provide a fundamental overview of the WB journey towards EU integration, highlighting the critical role of alignment with EU standards, especially in environmental policies and climate change mitigation. This alignment is seen as essential for the region's sustainable development, highlighting the importance of institutional reforms in environmental governance. Renner and Trauner (2009) highlight the EU's role in improving environmental standards and practices in candidate countries, illustrating the tangible impacts of EU policy transfer. In this context, WB countries, under the auspices of the "stabilization and association process," should adopt, put into effect, and enforce all 35 chapters of the EU acquis. Chapter 27, "Environment and Climate Change," is the largest and most demanding of the remaining chapters, involving adjustments and modifications to the WB's legal framework about the environment and climate change (Banja et al., 2020, p. 5). Chapter 27 also provides a solid foundation for WB to meet the EGD targets, particularly regarding a climate-neutral economy by reducing carbon emissions by 50% /55% by 2030 and achieving carbon neutrality by 2050 (Vuković & Mandić, 2018, p. 34). However, the "enlargement fatigue" slows down policy implementation and potentially hampers the advancement of environmental and climate policies in the WB peninsula (Economides, 2020; O'Brennan, 2014).

Existing literature finds the EU's role in guiding climate change mitigation and sustainable development efforts among its members and candidates is influential and complex (Becker et al., 2020; Brodny & Tutak, 2023; Çolak & Ege, 2013; Fura et al., 2017; Knez et al., 2022; Kryk & Guzowska, 2021; Pejović et al., 2021). Brodny and Tutak's (2023) research on the level of energy development and climate sustainability between 2010 and 2020 in the EU member states revealed that countries with long experience in the energy transition towards green energy sources, such as Scandinavian ones, perform best. The excellent performance of this group of countries is also highlighted in the study of Çolak and Ege (2013), assessing the EU member and candidate states performance in achieving the priorities of the EU 2020 Strategy. However, new EU, post-socialist countries such as Poland and Bulgaria have issues with energy transition associated with low growth and social problems, showing low performance (Brodny & Tutak, 2023, p. 362). In a similar research, Kryk and Guzowska (2021) attribute the variation in energy and climate sustainability performance among the EU member states to the disparities in the rate of compliance with the Europe 2020 strategy's objectives. These member states, mainly of Eastern Europe, confront existing energy/fuel mix economies, conflicting national interests and adverse economic conditions (Fura et al., 2017). However, across the EU, no country has met the targets for greenhouse gas emissions as defined in the EU institutional framework, with Bulgaria and Romania being of particular concern (Becker et al., 2020). Knez et al. (2022), investigating the climate change adaptation strategies in WB countries and Croatia, an EU member, found that the former suffers from a low level of implementation of specific environmental policies due to insufficient commitment of decision-makers to proceed with reforms relating to the field of climate change transition. Pejović et al. (2021) investigate the link between economic growth, energy consumption and carbon emissions in the 27 countries of the EU and the WB countries, underscoring that using renewable energy sources that the EGD promotes decreases CO_2 emissions level. Hence, WB countries' aspirations for early EU membership influence their climate policies and CO_2 emissions to transition to more energy-efficient technologies and processes and clean and renewable energy sources (Pejović et al., 2021).

3 Data and Empirical Approach

This research covers the period 1998–2022 on an annual scale for the ten countries located in the Balkan Peninsula in Europe.

3.1 Data Presentation

This study uses data covering ten Balkan countries, distributed into two regions. Region 0 includes the non-EU members Albania, Bosnia and Herzegovina (BiH), Montenegro, North Macedonia, and Serbia, while Region 1 includes the EU members Bulgaria, Croatia, Greece, Romania, Slovenia, and non-EU members (see Table 1).

Table 2 briefly describes the variables included in the empirical model, their coding, and data sources.

Table 3 presents statistics for the two regions, denoted as Region 0 and Region 1. The descriptive statistics cover the variables CO_2 emissions per capita, GDP per capita (Lngdpc and its square, Lngdpc_sq), as well as governance and regime index (Coc, Rul, Va, Gove, Plst, Rqu, Ldi).

The Variance Inflation Factor (VIF) metric is used to detect multicollinearity in our models. The VIF is found to be smaller than five (5), suggesting that this level of collinearity between independent variables is generally considered acceptable in our analysis.

The statistics reveal significant differences between the two regions regarding environmental impact (as indicated by CO_2 emissions), economic development (GDP per capita), and governance and democratic practices.

Region 1 appears more developed economically, with higher CO_2 emissions per capita—a possible indicator of higher industrial activity or less energy efficiency. It also scores higher on governance and democracy indices, suggesting better institutional quality. In contrast, Region 0, while having lower CO_2 emissions, indicating possibly lower economic activity or higher energy efficiency, faces challenges in governance and democratic practices, which could impact its long-term sustainable development.

Table 1 Regional Division of Target countries

Region	
0	1
Albania	Bulgaria
BiH	Croatia
Montenegro	Greece
North Macedonia	Romania
Serbia	Slovenia

Table 2 Variables description and coding

Variables	Description	Code	Source of data
Dependent variable			
Climate action	Annual CO_2 emissions per capita (tonnes)	CO_2	Our World in Data (2022)
Independent variables			
Governance indicators	A set of traditions and institutions by which authority in a country is exercised		
Control of corruption	Governance dimensions	*Coc*	Worldwide Governance Indicators (WGI)
Rule of law		*Rul*	
Voice and accountability		*Va*	
Political stability		*Plst*	
Government effectiveness		*Gov*	
Regulatory quality		*Rqu*	
Liberal democracy index	The aggregate index that describes features of democracy at the highest level	*Ldi*	V-Dem Dataset (V.10)
Income	The log of GDP per capita, PPP (constant 2017 international $)	*Lngdpc* *Lngdpc_sq*	World Bank-World Development Indicators

CO_2 Emissions Per Capita (co_2_per_capita)

Using the variable CO_2 emissions per capita over simply examining total emissions ensures a reasonable comparison between countries of the two regions. Population sizes differ both between and within regions; therefore, by standardizing the metric, CO_2 emissions per capita facilitates easier comparisons across countries and over time.

Region 0: The average CO_2 emissions per capita are lower (3.977 metric tons) than in Region 1, indicating potentially lower industrial activity or more efficient energy use. The standard deviation suggests variability among countries within this region.

Region 1: Higher CO_2 emissions per capita (6.207 metric tons), indicating higher industrial activity or energy consumption. The range is also wider, indicating significant emissions differences among the countries (see Fig. 1).

Post-2020, many regions have faced economic challenges, including the impacts of the COVID-19 pandemic, which might have slowed down industrial activity and emissions. However, the stability rather than a decline suggests that any reductions due to the economic slowdown, especially in Region 1, may have been offset by

Table 3 Descriptive statistics

Variable	Obs	Mean	Std. dev	Min	Max
Region 0					
Co2_per_capita	120	3.977	1.759	0.931	7.805
Lngdpc	119	8.346	0.553	6.819	9.220
Lngdpc_sq	119	69.964	8.969	46.495	85.002
Coc	99	–0.390	0.216	–0.856	0.012
Rul	95	0.019	0.278	–0.684	0.524
Va	99	0.047	0.171	–0.502	0.334
Gove	95	–0.250	0.349	–1.072	0.349
Plst	94	–0.183	0.398	–1.156	0.817
Rqu	99	–0.297	0.228	–1.021	0.317
Ldi	120	0.395	0.066	0.182	0.540
Region 1					
Co2_per_capita	120	6.207	1.780	3.740	10.327
Lngdpc	120	9.324	0.735	7.378	10.377
Lngdpc_sq	120	87.474	13.179	54.431	107.692
Coc	105	0.125	0.428	–0.511	1.052
Rul	105	0.558	0.231	–0.119	1.007
Va	105	0.671	0.262	0.262	1.191
Gove	105	0.367	0.438	–0.372	1.178
Plst	105	0.455	0.368	–0.379	1.304
Rqu	105	0.332	0.429	–0.266	1.112
Ldi	120	0.655	0.115	0.275	0.811

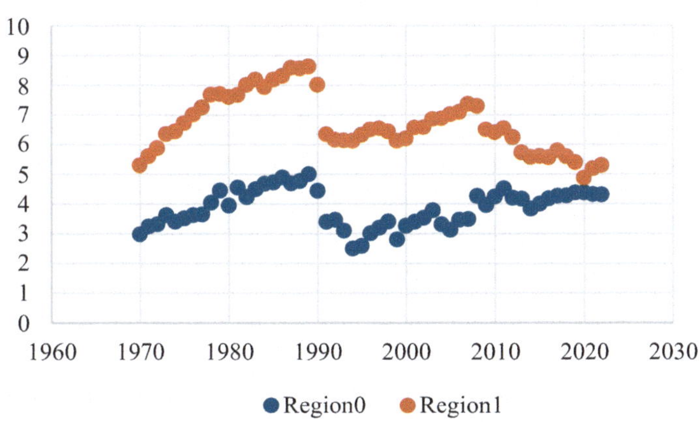

Fig. 1 CO_2 emissions per capita

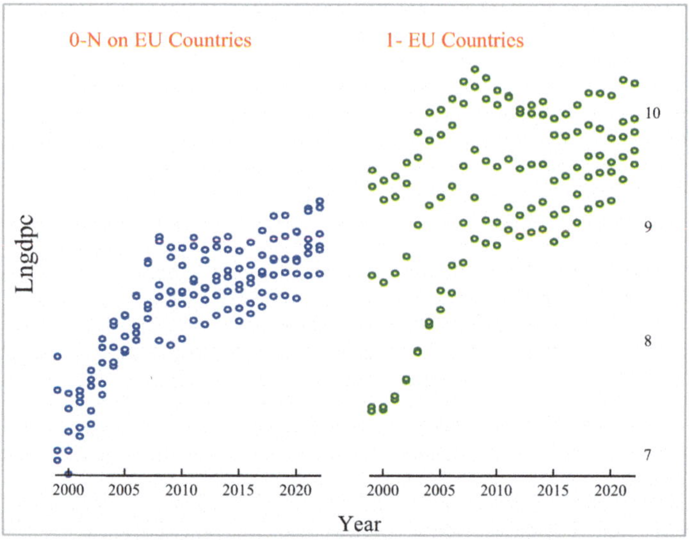

Fig. 2 GDP per capita by region

other factors, such as increased energy use in other sectors (e.g., increased heating or cooling due to people staying home more).

Environmental Kuznets Curve (EKC) Hypothesis

The Environmental Kuznets Curve (EKC) hypothesis posits that as a country's economy develops, emissions will initially increase and then decrease after reaching a certain level of economic maturity (Kuznets, 1955). To confirm the presence of the EKC, the paper's analysis typically examines for a significant positive coefficient for the initial GDP per capita term (indicating increased emissions with economic growth) and a significant negative coefficient for the squared GDP per capita term (indicating a decrease in emissions at higher levels of GDP). Hence, the hypothesis suggests a non-linear relationship between economic growth, technological innovation, and environmental policies, which mutually influence a country's environmental footprint over time and serve as a pivotal framework for understanding the dynamic relationship between economic development and environmental quality.

GDP Per Capita (Lngdpc) and Its Square (Lngdpc_sq)

GDP per capita specifies a standardized measure that allows for more meaningful effects across different countries and regions (Fig. 2).

These variables likely represent the natural logarithm of GDP per capita and its squared term, often used in economic models to assess the non-linear impacts of income on other variables.

Region 0: Lower average GDP per capita, with a mean log GDP of 8.346, reflects a generally lower economic development level than Region 1. The squared term's mean suggests the analysis considers the diminishing returns of income increases.

Region 1: Higher average GDP per capita (9.324 in log terms) indicates a more developed economy. The broader range in the squared term also points to significant income disparities within this region.

Governance and Regime Index

Several metrics to evaluate governance exist, and the most popular is the World Governance Indicators (WGI). WGI has gained significant popularity among researchers because they are accessible to a wide range of countries and offer a dependable evaluation of various aspects of institutional frameworks (Mengistu & Adhikary, 2011; Méon & Sekkat, 2007). This set of indicators evaluates six governance dimensions: control of corruption, rule of law, voice and accountability, government effectiveness, political stability, and regulatory quality (Kaufmann et al., 1999). These dimensions encompass all areas of governance, and the estimated values are scaled from –2.5 to 2.5. A high score on a specific governance indicator reveals strong governance in that area.

The liberal democracy index (Ldi) comes from the V-Dem database and is a novel approach for defining and quantifying democracy through a comprehensive and disaggregated dataset. Recently developed, it addresses numerous limitations found in traditional democracy indices (Clulow, 2019, p. 252). This index examines the constraints placed on governmental powers and the integrity of elections, where multiple institutional mechanisms ensure free and fair voting processes (Lührmann et al., 2020). This empirical analysis uses Ldi as an independent variable to evaluate whether the level of democratic consolidation influences climate change mitigation.

The country's Ldi rating categorizes its political system following the Regimes of the World (RoW) typology, in which a country can be categorized into four regime types: closed autocracies, electoral autocracies, electoral democracies, and liberal democracies (Morgan et al., 2019). Regimes in the Balkans range from electoral democracy to electoral autocracy, which captures contemporary political reality. A notable and significant decline in V-Dem's Ldi signifies either a democratic or autocratic regression. Conversely, any substantial and significant rise in the Ldi presents the liberalization of autocratic regimes or the strengthening of democratic systems (Lührmann et al., 2020, p. 11).

The general trend for non-EU Balkans in 2023, as recorded in the latest report of the V-Dem Institute (2024), shows a democratic increase in two of the five states (region 0) and democratic regression in three states, far beyond the liberal democracy. Notably, Albania and BiH are on the threshold to electoral autocracy, while Serbia is already electoral autocracy. Montenegro was an electoral autocracy and transitioned into electoral democracy by 2023, while North Macedonia overpassed its democratic breakdown and turned back to electoral democracy (Nord et al., 2024). Referring to EU Balkans (region 1), the same report characterizes them as electoral democracies.

Region 0: Shows generally lower scores in governance and Ldi, suggesting challenges in corruption, rule of law, government effectiveness, and political stability.

The negative means in several indicators imply issues that could hinder economic development and societal well-being.

Region 1: Demonstrates significantly higher scores across all governance and Ldi, indicating a more stable and effective governance structure, better rule of law, and higher levels of democracy and political stability. The positive means across these indices suggest a more conducive environment for economic growth and social development.

3.2 Econometric Analysis

This study uses Inverse Probability Weighting (IPW) regression in Average Treatment Effect (ATE) methodology to estimate the differences in CO_2 emissions depending on whether a Balkan country is part of the European Union (Region 1) or not (Region 0). Estimating ATE is often feasible even with limited data or resources, while IPW regression is a powerful tool in the ATE estimation context, especially for observational studies where randomization is not feasible. By using inverse probability weights derived from propensity scores, IPW regression helps to control for confounding and allows for an unbiased estimation of the average treatment effect, mimicking a randomized experimental design.

Framework of the Model

Treatment Model: A logit model is used to estimate the probability of each unit (in this case, a country) receiving the treatment (being an EU member). The predictors in the model include GDP per capita, the squared term of log GDP per capita and governance indicators. This model calculates the inverse probability of treatment weights.

$$\begin{aligned} P(Treatment = 1 \mid X) = logistic(&\beta_0 + \beta Lngdpc + \beta Lngdpc + \beta Coc \\ &+ \beta Rul + \beta_5 Va + \beta_6 Gove + \beta_7 Plst \\ &+ \beta_8 rq + \beta_9 Ldi) \end{aligned}$$

Outcome Model: A linear regression model is applied where the outcome (CO_2 emissions per capita) is regressed on the treatment status and log GDP per capita, the squared term of log GDP per capita and governance indicators. This model is adjusted by the weights obtained from the treatment model.

$$\begin{aligned} E(CO\_per\_capita \mid Treatment, X) = &\alpha_0 + \alpha Treatment + \alpha Lngdpc \\ &+ \alpha Lngdpc + \alpha Coc \\ &+ \alpha_5 Rul + \alpha_6 Va + \alpha_7 Gove + \alpha_8 Plst \\ &+ \alpha_9 Rqu + \alpha_{10} Ldi + \varepsilon \end{aligned}$$

Average Treatment Effect (ATE): The ATE provides the average effect of the treatment on the outcome variable across all units in the study. It is computed using the weighted outcome model and represents the difference in expected outcomes between treated and untreated units (Table 4).

$$ATE = E(CO\_per\_capita|Treatment = 1, X) - E(CO\_per\_capita|Treatment = 0, X)$$

Average Treatment Effect (ATE)

Average Treatment Effect (ATE) Region (1 vs 0): Balkan countries within the EU (Region 1) have an average CO_2 emission per capita that is 1.348411 units higher than that of the WB countries outside the EU (Region 0), with a statistically significant difference ($p = 0.020$). This suggests that EU membership, or the factors associated with it, might be linked with higher CO_2 emissions per capita.

Potential Outcome Mean (POmean) for Region 0: In the WB (non-EU countries), the average CO_2 emissions per capita are estimated to be 3.308975. This estimation is statistically robust ($p < 0.000$).

Outcome Model Estimates Without Treatment (OME0)

These coefficients describe the relationship between each predictor variable and CO_2 emissions per capita for WB countries (Region 0).

Lngdpc: One-unit increase in the natural logarithm of GDP per capita is associated with 31.81328 increase in CO_2 emissions per capita, which is statistically significant ($p = 0.001$).

Lngdpc_sq: One-unit increase in the squared natural logarithm of GDP per capita is associated with 1.71449 decrease in CO_2 emissions per capita, which supports the presence of an Environmental Kuznets Curve ($p = 0.002$).

The above estimates of the coefficients for GDP per capita and its square support the Environmental Kuznets Curve hypothesis, with emissions rising with wealth to a point and then declining.

Governance Indicators: The rule of law (Rul) and political stability (Plst) are significantly negatively associated with CO_2 emissions, suggesting that improvements in these areas could be linked to lower emissions in Region 0. Conversely, regulatory quality (Rqu) is positively associated with emissions.

Coc: The coefficient is -0.304 and is not statistically significant (p-value = 0.659). This suggests that controlling corruption does not have a significant direct impact on the dependent variable in this model.

Rul: The coefficient is –3.943 and is highly significant (p-value = 0.000), indicating a strong negative association with CO_2 emissions

Va: The coefficient is 0.640, and it is not statistically significant (p-value = 0.635), indicating a negligible direct impact of this variable on the dependent variable.

Gove: The variable has a coefficient of –0.319, which is not significant (p-value = 0.622). This implies that governance does not significantly affect CO_2 emissions.

Table 4 Results from the estimation of ATE model

Co_2_per_ capita	Coefficient	Std. err	z	P > |z|	[95% conf	Interval]
ATE						
Region						
(1 vs 0)	1.348	0.582	2.320	0.020	0.209	2.488
POmean						
Region						
0	3.309	0.540	6.130	0.000	2.250	4.367
OME0						
Lngdpc	31.813	9.273	3.430	0.001	13.638	49.989
Lngdpc_sq	−1.714	0.547	−3.130	0.002	−2.787	−0.642
Coc	−0.304	0.690	−0.440	0.659	−1.656	1.048
Rul	−3.943	0.659	−5.990	0.000	−5.235	−2.652
Va	0.640	1.349	0.470	0.635	−2.004	3.284
Gove	−0.319	0.648	−0.490	0.622	−1.590	0.952
Plst	−2.457	0.373	−6.590	0.000	−3.187	−1.726
Rqu	3.610	1.123	3.210	0.001	1.408	5.812
Ldi	−2.288	2.353	−0.970	0.331	−6.900	2.324
_cons	−140.913	39.031	−3.610	0.000	−217.413	−64.414
OME1						
Lngdpc	−18.936	4.424	−4.280	0.000	−27.606	−10.266
Lngdpc_sq	1.093	0.257	4.250	0.000	0.589	1.598
Coc	−0.928	0.743	−1.250	0.212	−2.385	0.528
Rul	1.660	0.483	3.440	0.001	0.714	2.607
Va	5.612	1.279	4.390	0.000	3.105	8.120
Gove	−0.630	0.695	−0.910	0.365	−1.992	0.732
Plst	0.494	0.317	1.560	0.119	−0.127	1.114
Rqu	−2.131	0.778	−2.740	0.006	−3.655	−0.607
Ldi	0.151	1.650	0.090	0.927	−3.083	3.385
_cons	83.250	19.101	4.360	0.000	45.813	120.687
TME1						
Lngdpc	4.195	0.802	5.230	0.000	2.623	5.767
_cons	−37.464	7.226	−5.180	0.000	−51.628	−23.301

Plst: The variable shows a significantly negative coefficient of −2.457 (p-value = 0.000), suggesting a strong negative impact of political stability on CO_2 emissions.

*Rqu***:** The variable shows a positive coefficient of 3.610, indicating a beneficial impact of regulatory quality on the dependent variable, with significance (p-value = 0.001).

Democracy Index

Ldi: The coefficient is –2.288 (p-value =0.331), indicating that liberal democracy does not have a significant impact on CO_2 emissions

Outcome Model Estimates with Treatment (OME1)

These coefficients describe the relationship between each predictor and CO_2 emissions per capita for Balkan countries within the EU.

lngdpc: A coefficient of −18.936 for lngdpc indicates that for a one-unit increase in the natural logarithm of GDP per capita for EU Balkan countries, there is an average decrease of 18.936 units in CO_2 emissions per capita, significant at $p = 0.000$.

lngdpc_sq : A coefficient of 1.093 for Lngdpc_sq indicates that for a one-unit increase in the squared natural logarithm of GDP per capita for EU Balkan countries, there is an average decrease of 1.093 units in CO_2 emissions per capita, significant at $p = 0.000$

The reversed signs of these coefficients compared to OME0 might reflect the impact of EU policies or economic structures that change how economic growth relates to emissions.

Governance Indicators*:* The governance dimension of voice and accountability (Va) is now significantly positively associated with emissions, which might reflect different environmental policies or enforcement mechanisms within EU member states (region 1).

Coc: The coefficient is –0.928, with a p-value of 0.212, which also indicates a lack of statistical significance, though the magnitude of the effect is larger compared to OME0.

Rul: The coefficient is 1.660, showing a positive relationship and being significant (p-value = 0.001). This opposite sign suggests different dynamics between regions.

Va: the coefficient is 5.612 and is significant (p-value = 0.000), suggesting a robust positive effect in this model setup.

Gove: the coefficient is –0.630, indicating a non-significant effect (p-value = 0.365). Similar to 'Coc', although the effect is more robust, it remains statistically insignificant.

Plst: the coefficient is 0.494, showing the opposite effect compared to OME0, which is not significant (p-value = 0.119), indicating that political stability does not have a significant effect in this model.

Rqu: the coefficient is –2.131, again showing the opposite effect compared to OME0 and is statistically significant (p-value = 0.006).

Democracy Index

Ldi: The coefficient is 0.151 (p-value = 0.927), further reinforcing the non-significance effect.

The differences in coefficients and their significance between OME0 and OME1 across these variables indicate different dynamics of CO_2 emissions relationships. The fact that the variables 'Coc', 'Gove', and 'Ldi' show little to no significant effects in both models might indicate their limited direct impact under the conditions tested, while the variables 'Lngdpc', 'Rul', and 'Plst' show notable effects and changes in sign.

Treatment Model Estimates (TME1)

Lngdpc: The positive coefficient suggests that countries with higher GDP per capita are more likely to be in the EU Balkans group, which could reflect the economic criteria for EU accession or the economic benefits of being an EU member.

These results could indicate that EU membership or the associated processes and standards may influence environmental outcomes and governance structures in complex ways. It's worth noting that EU countries may have more industry or energy consumption, leading to higher emissions, or it could be that EU integration has led to more rigorous emission reporting, which may not be as stringent in non-EU countries.

The findings suggest that EU Balkan countries have higher CO_2 emissions per capita than their Western Balkan counterparts, potentially due to the economic and regulatory differences associated with EU membership. The governance indicators show varying relationships with emissions in non-EU and EU settings, possibly reflecting the differing environmental policies, legal frameworks, and enforcement mechanisms. As the following section presents, the results indicate both the direct impact of economic development on CO_2 emissions and the significant role of governance and regulatory frameworks within these regional groupings.

3.3 Discussion

In the WB countries (Region 0), there is evidence supporting the EKC hypothesis, with emissions increasing and then decreasing with higher levels of economic development, hinging on the literature findings (Bilgili et al., 2016; Kacprzyk & Kuchta, 2020). However, in the EU Balkan countries (Region 1), the evidence contradicts the typical EKC pattern, potentially indicating that other factors associated with EU membership, such as environmental regulations, technology, and investment in cleaner energy, have altered this relationship or the level of democratization. Notably, as Eren (2022) pointed out while democratization initially reduces emissions, over time, it can delay environmental improvements as economies grow, thus raising the environmental costs associated with growth in democratic nations. Therefore, the results suggest that the EKC is present in the non-EU Balkan countries but not in the EU Balkan countries. This implies that economic development in the context of EU environmental standards and policies may have a different impact on CO_2 emissions than what the traditional EKC hypothesis would predict.

In WB countries (region 0), three dimensions of governance, the rule of law (*Rul*), political stability (*Plst*) and regulatory quality (*Rqu*) were found to hold a significant statistical relationship with CO_2 emissions. The observed negative link between the rule of law and emissions points out that a strengthened legal system and improved access to justice can lead to a decrease in CO_2 emissions and an enhancement of environmental conditions (Muhammad & Long, 2021; Sinha et al., 2021). The *First* empirical outcome validated the anticipated result; thus, political stability in WB countries is directly linked to lower environmental pollution. Stability extends the political horizon, encouraging leaders to adopt policies with short-term costs for long-term environmental benefits, a critical aspect of climate policy (Fredriksson & Neumayer, 2013, p. 16). Great political stability fosters an optimal environmental policy stringency (Fredriksson & Wollscheid, 2014, p. 56). In this regard, the EU's policy towards the Balkans, aimed at reform and stabilization, is crucial in this regard. However, delays in EU enlargement and external geopolitical factors, such as the Ukraine conflict, pose risks to regional stability and environmental health.

The variable of regulatory quality is positively related to the climate change variable, in WB countries, meaning enforcing the government's ability to formulate and implement sound policies and regulations that permit and encourage private sector growth, increase the CO_2 emissions level and pull-down WB countries' performance in climate action.

The findings for *Coc, Gove, Va* and *Ldi* reveal that there is not enough statistical evidence to conclude that the control of corruption, government effectiveness, voice and accountability, and the level of democratic consolidation have a significant impact on the dependent variable in our model, suggesting that improvements in these indices have only limited success in reducing CO_2 emissions. Lægreid and Povitkina (2018) explain a similar outcome in their empirical study for democratization and anti-corruption efforts, in the sense that the political mechanisms in such systems did not record a significant difference compared to the rest of the world.

In the EU Balkans (region 1), the rule of law and the regulatory quality are also associated significantly with CO_2 emissions but show an opposite effect compared to the OME0. The dimension of voice and accountability is positively and significantly related to the dependent variable. Von Stein (2022) states that voice and accountability contribute to environmentally friendly outcomes when voters recognize and prioritize environmental protection. Hence, in the EU Balkans, citizens appear to undervalue the importance of safeguarding their countries against the impacts of climate change. This oversight may be understandable, given that the last 15 years have been marked by the global economic crisis, the COVID-19 pandemic, and the Russian invasion of Ukraine, all of which have significantly stained daily life. Moreover, the effectiveness of the rule of law varies depending on government policies. When these are environmentally friendly or independent of political pressures and changes, the rule of law can be beneficial (Abid et al., 2021; Von Stein, 2022). In the opposite case, their outcomes can be detrimental. This appears to be the current situation in the EU Balkans.

The negative relationship between the regulatory quality and the CO_2 emissions underscores the significance of EU membership. This is because national governments of EU member states are required to adhere to EU regulations (the EU acquis). Governments in the EU are also committed to ensuring that private sector activities comply with both national and environmental laws, which support environmental sustainability. The above negative association is in alignment with the empirical results of Abid et al. (2021) and Bernauer and Koubi (2009). This might also explain the contrasting situation in the WB countries (region 0), where these states are incentivized rather than obligated to implement the EGD. Additionally, the "enlargement fatigue" has been slowing down the implementation of policies in this region, hindering green growth.

4 Conclusion

The paper examines the impact of the political landscape, EU membership, and economic growth on climate change mitigation in Balkan countries. Regimes in targeted countries range from electoral democracy to electoral autocracy, capturing the contemporary political reality. The literature review underscores that the relative empirical studies include more mechanisms and key factors in their research besides the level of democracy per se, which is an approach that this study also follows. These factors include the governance dimensions and stages of economic development, as the EKC hypothesis supports. Further, the conceptual analysis outlines the EU's role as a global leader in climate action, implementing the EGD to achieve net-zero greenhouse gas emissions by 2050 and integrating economic growth with sustainable resource use. It highlights the significant costs of achieving climate neutrality and the integration of climate law in adopting environmental standards, particularly in the WB countries, to ensure sustainable development and compliance with EU policies.

The study's empirical analysis incorporates the political regime and individual institutional variables that are considered to increase the regime's institutional stability and credibility and improve the government's ability to plan and implement effective policies limiting environmental pollution. The type of political regime found not to influence countries' environmental outcomes. The analysis of the effects of good governance dimensions on the CO_2 emissions levels was conducted based on comparative analysis for the EU and non-EU Balkans and reveals differences in statistical significance and intensity of impact. The clustering of the institutional indicators contributes to identifying certain governance aspects that influence countries' green growth. Notably, the rule of law and political stability enhance environmental outcomes in the non-EU Balkans, while a high level of regulatory quality leads to environmental degradation. On the contrary, an improved regulatory quality in the EU Balkans reduces CO_2 emissions. This highlights the significant impact of EU membership on environmental policy effectiveness since EU member states are bound by stringent regulations that enforce compliance from the private sector, promoting sustainability. This adherence to EU laws explains the disparities observed between EU members and WB countries, where the latter are merely incentivized and not mandated to align with EU environmental goals. The study's comparative analysis records that the emissions levels are lower in the WB countries than the EU Balkans, likely due to their lower industrial activity reflecting their lower economic development. However, over the last twelve years, the EU Balkans have reduced emissions to levels like the WB. This reduction highlights the impact of EU membership since, during this period, 3 out of 5 states of this group joined the EU. Also, this outcome is noteworthy considering the higher industrial activity and energy consumption in the EU Balkans, which positions them well for further decreases in environmental pollution in the region. The important finding is the critical role of EU regulatory frameworks in driving environmental improvements to meet the EGD goals. Voice and accountability and rule of law are significantly associated with environmental outcomes in the EU Balkans but reflect that citizens undervalue climate protection and the extent to which environmental government policies are influenced by political pressures. Finally, empirical results confirm the EKC hypothesis in the WB but not in the EU Balkans.

The policy implications of these findings suggest that governments in each group of countries need to strengthen their institutions in the specific governance dimensions to reduce environmental degradation from CO_2 emissions. Non-EU Balkans should prioritize implementing the EGD agenda, while the EU Ballans should focus on campaigns to highlight the importance of environmental sustainability.

The paper concludes with a recommendation for future research on how governance will aid Balkan countries in achieving EU environmental goals, once the necessary reforms are complete.

References

Abid, N., Ikram, M., Wu, J., & Ferasso, M. (2021). Towards environmental sustainability: Exploring the nexus among ISO 14001, governance indicators and green economy in Pakistan. *Sustainable Production and Consumption, 27*, 653–666. Elsevier B.V. https://doi.org/10.1016/j.spc.2021.01.024

Ahmad, M., Khan, Z., Rahman, Z. U., Khattak, S. I., & Khan, Z. U. (2021). Can innovation shocks determine CO2 emissions (CO2e) in the OECD economies? A new perspective. *Economics of Innovation and New Technology, Taylor & Francis, 30*(1), 89–109. https://doi.org/10.1080/10438599.2019.1684643

Akram, R., Chen, F., Khalid, F., Ye, Z., & Majeed, M. T. (2020). Heterogeneous effects of energy efficiency and renewable energy on carbon emissions: Evidence from developing countries. *Journal of Cleaner Production, 247*, 119122. https://doi.org/10.1016/j.jclepro.2019.119122

Ali, S., Akter, S., Ymeri, P., & Fogarassy, C. (2022). How the use of biomass for green energy and waste incineration practice will affect GDP growth in the less developed countries of the EU (A case study with Visegrad and Balkan countries). *Energies, 15*(7), 1–18. https://doi.org/10.3390/en15072308

Azam, M., Liu, L., & Ahmad, N. (2021). Impact of institutional quality on environment and energy consumption: Evidence from developing world. *Environment, Development and Sustainability, Springer, Netherlands, 23*(2), 1646–1667. https://doi.org/10.1007/s10668-020-00644-x

Banja, M., Đukanović, G., & Belis, C. A. (2020). Status of air pollutants and greenhouse gases in the Western Balkans -Benchmarking the accession process progress on environment. *Publications Office of the European Union, Luxembourg.* https://doi.org/10.2760/48321

Battig, M. B., & Bernauer, T. (2009). National institutions and global public goods: Are democracies more cooperative in climate change policy? *International Organization, 63*(2), 281–308. https://doi.org/10.1017/S0020818309090092

Bättig, M. B., & Bernauer, T. (2009). National institutions and global public goods: Are democracies more cooperative in climate change policy? *International Organization, 63*(2), 281–308. https://doi.org/10.1017/S0020818309090092

Becker, W., Norlén, H., Dijkstra, L., & Athanasoglou, S. (2020). Wrapping up the Europe 2020 strategy: A multidimensional indicator analysis. *Environmental and Sustainability Indicators, 8*. https://doi.org/10.1016/j.indic.2020.100075

Beeson, M. (2016). Environmental authoritarianism and China. In T. Gabrielson, C. Hall, J. M. Meyer & D. Schlosberg (Eds.), *The Oxford Handbook of environmental political theory* (pp. 1–15). Oxford University Press. https://doi.org/10.1093/oxfordhb/9780199685271.013.14

Bernauer, T., & Koubi, V. (2009). Effects of political institutions on air quality. *Ecological Economics, Elsevier B.V., 68*(5), 1355–1365. https://doi.org/10.1016/j.ecolecon.2008.09.003

Bilgili, F., Koçak, E., & Bulut, Ü. (2016). The dynamic impact of renewable energy consumption on CO2 emissions: A revisited Environmental Kuznets Curve approach. *Renewable and Sustainable Energy Reviews, Elsevier, 54*, 838–845. https://doi.org/10.1016/j.rser.2015.10.080

Brodny, J., & Tutak, M. (2023). Assessing the energy and climate sustainability of European Union Member States: An MCDM-based approach. *Smart Cities, 6*(1), 339–367. https://doi.org/10.3390/smartcities6010017

Cifuentes-Faura, J. (2022). European Union policies and their role in combating climate change over the years. *Air Quality, Atmosphere and Health, Springer, Netherlands, 15*(8), 1333–1340. https://doi.org/10.1007/s11869-022-01156-5

Clulow, Z. (2019). Democracy, electoral systems and emissions: Explaining when and why democratization promotes mitigation. *Climate Policy, Taylor & Francis, 19*(2), 244–257. https://doi.org/10.1080/14693062.2018.1497938

Çolak, M. S., & Ege, A. (2013). An assessment of EU 2020 strategy: Too far to reach? *Social Indicators Research, 110*(2), 659–680. https://doi.org/10.1007/s11205-011-9950-2

Congleton, R. D. (1992). Political institutions and pollution control. *Review of Economics & Statistics, 74*(3), 412–421. https://doi.org/10.2307/2109485

Dabrowski, M., & Muachenkova, Y. (2018). The Western Balkans on the road to the European Union. In *Policy Contribution, Vol. 38*. https://doi.org/10.1002/mmnd.18940380315

Economides, S. (2020). *From fatigue to Resistance: EU Enlargement and the Western Balkans, No. 17*. Berlin.

Eren, M. (2022). Different impacts of democracy and income on carbon dioxide emissions: Evidence from a panel quantile regression approach. *Environmental Science and Pollution Research, Springer, Berlin, 29*(47), 71439–71459. https://doi.org/10.1007/s11356-022-20805-x

European Commission. (2019). *Communication from the Commission to the European Parliament, the European Council, the Council, the European Economic and Social Committee and the Committee of the Regions*. The European Green Deal., European Commission, Brussels.

Frazer, S., Granius, M., Brinkerhoff, D. W., & McGregor, L. (2022). *Integrated governance: Achieving governance results and contributing to sector outcomes*. RTI Press.

Fredriksson, P. G., & Neumayer, E. (2013). Democracy and climate change policies: Is history important?. *Ecological Economics, Elsevier B.V., 95*, 11–19, https://doi.org/10.1016/j.ecolecon.2013.08.002

Fredriksson, P. G., & Wollscheid, J. R. (2014). Political institutions, political careers and environmental policy. *Kyklos, 67*(1), 54–73. https://doi.org/10.1111/kykl.12043

Fura, B., Wojnar, J., & Kasprzyk, B. (2017). Ranking and classification of EU countries regarding their levels of implementation of the Europe 2020 strategy. *Journal of Cleaner Production, Elsevier Ltd, 165*(2017), 968–979. https://doi.org/10.1016/j.jclepro.2017.07.088

Gilley, B. (2012). Authoritarian environmentalism and China's response to climate change. *Environmental Politics, 21*(2), 287–307. https://doi.org/10.1080/09644016.2012.651904

Güney, T. (2017). Governance and sustainable development: How effective is governance?1. *Journal of International Trade and Economic Development, 26*(3), 316–335. https://doi.org/10.1080/09638199.2016.1249391

Hannesson, R. (2022). Is There a Kuznets Curve for CO2-emissions? *Biophysical Economics and Sustainability, Springer International Publishing, 7*(2), 1–8. https://doi.org/10.1007/s41247-022-00099-w

Htike, M. M., Shrestha, A., & Kakinaka, M. (2022). Investigating whether the environmental Kuznets curve hypothesis holds for sectoral CO2 emissions: Evidence from developed and developing countries. *Environment, Development and Sustainability, Springer, Netherlands, 24*(11), 12712–12739. https://doi.org/10.1007/s10668-021-01961-5

Hussain, M., & Dogan, E. (2021). The role of institutional quality and environment-related technologies in environmental degradation for BRICS. *Journal of Cleaner Production, Elsevier Ltd, 304*, Article 127059. https://doi.org/10.1016/j.jclepro.2021.127059

Jahanger, A., Usman, M., & Balsalobre-Lorente, D. (2021). Autocracy, democracy, globalization, and environmental pollution in developing world: Fresh evidence from STIRPAT model. *Journal of Public Affairs*. https://doi.org/10.1002/pa.2753

Kacprzyk, A., & Kuchta, Z. (2020). Shining a new light on the environmental Kuznets curve for CO2 emissions. *Energy Economics, Elsevier B.V., 87*, 104704, https://doi.org/10.1016/j.eneco.2020.104704

Kaufmann, D., Kraay, A., & Mastruzzi, M. (2011). The worldwide governance indicators: Methodology and analytical issues. *Hague Journal on the Rule of Law, 3*(02), 220–246. https://doi.org/10.1017/S1876404511200046

Kaufmann, D., Kraay, A., & Zoido, P. (1999). Aggregating governance indicators. World Bank Policy Research Working Paper, No. 2195. https://doi.org/10.2139/ssrn.188548

Kim, S., Baek, J., & Heo, E. (2019). A new look at the democracy-environment nexus: Evidence from panel data for high- and low-income countries. *Sustainability (Switzerland), 11*(8), 1–14. https://doi.org/10.3390/su11082353

Kneuer, M. (2012). Who is greener? Climate action and political regimes: Trade-offs for national and international actors. *Democratization, 19*(5), 865–888. https://doi.org/10.180/13510347.2012.709686

Knez, S., Štrbac, S., & Podbregar, I. (2022). Climate change in the Western Balkans and EU Green Deal: Status, mitigation and challenges. *Energy, Sustainability and Society, Springer, Berlin, 12*(1), 1–14. https://doi.org/10.1186/s13705-021-00328-y

Kryk, B., & Guzowska, M. K. (2021). Implementation of climate/energy targets of the europe 2020 strategy by the eu member states. *Energies, 14*(9). https://doi.org/10.3390/en14092711

Kuznets, S. (1955). Economic growth and income inequality. *The American Economic Review, 45*(1), 1–28.

Lægreid, O. M., & Povitkina, M. (2018). Do political institutions moderate the GDP-CO2 relationship?". *Ecological Economics, Elsevier, 145*(November), 441–450. https://doi.org/10.1016/j.ecolecon.2017.11.014

Lah, O. (2017). Continuity and change: Dealing with political volatility to advance climate change mitigation strategies-Examples from the transport sector. *Sustainability (Switzerland), 9*(6). https://doi.org/10.3390/su9060959

Lau, L. S., Choong, C. K., & Eng, Y. K. (2014). Carbon dioxide emission, institutional quality, and economic growth: Empirical evidence in Malaysia. *Renewable Energy, Elsevier Ltd, 68*, 276–281. https://doi.org/10.1016/j.renene.2014.02.013

Lindvall, D. (2021). *Democracy and the challenge of climate change, No. 3*. International IDEA Discussion Paper, Stockholm, https://doi.org/10.31752/idea.2021.88

Lührmann, A., Maerz, S. F., Grahn, S., Alizada, N., Gastaldi, L., Hellmeier, S., & Hindle, G., et al. (2020). *Autocratzation surges - resistance grows. Democracy Report 2020*, Department of Political Science University of Gothenburg.

Lv, Z. (2017, February). The effect of democracy on CO2 emissions in emerging countries: Does the level of income matter? *Renewable and Sustainable Energy Reviews, 72*, 900–906. https://doi.org/10.1016/j.rser.2017.01.096

Mengistu, A. A., & Adhikary, B. K. (2011). Does good governance matter for FDI inflows? Evidence from Asian economies. *Asia Pacific Business Review, 17*(3), 281–299. https://doi.org/10.1080/13602381003755765

Méon, P.-G., & Sekkat, K. (2007). *Revisiting the relationship between governance and foreign direct investment, No. 07–13.* Brussels.

Morgan, R., Beger, A., & Glynn, A. (2019). *Varieties of forecasts: Predicting adverse regime transitions, No. 89.* V-Dem, Gothenburg, https://doi.org/10.2139/ssrn.3389194

Mudambi, R., & Navarra, P. (2002). Institutions and internation business: A theoretical overview. *International Business Review, 11*(6), 635–646. https://doi.org/10.1016/S0969-5931(02)00042-2

Muhammad, S., & Long, X. (2021). Rule of law and CO2 emissions: A comparative analysis across 65 belt and road initiative(BRI) countries. *Journal of Cleaner Production, Elsevier Ltd, 279*, Article 123539. https://doi.org/10.1016/j.jclepro.2020.123539

Nord, M., Lundstedt, M., Altman, D., Angiolillo, F., Borella, C., Fernandes, T., & Gastaldi, L., et al. (2024). *Democracy winning and losing at the Ballot.* University of Gothenburg.

North, D. C. (1990). *Insitutions.* Cambridge University Press, New York.

O'Brennan, J. (2014). 'On the slow train to nowhere?' The European Union, 'Enlargement Fatigue' and the Western Balkans. *European Foreign Affairs Review, 19*(2), 221–242. https://doi.org/10.1080/03932720701722993

Oberthür, S., & von Homeyer, I. (2023). From emissions trading to the European Green deal: The evolution of the climate policy mix and climate policy integration in the EU. *Journal of European Public Policy, 30*(3), 445–468. https://doi.org/10.1080/13501763.2022.2120528

Omri, A., & Ben Mabrouk, N. (2020). Good governance for sustainable development goals: Getting ahead of the pack or falling behind?. *Environmental Impact Assessment Review, Elsevier, 83*, 106388, https://doi.org/10.1016/j.eiar.2020.106388

Pata, U. K. (2018). Renewable energy consumption, urbanization, financial development, income and CO2 emissions in Turkey: Testing EKC hypothesis with structural breaks. *Journal of Cleaner Production, Elsevier Ltd, 187*, 770–779. https://doi.org/10.1016/j.jclepro.2018.03.236

Pejović, B., Karadžić, V., Dragašević, Z., & Backović, T. (2021). Economic growth, energy consumption and CO2 emissions in the countries of the European Union and the Western Balkans. Energy Reports. *No., 7*, 2775–2783. https://doi.org/10.1016/j.egyr.2021.05.011

Povitkina, M. (2018). The limits of democracy in tackling climate change. *Environmental Politics, Routledge, 27*(3), 411–432. https://doi.org/10.1080/09644016.2018.1444723

Renner, S., & Trauner, F. (2009). Creeping EU membership in south-east Europe: The dynamics of EU rule transfer to the Western Balkans.

Shkurti, A. (2019). Analysis of the Western Balkans power market prices within the ENTSO-E framework. *European Journal of Sustainable Development, 8*(1), 229–236. https://doi.org/10.14207/ejsd.2019.v8n1p229

Sikora, A. (2021). European Green Deal—legal and financial challenges of the climate change. *ERA Forum, The Author(s), 21*(4), 681–697. https://doi.org/10.1007/s12027-020-00637-3

Sinha, A., Sedai, A. K., Kumar, A., & Nepal, R. (2021). *Are autocracies bad for the environment? Global evidence from two centuries of data, No. 24/2021*, CAMA Working Paper, https://doi.org/10.2139/ssrn.3791763

Von Stein, J. (2022). Democracy, autocracy, and everything in between: How domestic institutions affect environmental protection. *British Journal of Political Science, 52*(1), 339–357. https://doi.org/10.1017/S000712342000054X

Tamazian, A., & Rao, B. B. (2010). Do economic, financial and institutional developments matter for environmental degradation? Evidence from transitional economies. *Energy Economics, Elsevier B.V., 32*(1), 137–145. https://doi.org/10.1016/j.eneco.2009.04.004

Vuković, A., & Mandić, M. V. (2018). *Study on climate change in the Western Balkans Region.* Sarajevo.

Wurster, S. (2013). Comparing ecological sustainability in autocracies and democracies. *Contemporary Politics, 19*(1), 76–93. https://doi.org/10.1080/13569775.2013.773204

You, W., Li, Y., Guo, P., & Guo, Y. (2020). Income inequality and CO2 emissions in belt and road initiative countries: The role of democracy. *Environmental Science and Pollution Research, Environmental Science and Pollution Research, 27*(6), 6278–6299. https://doi.org/10.1007/s11356-019-07242-z

Zhang, J. (2021). Environmental Kuznets Curve hypothesis on CO2 emissions: Evidence for China. *Journal of Risk and Financial Management, 14*(3), 1–16. https://doi.org/10.3390/jrfm14030093

Smart Grid ETFS: Evaluating Risk, Return, and Diversification Benefits in Sustainable Investment Portfolios

Cristiana Tudor and Robert Sova

Abstract The smart grid plays a pivotal role in advancing sustainability and achieving the goals of the 2030 Agenda for Sustainable Development. By integrating advanced digital technologies smart grids improve the efficiency and reliability of electricity transmission, while supporting large-scale renewable energy integration. This paper analyzes the financial landscape of smart grid technologies through a comprehensive examination of Exchange-Traded Funds (ETFs) that invest in this sector. Using portfolio optimization techniques, including Monte Carlo simulation and efficient frontier analysis, the study evaluates the risk-return profiles and diversification benefits of smart grid ETFs compared to traditional diversified portfolios. The results show that smart grid ETFs like GRID exhibit annualized returns of approximately 20% with a volatility of around 25%, which is significantly higher than the returns of traditional energy sector ETFs like XLE, which show a return of 8% but with a higher volatility of around 35%. This study provides insights for investors and policymakers by demonstrating that smart grid ETFs offer a strategic opportunity to increase portfolio performance while aligning with sustainable investment objectives.

Keywords 2030 agenda · Minimum Variance Portfolio (MVP) · Monte Carlo simulation · Portfolio diversification · Portfolio optimization · Sharpe ratio · Single Factor Model (SFM) · Tangency Portfolio (TP) · Treynor ratio

Jel Classification Code C58 · G11 · G15 · G17

C. Tudor (✉) · R. Sova
Bucharest University of Economic Studies, Bucharest, Romania
e-mail: cristiana.tudor@net.ase.ro

R. Sova
e-mail: robert.sova@ase.ro

I. Bartuseviciene et al. (eds.), *Building Economic Resilience*, Contributions to Economics, https://doi.org/10.1007/978-3-031-96428-2_11

1 Introduction

The integration of advanced digital technologies with the electrical grid, commonly referred to as smart grids, represents a transformative advancement in the global pursuit of sustainability. Smart grids align with the goals of the 2030 Agenda for Sustainable Development by facilitating more efficient electricity transmission, enhancing energy service reliability, and enabling the large-scale integration of renewable energy sources (Amin & Wollenberg, 2005; Fang et al., 2012). Through real-time data monitoring and automation, smart grids optimize electricity distribution, significantly reducing energy losses and improving overall system resilience (IEA, 2011; Vaccariello et al., 2021). This makes smart grids essential for modern energy systems in their capacity to balance supply and demand while incorporating distributed energy resources.

As global efforts to meet ambitious energy and environmental targets intensify, smart grid technologies have gained substantial importance not only for their technological advancements but also as a compelling financial opportunity. Exchange-Traded Funds (ETFs) that focus on companies developing and operating smart grid technologies allow investors to gain exposure to this rapidly growing sector. These ETFs offer the potential for investors to benefit both financially and contribute to the transition to sustainable energy systems. The confluence of increasing regulatory support for clean energy, technological advancements, and rising demand for decentralized power production creates a promising environment for smart grid investments.

From an investment perspective, smart grids play a dual role. They are not only instrumental in achieving environmental and energy objectives, but they also serve as a catalyst for economic growth and social inclusivity (IRENA, 2019). The introduction of smart grid ETFs provides investors access to companies driving this transition, offering opportunities to capitalize on the projected growth of the sector. Moreover, these ETFs provide a platform for investors looking to align their financial objectives with sustainability and ethical considerations, contributing to the global energy transition while potentially generating significant returns.

Despite the recognized potential of smart grid technologies, there remains a gap in comprehensive financial analyses specifically focused on smart grid ETFs. The financial community has not fully explored the risk, return, and diversification characteristics of these ETFs compared to traditional energy or technology sectors. This study aims to fill this gap by analyzing the risk-adjusted performance, tracking error, and downside risk of smart grid ETFs, as well as assessing the diversification benefits these ETFs offer when integrated into traditional investment portfolios. The research also seeks to understand how portfolio optimization strategies—such as the Minimum Variance Portfolio (MVP) and Tangency Portfolio (TP)—can be applied to maximize returns while minimizing risks for different investor profiles.

The paper is structured as follows: the next section provides a comprehensive review of the literature on smart grid technologies, ETF performance, and portfolio optimization. Following that, the methodology section outlines the data and models used in the analysis. The results section presents the findings from portfolio optimization and performance metrics, and the final section discusses the implications of these findings for sustainable investments and policymaking.

2 Literature Review

The evolution of the smart grid concept has been extensively documented in academic literature, which underscores its potential to revolutionize the energy sector (Amin & Wollenberg, 2005; Fang et al., 2012). Smart grids leverage technologies such as automation, real-time data management, and decentralized energy production to optimize electricity delivery and consumption (Farhangi, 2010; Gungor et al., 2011). These advancements align closely with global sustainability initiatives, particularly the Sustainable Development Goals (SDGs), which emphasize affordable and clean energy, innovation, and infrastructure development (United Nations, 2015). The deployment of big data, artificial intelligence (AI), and edge computing further enhances the operational efficiency and reliability of smart grids, positioning them as essential components of future energy systems (Yao et al., 2022). The extant literature consistently supports the notion that smart grid advancements are integral to achieving global sustainability initiatives, particularly the SDGs (Olatunde, 2024; Kumar et al., 2021; Fang et al., 2023; Guo et al., 2023; Haque et al., 2023).

Beyond their technological importance, smart grids have become a significant area of focus for investors interested in socially responsible investing (SRI) and environmental, social, and governance (ESG) principles. SRI integrates ESG criteria into investment decisions, allowing investors to align their portfolios with ethical and sustainable practices. The growing demand for SRI has driven investment in sectors that promote environmental stewardship and social responsibility (Liu et al., 2021; Tolliver et al., 2020). As a result, ETFs focused on smart grid technologies have emerged as attractive vehicles for investors seeking to support the transition to renewable energy while capturing the sector's growth potential.

Several studies have examined the financial performance of renewable energy investments, emphasizing their risk-return profiles and diversification benefits within traditional portfolios (Bohl et al., 2013; Henriques & Sadorsky, 2008; Tudor, 2024). Smart grid ETFs are uniquely positioned to offer diversification benefits due to their ability to manage the distributed and variable nature of renewable energy sources. These ETFs provide a mechanism for investors to hedge against volatility in broader markets, particularly as renewable energy becomes a more significant portion of the global energy mix (World Economic Forum, 2022).

Recent literature has increasingly focused on portfolio optimization strategies, particularly the Minimum Variance Portfolio (MVP) and the Tangency Portfolio (TP), to enhance risk-adjusted returns in portfolios that include renewable energy exchange-traded funds (ETFs). These strategies are particularly relevant given the growing interest in sustainable investments and the unique risk-return profiles associated with renewable energy assets. One notable study by Jisma et al. (2023) explores the application of the Tangency Portfolio and the Black-Litterman model to optimize asset allocation in energy sectors, highlighting the importance of balancing renewable and fossil fuel sources to achieve optimal risk-return outcomes This approach allows investors to strategically allocate their resources in a manner that maximizes expected returns while minimizing risk, which is crucial in the volatile renewable energy market. Additionally, Pizzutilo and Gleason (2023) discuss the implications of investing in renewable energy equities, emphasizing the evolving nature of risk and return profiles as the sector matures and more investment options become available Their findings suggest that traditional portfolio optimization methods, such as MVP and TP, could be adapted to better capture the dynamics of renewable energy investments, particularly as these assets become more integrated with conventional energy markets. Moreover, the work of Tudor (2023) presents a multifaceted risk-return analysis of green hydrogen equity investments, which can be incorporated into broader renewable energy portfolios. This study underscores the necessity of employing sophisticated portfolio optimization techniques to navigate the complexities and risks associated with emerging renewable technologies. The performance evaluation of renewable energy ETFs is also addressed by Saleem and Al-Hares (2018), who analyze the market efficiency of these funds compared to traditional energy investments and conclude that both categories are weak-form inefficient and present long memory in their volatility.

Furthermore, the research by Henriques et al. (2022) proposes a hybrid approach that combines Data Envelopment Analysis (DEA) with multi-objective portfolio models to identify efficient portfolios within the energy sector. This methodology aligns well with the principles of MVP and TP, as it seeks to optimize the selection of assets based on their performance metrics, thereby enhancing overall portfolio efficiency.

However, studies specifically focused on portfolio optimization strategies that include smart grid exchange-traded funds (ETFs) remain scarce, despite the growing importance of this sector in sustainable investing. One significant contribution is the work of Zhao et al. (2022), which presents a learning-to-rank-based investment portfolio optimization framework specifically tailored for smart grid planning. This study emphasizes the importance of optimizing investment portfolios to ensure the efficient allocation of resources in smart grid infrastructure projects, which are characterized by substantial investments and long construction periods. Additionally, Liu et al., (2023) explore a multistep iterative ranking learning method for optimal project portfolio planning in the context of smart grids. Their findings suggest that integrating advanced optimization techniques can significantly enhance the decision-making process regarding investments in smart grid projects, thereby improving overall portfolio performance. This aligns with the principles of MVP and TP, which aim to minimize risk while maximizing returns.

Consequently, while significant advancements have been made in optimizing portfolios within the renewable energy sector, the specific application of these strategies to smart grid ETFs remains relatively underexplored. This presents a compelling opportunity for further investigation, particularly as the integration of smart grid technologies into investment portfolios aligns with the growing emphasis on sustainable finance and the evolving complexities of the global energy landscape.

3 Material and Method

3.1 Data

The study encompasses an analysis period from January 2020 to March 2024, focusing on smart grid ETFs and their performance metrics relative to traditional equity investments. Specifically, this research includes several key ETFs, as follows:

1. **GRID (First Trust NASDAQ Clean Edge Smart Grid Infrastructure Index Fund)**: This ETF seeks to track the performance of companies engaged in the development and deployment of smart grid technologies, including electric meters, devices, networks, energy storage, and related technologies.
2. **SIMS (Global X Autonomous & Electric Vehicles ETF)**: Although primarily focused on autonomous and electric vehicle technologies, SIMS contributes to the analysis by investing in companies that develop technologies critical to smart grid infrastructure, particularly in terms of energy management systems and the integration of electric vehicles into grid networks. Electric vehicles play a key role in demand-side management and energy storage, which are integral components of smart grid functionality.
3. **SPY (SPDR S&P 500 ETF Trust)**: This widely-used ETF tracks the S&P 500 Index, providing exposure to a broad range of U.S. large-cap stocks, serving as a benchmark for traditional equity investments.
4. **EFA (iShares MSCI EAFE ETF)**: This ETF offers exposure to large- and mid-cap stocks in developed markets outside of the United States and Canada, providing a measure of international equity market performance.
5. **XLE (SPDR Select Sector Fund - Energy Select Sector)**: This ETF targets the energy sector within the S&P 500, including companies involved in oil, gas, and energy equipment and services, which are relevant for comparison due to their focus on traditional energy infrastructure.
6. **EEM (iShares MSCI Emerging Markets ETF)**: This ETF provides exposure to large- and mid-cap stocks in emerging market economies, offering insights into market dynamics and growth potential outside of developed markets.

These ETFs were chosen to represent a diverse range of investment opportunities, including smart grid technologies, traditional energy infrastructure, and broad-market benchmarks, to facilitate a comprehensive analysis of risk, return, and diversification benefits. Data for all ETFs were sourced from the Yahoo Finance platform, a reliable financial database, ensuring accuracy and consistency.

Utilizing the R programming environment, the study employs extensive financial modeling and portfolio optimization techniques.

3.2 Single Factor Models (SFM) with Alternative Market Factors

The primary reason for estimating the Single Factor Model (SFM) is to understand the relationship between the returns of smart grid ETFs (such as GRID and SIMS) and various market ETFs (SPY, EFA, and XLE). By doing so, we can assess the sensitivity of these smart grid ETFs to broader market movements and evaluate their performance on a risk-adjusted basis. This analysis is crucial for investors who are considering smart grid ETFs as part of their portfolio, as it provides insights into how these ETFs behave relative to well-established market benchmarks. The choice of SPY, EFA, and XLE as factors is deliberate to cover a broad spectrum of market conditions: SPY represents the overall U.S. market, EFA captures the performance of developed markets outside the United States and Canada, and XLE focuses on the energy sector, which is relevant due to its traditional energy infrastructure.

However, EEM (iShares MSCI Emerging Markets ETF) was not included as a factor despite its global exposure and relevance to energy and infrastructure sectors. This decision is based on the distinct market dynamics and risk profiles associated with emerging markets, which may introduce additional volatility and complexity into the model. Emerging markets are characterized by higher economic and political risks, which can lead to significant deviations in performance compared to developed markets and the energy sector. Including EEM as a factor could obscure the specific sensitivities of smart grid ETFs to the more stable, established market benchmarks provided by SPY, EFA, and XLE. By focusing on these three factors, the analysis remains concentrated on understanding the core relationships between smart grid technologies and broader, more predictable market movements, ensuring clearer insights into their risk-adjusted performance.

The SFM for each smart grid ETF is specified as:

$$R_{\{ETF,t\}} = \alpha + \beta \cdot R_{\{M,t\}} + \epsilon_t$$

where:

- $R_{\{ETF,t\}}$ is the return of the ETF at time t,
- α is the intercept term representing the alpha of the ETF,
- β is the slope coefficient representing the beta of the ETF with respect to the market factor,
- $R_{\{M,t\}}$ is the return of the market factor (i.e., SPY, EFA, or XLE) at time t,
- ϵ_t is the error term.

The estimation of the Single Factor Model (SFM) is performed using Ordinary Least Squares (OLS) regression, assuming that the error term follows a normal distribution with a mean of zero and constant variance (homoscedasticity). Additionally, it is assumed that the returns of the ETFs and the market factors exhibit no autocorrelation.

Several key performance metrics are calculated from the estimated model:

- Alpha (α): Indicates the SG ETF's performance relative to the market factor, adjusted for risk.
- Beta (β): Measures the sensitivity of the ETF's returns to the returns of the market factor.
- R-squared: Represents the proportion of variance in the SG ETF's returns explained by the market factor.
- Tracking Error: Measures the standard deviation of the difference between the SG ETF's returns and the market factor's returns.
- Information Ratio: Calculates the risk-adjusted return of the SG ETF relative to the market factor.
- Treynor Ratio: Evaluates the risk-adjusted return of the SG ETF using beta as the risk measure.
- Sharpe ratio: Evaluates the risk-adjusted return of the SG ETF using total risk proxied by the standard deviation.

The estimated alphas and betas provide insights into the risk-return characteristics of the smart grid ETFs relative to the market factors. High beta values indicate higher volatility, while positive alpha values suggest superior risk-adjusted performance. By using SPY, EFA, and XLE as factors, we capture different dimensions of market exposure: SPY represents the broad U.S. equity market, EFA covers developed international markets outside the United States and Canada, and XLE focuses on the energy sector, providing a comprehensive analysis of the smart grid ETFs' performance across different market conditions. This multi-faceted approach allows investors to better understand the dynamics of smart grid ETFs and their potential role in diversified investment portfolios.

3.3 Portfolio Optimization

To evaluate the potential performance of smart grid ETFs within a diversified investment portfolio, this study employs Monte Carlo simulation, a powerful tool for generating a wide array of portfolio configurations and evaluating their expected returns and risks (Brandimarte, 2014; Ross, 2004; Wang, 2012). The Monte Carlo method allows for an extensive exploration of potential portfolio combinations, providing robust insights into optimal asset allocations under varying market conditions (McLeish, 2011; Rubinstein & Kroese, 2016; Zio, 2013). Additionally, by simulating thousands of possible scenarios, the Monte Carlo method can help investors understand the range of potential outcomes and risks associated with investing in smart grid ETFs. This approach can assist in making more informed decisions when constructing a diversified investment portfolio.

In this study, the portfolio optimization process involves constructing 50,000 distinct portfolios, each consisting of a combination of six assets, including smart grid ETFs. The asset weights for each portfolio are randomly generated, ensuring an equal likelihood for all possible portfolio configurations. This randomness, combined with the large number of portfolios, allows for a comprehensive exploration of the portfolio space, enabling identification of optimal risk-return trade-offs.

The expected return of each portfolio (Rp) is calculated as the weighted sum of the individual asset returns, using the following equation:

$$R_p = \sum_{j=1}^{n} w_i \mu_i \tag{1}$$

where R_p is the portfolio return, w_j is the weight of asset i, and μ_j is the expected return of asset i.

The risk of each simulated portfolio is measured by the standard deviation of returns, calculated using the covariance matrix (Σ) of asset returns. This matrix captures the correlations between the assets within the portfolio. The risk for each portfolio (σ_p) is computed using the following formula:

$$\sigma_p = \sqrt{w^T \sum w} \tag{2}$$

where σ_p is the portfolio standard deviation, w is the vector of asset weights in the portfolio, and Σ is the covariance matrix of asset returns.

The simulation identifies the Efficient Frontier (EF), which represents the set of portfolios offering the highest expected return for a given level of risk. Within this set, two key portfolios are of particular interest: the Minimum Variance Portfolio (MVP) and the Tangency Portfolio (TP).

The Minimum Variance Portfolio (MVP) is determined by identifying the portfolio with the lowest overall risk, which is characterized by the minimum standard deviation of returns among all simulated portfolios. This involves an exhaustive examination of the generated portfolios to select the one that exhibits the smallest portfolio variance. The optimization process leverages the covariance matrix of asset returns to compute the risk for various weight combinations, ultimately identifying the optimal asset allocation that achieves the minimum risk. This ensures that the portfolio is fully invested while minimizing exposure to volatility. For risk-averse investors, the MVP plays a crucial role as it allows them to participate in the market while reducing the risk of extreme losses. By focusing on minimizing variance, the MVP tends to allocate assets in a way that avoids high-volatility securities, making it a preferred option for those who prioritize stability over potentially higher returns. In the context of a diversified investment strategy, the MVP offers a foundational portfolio that can serve as a hedge against more aggressive, high-risk investments. The low-risk nature of the MVP makes it a valuable methodological tool in constructing balanced portfolios, helping investors to meet their risk tolerance while achieving steady, albeit lower, and returns. Its inclusion ensures that the overall portfolio risk is controlled, preventing confounding outcomes that could arise from overexposure to volatile assets.

Conversely, the Tangency Portfolio (TP) is identified by locating the portfolio with the highest Sharpe ratio, representing the optimal risk-adjusted return. The Sharpe ratio is calculated as the ratio of the portfolio's excess return over the risk-free rate to its standard deviation. The TP provides the optimal risk-adjusted return, balancing high returns with a manageable level of risk. This portfolio is particularly suited for growth-oriented strategies, maximizing returns for a given level of risk.

As such, the MVP is derived by minimizing the portfolio variance using the covariance matrix, while the TP is determined by maximizing the Sharpe ratio. These optimization techniques provide investors with critical insights into how to structure their portfolios to achieve specific investment goals, whether it be minimizing risk or maximizing returns adjusted for risk.

Monte Carlo simulation is well-suited for this analysis because it enables the generation of a large number of portfolio configurations, thus offering a robust evaluation of smart grid ETFs. By simulating 50,000 portfolios, a comprehensive understanding of the range of potential outcomes for investors is achieved. Additionally, the use of the MVP and TP optimization techniques provides clear insights into how portfolios can be structured to meet specific investment objectives, whether minimizing risk or maximizing risk-adjusted returns, ultimately leading to more informed decision-making and better portfolio performance within financial markets.

The identification of the MVP and TP is carried out using R programming, which queries the simulated portfolio dataset to find the configurations that satisfy the criteria for minimal variance and maximum Sharpe ratio. The use of advanced computational techniques ensures that the results are accurate and reflective of real-world market conditions. The Monte Carlo simulation process, combined with portfolio optimization, provides a thorough analysis of how smart grid ETFs can enhance risk-adjusted returns within a sustainable investment framework.

4 Empirical Results and Discussion

4.1 Exploratory Analysis

The descriptive statistics for the six ETFs (SPY, EFA, EEM, XLE, GRID, and SIMS) employed in this study are provided in Table 1.

Each ETF has 1339 observations with no missing data, ensuring the analysis is based on a complete dataset. The arithmetic mean returns for all ETFs are positive, with GRID showing the highest mean return (0.0008), followed by SPY and XLE (both with 0.0006), and then EFA, EEM, and SIMS (each with 0.0003). The median

Table 1 Descriptive statistics

	SPY	EFA	EEM	XLE	GRID	SIMS
Observations	1339	1339	1339	1339	1339	1339
NAs	0.0000	0.0000	0.0000	0.0000	0.0000	0.0000
Minimum	−0.1159	−0.1164	−0.1333	−0.2249	−0.1393	−0.1176
Quartile 1	−0.0049	−0.0053	−0.0067	−0.0099	−0.0069	−0.0091
Median	0.0008	0.0007	0.0008	0.0009	0.0012	0.0003
Arithmetic Mean	0.0006	0.0003	0.0001	0.0006	0.0008	0.0003
Geometric Mean	0.0005	0.0002	0.0000	0.0003	0.0007	0.0001
Quartile 3	0.0072	0.0066	0.0076	0.0115	0.0088	0.0098
Maximum	0.0867	0.0813	0.0775	0.1487	0.1041	0.1089
SE Mean	0.0004	0.0003	0.0004	0.0006	0.0004	0.0005
LCL Mean (0.95)	−0.0001	−0.0003	−0.0006	−0.0006	0.0000	−0.0007
UCL Mean (0.95)	0.0013	0.0010	0.0009	0.0018	0.0017	0.0012
Variance	0.0002	0.0001	0.0002	0.0005	0.0003	0.0003
Stdev	0.0130	0.0122	0.0139	0.0226	0.0159	0.0176
Skewness	−0.8263	-1.1837	−0.9945	−0.9343	−0.9686	−0.4068
StdDev Sharpe (Rf = 0%, p = 95%)	0.04779	0.02801	0.008796	0.02469	0.05362	0.01717

returns are close to the arithmetic means, indicating a relatively symmetric distribution of returns for each ETF around their central tendency. Quartile 1 and Quartile 3 provide insights into the spread of the middle 50% of returns, showing that SPY and GRID have narrower interquartile ranges compared to XLE, which has the widest spread.

The standard deviation (Stdev) highlights the volatility of the ETFs, with XLE exhibiting the highest volatility (0.0226) and EFA the lowest (0.0122). The minimum and maximum values show the range of returns, with XLE again showing the most extreme values, having the highest maximum (0.1608) and the lowest minimum (−0.2249), indicating significant price swings. GRID and SIMS have lower extremes compared to XLE, suggesting they are less volatile.

The skewness values indicate the asymmetry of the return distributions. All ETFs exhibit negative skewness, meaning there are more frequent small positive returns and fewer but larger negative returns. SPY and EFA have the highest negative skewness, indicating a greater likelihood of extreme negative returns compared to GRID and SIMS, which have lower skewness values.

The Sharpe ratio, calculated for each ETF with a risk-free rate of 0%, provides insight into the risk-adjusted performance of the assets under study. Among the ETFs, GRID demonstrates the highest Sharpe ratio of 0.05362, suggesting that despite its volatility (as reflected by its standard deviation of 0.0159), it offers superior returns when adjusted for total risk. This indicates that GRID may provide the best risk-adjusted returns, making it an attractive option for investors seeking exposure to smart grid technologies while balancing risk and reward.

SPY, a broad-market U.S. ETF, also shows a relatively strong Sharpe ratio of 0.04779, underscoring its consistent risk-adjusted performance in a large, diversified portfolio. EFA, which represents international developed markets, exhibits a lower Sharpe ratio of 0.02801, indicating that although it has lower volatility (standard deviation of 0.0122), its risk-adjusted return is not as competitive compared to U.S. markets and the smart grid-focused ETFs.

SIMS, with a Sharpe ratio of 0.01717, underperforms relative to GRID and SPY, suggesting that despite its focus on electric and autonomous vehicle technologies, its risk-adjusted return is lower, likely due to its relatively higher volatility (0.0176). Similarly, XLE, an energy sector ETF, has a Sharpe ratio of 0.02469, reflecting the high-risk nature of the traditional energy sector as shown by its substantial standard deviation of 0.0226.

Lastly, EEM, the emerging markets ETF, has the lowest Sharpe ratio at 0.008796, indicating poor risk-adjusted performance. This aligns with its higher volatility (standard deviation of 0.0139) and lower returns, which is due to the inherent risk and instability present in emerging markets.

These descriptive statistics provide a detailed snapshot of the performance and risk characteristics of the six ETFs, offering valuable insights for investors looking to understand the behavior of these assets in their portfolios.

The scatter plot of risk and return, shown in Fig. 1, illustrates the annualized returns and risks (standard deviation) for the six ETFs: SPY, EFA, EEM, XLE, GRID, and SIMS.

GRID exhibits the highest annualized return, approximately 20%, with moderate risk around 25%, making it an attractive option for investors seeking high returns with moderate volatility. SPY shows a balanced risk-return profile with a return of about 14% and a risk around 22%, indicating it offers relatively high returns with substantial risk. EFA, representing developed international markets, provides a return of around 7% with a risk below 20%, offering moderate returns with significant risk compared to GRID and SPY, suitable for investors seeking stability with international exposure. EEM, which focuses on emerging markets, has the lowest return with a higher risk than EFA, indicating inferior performance over the analysis period. XLE, representing the energy sector, has a return of about 8% but comes with the highest risk at around 35%, reflecting significant price swings in the energy market. SIMS, another smart grid ETF, shows a return of about 5% with a risk close to 30%, offering inferior performance compared to SPY and EFA. This plot helps investors compare the ETFs' performance, highlighting GRID as a high-return, high-risk option, while SPY and EFA provide more balanced choices.

The downside risk measures for the six ETFs (SPY, EFA, EEM, XLE, GRID, and SIMS) provide a comprehensive view of the potential risks associated with negative returns, which is crucial for investors focused on risk management (Table 2).

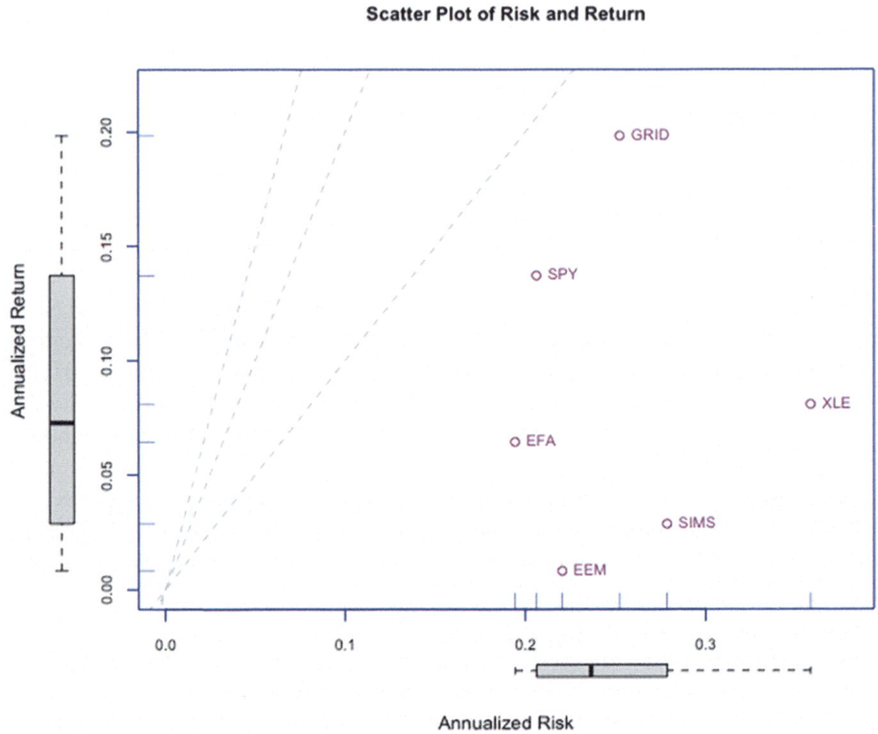

Fig. 1 Scatter plot of annualized risk and return for the six ETFs

Table 2 Downside risk measures for the six ETFs

	SPY	EFA	EEM	XLE	GRID	SIMS
Semi Deviation	0.0097	0.0092	0.0104	0.0167	0.0118	0.0128
Gain Deviation	0.0087	0.008	0.0089	0.0152	0.0104	0.0115
Loss Deviation	0.0109	0.0103	0.0111	0.0182	0.013	0.0129
Downside Deviation (Rf = 0%)	0.0094	0.009	0.0103	0.0164	0.0115	0.0126
Maximum Drawdown	0.3575	0.3572	0.4195	0.6635	0.4291	0.4575
Historical VaR (95%)	–0.0184	–0.0168	–0.0203	–0.0323	–0.0228	–0.0274
Historical ES (95%)	–0.032	–0.029	–0.0322	–0.0523	–0.0367	–0.0399
Modified VaR (95%)	–0.0203	–0.0198	–0.0229	–0.0359	–0.0256	–0.0284
Modified ES (95%)	–0.0475	–0.0527	–0.0569	–0.0866	–0.0639	–0.0533

Semi deviation, which measures the standard deviation of all negative returns, shows that XLE and SIMS exhibit the highest values (0.0167 and 0.0128, respectively), indicating higher downside volatility. SPY and EFA have the lowest semi deviations (0.0097 and 0.0092), suggesting lower downside risk.

Gain deviation, reflecting the standard deviation of all positive returns, also highlights XLE with the highest value (0.0152), followed by SIMS (0.0115), pointing to greater variability in positive returns. SPY and EFA again show lower gain deviations (0.0087 and 0.0080), indicating more consistent positive returns.

Loss deviation, focusing solely on negative returns, underscores XLE's significant downside risk during 2020–2024 with the highest value (0.0182). SPY and EFA maintain lower loss deviations (0.0109 and 0.0103), reinforcing their lower risk profile.

Downside deviation measures further emphasize XLE's higher risk, with values of 0.0164 across the board. SPY and EFA have the lowest downside deviations (0.0094 and 0.0090), indicating minimal risk of returns falling below zero.

Maximum drawdown, which indicates the largest peak-to-trough decline, reveals XLE's vulnerability with a maximum drawdown of 0.6635, the highest among the ETFs. SPY and EFA show lower drawdowns (0.3575 and 0.3572), suggesting better resilience during market downturns.

Historical VaR (95%), which estimates the maximum expected loss with 95% confidence, shows XLE with the highest risk (-0.0323), while SPY and EFA exhibit lower values (-0.0184 and -0.0168). Historical ES (95%), which measures the average loss exceeding VaR, also places XLE at the highest risk (-0.0523), with SPY and EFA at lower risks (-0.032 and -0.029).

Modified VaR and ES, adjusting for skewness and kurtosis, indicate XLE's substantial risk (-0.0359 for VaR and -0.0866 for ES). SPY and EFA again demonstrate lower risk levels (-0.0203 for VaR and -0.0475 for ES), making them more appealing for risk-averse investors.

Overall, these downside risk measures underscore the differences in risk profiles among the ETFs. SPY and EFA consistently exhibit lower downside risk, making them suitable for conservative investors. XLE, with the highest values across multiple risk metrics, highlights substantial volatility and potential for large losses. GRID and SIMS present moderate downside risk, with GRID slightly outperforming SIMS in some measures. These insights are essential for investors aiming to align their portfolios with their risk tolerance and investment goals.

4.2 *Results of Single Factor Models (SFM) Estimation*

Table 3 report the estimation results for the Single Factor Model (SFM) using SPY, EFA, and XLE as factors.

Both smart grid (SG) portfolios, represented by GRID and SIMS ETFs, exhibit high correlations with SPY and EFA. This high correlation indicates strong ties to the broader equity market movements. Specifically, the correlation coefficients for

Table 3 Estimation results for the Single Factor Model (SFM)

Metric	GRID to SPY	SIMS to SPY	GRID to EFA	SIMS to EFA	GRID to XLE	SIMS to XLE
Alpha	2E-04	–4E–04	5E-04	–1E-04	6E-04	0
Beta	1.0682	1.1667	1.1549	1.1913	0.4325	0.4819
R-squared	0.7604	0.7452	0.7892	0.6898	0.3768	0.3844
Annualized alpha	0.0544	–0.1021	0.1262	–0.0295	0.1633	–0.0017
Correlation	0.872	0.8632	0.8884	0.8306	0.6138	0.62
Tracking error	0.1244	0.1448	0.1198	0.1596	0.2849	0.2869
Active premium	0.0611	–0.1085	0.1337	–0.0359	0.1174	–0.0522
Information ratio	0.4908	–0.7494	1.1158	–0.2251	0.412	–0.1821
Treynor ratio	0.1856	0.0246	0.1717	0.0241	0.4585	0.0595

GRID with SPY and EFA are 0.872 and 0.8884, respectively, while SIMS shows correlation coefficients of 0.8632 with SPY and 0.8306 with EFA. These high values suggest that the performance of smart grid ETFs is closely aligned with these broader market indices.

The beta values for both GRID and SIMS are greater than one when compared to SPY and EFA, indicating higher volatility relative to these benchmarks. For instance, GRID has a beta of 1.0682 with SPY and 1.1549 with EFA, while SIMS has even higher betas of 1.1667 with SPY and 1.1913 with EFA. These elevated beta values highlight the increased sensitivity of smart grid ETFs to market fluctuations, implying that they are more volatile than the market indices.

When examining XLE as a factor, GRID and SIMS show different dynamics. For GRID, the beta is 0.4325, indicating lower sensitivity to the energy sector compared to the broader market indices, while SIMS has a beta of 0.4819. These beta values with respect to XLE suggest that while smart grid ETFs are somewhat influenced by the energy sector, their volatility relative to XLE is less pronounced than their volatility relative to SPY and EFA.

When examining performance indicators, GRID generally shows positive metrics compared to SIMS and the benchmarks (SPY and EFA). Specifically, GRID exhibits a positive alpha (when compared to SPY and EFA, indicating that it has outperformed the market on a risk-adjusted basis. Conversely, SIMS shows negative alpha values, indicating underperformance. GRID also demonstrates a higher active premium (0.0611) relative to SIMS (–0.1085), suggesting better returns above the benchmark. The information ratio for GRID is 0.4908, significantly higher than that of SIMS (–0.7494), reflecting better risk-adjusted returns. Similarly, the Treynor ratio for GRID (0.1856) surpasses that of SIMS (0.0246), indicating more efficient performance per unit of market risk.

In relation to XLE, GRID shows an alpha of 0.0006, a beta of 0.4325, and a Treynor ratio of 0.4585. These metrics indicate that GRID has a low but positive excess return relative to the energy sector and performs efficiently in terms of risk-adjusted returns. SIMS, on the other hand, shows an alpha of 0, beta of 0.4819, and a Treynor ratio of 0.0595, indicating underperformance compared to GRID when using XLE as the benchmark.

4.3 Optimization Results

The results of the portfolio optimization, which includes the identification of the Minimum Variance Portfolio (MVP) and the Tangency Portfolio (TP), provide valuable insights into the optimal allocation of assets to achieve specific investment objectives. The optimization utilized six ETFs: EEM, EFA, GRID, SIMS, SPY, and XLE. The allocations in each ETF for both efficient portfolios are detailed in Table 4, along with their annualized expected return, risk, and Sharpe ratios.

The MVP aims to minimize the portfolio's total risk (standard deviation) while ensuring it is fully invested. The MVP has an expected return of 11.4%, a risk (standard deviation) of 19.4%, and a Sharpe ratio of 0.585. While a Sharpe ratio below 1 indicates moderate performance, it still reflects a positive risk-adjusted return, especially considering the conservative nature of the MVP, which prioritizes risk minimization over aggressive returns This portfolio allocates the highest weight to EFA (46.6%) and SPY (42%), indicating a preference for diversified international and U.S. market exposure, with minimal allocation to GRID (1.33%), SIMS (0.845%), and XLE (0.207%), reflecting their higher volatility. The significant weights in EFA and SPY suggest a conservative approach aimed at minimizing risk through diversification across stable, large-cap international and U.S. equities.

The TP, or the portfolio with the highest Sharpe ratio, maximizes the risk-adjusted return. The TP has an expected return of 21.0%, a risk of 23.8%, and a Sharpe ratio of 0.884. While the Sharpe ratio is below 1, indicating some variability in performance, it remains relatively strong given the high returns and moderate risk level of the portfolio. This portfolio allocates a substantial weight to GRID (74.9%), indicating its high expected return despite higher volatility. SPY and EFA have moderate allocations (13.3% and 3.99%, respectively), while EEM, SIMS, and XLE have lower

Table 4 Efficient portfolios

	EEM	EFA	GRID	SIMS	SPY	XLE	Return	Risk	Sharpe Ratio	Treynor Ratio
TP	0.0202	0.0399	0.749	0.0127	0.133	0.0453	0.210	0.238	0.884	0.2072
	EEM	EFA	GRID	SIMS	SPY	XLE	Return	Risk	Sharpe Ratio	Treynor Ratio
MVP	0.0904	0.466	0.0133	0.00845	0.420	0.00207	0.114	0.194	0.585	0.1160

weights, reflecting a more aggressive investment strategy focused on maximizing returns. The significant weight in GRID highlights its dominant role in driving the high-risk-adjusted returns of the TP, making it an attractive option for investors willing to accept higher volatility for greater potential gains.

Summing up, both the MVP and TP outperform most of the individual ETFs in terms of their annualized Sharpe ratios, demonstrating the benefits of diversification and optimization. The MVP, with an annualized Sharpe ratio of 0.585, offers a better risk-adjusted return than most individual ETFs (except SPY and GRID), providing a stable option for conservative investors who prioritize risk minimization. In contrast, the TP, with an annualized Sharpe ratio of 0.884, significantly exceeds all individual ETFs, including the high-performing GRID and SPY, by effectively balancing GRID's high returns with the stability of SPY and EFA.

Furthermore, the Treynor Ratio (TR), computed relative to SPY as the benchmark, provides a nuanced assessment of the portfolios' risk-adjusted returns in relation to their systematic risk (beta). The Tangency Portfolio (TP) exhibits a Treynor ratio of 0.2072, indicating superior performance when compared to the Minimum Variance Portfolio (MVP), which holds a Treynor ratio of 0.1160. Notably, the TP outperforms individual ETFs, with GRID to SPY showing a Treynor ratio of 0.1856. This underscores the TP's ability to deliver enhanced systematic risk-adjusted returns through its strategic allocation to GRID. Although the MVP adopts a more conservative approach, it still surpasses ETFs such as SIMS to SPY (Treynor ratio of 0.0246) and XLE to SPY (Treynor ratio of 0.0595), underscoring its efficacy in achieving a balanced trade-off between risk and return.

Figure 2 graphically depicts the MVP and TP on the efficient frontier, which shows the set of optimal portfolios offering the highest expected return for a given level of risk. The efficient frontier demonstrates the trade-off between risk and return for the generated portfolios. The TP is located at the top of the efficient frontier, indicating the highest Sharpe ratio, while the MVP is positioned at the point with the lowest risk.

4.4 Discussion

The optimization results highlight distinct strategies for different investment goals. The MVP, with its focus on minimizing risk, leans heavily toward stable, diversified ETFs like EFA and SPY, making it suitable for risk-averse investors seeking consistent returns. In contrast, the TP, with its emphasis on maximizing risk-adjusted returns, allocates significantly to GRID, reflecting its potential for high returns despite higher risk, making it ideal for more aggressive investors willing to tolerate greater volatility for higher potential gains.

The substantial allocation to GRID in the TP underscores the critical role of smart grid ETFs in achieving superior risk-adjusted returns. Smart grid technologies, which include advancements in energy storage, efficiency, and management, are pivotal for the transition to a more sustainable energy infrastructure. As such, ETFs like

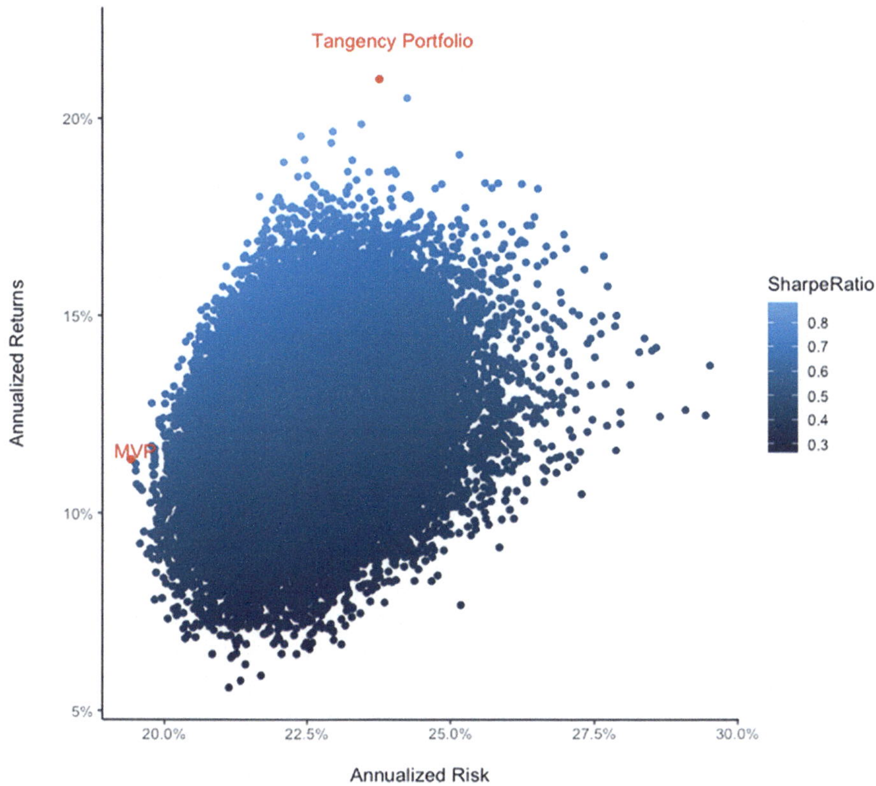

Fig. 2 Location of MVP and TP within the 50,000 6-asset portfolios

GRID, which invest in companies developing and implementing these technologies, offer significant growth potential. The high expected return and the allocation in the TP suggest that investors recognize the value and growth prospects of smart grid technologies.

SIMS, although having a lower allocation in both the MVP and TP, still contributes to the diversification of the portfolio. The inclusion of both GRID and SIMS in the optimized portfolios highlights the importance of incorporating smart grid ETFs for capturing the benefits of technological advancements in the energy sector. These ETFs not only provide exposure to innovative companies but also align with broader sustainable investment goals.

Overall, these optimization results underscore the importance of understanding the risk-return profile and the role of each ETF in achieving a balanced, diversified portfolio tailored to specific investment objectives. Smart grid ETFs, particularly GRID, play a crucial role in enhancing portfolio performance by offering high growth potential and aligning with the increasing emphasis on sustainability in investment strategies. The growth potential of smart grid technologies is driven by their pivotal role in the modernization of energy infrastructure, which is essential for facilitating the global transition toward cleaner, more efficient energy systems. As the demand for sustainable and decentralized energy solutions grows, smart grid companies are well-positioned to benefit from both regulatory support and market expansion. Additionally, these ETFs provide investors with exposure to a sector that aligns with environmental, social, and governance (ESG) principles, allowing for both financial returns and the opportunity to support responsible investing. This dual benefit of growth and sustainability makes smart grid ETFs, such as GRID, particularly valuable in portfolios seeking to achieve superior risk-adjusted returns while adhering to long-term sustainability goals.

Current findings that underscore investors' recognition of the value and growth prospects of smart grid technologies is supported by recent studies. These studies highlight the increasing importance of smart grid investments in achieving superior risk-adjusted returns, reflecting the broader trend toward sustainable energy solutions. Ma et al., (2018) discuss the influential factors driving industrial consumers' adoption of smart grid technologies, emphasizing that the return on investment (ROI) improves with enhanced functionalities of the smart grid. This finding aligns with the notion that as smart grid technologies evolve, they become more attractive to investors, thereby increasing their expected returns and justifying their allocation in optimized portfolios. Also, Giannelos et al. (2023) model smart grid technologies within optimization problems for electricity grids, suggesting that the integration of these technologies can lead to significant improvements in efficiency and reliability Their research indicates that smart grid investments are beneficial for operational performance and present substantial growth potential, which is likely to attract investor interest and enhance portfolio performance. Additionally, a recent study on efficiency metrics by Zaman (2024) highlights the critical role of technology infrastructure investments in improving grid reliability and energy efficiency. The findings suggest that increased investments in smart grid technologies can lead to enhanced performance metrics, further supporting the idea that these investments are recognized by investors as valuable opportunities for achieving high returns.

Furthermore, Dutra et al. (2019) explore the transition to smart homes facilitated by smart grid technologies, noting that government support and demand-response pricing mechanisms are driving the growth of smart grid applications. This trend indicates a growing recognition of the economic potential of smart grids, which is likely to influence investor behavior and portfolio allocations toward these technologies.

Additionally, Gwerder et al. (2019) assess the influence of regulatory and market factors on investment levels in smart grids, emphasizing the need for substantial investments to facilitate the transition to cleaner energy systems. Their findings suggest that as the regulatory landscape evolves to support smart grid technologies, investor confidence will likely increase, leading to higher expected returns and greater allocations in portfolios, which is in line with the current findings.

These converging insights from recent studies reinforce the conclusion that smart grid technologies not only hold immense potential for improving energy efficiency and grid reliability but also represent a highly attractive investment opportunity. As investors increasingly acknowledge the long-term value and growth prospects of these technologies, their inclusion in optimized portfolios is likely to gain momentum, driving further integration of smart grid solutions in sustainable investment strategies.

5 Conclusion

This study provides a comprehensive financial analysis of smart grid ETFs, highlighting their risk, return, and diversification benefits. The findings indicate that smart grid ETFs like GRID and SIMS exhibit substantial volatility but also offer potential for significant returns. When incorporated into traditional investment portfolios, these ETFs enhance the risk-return profile, providing valuable diversification benefits.

The results underscore the strategic importance of smart grid ETFs in sustainable investment portfolios. These funds enable investors to access the expanding smart grid sector, allowing them to capitalize on its growth while benefiting from improved portfolio diversification and the potential for elevated returns. Furthermore, the study reveals that smart grid ETFs offer superior returns relative to their associated risks compared to traditional energy ETFs and broader market indices. The Single Factor Model (SFM) analysis highlights that, despite their significant correlation with market indices, smart grid ETFs possess distinct risk-return characteristics that render them valuable assets in diversified portfolios.

While this research provides key insights, several limitations warrant further investigation. The analysis was conducted over a relatively short time horizon, which may not fully capture the long-term performance and evolving nature of smart grid ETFs. Future studies should extend the timeframe to better understand trends over multiple market cycles. Additionally, the study does not incorporate assumptions or forecasts regarding future market behavior, which may limit its applicability in predicting future outcomes. Further research should consider incorporating predictive models that account for potential shifts in market conditions and technological advancements. Moreover, there is significant potential to explore the influence of macroeconomic factors on smart grid ETF performance and examine the broader category of renewable energy ETFs to offer a more comprehensive understanding of sustainable investment strategies. While this research provides key insights, several limitations warrant further investigation. The analysis was conducted over a relatively short time horizon, suggesting that future studies should extend the timeframe to capture long-term market trends. Moreover, there remains significant potential for future research to explore the influence of macroeconomic factors on the performance of smart grid ETFs and to examine the broader category of renewable energy ETFs, thereby providing a more comprehensive understanding of sustainable investment strategies.

The implications of this research are multifaceted, extending to both investors and policymakers. For investors, smart grid ETFs represent a vital mechanism for gaining exposure to the rapidly expanding smart grid sector, while also contributing to portfolio diversification and enhancing risk-adjusted returns. This study confirms that these ETFs are well-positioned to capitalize on the global shift toward renewable energy, offering financial rewards that align with sustainability objectives.

For policymakers, the findings provide essential evidence supporting the further development and adoption of smart grid technologies. By encouraging investments in these areas, policymakers can align financial markets with sustainability goals, facilitating the transition to a low-carbon economy. Moreover, as smart grid infrastructure continues to evolve, its integration into investment portfolios will likely play a critical role in advancing both economic and environmental objectives.

In conclusion, this paper not only provides a detailed assessment of the financial performance of smart grid ETFs but also emphasizes their importance in sustainable investment strategies. As the global energy landscape continues to transform, smart grid ETFs stand out as a promising tool for both investors seeking long-term returns and policymakers aiming to foster sustainable development. Given the sector's growth potential and the unique characteristics of these ETFs, this study serves as a foundation for future research, which should further explore the long-term performance and macroeconomic impacts on smart grid and other renewable energy ETFs.

Acknowledgements This work was partially funded by the EU's NextGenerationEU instrument through the National Recovery and Resilience Plan of Romania - Pillar III-C9-I8, managed by the Ministry of Research, Innovation and Digitalization, within the projects entitled „Non – Gaussian self – similar processes: Enhancing mathematical tools and financial models for capturing complex market dynamics", contract no. 760243 /28.12.2023, code CF 194/31.07.2023 and „A Study of Consumer Trust in Online Reviews and Social Media Comments in the Age of Artificial Intelligence", contract number 760248/28.12.2023, code CF 158/31.07.2023.

References

Amin, S. M., & Wollenberg, B. F. (2005). Toward a smart grid: Power delivery for the 21st century. *IEEE Power and Energy Magazine, 3*(5), 34–41.

Bohl, M. T., Kaufmann, P., & Stephan, P. M. (2013). From hero to zero: Evidence of performance reversal in the stock market. *Journal of Empirical Finance, 21*, 102–121.

Brandimarte, P. (2014). *Handbook in Monte Carlo simulation: Applications in financial engineering, risk management, and economics*. Wiley.

Dutra, M., Anjos, M., & Digabel, S. (2019). A general framework for customized transition to smart homes. *Energy, 189*, Article 116138. https://doi.org/10.1016/j.energy.2019.116138

Fang, X. (2023). Energy management system technology in smart grid. *Highlights in Science Engineering and Technology, 76*, 328–336. https://doi.org/10.54097/x5ch4d78

Fang, X., Misra, S., Xue, G., & Yang, D. (2012). Smart grid—The new and improved power grid: A survey. *IEEE Communications Surveys & Tutorials, 14*(4), 944–980.

Farhangi, H. (2010). The path of the smart grid. *IEEE Power and Energy Magazine, 8*(1), 18–28.

Giannelos, S., Borozan, S., Aunedi, M., Xi, Z., Ameli, H., Pudjianto, D., & Štrbac, G. (2023). Modelling smart grid technologies in optimisation problems for electricity grids. *Energies, 16*(13), 5088. https://doi.org/10.3390/en16135088

Gungor, V. C., Sahin, D., Kocak, T., Ergut, S., Buccella, C., Cecati, C., & Hancke, G. P. (2011). Smart grid technologies: Communication technologies and standards. *IEEE Transactions on Industrial Informatics, 7*(4), 529–539.

Guo, T., Du, H., Li, N., & Palaoag, T. (2023, November). Exploration of sustainable development strategies and applications for grid management in smart communities. In *Proceedings of the 4th international conference on modern education and information management, ICMEIM 2023, September 8–10, 2023.* Wuhan, China.

Gwerder, Y., Figueiredo, N., & Silva, P. (2019). Investing in smart grids: Assessing the influence of regulatory and market factors on investment level. *The Energy Journal, 40*(4), 25–44. https://doi.org/10.5547/01956574.40.4.ygwe

Haque, A., Hussain, M. N., Ali, M. S., Khan, M. Y. A., & Halim, M. A. (2023). Technical and economic challenges and future prospects of a smart grid-a case study. *Control Systems and Optimization Letters, 1*(3), 186–193.

Henriques, C., Neves, M., Castelão, L., & Nguyen, D. (2022). Assessing the performance of exchange traded funds in the energy sector: A hybrid dea multiobjective linear programming approach. *Annals of Operations Research, 313*(1), 341–366. https://doi.org/10.1007/s10479-021-04323-6

Henriques, I., & Sadorsky, P. (2008). Oil prices and the stock prices of alternative energy companies. *Energy Economics, 30*(3), 998–1010.

IEA (International Energy Agency). (2011). Technology roadmap: Smart grids. Retrieved from https://www.iea.org/reports/technology-roadmap-smart-grids

IRENA (International Renewable Energy Agency). (2019). Innovation landscape brief: Smart charging for electric vehicles. Retrieved from https://www.irena.org/publications/2019/May/Innovation-landscape-brief-Smart-charging

Jisma, M., Mohan, V., & Thomas, M. S. (2023). Risk-return optimised energy asset allocation in transmission-distribution system using tangency portfolio and Black-Litterman model. *IET Energy System Integration, 5*(3), 290–306.

Kumar, P., Kasinathan, P., Elavarasan, R., Ramanathan, V., Anandan, R., Subramaniam, U., & Hossain, E. (2021). A comprehensive review on sustainable aspects of big data analytics for the smart grid. *Sustainability, 13*(23), 13322. https://doi.org/10.3390/su132313322

Liu, C., Li, X., Liang, J., Sheng, K., Kong, L., Peng, X., & Zhao, W. (2023). A multistep iterative ranking learning method for optimal project portfolio planning of smart grid. *International Transactions on Electrical Energy Systems, 2023*, 1–10. https://doi.org/10.1155/2023/1358099

Liu, Y., Ren, S., & Wang, Y. (2021). Environmental, social, and governance (ESG) performance and firm value: The moderating role of disclosure. *Asia-Pacific Journal of Financial Studies, 50*(2), 178–205.

Ma, Z., Jôrgensen, B., & Asmussen, A. (2018). Industrial consumers' smart grid adoption: Influential factors and participation phases. *Energies, 11*(1), 182. https://doi.org/10.3390/en11010182

McLeish, D. L. (2011). *Monte Carlo simulation and finance* (Vol. 276). Wiley.

Olatunde, T. (2024). The impact of smart grids on energy efficiency: a comprehensive review. *Engineering Science & Technology Journal, 5*(4), 1257–1269. https://doi.org/10.51594/estj.v5i4.1016

Pizzutilo, F., & Gleason, K. (2023). Portfolio performance implications of investment in renewable energy equities: Green versus gray. *Corporate Social Responsibility and Environmental Management, 30*(6), 2990–3005. https://doi.org/10.1002/csr.2533

Ross, J. G. (2004). Risk and uncertainty in portfolio characterisation. *Journal of Petroleum Science and Engineering, 44*(1–2), 41–53.

Rubinstein, R. Y., & Kroese, D. P. (2016). *Simulation and the Monte Carlo method*. Wiley.

Saleem, K., & Al-Hares, O. (2018). Measuring the market efficiency of energy exchange-traded funds (ETFS). *Theoretical Economics Letters, 8*, 1247–1256. https://doi.org/10.4236/tel.2018.86082

Tolliver, C., Keeley, A. R., & Managi, S. (2020). Green bonds for the Paris Agreement and sustainable development goals. *Environmental Research Letters, 15*(11), Article 114013.

Tudor, C. (2023). Enhancing sustainable finance through green hydrogen equity investments: A multifaceted risk-return analysis. *Risks, 11*(12), 212.
Tudor, C. (2024). Opportunities in clean energy equity markets: The compelling case for nuclear energy investments. *Journal of Business Economics and Management, 25*(5), 960–980.
United Nations. (2015). Transforming our world: The 2030 Agenda for Sustainable Development. Retrieved from https://sdgs.un.org/2030agenda
Vaccariello, E., Leone, P., Canavero, F. G., & Stievano, I. S. (2021). Topological modelling of gas networks for co-simulation applications in multi-energy systems. *Mathematical and Computer Modelling of Dynamical Systems, 27*(1), 65–84.
Wang, H. (2012). *Monte Carlo simulation with applications to finance.* CRC Press.
World Economic Forum. (2022). Here's why we need a smart grid — and how we build one. Retrieved from https://www.weforum.org/agenda/2022/10/smart-grid-energy-renewables/
Yao, L., Liu, Z. & Chen, S. (2022). Advanced digital technologies in digitalized smart grid. *Frontiers in Energy Research.* Retrieved from https://www.frontiersin.org/articles/https://doi.org/10.3389/fenrg.2022.00029/full
Zaman, K. (2024). Efficiency metrics: assessing the impacts of grid reliability on energy efficiency in smart systems. *Energy Research Letters, 5*(Early View). https://doi.org/10.46557/001c.94671
Zhao, W., Liu, X., Wu, Y., Zhang, T., & Zhang, L. (2022). A learning-to-rank-based investment portfolio optimization framework for smart grid planning. *Frontiers in Energy Research, 10.* https://doi.org/10.3389/fenrg.2022.852520
Zio, E. (2013). *The Monte Carlo simulation method for system reliability and risk Analysis.* Springer Series in Reliability Engineering.

The manufacturer's authorised representative in the EU is Springer Nature Customer Service Centre GmbH, Europaplatz 3, 69115 Heidelberg, Germany. If you have any concerns regarding our products, please contact ProductSafety@springernature.com

Printed and bound by CPI Group (UK) Ltd, Croydon, CR0 4YY
30/09/2026
02225507-0013